Renzo Piano

Massimo Dini

Renzo Piano

Projects and buildings 1964-1983

Electa/Rizzoli
New York

Translation
Richard Sadleir

To the memory of my father,
who taught me, from boyhood onwards,
the love of building.
R.P.

Library of Congress Cataloging in Publication Data
Piano, Renzo.
Renzo Piano, projects and buildings, 1964-1983.
Italian ed. published as: Renzo Piano, progetti e architetture, 1964-1983.
Bibliography: p.
1. Piano, Renzo. 2. Architecture, Modern-20th
century-Italy. I. Dini, Massimo. II. Title.
NA1123.P47A4 1983 720'.92'4 83-42993
ISBN 0-8478-0513-1 (pbk.)

First published in 1984 in the United States of America by
RIZZOLI INTERNATIONAL PUBLICATIONS, INC.
712 Fifth Avenue, New York, New York 10019

Printed in Italy

Contents

C.1

Introduction

In the midst of many doubts, Renzo Piano is certain that the architect is on the decline, at least in terms by which his work has hitherto been conceived. It is no longer sufficient to update the catalogue of expressive tricks or renew the style code; it is the architect himself that needs to be redesigned. At the most delicate moment, on the brink of entering the microelectronic village, he finds the ground removed from beneath him. He is no longer able to build or invent. In short, unable to play architect. Art, though mannered, becomes his refuge and often deteriorates into pure slight of hand, formal arabesques lacking substance. As his field of competence gradually shrinks, so does his bargaining power disappear and his social usefulness tends to become void. The outcome is that the architect's role today is of no use to anyone or anything. He may just as well bow out.

So what is to be done? Is there any solution to this dramatic identity crisis? Piano does not lay claim to an exact diagnosis, but does suggest a possible therapy. "One of my deepest convictions," he declares, "is that the architect should first design his own working instruments, his technical and disciplinary equipment. This is a sort of return to one's origins which is further justified today in the light of conventionalism and mass production of the conceptual process. If one does not intervene in the making of instruments, in its processes, we risk having our work relegated to the periphery where there is only space for ineffective and nostalgic operations."

Reappropriation of the work instruments; mastery in handling the materials and techniques of construction; the reformulation of the professional role is the goal of a tortuous journey back through the mythical countries of craftsmanship, the craft of building before everything else. This may well be the only formula which can heal the schizophrenic syndrome of contemporary architecture, close the ever-widening gap between humanistic and scientific culture, between thought and action, conceptual and manual work. Returning to the roots and establishing a solid and concrete basis is one way to restore the craft with substance, rescuing it from the self-indulgence of formalism. Designing means building, and the various fields of expertise have to be recombined, the roles in the creative process integrated.

The folklore of craftsmanship is irrelevant. As the Genoese Piano sees it there is nothing sentimental or regressive about the journey in memory. We cannot free ourselves from the feeling of non-fulfilment simply by travelling back through time. Hurtling forward as we are towards the wonderland of data processing, it would be absurd to ignore technological progress. The problem is twofold, to reestablish the importance of "making," the craft mentality, and also to acquire an up-to-date and effective manipulation of the instruments based on the most sophisticated technological results, something that has been for too long the exclusive preserve of specialized industry, of the "pure technicians."

Hence the high-tech label that is all too hastily attached to Renzo Piano's work (the dominant reference being, of course, his most popular creation the Centre Pompidou, the spaceship catapulted into the center of Paris) and the image of the architect as a standard-bearer of technological extremism. Is this interpretation correct? "Absolutely not. The choice of technology is implicit in the choice to build. Even the use of stone corresponds to a precise technological option. It is simply that in an advanced period like our own materials are available with high levels of cohesion and durability that are easily worked and handled. It is culturally a mistake to reject the opportunity to mould an architectural language using all this potential. It is questionable even to make an issue of it. An architect, a builder, cannot help but use technological methods when it meets the design requirements."

What especially needs clarifying is the underlying confusion. Advanced technology does not necessarily mean *hard* technology, something harsh and aggressive, the deployment of complex contraptions and large scale machinery. While it is true that the two often coincide in the reality of urban development, it is also true that high technology can be directed toward *soft* objectives. It is a question of mental rigor. When examining one of Piano's recent designs, the travelling exhibition for IBM, the innovatory technologies are used in such a minute, exploded fashion that in the end the aesthetic object acquires an almost organic aspect. It is essential for us not to become conditioned by technological evolution but to bend it to the needs of the community, to miniaturize it and adjust the scale to ecological models. "You can become a slave to stone, just as you can concoct an outsized boorish, Fascist design even when you have renounced the use of its current vocabulary."

Piano's progress has taken all sorts of twists and turns. His works include an automobile, museum, new buildings and restorations, but throughout its variety one constant is apparent: the way he draws on technological know-how. Transcribed into cultural terms this means seeking to progress beyond one of the classic conflicts of modern art, the clash between creativity and science. Without the support of scientific developments, the aspiration of new architectural frontiers is destined to remain in the limbo of manifestoes and declarations. It is here that the long haul begins, with all that this implies about the science of construction. The technological instruments are varied, complex, continually evolving; mastering them calls for a very high level of competence.

So, the scientific approach; but along which lines? Certain artists have followed mathematical parameters, or contemporary composers for instance; others have taken social guidelines; or sought a point of reference in following nature's principles; all various ways of escaping the hazards of the gratuitous and the random. But from the beginning, even from the time of the space frames he invented in the workshop, Piano has followed a clearly defined path. Another question arises on how to fit the various principles into the reality of designing, of searching for what is involved in making architecture scientific. "I quite realize," says Piano, "that my attitude may seem naive. I mean that the scientific reference itself is not enough to resolve the riddle of architecture. But science also means first-hand observation, analysis and decipherment of the physical environment. So, the effort should not consist of morphological reproduction, a mimetic representation of the natural world. This would be an academic operation, just like the revival of the arch and column. The problem is to dissect and memorize the structural factors, the visible aspect of constructional processes."

Nature is the magnetic pole, the atlas through which to leaf. But it is also necessary to be well-equipped to venture along the paths of cosmic archetypes. Two elements appear indispensable: a taste for methodological experimentation and a refined but not overwhelming understanding of techniques; calculation plus verification, computer plus trial and error, theory and practice; two dimensions that in Piano's design work overlap and intertwine continually. There is the abstract, cerebral aspect (the mathematical model) and the practical manual aspect (experiment). It is in its execution that the reference to the organic world becomes immediate, spontaneous.

At this point the identity of the new architect acquires a firmer outline. Building means starting from scratch, with a blank sheet, with matter and its laws, it means creating; though when the time comes to put creation into practice that it cannot follow fanciful paths but has to manifest itself in carefully detailed plans, continually referring to its intimate relationship with the biological universe. The architect is the investigator of nature, and architecture a painstaking research, a patient transcription of arcane structural homologues. It is no accident that the feeling we get from Piano's most recent designs is of biotechnological architecture, as if there was a symbiosis of high-tech and physical reality. We can see this in two significant examples, the flower shaped joint that unites, virtually fuses, the wooden and aluminum elements (the design for the IBM exhibition) and in the leaf shaped ferrocement screen that filters sunlight by multiple refraction (the design for the Menil Collection in Houston).

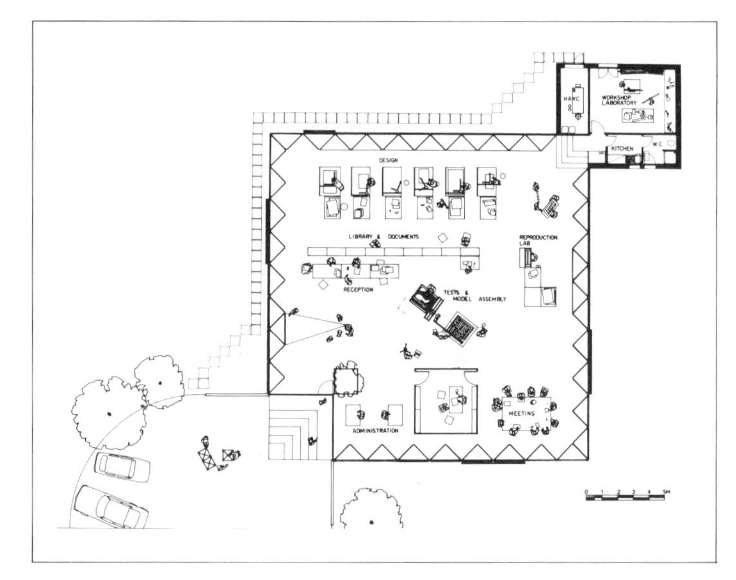

Plan of the studio/workshop (1968) in the hills of Genoa.
Interior of the studio/workshop.

Plan of the present studio/workshop in Genoa, containing a TV studio and lightweight equipment for structural experiments.

Most of the Genoa work team.

It is the naturalistic theme that inspires the engineering solution. "The tree system is based on a continual refraction of light between leaves creating areas of shadow without impeding ventilation. Basically the Houston screens are no more than large leaves geometrically arranged so as to leave passage for air but also to exclude the ultraviolet rays that would damage the works of art."

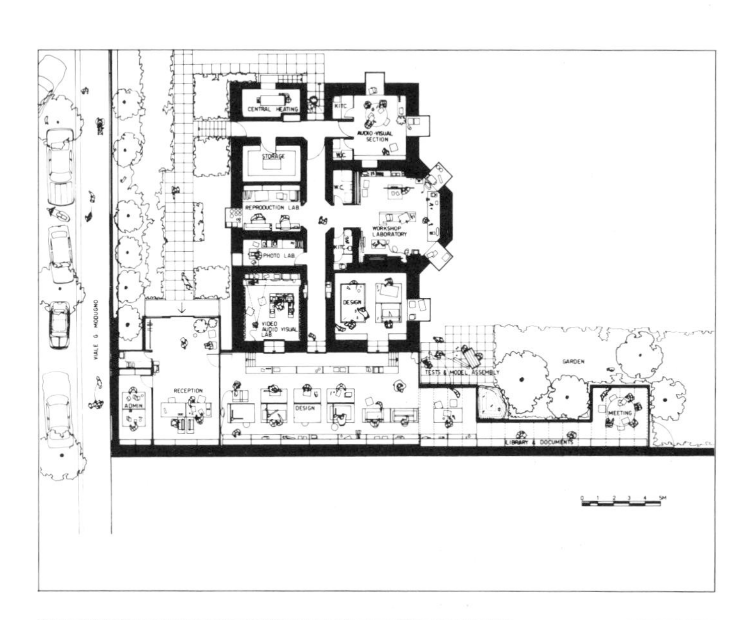

Thus creation is at the juncture of past and future, the banal and sophisticated, the ritual and futuristic technology; it is a way of reducing elaborate, intricate realities to their essential expression. Can this be considered an aesthetic operation? Piano distrusts the term "art." Indeed, he often uses it disparagingly as a synonym for something freakish or stagey. "Building is the most wonderful work in the world, but architecture and architects need debunking. Of course you can indulge in emotion and gestures but only when you possess a sufficiently strong mastery to guide and discipline you as if by invisible strings. It is a much easier life being an artist than being a bricklayer, someone who builds piece by piece exploring methodically." Far from being sorcery, a sacred mystery, art is the sublimation of craftsmanship, the fusion of idea and act. This is why the Genoa-Pegli workshop has an atmosphere unlike that of an architectural office: it is a miniature building site, a craftsman's workshop (fitted out for travel into the electronic future) where the architectural product is perennially unfinished, "work in progress," and where there is no separation of roles.

But research into construction is not enough. Slipshod inaccuracy is a constant hazard of architectural experimentation. Hence the need to firmly anchor the profession to objective premises: scientific discipline on the one hand, and human discipline on the other. Enclosed in an ivory tower, the run-of-the-mill architect is cut off from the world and he designs mechanically, without knowing people's true needs. The only way to reestablish contact is to leave the drawing board and go into the streets, onto the building sites. This is where you learn to interpret what is necessary in everyday living and render a service to architecture. Also in this respect Piano's work qualifies as a multidisciplinary activity, welding together the technological and social worlds which are all too often in conflict. "Architecture must fully commit itself to understanding technology, experimenting with its instruments. It must also take the pulse of people's real needs, participating in community organizations that economically and actively involve the people concerned, giving them, both literally and figuratively, a say in their own homes. This is the exact opposite of what happens with wordy, demagogic and participatory assemblies."

This is what underlies the idea of the Neighborhood Workshops, born in the wake of Piano's exhausting Beaubourg achievement. It is

Testing in the experimental workshop.
Magda Arduino in the video workshop.

a significant breakthrough: from the mass cultural stance characterized by an extreme simplification of design, to a more careful and thorough analysis of the social dimension embodied in the mobile workshops (with the help of his wife, Magda Arduino) for the rehabilitation of ancient town centers. It is based on two key elements: the use of soft technologies and participation of the future occupants. There is optimism and ingeniousness in this challenge to the traditional building industry. Its underlying theory is that to rehabilitate the existing, there is no need for heavy-handed intervention (bulldozers, mass excavations, demolitions, etc.). All that is needed is to reduce in scale advanced technologies and rekindle the awareness of the inhabitants. Participatory design has been developed throughout the years, its operational terms defined and the conviction that environmental culture must grow out of the reawakened sensibilities of its inhabitants that has always remained unchanged. "The crux of participatory work," Piano has said, "lies in the widespread non-culture of housing. Public provision is clearly an important social conquest, but at the same time it generates passiveness, fostering the welfare mentality." And so the architect-builder becomes transformed into the architect-general practitioner. He has another social mission to fulfil: to stimulate social demand and seek to satisfy it in all its scope and variety. It is pointless to conjure up demagogical Utopias; what counts is direct action. Piano's is an architecture of connection, one that tries to create contacts and demolish divisions, barriers; an architecture that fights against the current and is hard to classify amid all the shooting stars of contemporary architecture. We have to proceed by exclusion: rejection of the restoration of formalism, rejection of mannerism, rejection of exhibitionist iconography. All this boils down to stating that we are at the opposite pole of postmodernism, which is sweepingly dismissed by Piano as an "aberrant phenomenon," one that places the creative impulse before construction technique and tries to redirect the new generation along the path of aestheticism.

A study of his cultural background also fails to fully account for Piano's achievement. Of course his international apprenticeship has left a profound mark on his approach to design, but it is useless to go hunting for quotes, stylistic references, coded allusions. It is a question of methodology, not of architectural forms. In this sense Piano is always ready to acknowledge the debts to his masters, from Frei Otto for his experimental work and curiosity about the natural world, to Z.S. Makowsky for his mathematical approach; from Pierluigi Nervi to Jean Prouvé for their fusion of conceptual gestation and execution, concept and craftsmanship; from Franco Albini for "he taught me to be methodical, to be stubborn and to reject the slipshod" to Marco Zanuso from whom he learned how to

handle materials; his apprenticeship in Philadelphia with Louis Kahn taught him an extraordinary dedication to work, rather than Kahn's approach.

These are important reference points but perhaps they are not decisive or are not sufficient to reduce the distance between Piano and the rest of the architectural world. There is another experience that may have well been decisive, an emotional one which goes back to the beginning of his professional training when he worked alongside his father, a building contractor. It was on the site that the youthful architect learned the rudiments of his experimental and craftsmanlike philosophy, his taste for execution, the love of building. That love later became embodied in a whole gamut of membranes he designed: light, translucent, almost gothicized veils which become symbolic of a seemingly childlike creativity. "The membrane is simply the deformation of an elastic surface, and precisely because of this it expresses clearly the way it functions. The link between the form and the conditions — structural, material, technical — immediately determine it. If this relation does not exist or is not legible, then the architecture becomes academic." The membrane is both a formal element and also the key to an architectural language that rejects division and accepts the risks of difference.

While it is difficult to do an inventory of Piano's architecture, establishing a network of precise interconnections, it is equally difficult to trace a common thread throughout his course as a designer, from the "liberated boxes" of the sixties to the sophisticated designs for the Houston museum and the Milan exhibition complex by way of the Beaubourg. The fact is that aesthetic parameters count for little: the method and the mental outlook are different; the architectural outcome finds its ratification in the degree to which it was conceived. Each design constitutes a separate history instead of being just a stage in a consistent artistic development. Yet despite this range of typological solutions, it is possible to distinguish a focal point, not formally but perhaps in the lengthy and, at times tortuous, exploration of evolving space. In the beginning it was merely a primary structure, an empty shell, but as it developed it became transformed into malleable material, one that could be moulded with gentle touches without the architect's intervention ever being translated into exhaustive all-embracing forms.

Space is time — a non-photographable reality — yet it is fluctuating, dynamic, kaleidoscopic; it is light, air, wind, color, nature; something magical, like a fantasy city of crystal. "Paxton's Crystal Palace was not just a beautiful object, poetic in its transparency, its integration into nature. It was also the result of

The work team of the Paris studio: the whole team, including the Houston members. About 30 people who often move from one studio to the other.

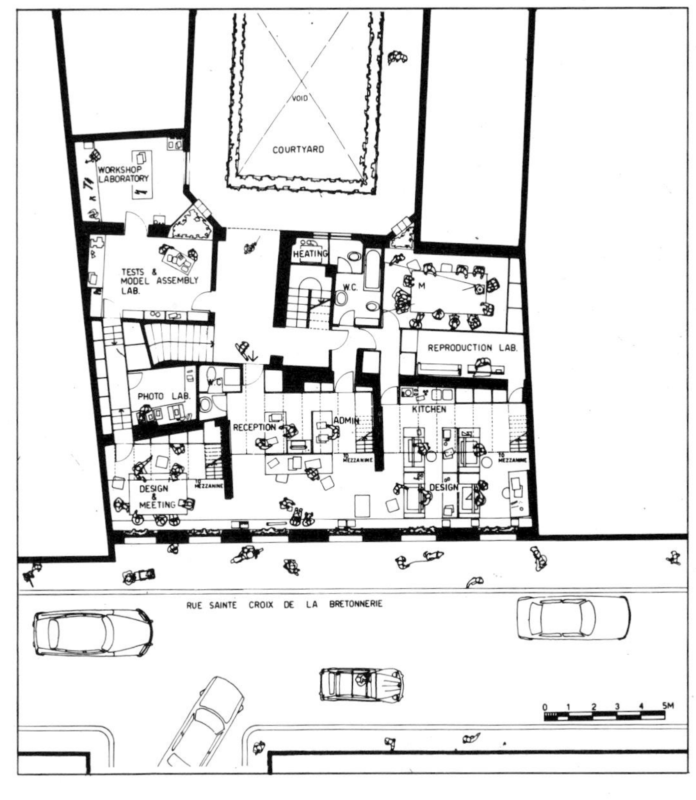

Plan of the Paris studio, in the historic center of Le Marais.

The Paris studio seen from Rue St.-Croix-de-la-Bretonnerie.

painstaking perfection of construction systems, intelligent building in which you always find the reasoning behind the formal appearance."

The same image is evoked in the design for the Milan exhibition complex which is raised to a level of symbolic space embodying functionality and spectacle. It is an everyday familiar interior and yet one that is arcane, magical, with an elusive ground floor plan; a world both real and imaginary that realizes Reyner Banham's Utopia: the well ordered environment. Order and disorder, symmetry and asymmetry: in the shadow of the harmonious roofs, made of identical construction pieces, endlessly repeated, a most unexpected Disneyland, a realm of freedom is revealed. Just as in the book of nature, is not repetition the poetic key to the honeycomb, the structure of crystals, the organization of the molecule? Is not the universe governed by geometrical laws? The roof here is like a gigantic crystal, except that, just as in planetary systems, the inflexible sequence breaks down after a point and we find the dissonant element that scatters the elementary particles and generates chaos.

Is this the final goal of the journey? Perhaps. Yet it may be that Piano, like a questing voyager, will suddenly decide to take hold of the helm again and set sail for unchartered shores. His story, as those who know him can tell, is of architecture and the sea. Behind the appearance of detachment, there has always been the spirit of the trailblazer, the desire to measure himself against the impossible. This is why his adventure as a designer presents itself in retrospect as a sequence of enigmas: yesterday the mystery of materials, today evolving space and tomorrow, perhaps, "built nature." "Now that the crazy postwar urban expansion is over, we increasingly find in the towns the phenomenon of building onto the built. During this recovery we occasionally come across countryside, true oases, spared by the concrete tide. Here a problem arises: is there any sense in deluding ourselves that we can find a natural dimension in these tiny islands now being absorbed into the urban fabric? I do not think so. We must try to imagine a built nature which merges and blends with the city. In the conversion of the Schlumberger works in Paris we focused on the theme of the garden that enfolds, assails the surrounding buildings, but that at the same time conceals underground parking for a thousand cars, a forum and areas for collective activities. The construction does not have to obliterate nature, only nature has to be invented and designed, it is a new typology. The comeback of nature over the city is possible through a careful, painstaking, methodical recovery of these islands that have survived the holocaust. Of course it is not a question of creating bogus 'natural' panoramas but of interpreting the garden in an urban key. I feel this is the most authentic solution."

Riddles, always riddles; but luckily with messianic affirmations of the coming of the heavenly city. Riddles formulated in a language everyone understands, hammered out (no accident this) in a workshop where architects from nine different nations work side by side.

Massimo Dini

1964-1965 Genoa, Italy
Reinforced polyester space frames

Architects: Studio Piano

The discovery of materials

Piano's architectural adventure began in the mid-sixties with a space frame organized in perfectly symmetrical patterns, a rhapsody of signs: a continuum of identical square-based pyramidal elements, assembled to form an orthogonal grid; above them, joining the tops of the pyramids, another tubular grid of steel. Like the facets of quartz it was not just an academic exercise. It reflects the lessons learned in London at the workshop of Makowsky, then the director of the Battersea College of Technology. ("With his pyramidal sequences Makowsky was pursuing a dream of perfection: through optical and mechanical systems he verified the stresses and checked the tensions of plastics.") This delicate three-dimensional network represents the first stage in a long quest, the study of materials, the way to manipulate them, mould them, structure them. The choice of plastic was in itself significant, a sort of challenge: reinforced polyester which of all plastic materials can boast of properties closest to metal, it has a coefficient of elasticity which is merely one-twentieth that of steel, but it is up to the designer to overcome the technical obstacles without showing any signs of restriction on the expressive level. But this was still in the experimental phase. "I feel," Piano was later to declare, "that the architect has to have a scientific understanding of a material, of its possible transformations, of its behavior. This discipline, far from being rigid, is one of the architect's fundamental tools." Even then he was making contact with the concrete, manual discovery of materials in the course of a natural transition following his experience on the construction site alongside his father, also a builder.

This first experience of craftsmanship had already revealed his love of building. It is easy to see how the *esprit de géométrie* which characterizes the structural arrangement acquires features which are anything but rigid: the plastic covering, so fine and light (the modular unit weighs less than 10 kg) suggests randomness, as if the object could go on multiplying itself endlessly or else come to a halt. More like embroidery than framework, it only seemingly is a static structure, but one that in reality may vary in keeping with the needs of its setting. Its symmetry is ephemeral, soft, to the point of becoming fluid.

2

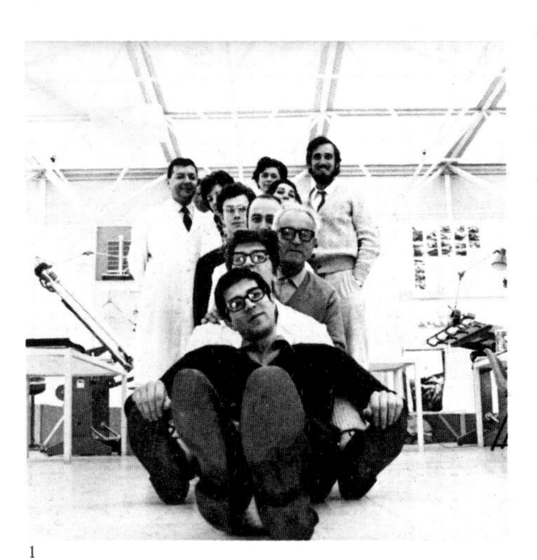

1

"I feel that the architect has to have a scientific understanding of a material, of its possible transformations, of its behavior."

1. Studio Piano in 1968.

2. Structural tests conducted in a laboratory of the University of Surrey in collaboration with Z.S. Makowsky.

3. Travelling exhibition pavilion consisting of a reinforced polyester pyramidal space frame.

4. Research involves utmost simplicity of detail into weight reduction.

5. Arch of reinforced polyester pyramids.

6. Each piece in this structure weighs 12 kg and is easy to handle.

3

4

5

6

1965 Genoa, Italy
Woodworking shop

The love of building

Architects: Studio Piano
with the collaboration of R. Foni, M. Filocca, L. Tirelli

Contractors: E. Piano Contractors

This is another structural model with a geometrical matrix: a woodworking shop. The components serve as support structure and wall-screen. The steel lozenges are bolted together. The scheme consists of a barrel vault (net span of 18 m) in which the lines of force intersect, running vertically from the central directrix of the fold in the elements and diagonally from the joints between the lozenges. It is this complex intersecting of planes that reveals a qualitative advance. The arrangement becomes less austere, enriched with delicate modulations and amber-tinted reflections. Moreover, the clustering of the molecule of the space frame is only provisional and does not exclude further development. The modular elements are rigorously standardized, but by modifying the angle of the central fold it is possible to vary the geometrical pattern of the grid and the net span of the barrel vault. The workshop consists of structural elements in steel sheeting (weight 25 kg, thickness 12/10 mm), produced by a process similar to those used in the automobile industry.

Piano envisages the woodworking shop as an open-ended structure, whose size can be fixed as necessary, like a magic box, which can be extended or contracted by routine operations. This is the distinctive feature of his early designs. The architectural product, instead of appearing as a finished product, is a "work in progress," a provisional and open-ended spatial whole. What counts first of all is the creative process, the mastery of materials and tools of the productive cycle: the love of building. It is this that drives him to invent and to venture into areas outside the usual spheres of traditional architecture.

This is a significant step forward; Piano is learning his job but already he is interpreting it in his own fashion, projecting himself into the future through the technological option, and at the same time redeeming "lost time" through rediscovery of the role of architect-builder. All this was an experiment in craftsmanship conducted in Genoa where, after his studies at the Milan Polytechnic, he was progressively concentrating his professional activity in collaboration with his brother who had inherited their father's construction firm.

Hand plus head, work plus thought, creativity plus execution; with all the consequences this involves on the aesthetic level, "it is no longer possible to reconnect the structural, constructional and technological aspects to the purely instrumental role. Since the above aspects intervene in any highly articulated design process, they modify and define the basic assumptions of design. In reality the level of complexity of the final product is largely conditioned even in its functional aspects, by a set of so-called technological aspects."

7

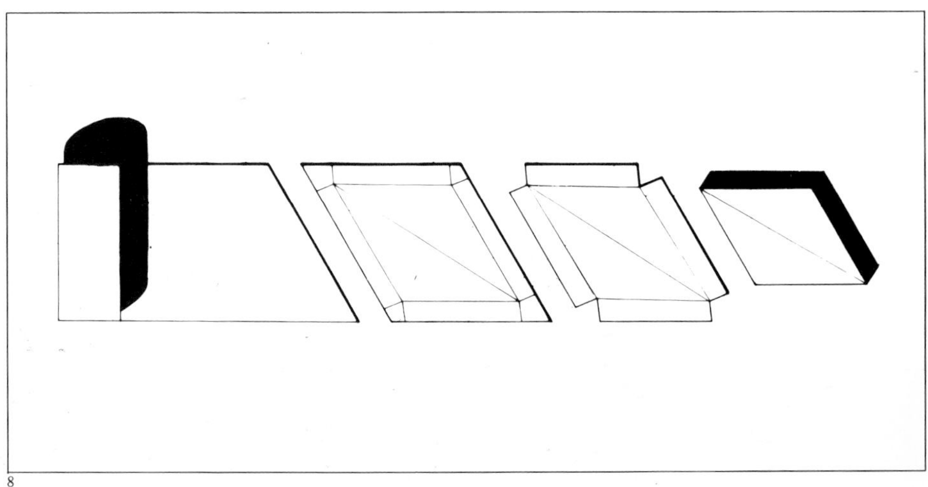

8

The architectural product instead of appearing as a finished product is a "work in progress," a provisional and open-ended spatial whole.

7. The basic structural element is made of sheet metal produced by simple bending.

8. Scheme for cutting and bending, starting from a roll of sheet metal.

9. Interior of the workshop.

10. Exterior.

9

10

1966 Genoa, Italy
Prestressed steel and reinforced polyester structure

Pent-up energy

18 Client: IPE - Genoa
Architects: Studio Piano with F. Marano
Contractors: E. Piano Contractors

The visual impression of the undulations of the membrane, which is elastic and translucent, is of a wavy sea. The suggestion of the marine world is more than a mere allusion in Piano's architectural vocabulary, it is an iconographical sign, or even a ritual symbol. It supplies a key to the structure. "Building boats has taught me much. You make use of the dynamics of materials. Apart from the keel, which is cut out, the woodwork is bent into shape. In a wreck, you always clearly see how the wood has burst open, showing the restrained energy. Whatever material is set in tension the effect is magnificent. This dynamic is the basis of pretensing, of precompression. And when a material is moulded there is always a gain. Construction also has a very powerful effect on memory. When I built my first boat, I had built up a storage of information about material and its process of transformation."

The marine archetype also relates to exploration for Piano, experimenting and verifying, but never taking extreme risks, feeling his way cautiously, with pragmatic rigor and scientific method. This emerges clearly in this prestressed steel and polyester structure, in which he devoted great care to planning the phases of assembly and mounting, the equipment needed for on site production. Yet the design does not call for any great technological resources. On the contrary, assembly is simplified to the point that a one-ton jib crane can take care of everything. There is no waste of technological resources, behind it there is systematic research based on experimental method. "This was, quite literally, a home-made design. I even took over the living-room with a full-scale section, a gigantic structure whose tensions I calculated by using springs, without calling in the engineer." The results are tangible, ranging from structural optimization (average weight of the whole enclosure is 8.7 kg/m^2) to regulation of the tensions. The problem here was to control the non-elastic deformability of the plastic material and the dimensional variation caused by changes in temperature. The solution consisted of a highly articulated system of retrieval tensions.

The formal structure is extremely simple, a minimal box-enclosure which can, however, be extended in any direction (through a process of temporarily suspending the tensions), compact yet traversed by hidden vibrations, elementary yet elegant. There is nothing contrived about the elegance: "Elegance and beauty are closely bound up with the strict requirements of the material. It takes a hell of a lot of hard work to achieve simplicity. Simplicity cannot be the starting point but the goal of our work. I have never sat down at the drawing board with elegance as my specific aim. If it is there, it is something I achieve as I am working on my material."

Here we already find a concern with light, the balancing of natural and artificial light. The covering membrane (made up of reinforced polyester panels measuring 2.50 m^2) absorbs about 30% of the light, so that transparency in relation to outside light touches 70%. This is yet another channel through which his architectural vocabulary progressively attained harmony with the external environment.

"Building boats has taught me much. You make use of the dynamics of materials. Apart from the keel, which is cut out, the woodwork is bent into shape. In a wreck, you always clearly see how the wood has burst open, showing the restrained energy. Whatever material is set in tension the effect is magnificent."

11, 12. Structural study model of the membrane geometry.

13. Full-scale experimental structure to measure stress on cables and masts. Practical experiment alongside mathematical calculation is Piano's regular working practice.

14, 15. Plans of the industrial complex in first and second phases of construction.

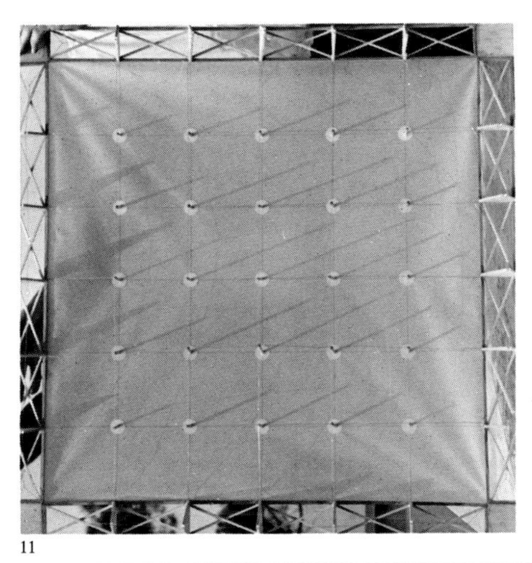

11

12

13

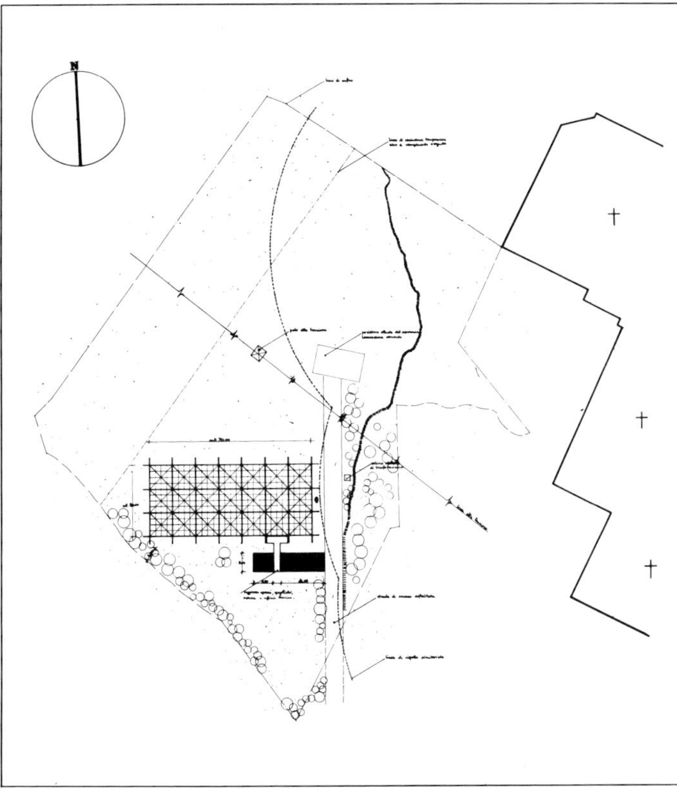

14

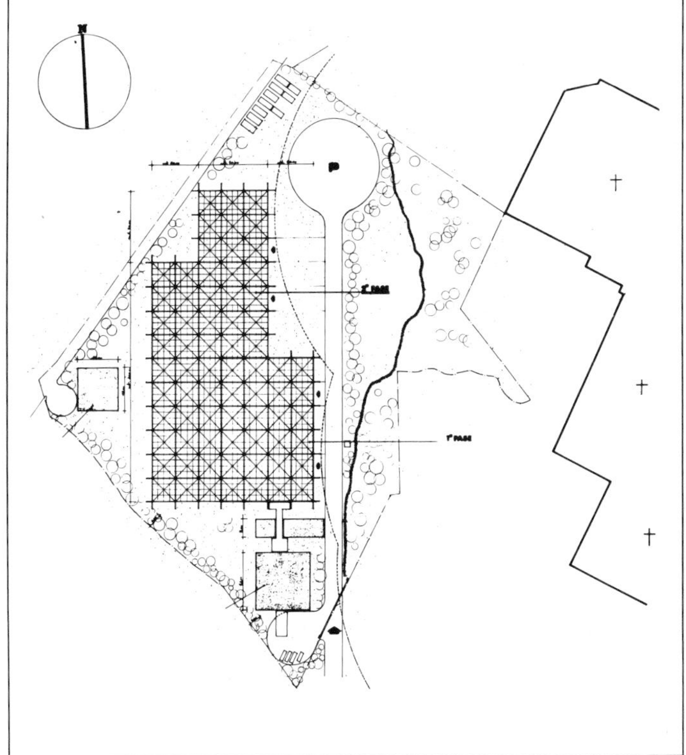

15

16. The prestressed membrane seen from above.

17. Mould detail at attachment point of strut to membrane.

18. Detail of corrugation of the membrane at point of major stress concentration.

19. Section of the structure: span 10 m x 10 m.

20. Detail of pillar holding pretensing cables.

16

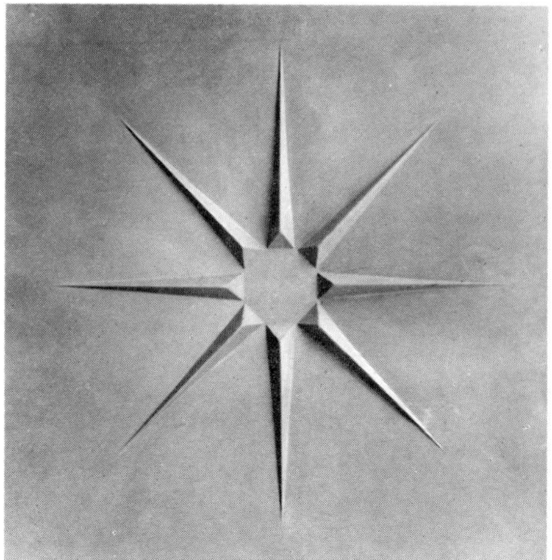

17

18

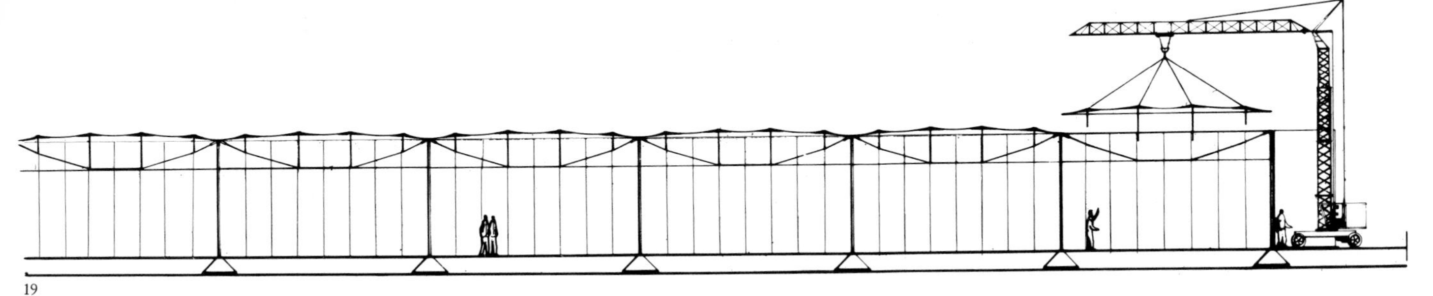
19

20

21. The reinforced polyester membrane is tensioned by vertical metal masts. Total weight of construction, 9.8 kg/m².

22. Detail of attachment of prestressing masts to pillar.

23. Mounting the structure.

24. Attachment of the reinforced polyester membrane to the support and prestressing steel frame.

10000
2500 2500 2500 2500
2500 2500 2500
1250 2500 2500 2500 1250

21

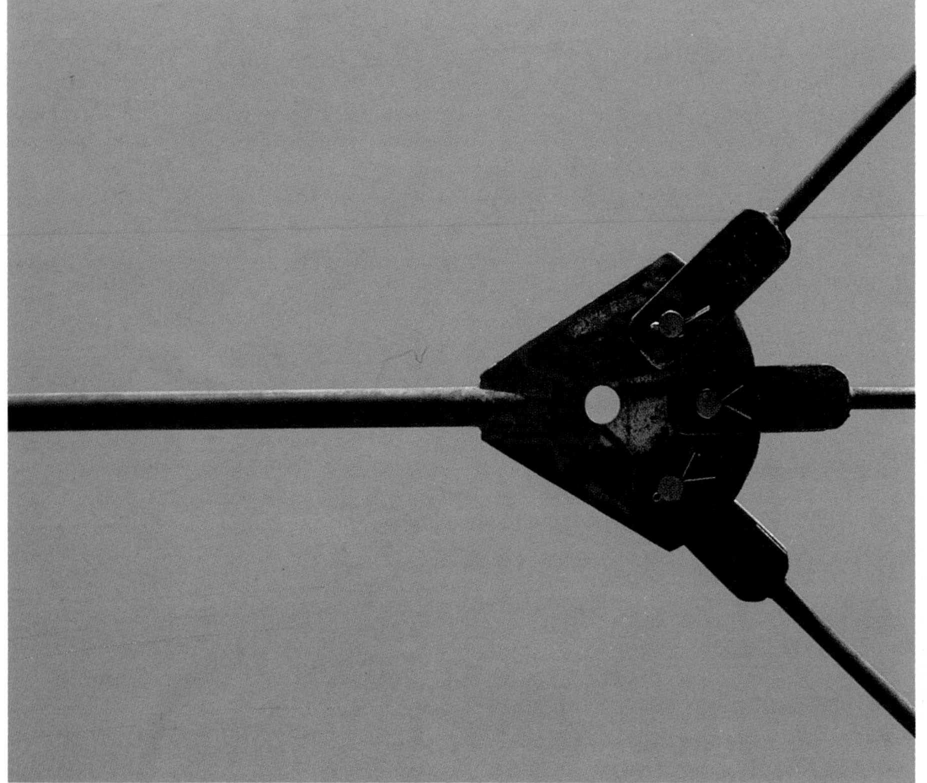

22

23

24

25. View inside the construction: the polyester membrane allows 70% of external light to filter through.

26. Sealing of external joints of covering after prestressing.

25

25

26

1967 Milan, Italy
Shell structural systems:
a pavilion for the XIV Triennale

Designing the instruments

26 Client: Milan Triennale
Architects: Studio Piano
with F. Marano, O. Celadon, G. Fascioli

From the corrugated surface to the shell, Piano's architectural language begins to move away from geometry and the canons of symmetry in search of more complex spatial flows. The threshold passed is the structural definition of the shell: a simple form that can be dissected into similar components by extending the range of mass production beyond the usual boundaries. "I am a practical person," says Piano, "an artisan of technology. If I want to achieve a goal, I am restless until it is done. If the means cannot be found, perhaps the goal itself is mistaken."

He proceeds by trial and error combining scientific discipline with experimental inventiveness: concept calculation, development of models and prototypes in the workshop, a verification of architectural space. The shell structure theoretically can be shaped to an immense variety and complexity of forms. The industrial production depends more on the characteristics of the plant rather than on the features of the structural element. It is necessary to get beyond the concept of an industrially produced element as an inevitably standardized element.

In this challenge what is at stake is a different idea of space, a dynamic, undefined space which rejects classical design schemes; a psychological space, so to speak, not crystalized in pure geometrical forms, and completely realized in the workshop. This shell structure provides a typical instance of Piano's design procedure. "Once, when architecture really was a craft, the architect used to design his work instruments before he designed the actual buildings. Nowadays, in order to express oneself, it is absolutely necessary to 'edify' these instruments, which are at present in the hands of 'uncultivated' and corporative operators. Form, if it ever is to emerge, must also emerge from this reappropriation of the 'cultural' and material instruments of building."

One of the procedures followed is the study of elastic forms under pressure: the plaster models are made by using elastic moulds that reproduce, with sufficient exactness, an elastic membrane in simple tension, a form which, when inverted, reproduces a continuous membrane with shell-type structural behavior. By varying the constraints of elastic forms and modifying the tensions, it is possible to carry out experiments in free-form shell structures. On the production level, a complex procedure was devised: working on the model (generally on a scale of 1:10) the entire surface of the membrane was divided into a number of sections, each different from the others in form and curvature; using an apparatus for the reading of the coordinates of each point of the element on the model, the data related to each section was transmitted to an adjustable mould supported on 36 pistons which immediately reproduced the form provided by the reading in full size. This mould, adapted to the concave form provided by the model, was then used to make the structural shell element.

This lengthy research finally led to the design (put forward by Marco Zanuso) for the outer pavilion of the XIV Milan Triennale, a macrostructure with a rigid continuous membrane, to be set on a site of about 2500 m^2, resting on the ground along a number of main corrugations. The materials used for the construction were a double layer of rigid polyester and expanded polyurethane, with areas of restricted light absorption to accentuate the feeling of depth and indeterminacy of the spatial organism. The design was rejected. One critic commented: "Considering the scheme which was finally adopted, this design by Piano was an opportunity thrown away by the Triennale, which could have made a real contribution to Italian research by accepting a completely new structure." Meantime the geometrical emblem had been broken, leaving the way open to expressive solutions which mimicked biological forms by recycling them in imaginative ways.

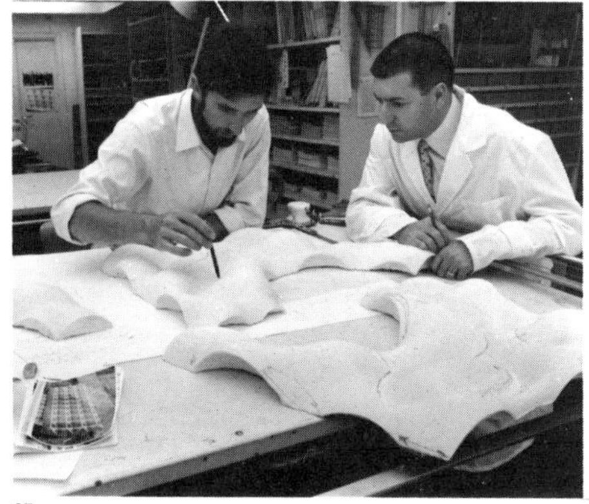
27

"Once, when architecture really was a craft, the architect used to design his work instruments before he designed the actual buildings. Nowadays, in order to express oneself, it is absolutely necessary to 'edify' these instruments, which are at present in the hands of 'uncultivated' and corporative operators."

27. Flavio Marano with Renzo Piano working on the structural test model.

28, 29. Morphological studies of the shell structure.

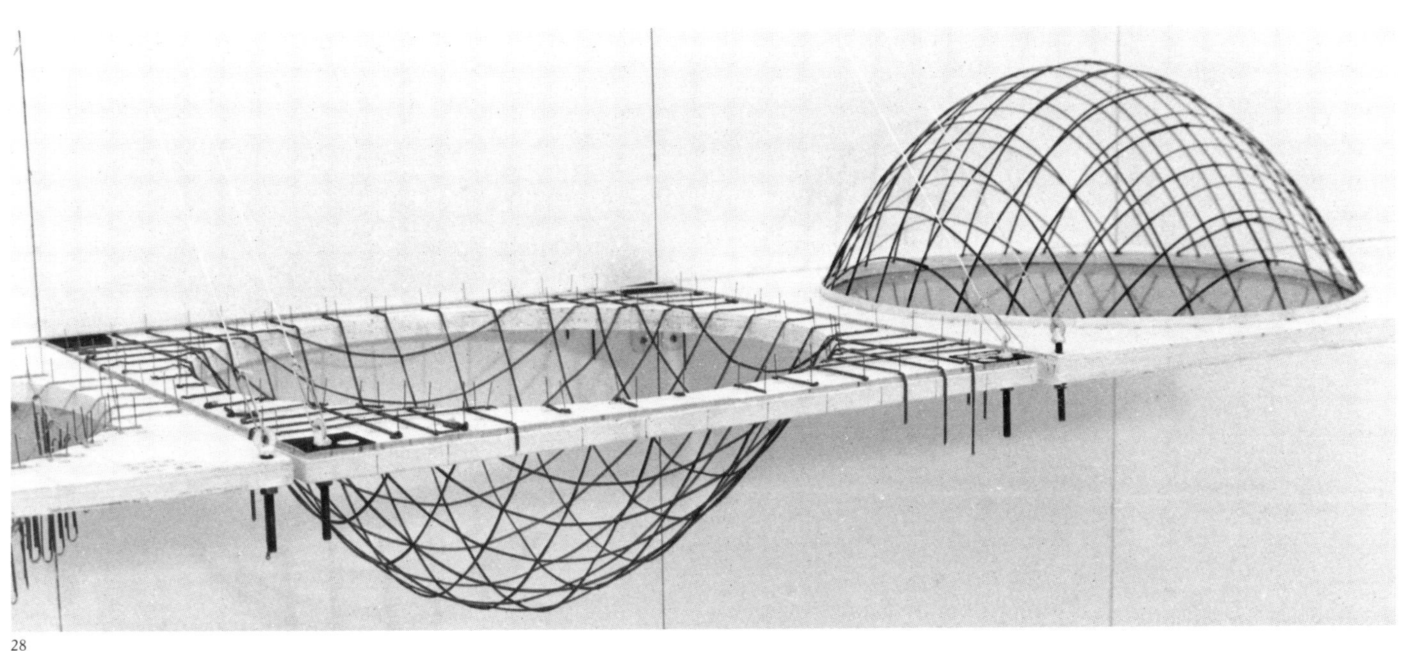

28

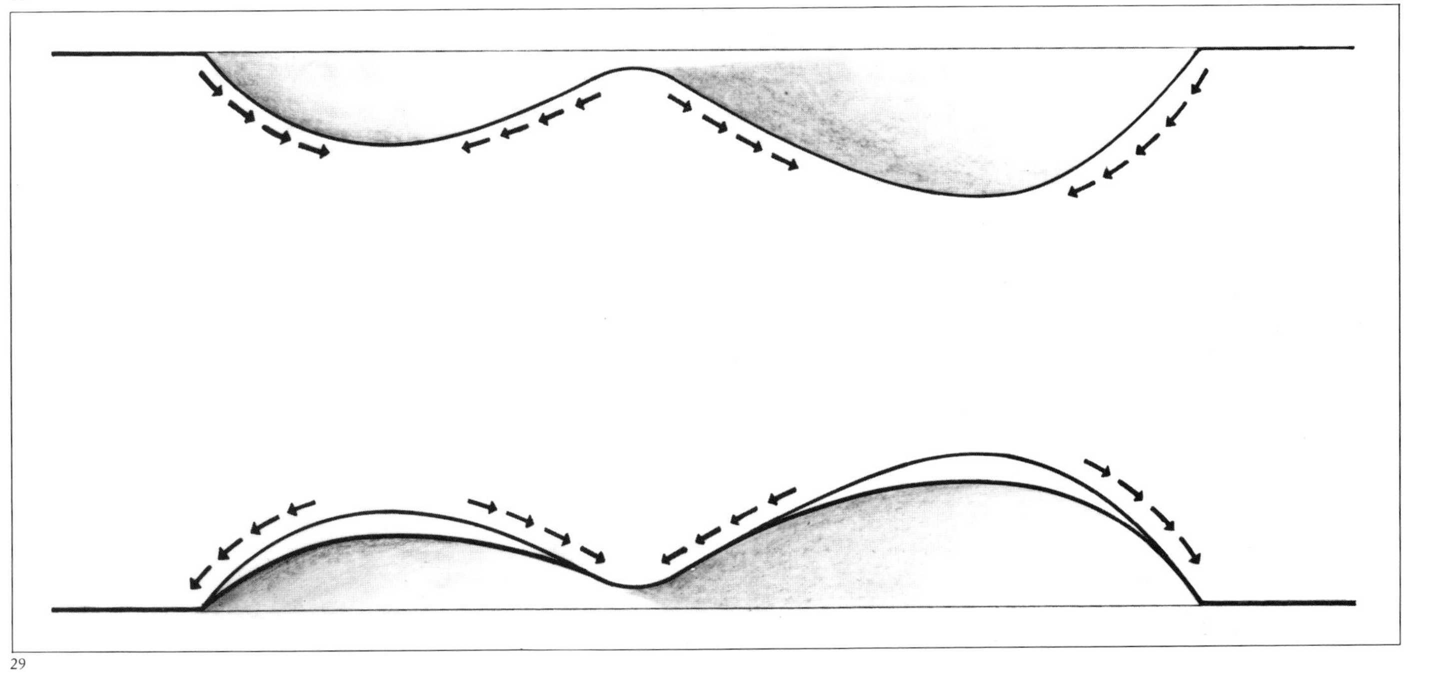

29

30. Studies of the membrane.

31. Studies for the XIV Milan Triennale pavilion.

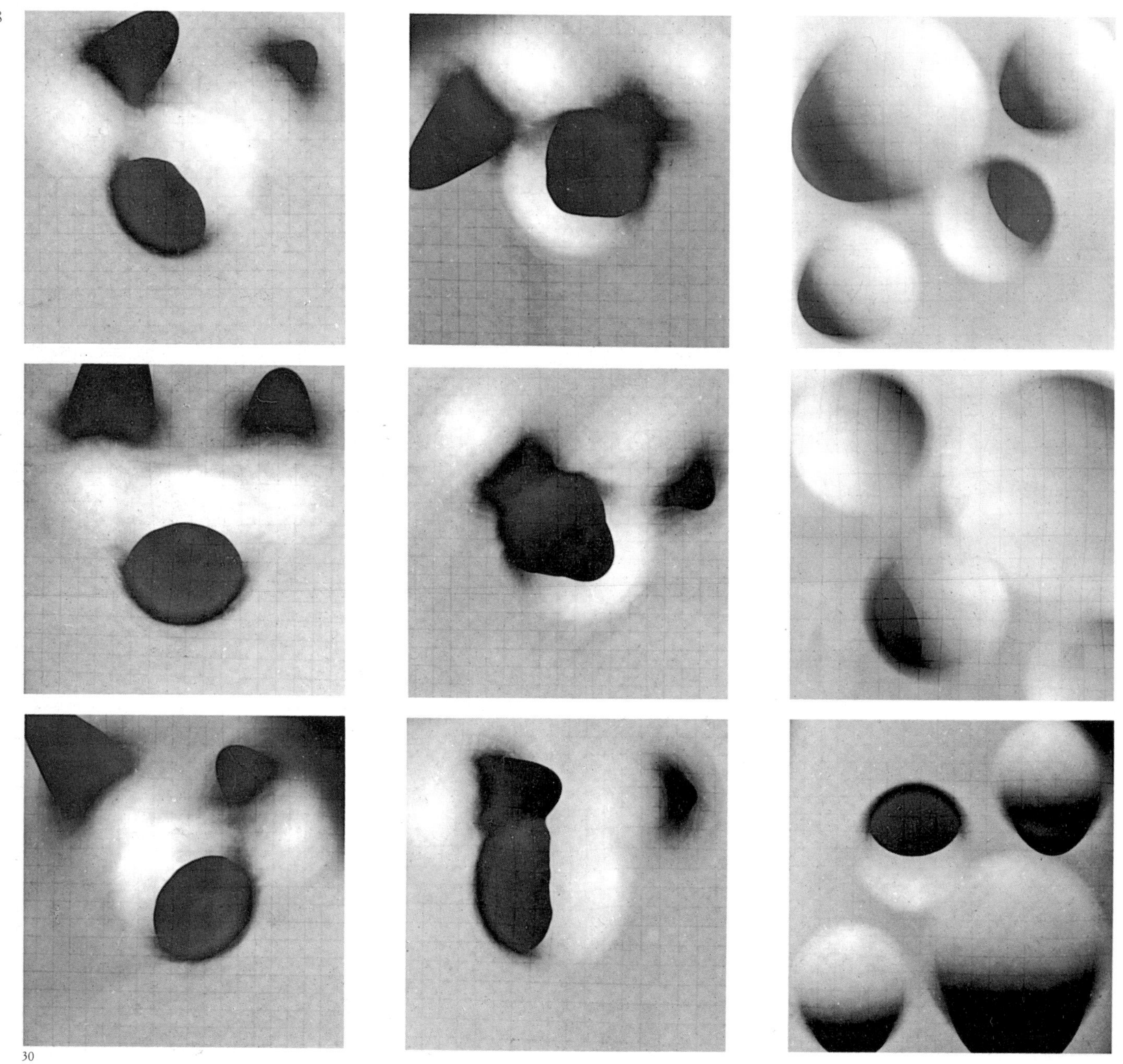

29

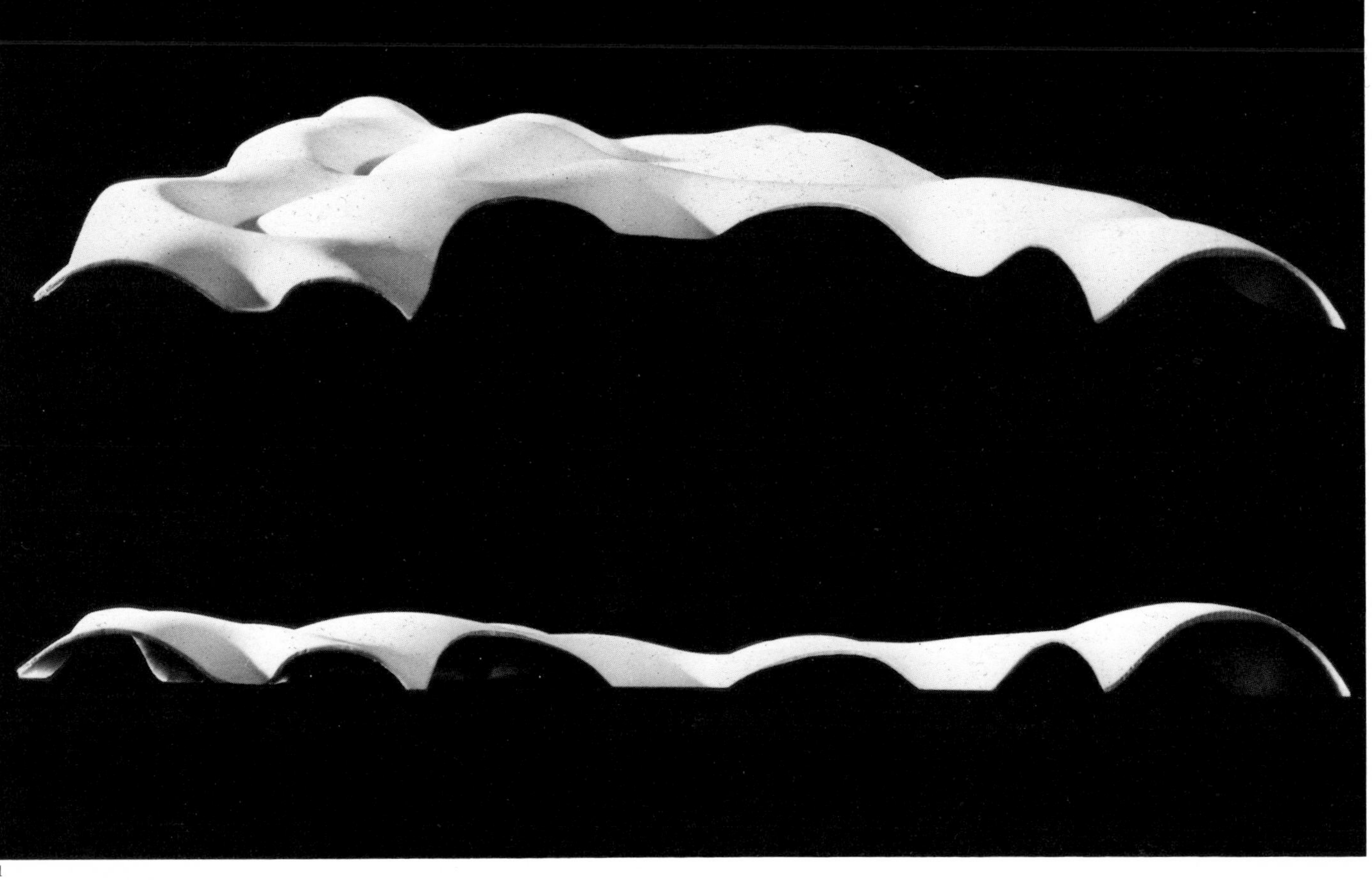

31

32. Gauge for transfer of the form from the models to the modifiable mould.

33. Detail of the modifiable mould piston-system.

34. Structural study with polarized light.

35. Transfer system of membrane form from the model to the modifiable mould.

36, 37. Assembling the elements of the shell structure for a test structure.

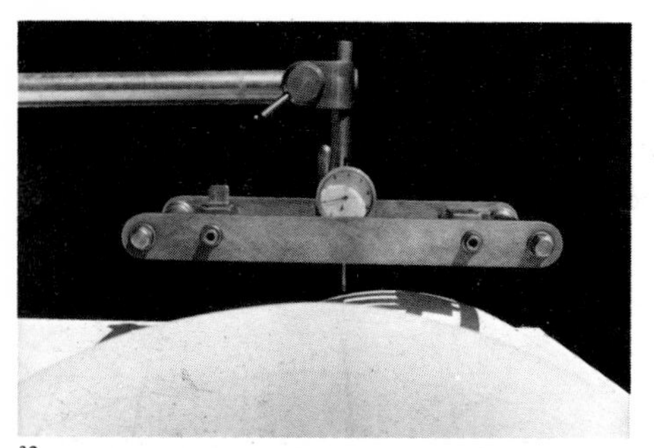

32

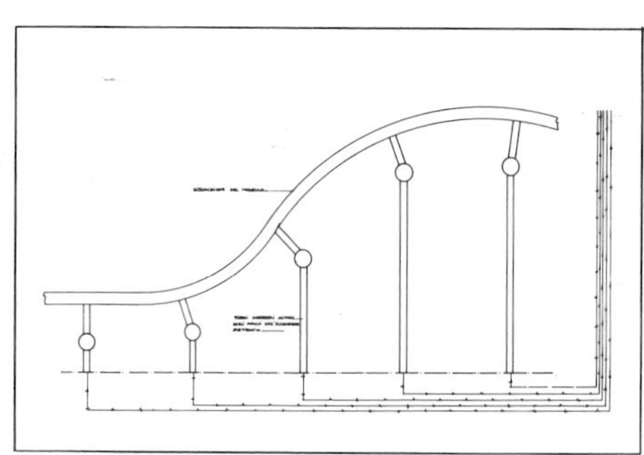

33

34

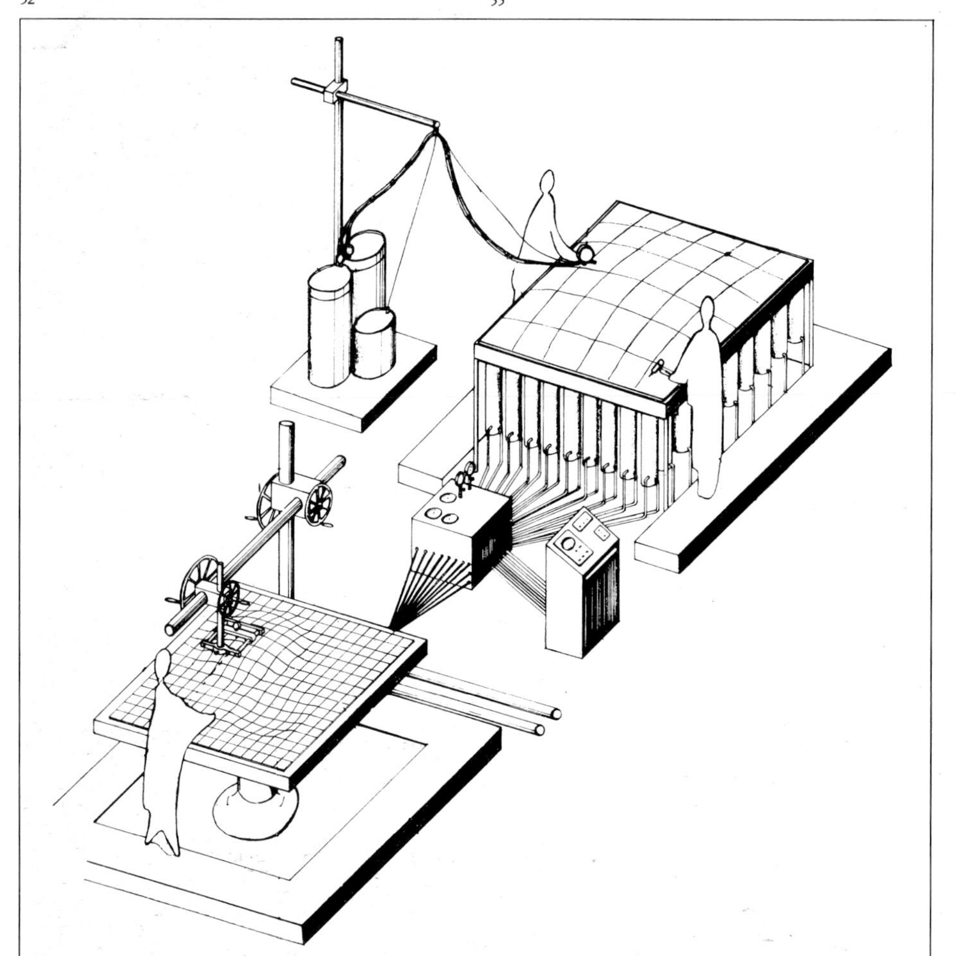

35

36

37

1969-1970 Osaka, Japan
Italian Industry Pavilion at the Osaka Expo

Calculation and experimentation

Client: Italpublic, Rome
Architects: Studio Piano
with F. Marano, G. Fascioli, G. Queirolo, T. Ferrari
Engineers: SERTEC Engineering
Contractors: E. Piano Contractors

The ancient and the futuristic, the transitory and the unchanging, craftsmanship and technology come together and merge in the city of Renzo Piano. In the Italian Industry Pavilion designed for the Osaka World Fair all these various facets come together in a single image. The great container – a prestressed structure of steel and reinforced polyester – is solid and compact, yet its rigidity is only relative, ephemeral. Like the circus big top, once the show is over it can be carried away and set up again elsewhere. The pavilion was built of prefabricated parts in Italy then shipped to Japan, set up for 60 days and then dismantled once the fair was over. Its three-dimensional enclosure conjures up images of circus marquees, the canopies of Mongol tents, the flimsy shelters of desert nomads. The thickness, the substantiality of the materials is almost an illusion.

Osaka marked an important stage. It signified Piano's definitive mastery of construction site problems, and also the development of a working method based on experiment and continual checking of practical results by using sophisticated technology. The calculation of the pre-tensioning values was achieved with a computer that calculated a wide range of extreme conditions related to wind dynamics and seismic phenomena. This optimizes the use of materials, standardizes elements, reduces weight and the number of components. Once the building is taken down it can be packed into about fifteen containers.

Osaka was not just an experiment contributing to research into tensile frames and special materials. The choice of a plastic covering for the metal framework fulfilled precise requirements for a very simple reason. Because of its low coefficient of elasticity, plastic materials are liable to deformation. This means that any structural system of this type subjected to pressure tends to deform, to alter the original geometrical scheme. This is the impression given by the pavilion in which the membrane, at bursting point, seems to have been halted, penned in by a web of cables and rods. These are the key elements not just in building up the structure but also in striving for expressiveness.

Technological virtuosity? Not just that. The incisions in the plastic membrane suggest the ribbing of leaves or geological patterns. The daytime lighting of the exhibition area because of the pavilion's translucency suggests natural illumination.

38

39

The great container is solid and compact, yet its rigidity is only relative, ephemeral. Like the circus big top, once the show is over it can be carried away and set up again elsewhere.

38. Prestressed reinforced polyester panel.

39. Load tests of reinforced polyester panel: the interaction of design and experiment is a constant feature of Piano's procedure.

40. Preparatory drawings for the Italian Industry Pavilion in Osaka.

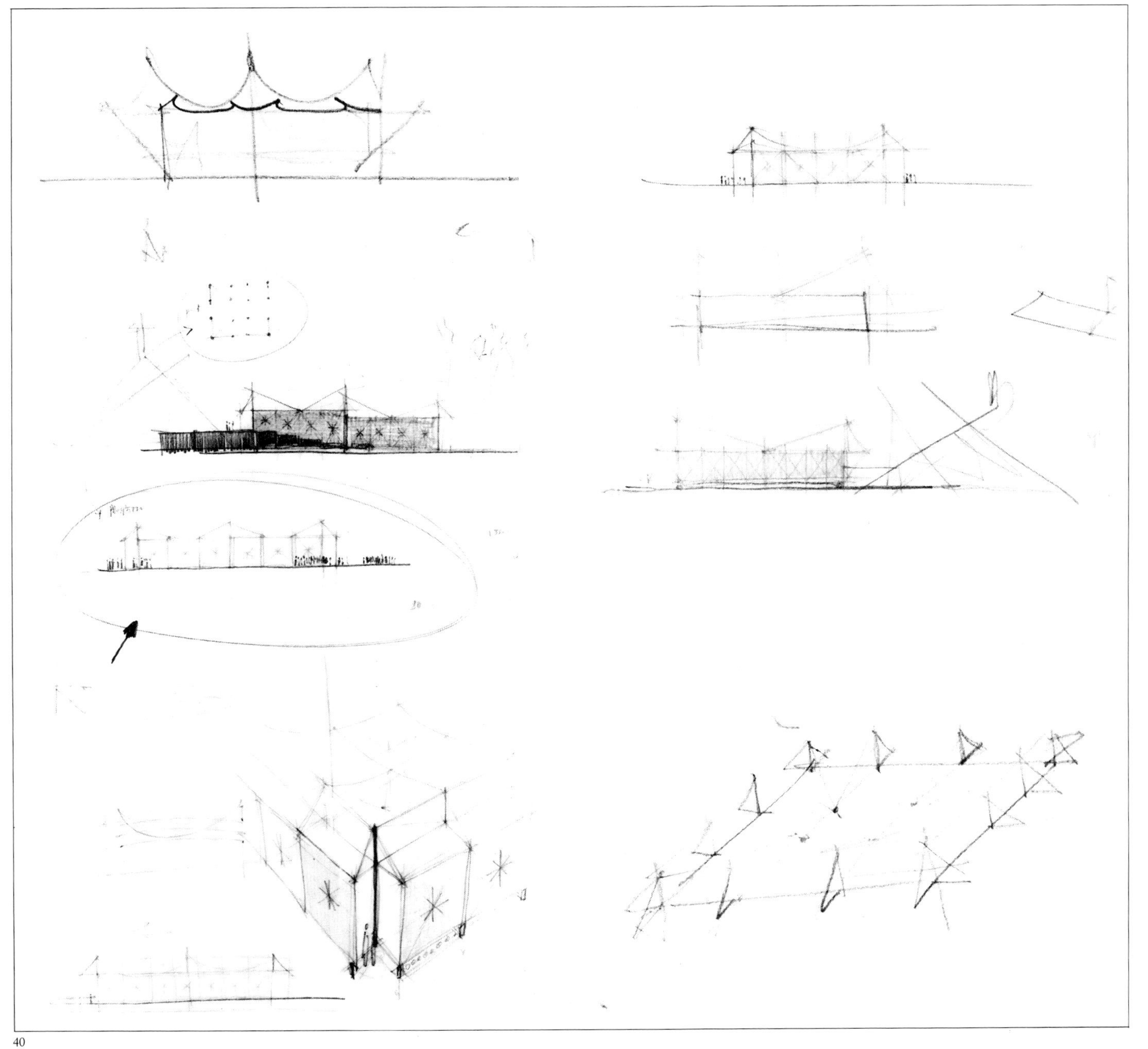

40

41. Section of panel made of two surfaces of reinforced polyester and an intermediate air chamber.

42. General axonometric scheme of the structure.

43. Italian Industry Pavilion in Osaka.

44. Detail of attachment of metal frame to reinforced polyester membrane.

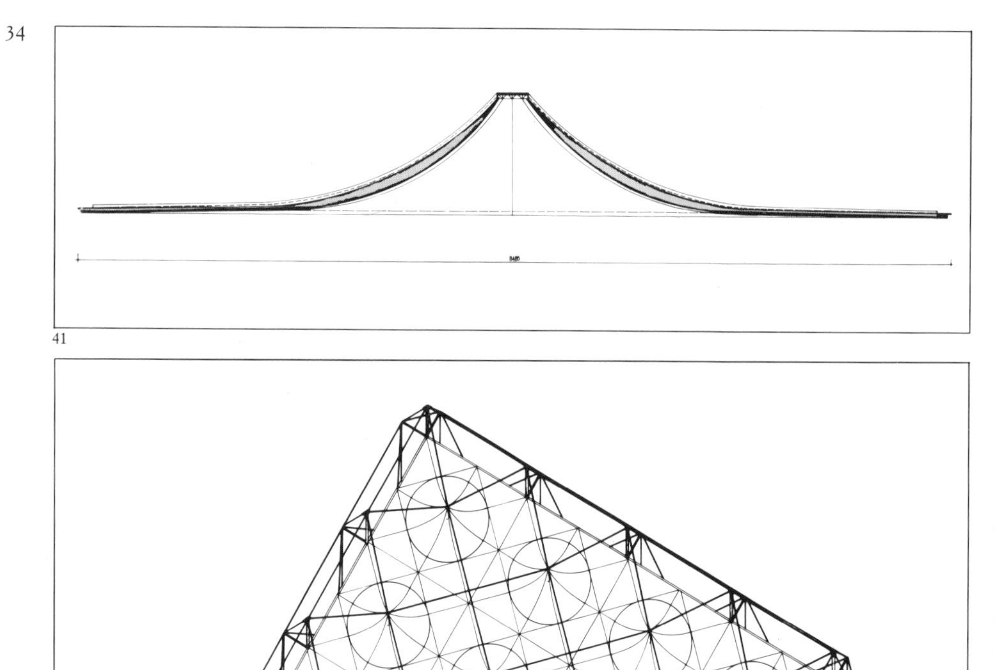

41

42

43

44

45. Construction drawings for the prestressed metal frame.

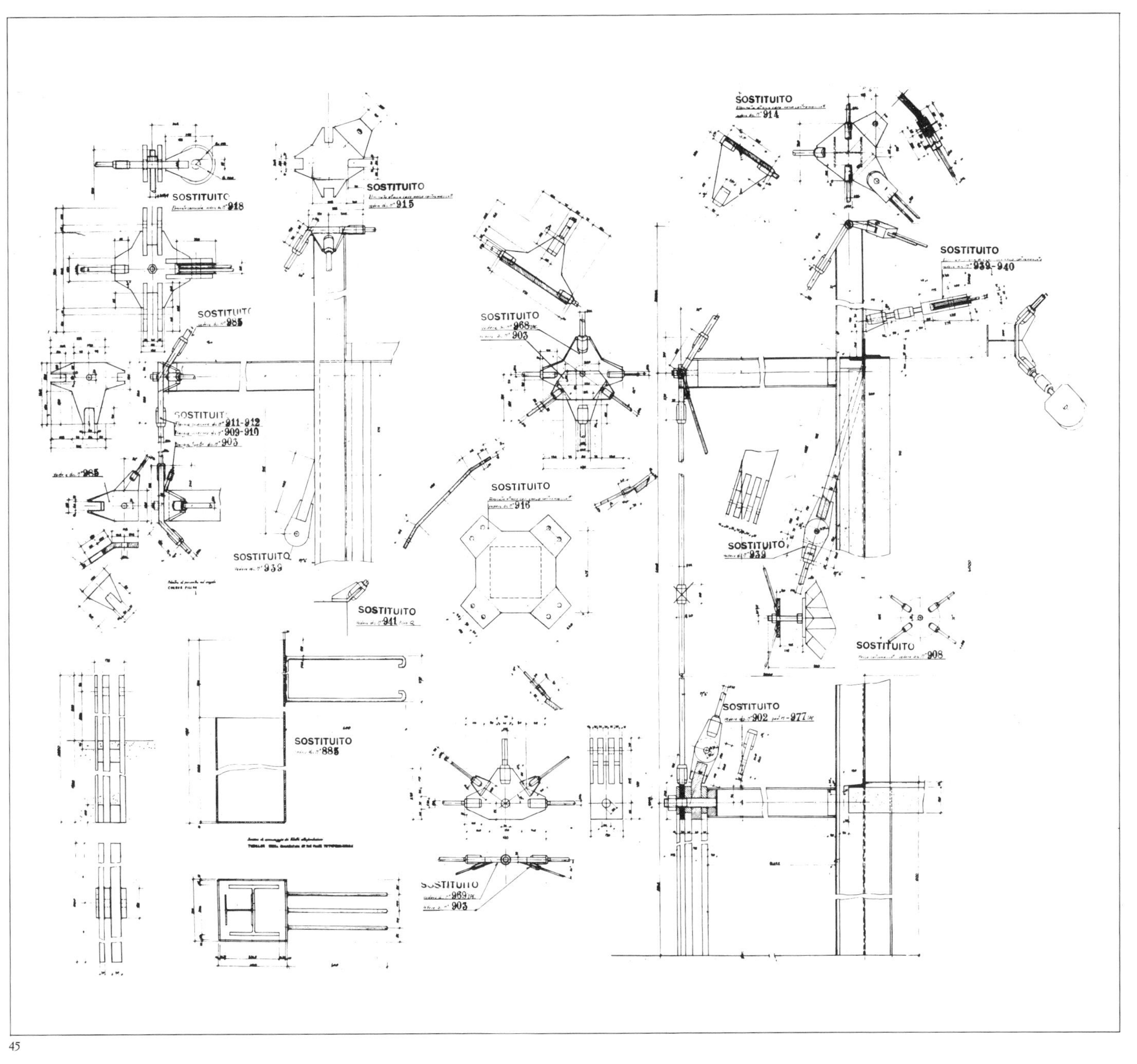

45

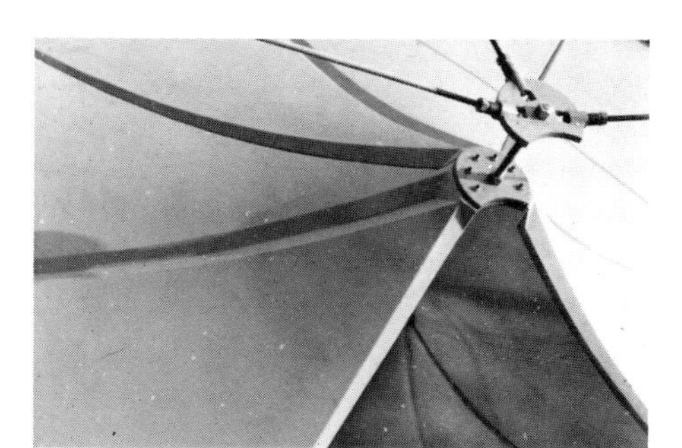

46

46. *Detail of joint connecting steel and polyester.*
47. *Geometrical scheme of the structure.*

48. *Detail of the membrane tensed by the external metal structure.*

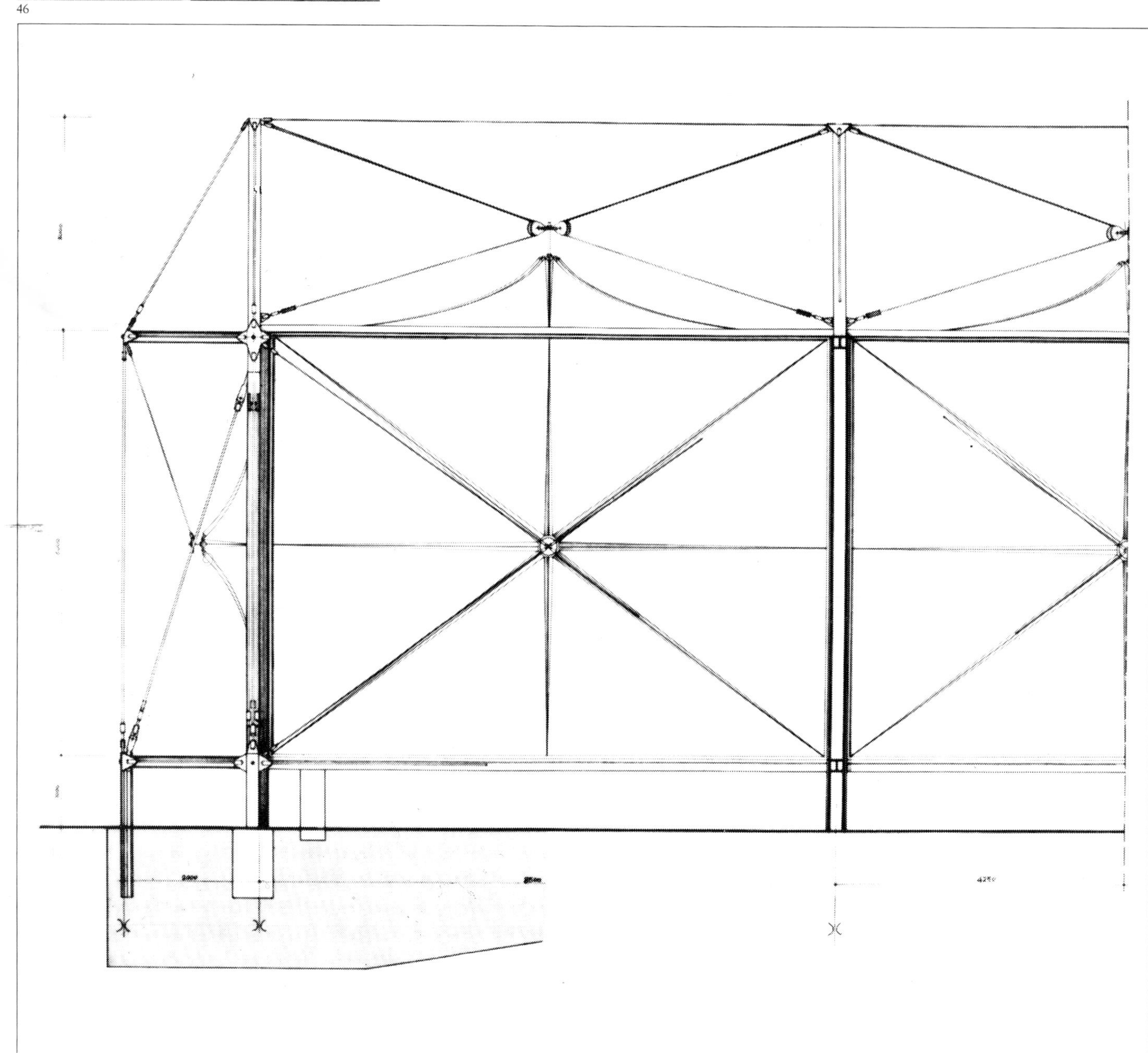

47

74. *Comparative diagram for production of an automobile: (a) using the traditional system and (b) the VSS prototype methods.*

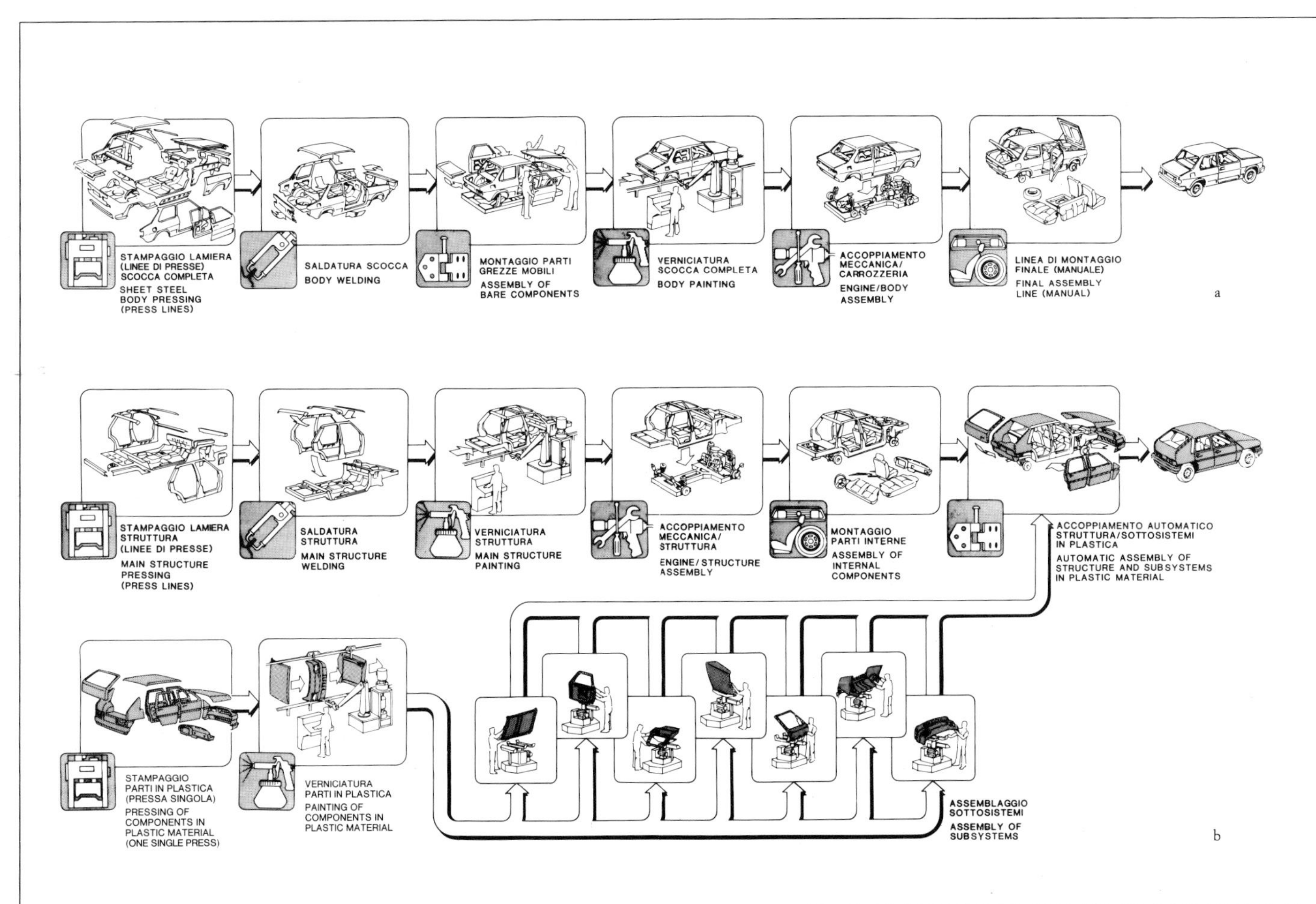

74

73. *Design of the substructure of the diaphragm.*

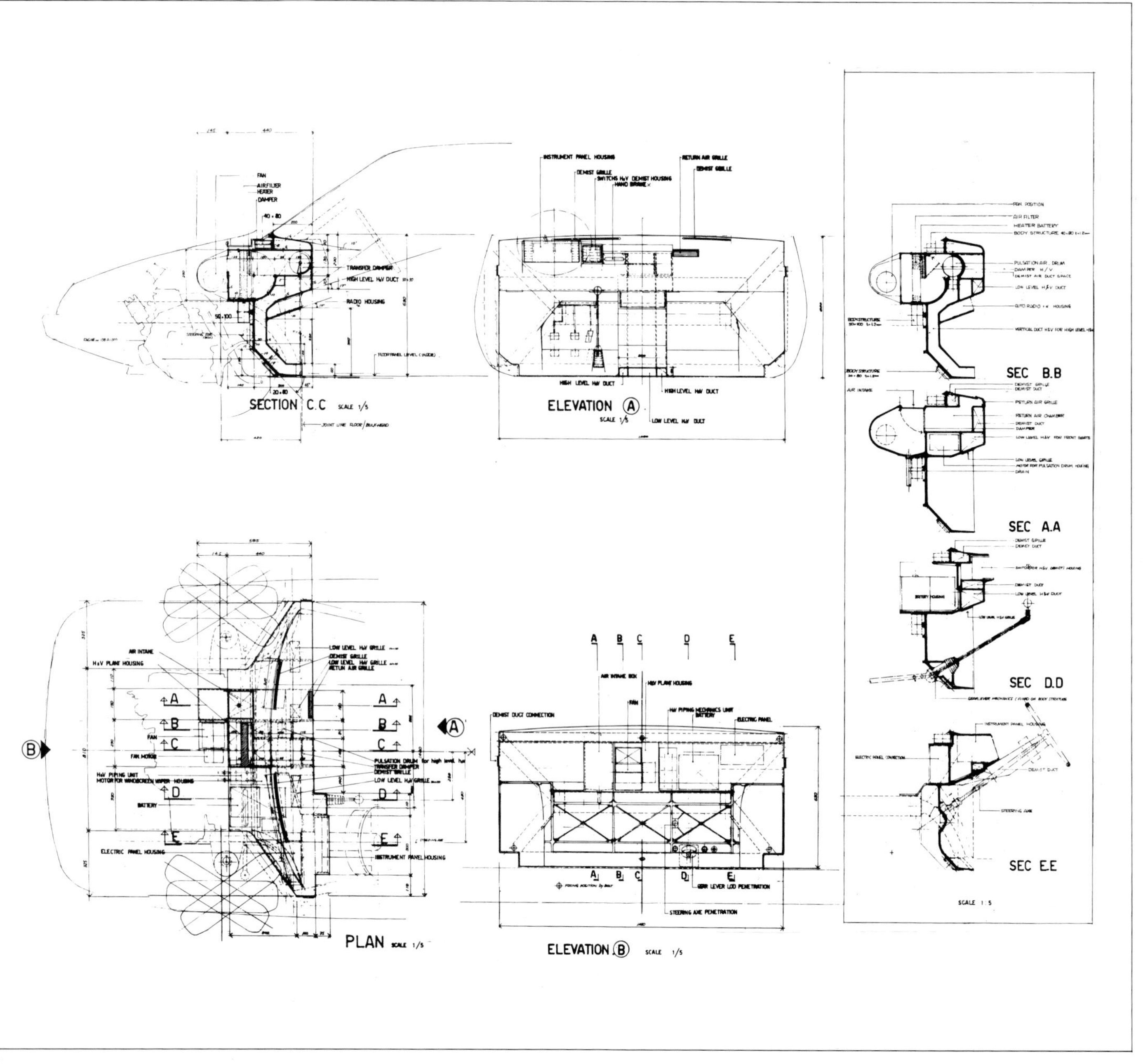

69. *Section of a door with steel core and polycarbonate skin.*

70. *Polycarbonate door components.*

71. *Structural study of the deformability of the trunk.*

72. *Attachment details of plastic shell to bearing frame.*

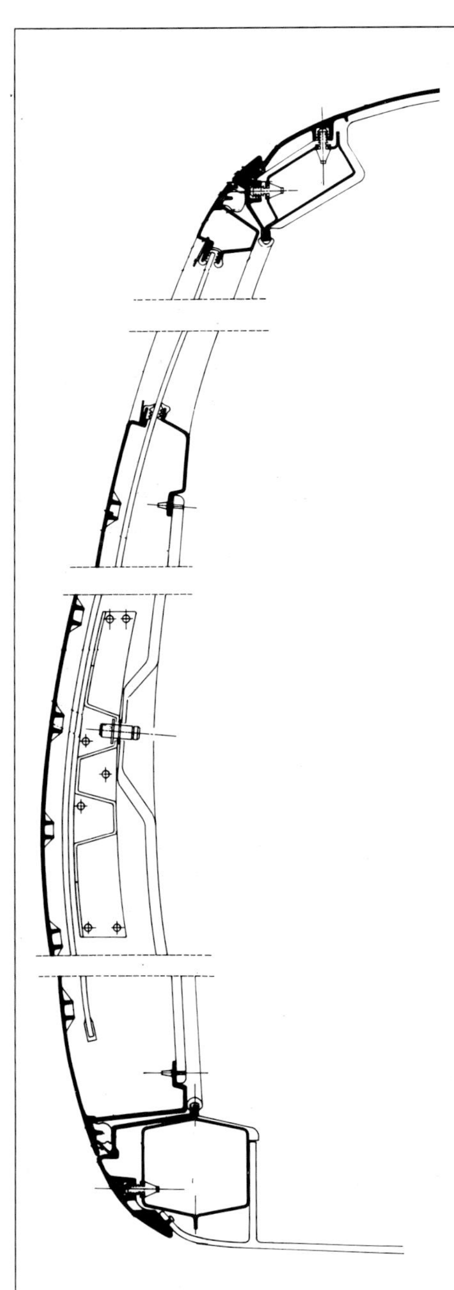

69

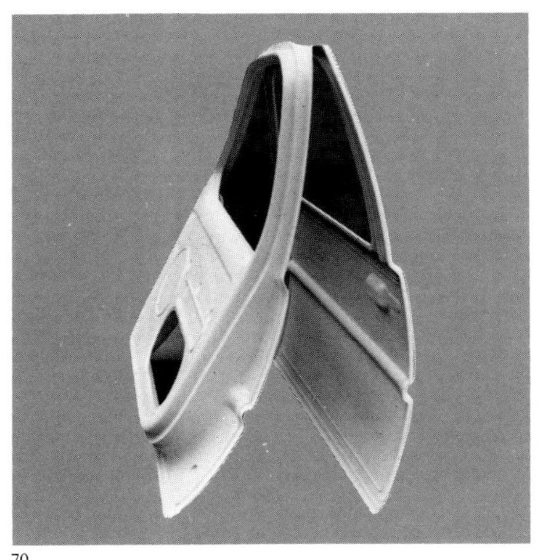

70

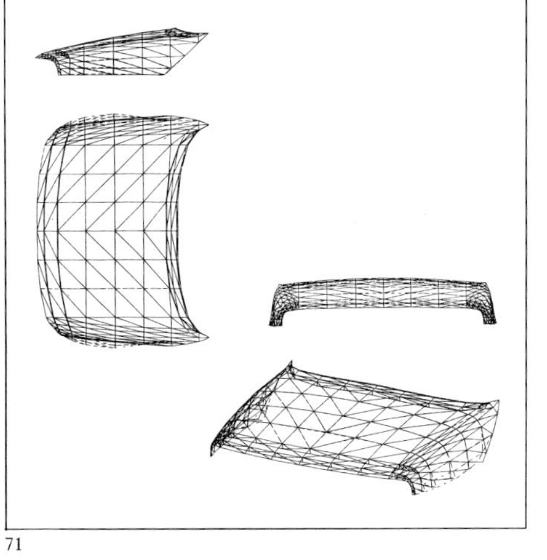

71

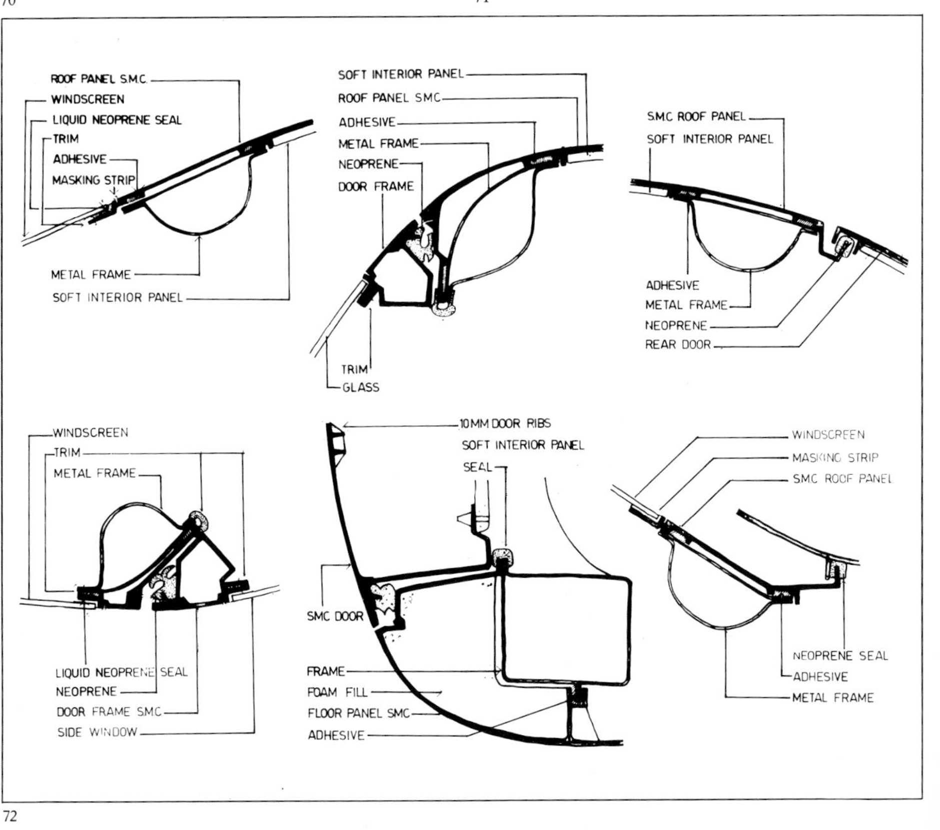

72

68. General scheme of plastic components of the vehicle's shell.

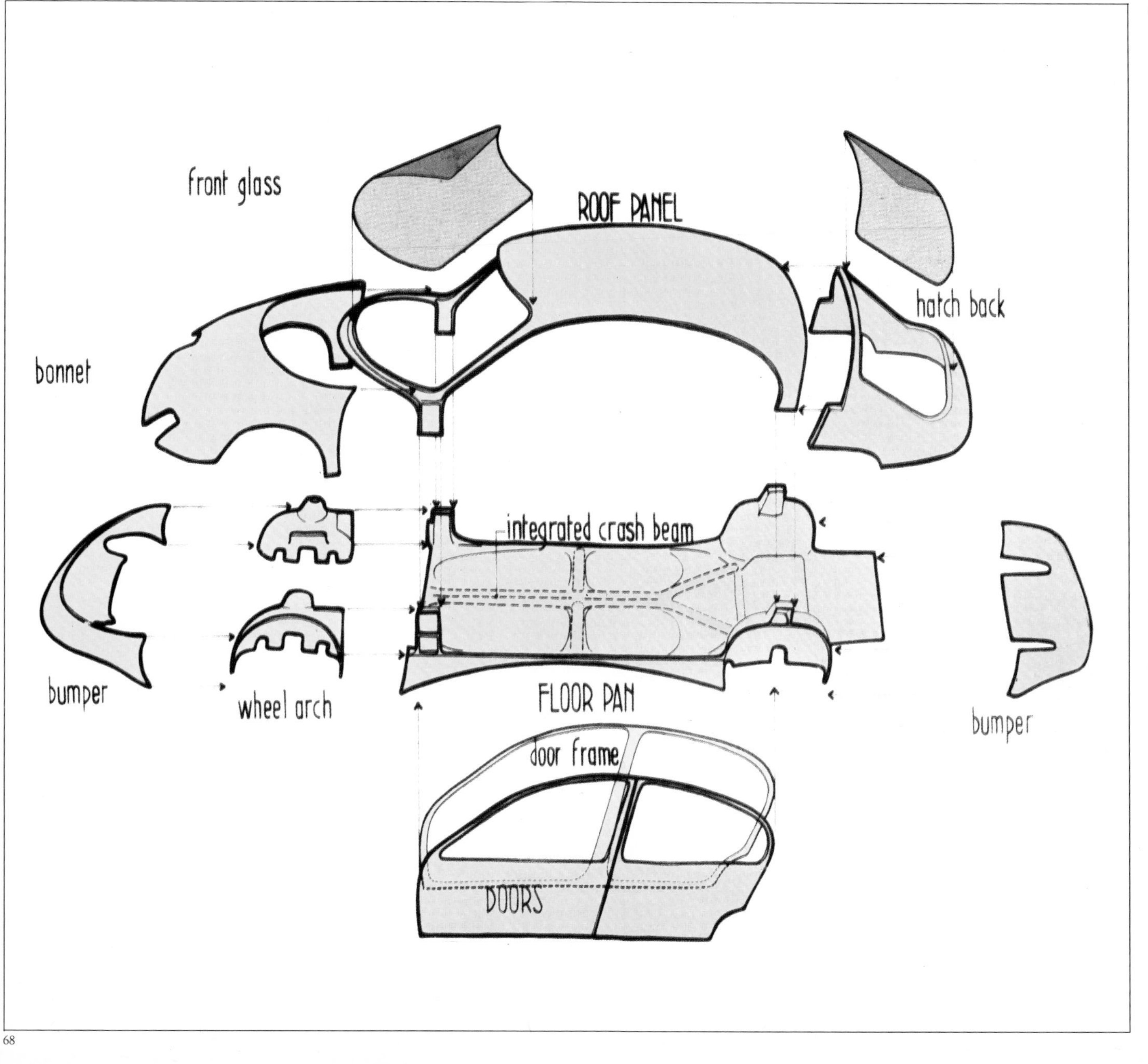

57. Schemes of different types of coachwork applied to a single frame.

58. Section of the top with suggested ventilation system.

59. Coachwork components in plastic.

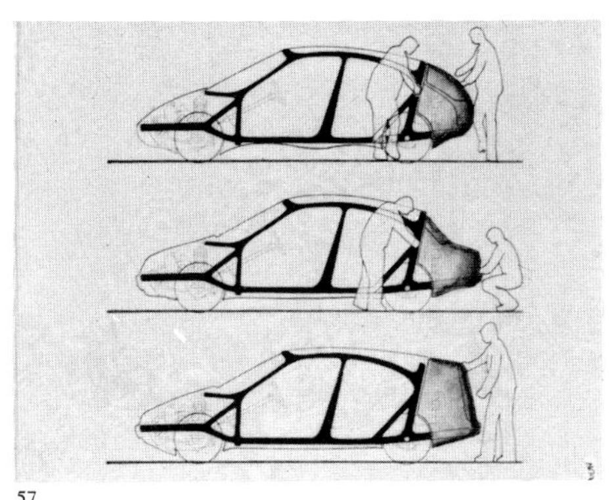

57

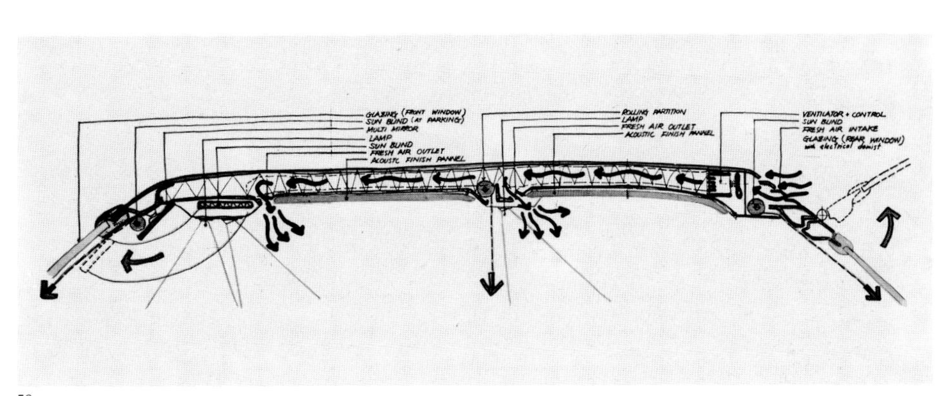

58

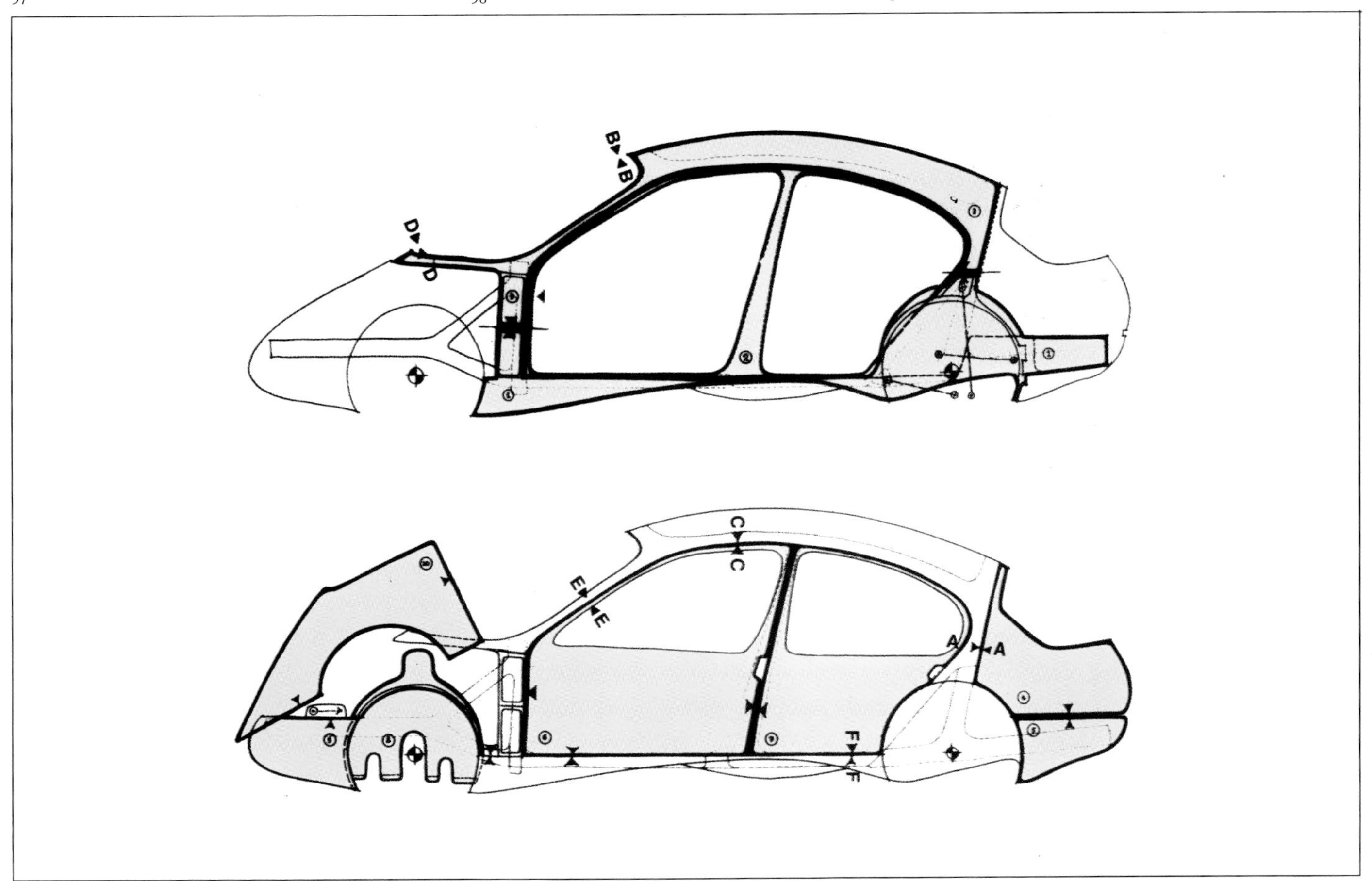

59

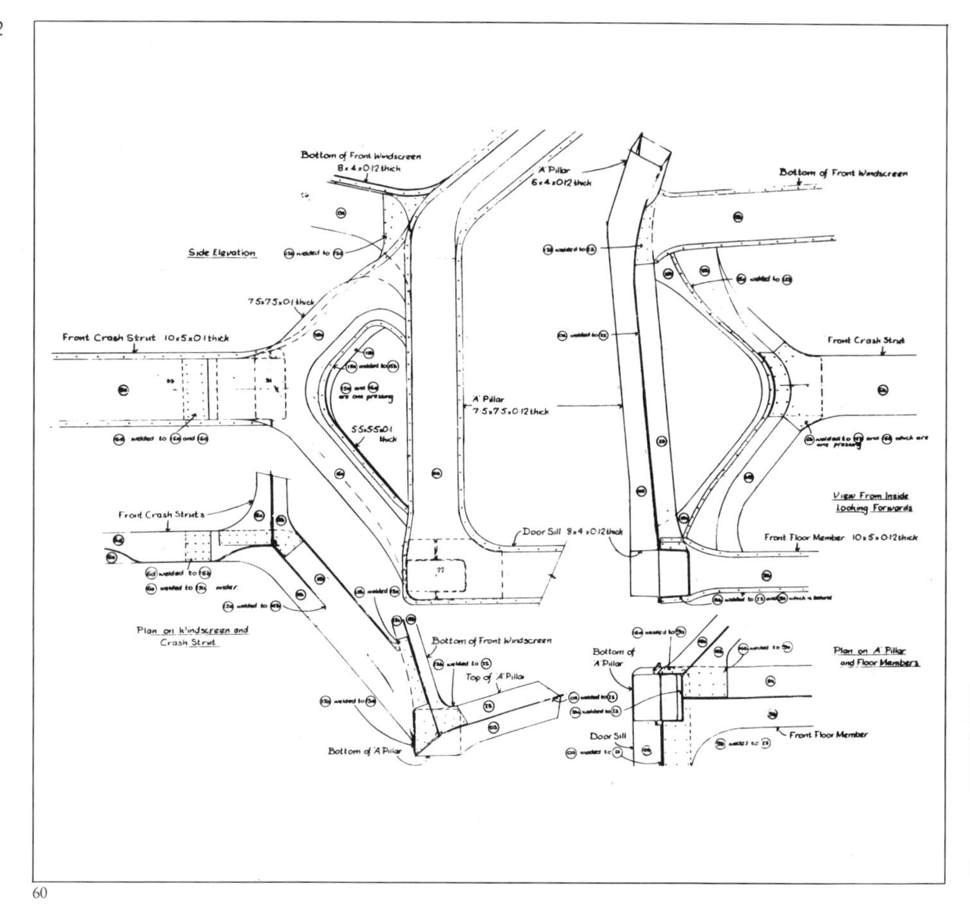

60

60. Assembly plan for elements of the steel frame.

61

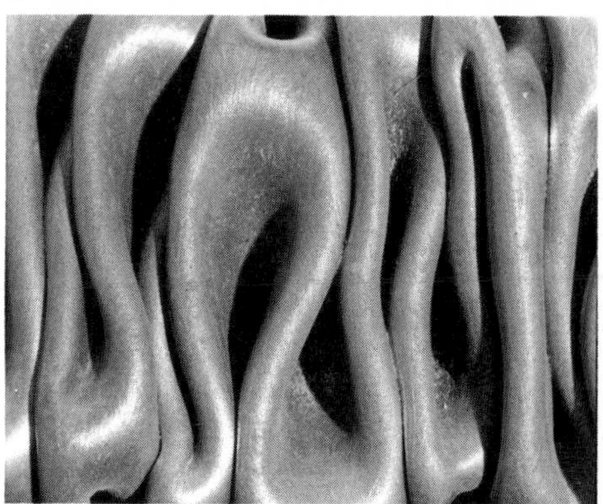
62

61. Assembling one of the steel trial structures.
62. Section of structure buckled in testing.

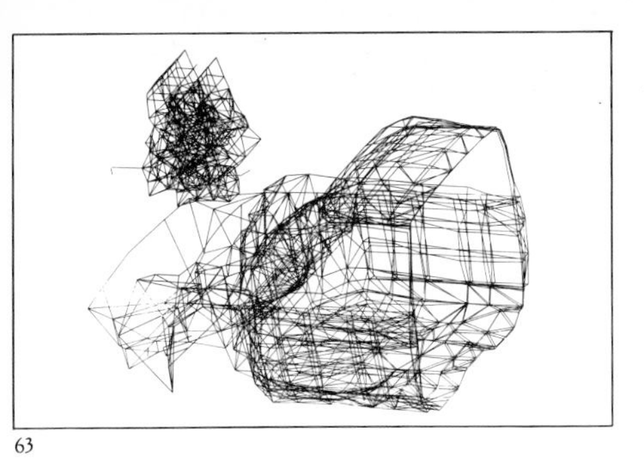

63

63. Plotter pattern of buckling in case of shock to the front of coachwork.

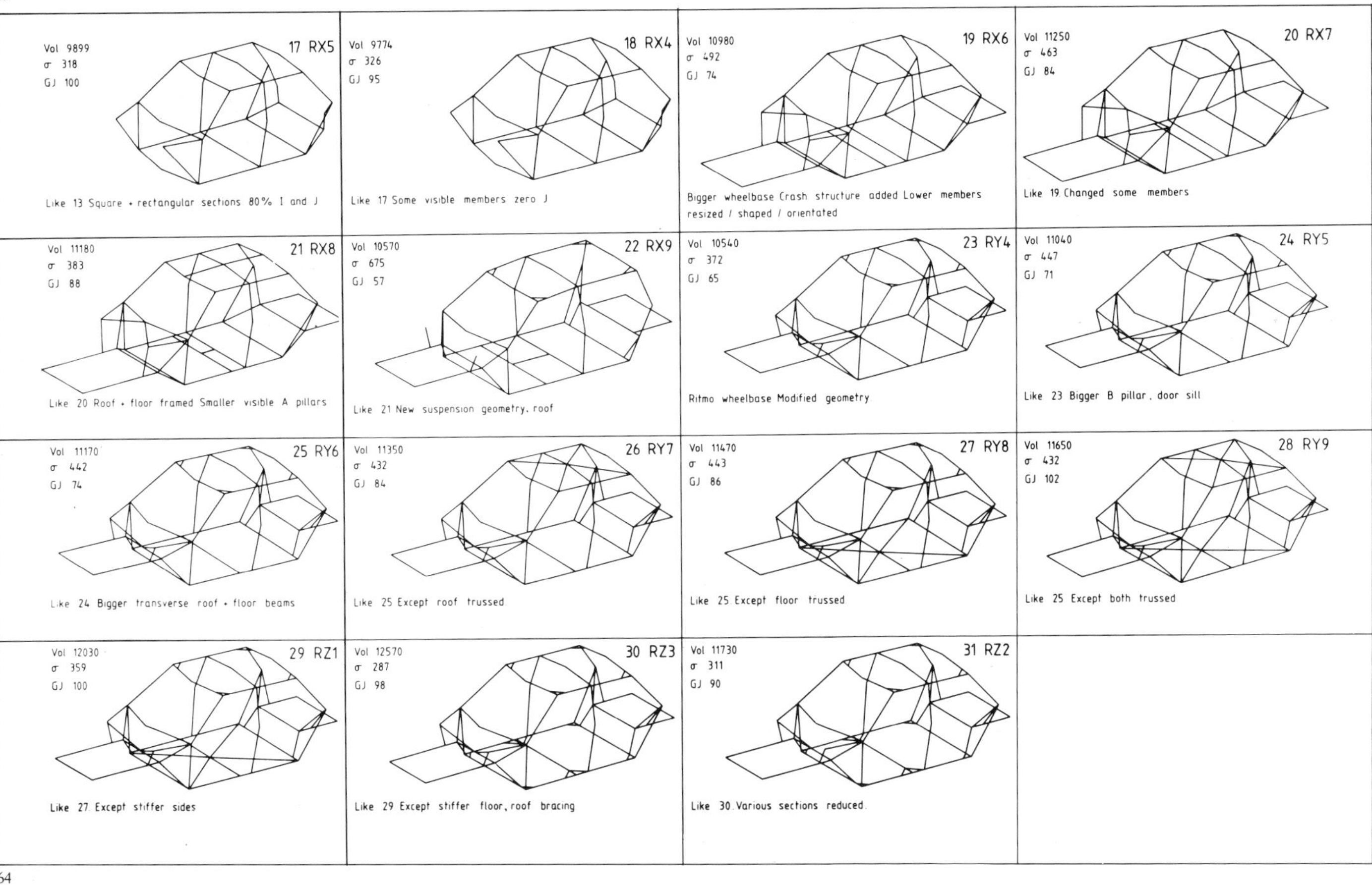

64

64. Basic geometrical schemes for mathematical studies of structure.

65. *Diagram of components' material properties.*

66. *Perfecting the vehicle's covering* (a) *and wind tunnel tests* (b).

67. *Structural scheme for attaching polycarbonate cover to metal bearing frame.*

EXTERNAL PANELS	STEEL	ALUMINIUM	S.M.C.	POLYPROPYLENE	R.P. FOAM	POLYURETHANE	STX ?	NOTES
	H R G P B	M D F P F	L R VG VG G	L N VG VG G	VL B VG VG G	L N VG VG G		WEIGHT – HEAVY H, MEDIUM M, LIGHT L, VERY LIGHT VL
BUMPERS								
FRONT SECTION								REPAIR (RELATIVE) NO N, DIFFICULT D, REASONABLE R, BETTER B
BULKHEAD								FORMING FAIR F, GOOD G, VERY GOOD VG
FLOOR								INTEGRAL FORMING POOR P, VERY GOOD VG
ROOF								DURABILITY BAD B, FAIR F, GOOD G
DOORS								PAINTING ALL MATERIALS WILL ACCEPT A PAINT FINISH, BUT IN SOME CASES THE METHOD OF APPLICATION AND QUALITY OF FINISH WOULD DIFFER; PANEL BREAKDOWN THIS IS RELATED TO REPAIRABILITY
REAR SECTION								MATERIAL

65

66 a

b

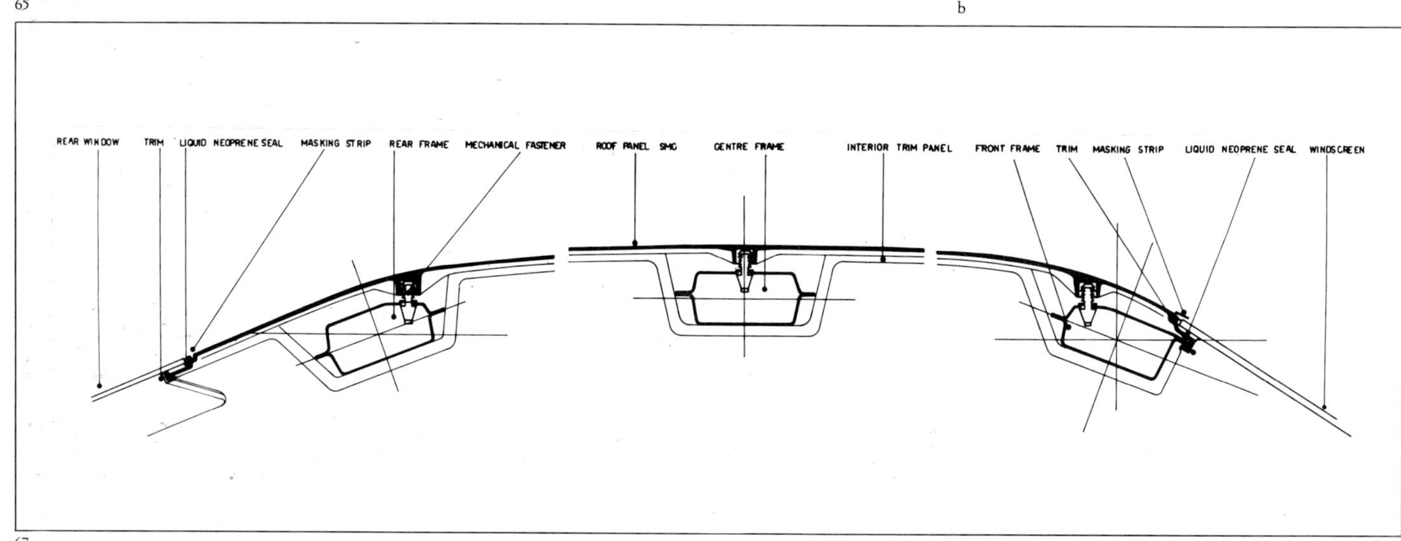

67

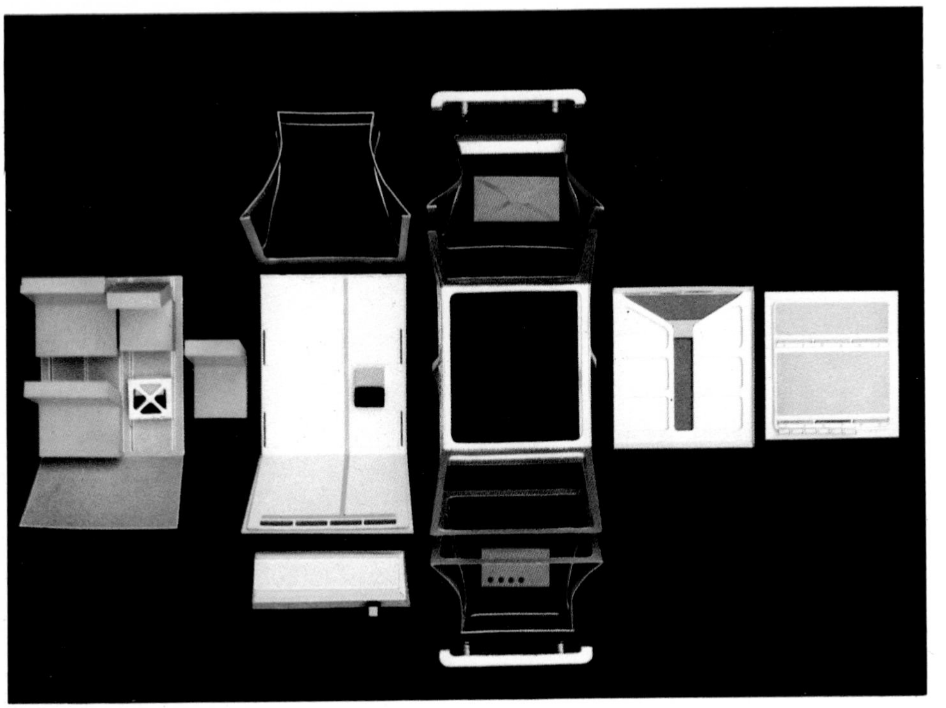

55

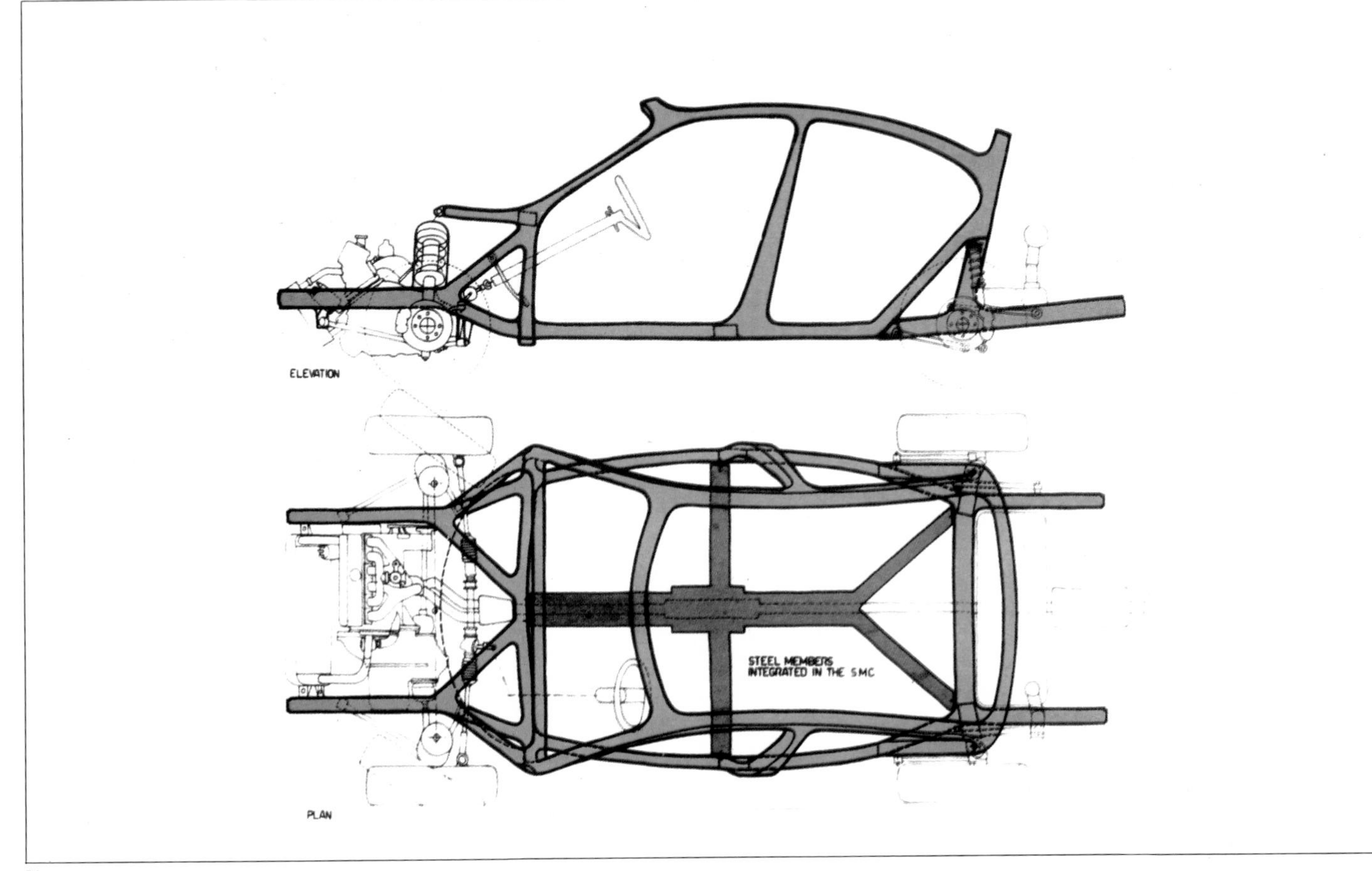

56

55. Initial elements of the vehicle's components.
56. Scheme of the steel structural frame.

The basic question of whether there is any place for imagination in big industry is still open. This could well be a role played by tomorrow's architects: to rekindle creativity within industry.

well be a role played by tomorrow's architects: to rekindle creativity within industry, a creativity that is all too often blunted by the logic of the market. "At this point it has to be decided whether the automobile industry wants to treat the user as an adult or not. I feel that in the long run faith in the public, confidence in their ability to understand innovations, even in automobile forms, is likely to pay off."

49. Peter Rice working on a structural trial model.

50. Working model for optimization of the structural frame.

51. Nori Okabe working on a full-scale drawing.

52. One of the first schemes for separating the structure from the coachwork.

53. VSS scheme.

54. Wind tunnel tests.

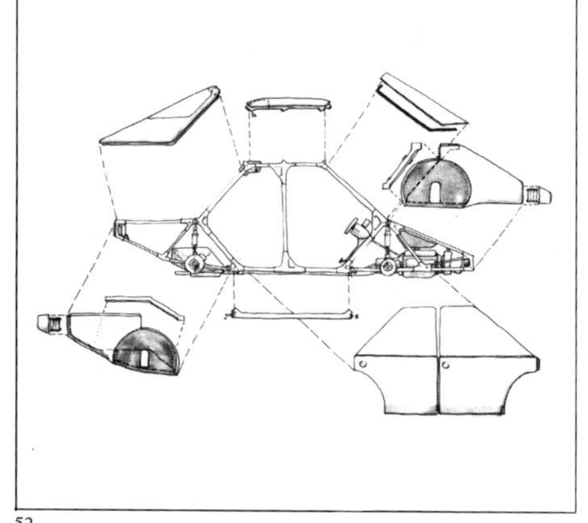

52

54

50

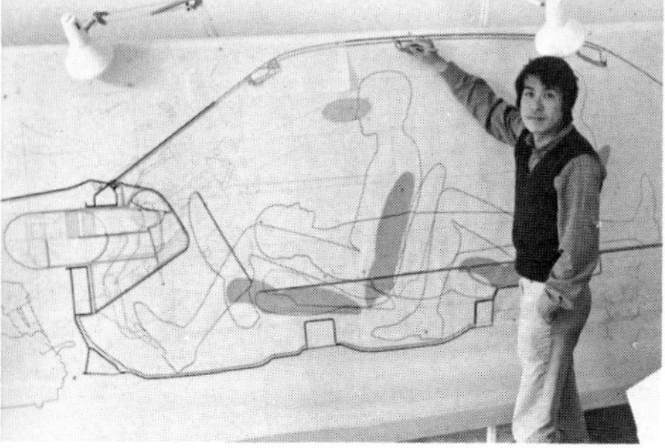

51

53

1978-1980 Turin, Italy
Fiat VSS experimental vehicle

38 Client: Fiat Auto S.p.A., Turin/IDEA Institute
Coordination: G. Trebbi/IDEA Institute
Architects: Piano & Rice & Associates
with L. Abbot, S. Ishida, N. Okabe, B. Plattner, A. Stanton, R. Verbizh
IDEA Institute
with S. Boggio, F. Conti, O. Di Blasi, W. De Silva, M. Sibona
Engineers: Ove Arup & Partners (T. Barker and M. Manning)
Acoustics: S. Brown Associates

49

Beyond styling

In the summer of 1978 Nicola Tufarelli, then managing director of Fiat, called Renzo Piano and Peter Rice and gave them the special task to invent the car of the nineties. The proposal was ambitious and the impulse behind it revolutionary. To transform the image of the automobile was the underlying concept, restyling was not enough. A breakthrough was called for, one that would change the basic idea of the motor-car, going well beyond the boundaries of design. The overriding objective to be achieved was a weight-reduction of at least 20% which would in its turn ensure notable fuel savings. A stiff challenge but Piano and Rice took it on. This led to the creation of the Institute of Development in Automotive Engineering (IDEA) in Turin, with Franco Mantegazza as managing director, Piano as president and Rice as vice-president, a sort of works office. The budget was 3 billion lire (3.25 million dollars) spread over a three-year plan.

It was the beginning of a remarkable adventure in design and engineering, an ideal challenge for an architect like Piano who rejects any compartmentalization of the creative process. "I began by spending day after day in the factory, studying the assembly under the guidance of Dante Giacosa, who acted like a 'father-in-design' to me. In the automobile works all the various phases of the execution process come together. It is a great school for any architect."

The development of a design was the outcome of close team-work. The research team was made up of specialists of different nationalities and backgrounds: architects, mathematicians, physicists, chemists, engineers and many others. It was multi-disciplinary achievement in collaboration, a point where different scientific skills converged, displaying the innovatory, anti-parochial nature of the design effort, all the more significant because the automobile world is so traditionally closed to outside interference.

The basic criterion of the car lies in the separation of the function of the mechanisms and the protection of the passengers. This logically leads to structuring the vehicle in separable and interchangeable components, following a design procedure already applied in the field of electronics and tried out by Piano himself in the great machine of Beaubourg.

There are four basic canons which the VSS prototype had to meet: weight, durability, safety and comfort. Weight was a decisive issue. Piano suggested that sheet metal should be discarded for the coachwork in favor of different materials, lightweight yet tough, like certain plastics and their compounds (polycarbonates, SMC). But these have a serious drawback in their lack of torsional rigidity and offer inadequate protection in case of accident. The solution was a metal structure: a bearing frame of galvanized steel capable of absorbing shock through the material's progressive collapse. The structure was optimized according to a mathematical pattern, giving an overall weight loss of 20% less than a traditional car made of sheet metal.

The polycarbonate skin also proves to have appreciable advantages in terms of durability. Unlike steel, which is corroded by atmospheric conditions, these synthetic materials are rust-proof. This means that the VSS could last over twenty years. It would also be much less noisy for the passengers, since plastics vibrate on a lower frequency than sheet metal. Because of the continuity of material between the engine and the shock-absorbers, the prototype gives one the sensation of riding in a sound box.

Will the car of the nineties be modelled on the VSS? At the end of the long study, conducted simultaneously on the experimental level and the mathematical-analytical level with comparisons between tests and calculations for each element of the prototype, some clear guidelines emerged: (1) separation of the bearing function (structure) and form (coachwork) would make it possible to decentralize the production cycle and replace the assembly line with workpoints for the manufacture of separate units (independent subsets), which can be brought together and assembled at a later stage; (2) by retaining the central framework unchanged, it would be possible to make endless changes to the range of models offered with minimal investment costs. The prototype hinges entirely on this evolutionary principle. Seen this way the car is no longer a finished object, complete and perfect, but a technologically flexible tool whose typology can be adapted to the individual requirements of the user.

The question of industrial feasibility is obviously more complex. Yet the practical effects of this study have so far been by no means negligible. About 30% of the contents of the study will be channelled into Fiat's 1983 series production. But the experiment has been suspended, without further development. "Unfortunately the cultural breakthrough was followed by a certain regression," explains Piano. "Fiat felt the need to concretely include the research into a prototype. But this prototype had its problems: while it did weigh 20% less than the *Ritmo* model, it did not manifest design innovations, providing a domesticated image in keeping with current criteria."

What remains today of the VSS venture, as Franck Renevier has written, is "the attempt to provide a new view of the mass produced car from the outside, to completely rethink its status outside the established patterns within the company and the pressing needs of commercial production." But the basic question of whether there is any place for imagination in big industry is still open. This, according to Piano, could

37

75

75. Road test: the vehicle achieved weight reduction of 80 kg and high levels of soundproofing.

76

76. Final VSS prototype.

1980-1981 Cremona, Italy
Arvedi tubular structural system

Client: Arvedi S.p.A.

Architects: Piano & Rice & Associates/ Building Workshop S.r.l. with S. Ishida, O. Di Blasi

Engineers: P. Rice assisted by H. Bardsley with Arvedi technical department with engineers Gosio and Galli

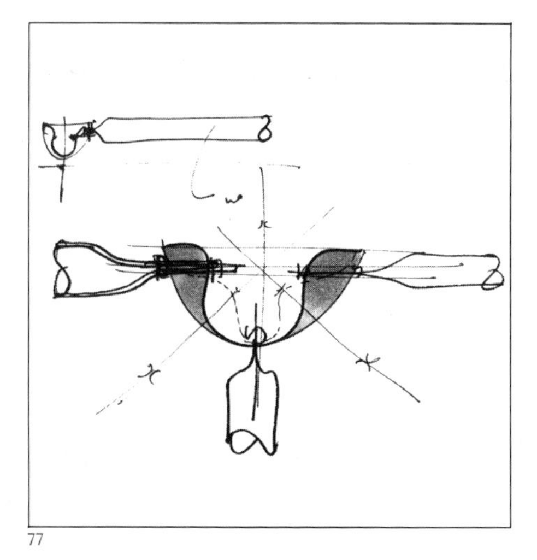

77

Exploration of the joint

The great *tableau* constructed for the Cremona trade fair can be seen in two ways. One approach is to describe the spectacular entrance to the fair. This was composed of two key elements: (1) a platform of metal struts used in vertical projection; (2) a canopy fixed to the structural frame without intermediate mountings fitted under the *tableau*.

The latter element acted as a counterpoint. It provided shelter for the public queuing up and defined a meeting place; like a shady pinnacle, delicate and subtle, it softens the rigorous geometry and gives a visual message to the whole, a protective shell of architectural symbols unmistakably remote, ancestral and different from the technological landscape.

Piano was invited to visit the Arvedi factory in Cremona, and it was here, as he observed the way the piping was made and the complex relations between rods and nodes, that he developed the idea for a special type of joint. The joint that was to constitute the prototypal element of the structure for the Cremona fair.

The study was a collaboration between Studio Piano, Peter Rice and the engineers of the Arvedi steel and piping factory, and it intended to invent a new system of construction. Why such concern for a detail for a mere accessory? "It is frequently a mistake to start from the general and so descend to the particular. Frankly I cannot understand the kind of architect who draws general sketches and then tells the engineers to look after the rest. This is a dichotomy, a schizophrenic syndrome. Architecture is a whole, and has to be approached carefully from every side. Otherwise it ceases to be architecture."

After endless attempts, a system of connecting up the tubular segments was devised that was markedly more economical and functional than those currently in use. Moreover, the joint also offered advantages in terms of durability and could perform a load-bearing function, supporting the weight of complex tubular systems.

Trials and tests were carried out by following a many sided multi-disciplinary approach ranging from architectural design to mechanical operations. At the end of this lengthy phase involving operations in the workshop, in the laboratory and at the drawing board the new joint was ready. First the rod is made cone-shaped by cold-plasticizing the material, then the filled sheet metal node is pierced; a plug of reinforced concrete, which can be removed permitting access for maintenance work, and playing a structural role by making the node indeformable. The goal has been achieved: a few structural elements suffice to form a complex framework.

The great screen of the Cremona fair is the application on a very large scale of the construction system conceived in the Arvedi works (the Arvedi Space Frame System). An elementary system capable of bracing multi-functional complexes. The fair's entrance structure acts as a vehicle for advertising, presents visual and aural messages; it acts as a spatial backdrop delimiting and underscoring the proportions of the great inner concourse, the true backbone of the fair ground; it is a graphic symbol, playful and flamboyant, of the great trade fair.

The joint, inserted into this landscape, becomes charged with symbolical features. It is the link uniting architecture and industry, technology (the structural web) and the organic world (the canopy, a great butterfly, a sail billowing in the wind, a sinuous shell), a sign both expressive and conceptual. This will also be one of the features of the Parisian Universal Exhibition in 1989, on the theme of *Les chemins de la liberté*. In this case the proportions are going to be macroscopic. The screen, an immense mobile and luminescent wall, unfolds on the scale of the city; it flanks the Seine and sums up the entire audiovisual catalogue of the exhibition, offering itself to the view of 50,000 visitors.

"It is frequently a mistake to start from the general and so descend to the particular. Frankly I cannot understand the kind of architect who draws general sketches and then tells the engineers to look after the rest. This is a dichotomy, a schizophrenic syndrome."

77. Preparatory drawing of the joint.

78. Perfecting the prototype.

79. Terminal section of the tube showing the thickening of materials at the joint node.

80. Mounting the structural node.

81. Elevation of the entry to the Cremona fair made experimentally with the Arvedi tubular system.

78

79

80

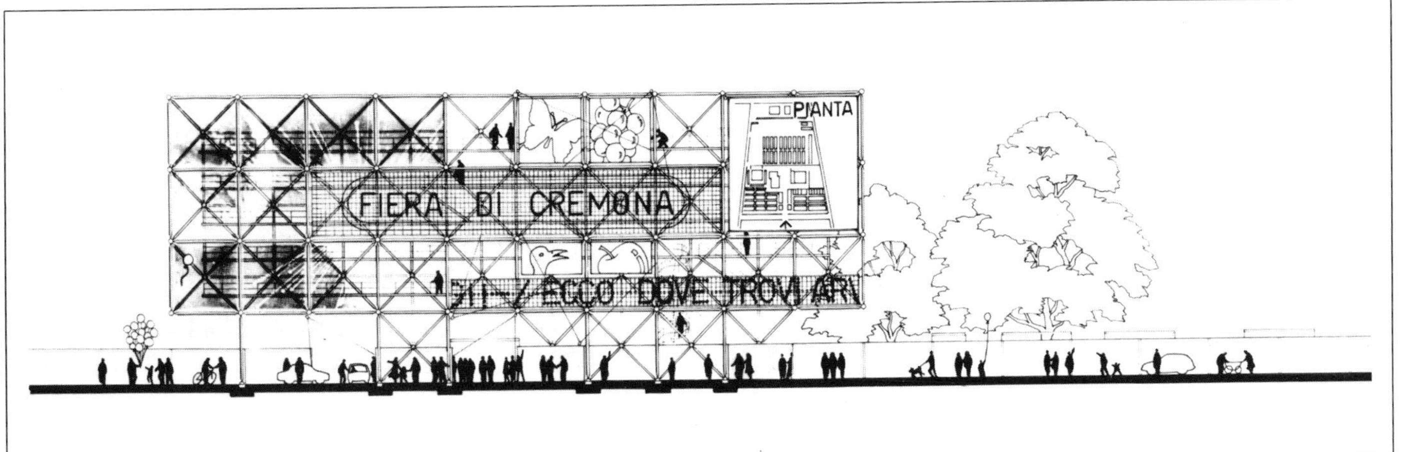

81

82, 83. Entrance to the Cremona fair.

84. Plan of entrance to the Cremona fair.

82

83

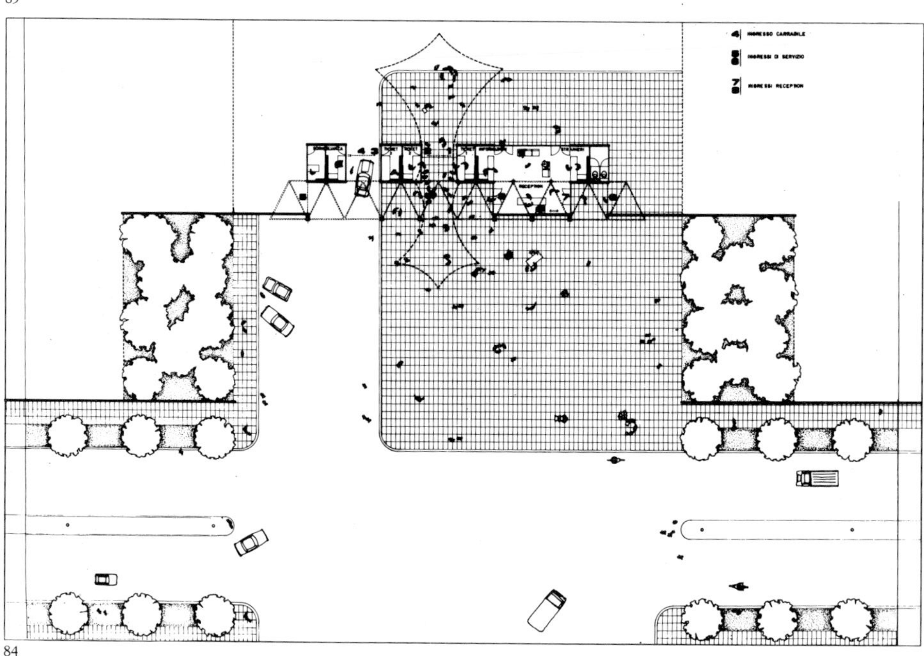

84

85. Prototype of the structural node: the inner part in cement prevents deformation of the hemispherical cap which is subjected to axial stress.

85

1966 Pomezia, Rome, Italy
Mobile structure for sulfur extraction

Architects: Studio Piano
Contractors: E. Piano Contractors

The mobile factory

Think of the city as a crystalline structure, geometrized, made up of detachable elements (suburb, district, etc.); imagine dismantling the works bit by bit and reassembling the ingredients elsewhere, shifting the center of gravity of urban life. In short, imagine a nomadic city, its map shifting, continually changing, flowing together and scattering apart, following the flux and reflux of the community's needs and feelings.

Is such a city feasible? Some of Renzo Piano's space frames indicate the possibility, volumes that can be dismantled at will forming a miniature model of the mobile city, the city-construction site, ceaselessly renewing, self-building, self-destroying.

The factory for processing sulfur ore constructed at Pomezia in 1966 is a structure braced by a network of rhomboidal reinforced polyester elements (a material unaffected by sulfur fumes), easily modifiable and capable of moving along the path of mining operations. To ensure mobility the factory is set on a continuous foundation system so that the standard panels (each weighing 14 kg) can be dismantled at one end of the mine and reassembled at the other end. The structural framework is a barrel vault made rigid by three cross-arches: two diagonals along the joints between the panels and one along the longitudinal bend-lines of each floor panel. Given the lightness of the vault, a steel strip is used to anchor it to the base. The overall cost is minimal, a contributing factor being that the interior of the factory receives light through the translucent enclosure of plastic panels.

The operation for sulfur extraction is a capsule, a technological microcosm, travelling, or rather crawling, across the landscape. Order is not static; indeed it is the essential condition ensuring the functionality, manageability and the mobility of the factory. Movement is not the end in itself but related to the requirements of the specific case. "Knowing a job, knowing how to build, meeting the client's needs, society's needs – that is what it's all about."

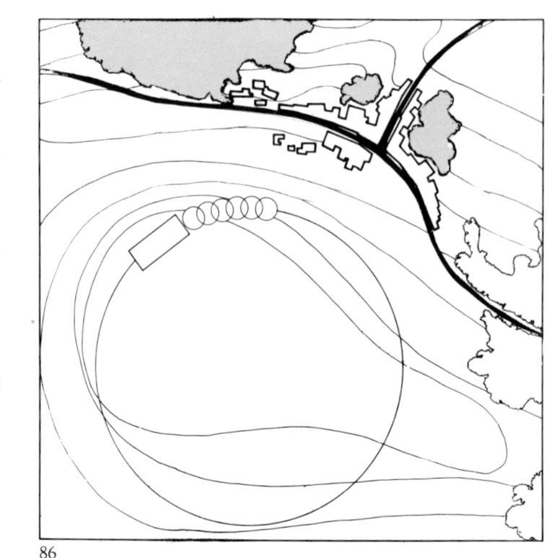

86

87

Imagine a nomadic city, its map shifting, continually changing, flowing together and scattering apart, following the flux and reflux of the community's needs and feelings. Is such a city feasible?

86. Scheme of movement of the factory along the sulfur mine.
87. Phase of assembly.

88. Structural detail.

88

89. Plan and elevation of the mobile factory's structure.

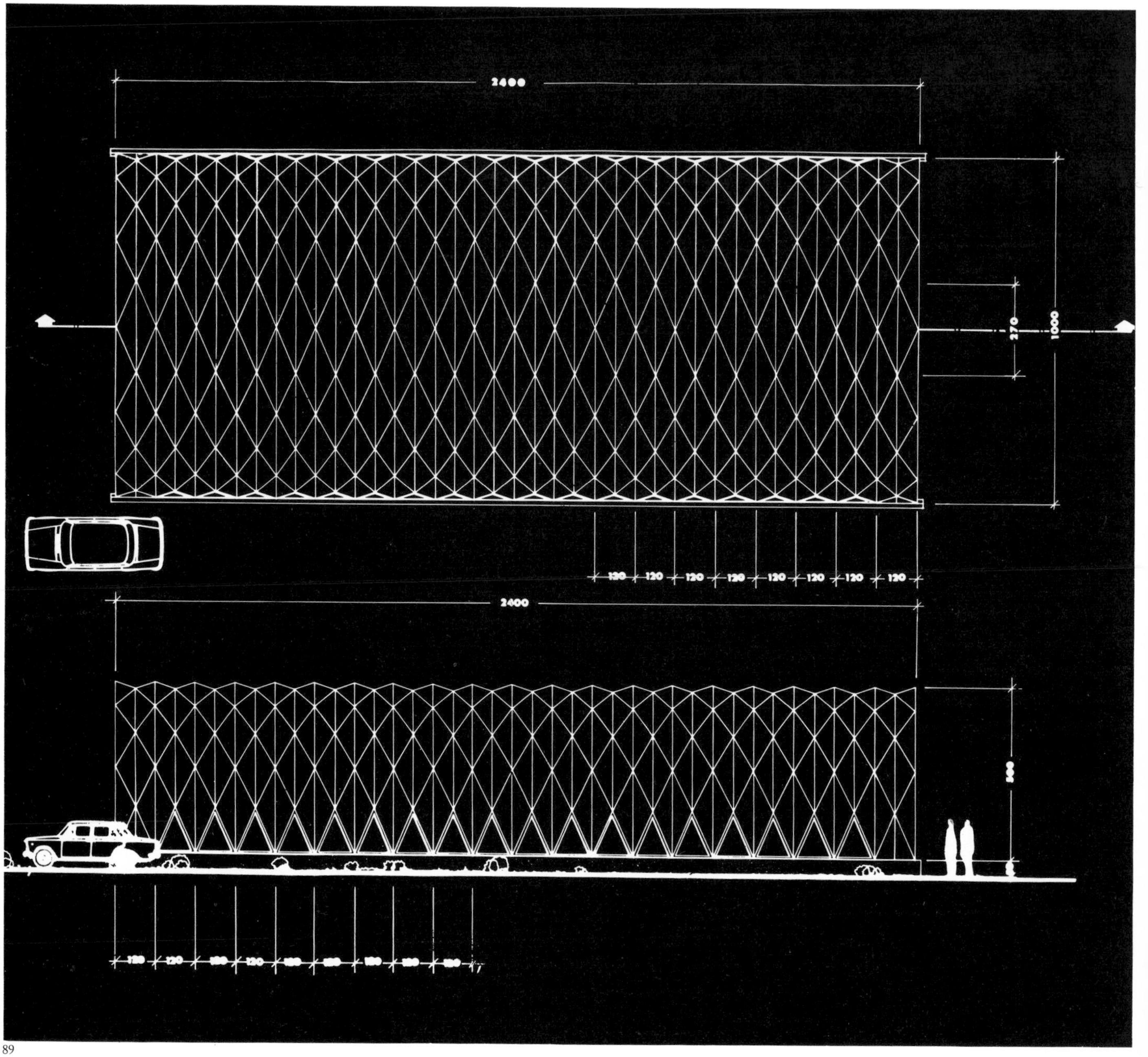

89

90. Exterior.

90

1970 Washington D.C., USA
Standardized hospital module

Client: ARAM (Association for Rural Aids in Medicine), Washington, D.C.
Architects: Studio Piano & Rogers with M. Goldschmied, J. Young, P. Flack

The open hospital

The traditional image of the hospital is closed, inflexible, immobile, centralized and absolute reflecting a certain idea of medicine and medical practice. It would be realistic to imagine a different kind of organizational structure, one that is open, flexible, mobile, decentralized and relative. Piano proves it is feasible in the design of the ARAM module devised in collaboration with the London based firm of Richard Rogers and a team of specialists.

The basic idea is that the hospital is now an institutional machine incapable of meeting the ever-changing requirements of the community. There has to be a change of direction by transforming the clinic into a flexible system; in brief, a passage from the absolute to the relative.

On the operational level, it is proposed to create a standard module that incorporates the most sophisticated hospital equipment and which decentralizes less complex facilities (from paramedical equipment to the wards themselves) into the existing environment where the module is to be installed.

From this viewpoint, the hospital space is no longer frozen, ordered, geometric, but open-ended, developing continually, becoming multidimensional.

The first requirement, in this case, is for the sanitary capsule to be flexible, easily dismantled and reassembled. In the ARAM module everything is arranged so that assembly and any adjustments can be carried out by unskilled workmen under the guidance of a small team of technicians using cheap, lightweight standardized components, elementary joining systems, a crane incorporated in the structural complex, etc.

Simplified to the utmost, the hospital unit is self-contained, adaptable and therefore dynamic, capable of being easily transported.

The service module is planned for a maximum of 200 beds: beyond this limit, Piano says, a hospital tends to become an anonymous entity, and loses the flexibility needed to meet community needs. The nature of the ARAM module, its open structure and its degree of reliability is subject to certain factors: (1) interaction with the local population; (2) the degree of development of technology and services in the various local situations.

These two variables can make a notable difference in the efficiency of the hospital laboratory. If the module is installed with an adequate multidisciplinary work force in selected urban or rural situations it can help about one hundred thousand people.

"The ARAM module," explains Piano, "is a technical constant, an instrument for community use, distinct from the image of the hospital and it permits a flexible contribution to community resources." As a standard unit, the module can be produced in series and distributed everywhere, a travelling technological structure at the service of a new electronic city, a Third World metropolis, provided, of course, that the doctor-scientist is disposed to revise his own role and become mobile.

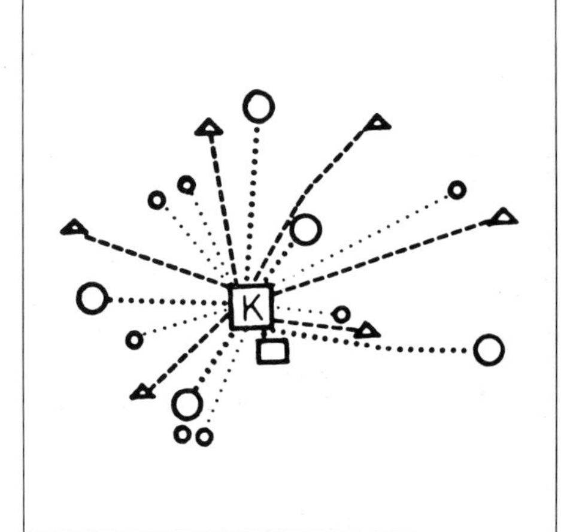

91

The hospital is now an institutional machine incapable of meeting the ever-changing requirements of the community. There has to be a change of direction by transforming the clinic into a flexible system; in brief, a passage from the absolute to the relative.

91. Scheme of interaction between the sanitary capsule and secondary services distributed over the district.

92. Section of the sanitary capsule indicating the central area served by the upper and lower levels.

93. Capsule's assembly method.

94. The ARAM sanitary capsule is a nucleus containing the most sophisticated part of the hospital. The wards are instead made of less sophisticated structures distributed over the neighborhood. Pilot studies for its application have been carried out for urban and rural environments.

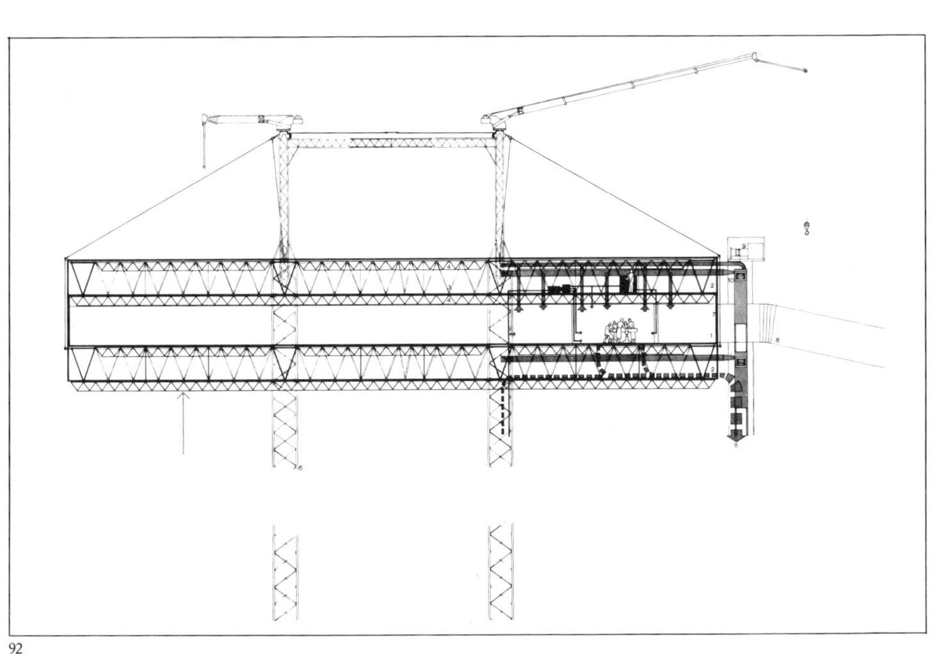

92

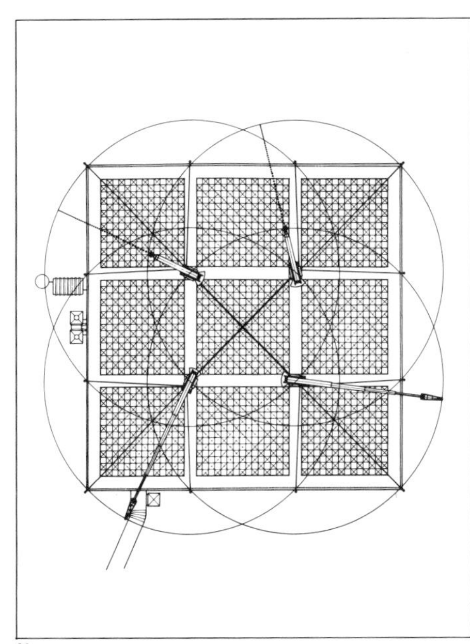

93

94

1978 Dakar, Senegal
Mobile construction unit for Senegal

Building in Africa

60 Client: UNESCO; Dakar regional office; M. Senghor; Breda of Dakar
Architects: Piano & Rice & Associates with R. Verbizh, O. Dellicour, S. Ishida

Whenever Renzo Piano has finished a design or architectural project he amuses himself by pulling apart its conceptual pattern, destructuring its nodal points and dismantling its elements. Then, in his next effort he fits the pieces of the puzzle together again combining and manipulating them with other pieces so as to create a new montage, a new molecular structure in which the differences are more apparent than the analogies. The project requested by the president of Senegal, Leopold Senghor, for a program of public aid for self-build reflects an unusual approach to architectural research; a true jigsaw puzzle. Piano's solution is simple. The objective is to make prefabricated systems for the villages in the interior of the country. The systems could have been imported, but it would prove costly, so they were built on the spot. "It is easier to transport the production equipment than the people and the products," Piano concluded. The problem was solved by small travelling factories, in line with Senghor's own suggested policy of decentralization (already tried out with mobile ophthalmic units). The local population provides the raw materials. Piano's staff analyzes the construction material and supplies instructions to start production, afterwards they visit the various construction sites scattered across the territory. The inhabitants transform the construction unit into a fixed, self-managed structure, capable of harmonizing the evolution of housing with the realities of the environment. The habitat, in the plains of Senegal, is a menace but also a mine, "in some arid zones we have actually planted vegetation to provide the right kind of fibers for building houses."

Senghor himself, Piano recalls, was enthusiastic in support of the project, "his aim was to continue the memory of local culture. 'Every old man that dies,' he used to say, 'is a library burnt.' This project was undoubtedly a way to fix the memory of these things. If it has failed to make much progress, this is mainly due to the resistance of the local authorities, restricted by their bureaucratic views."

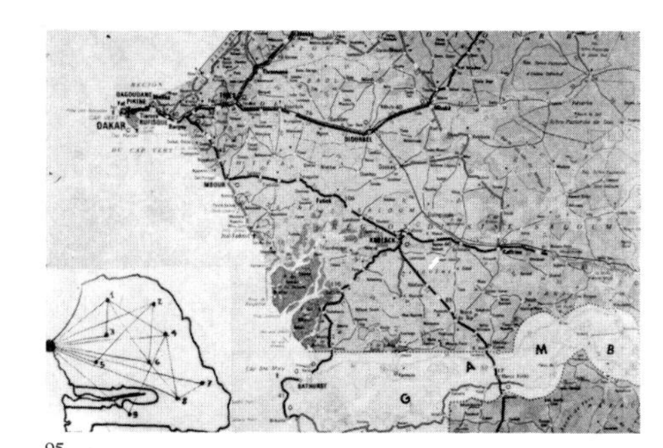

95

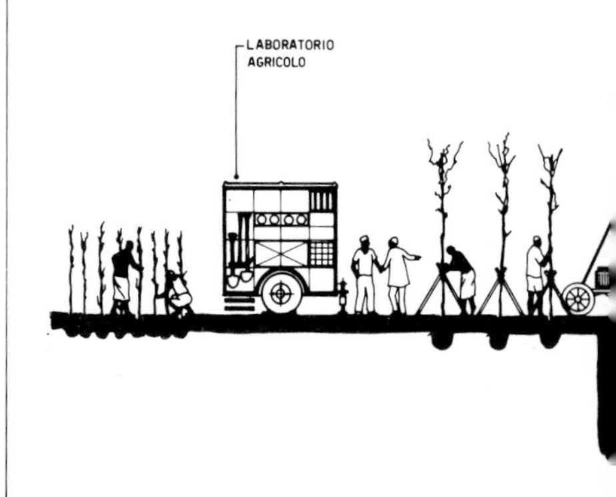

96

"Leopold Senghor's aim was to continue the memory of 'ocal culture. 'Every old man that dies,' he used to say, was a library burnt.' This project was undoubtedly a vay of perpetuating African culture."

95. Area of Senegal where the mobile workshop operates.
96. The mobile workshop proposal for self-building in Senegal. The workshop includes an agricultural facility for planting vegetation to be used in construction, a mobile library, a training school, a laboratory for stabilizing clays and other earths used in construction.
97. This design is a publicly subsidized self-build program carried out by UNESCO for Senegal.

97

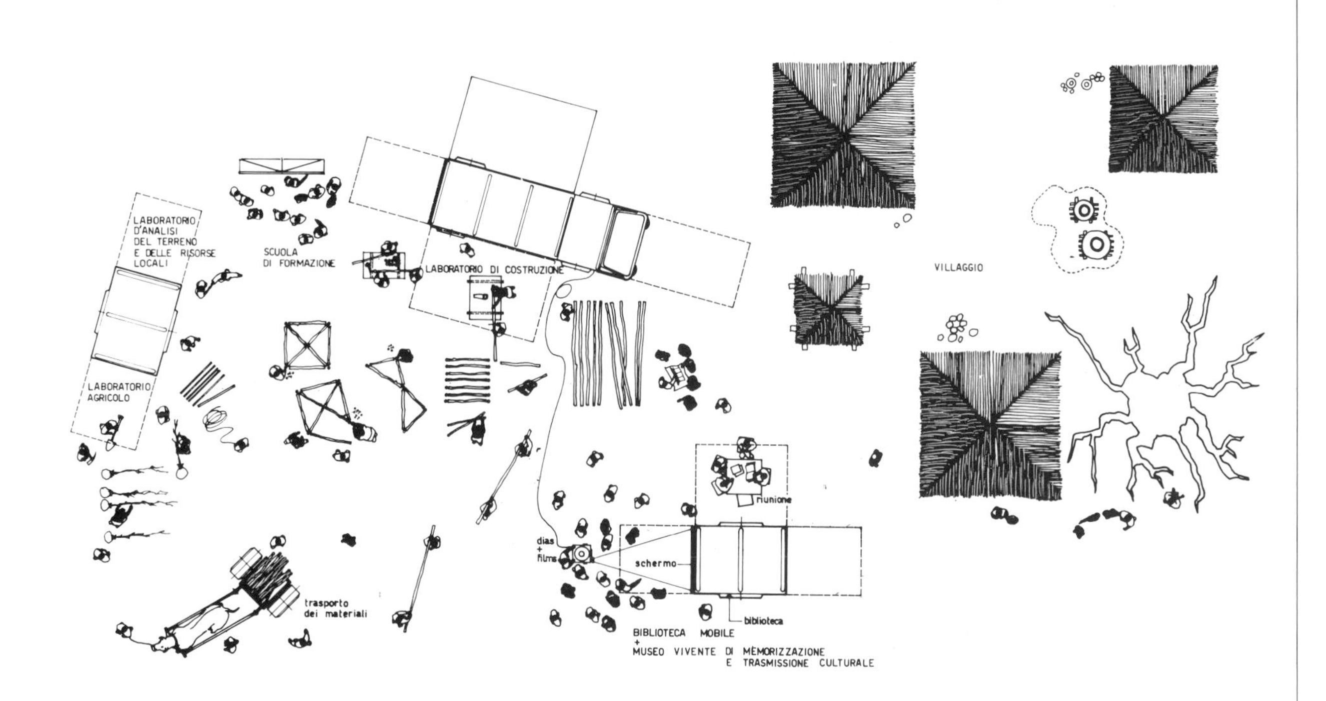

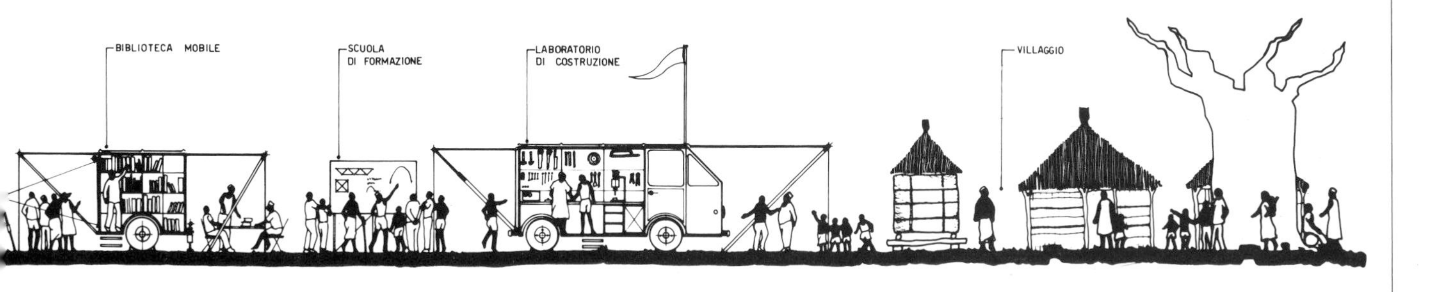

1978 Turin, Italy
Transport vehicle

62 Client: IDEA S.p.A.
Architects: Piano & Rice & Associates
with S. Ishida, N. Okabe
IDEA (Institute of Development in Automotive Engineering)
with F. Mantegazza, W. De Silva

A primary vehicle

Renzo Piano's city is made up of variables, of deviations from the norm, of unfinished architectural objects and alternative means of transport, such as this "Flying Carpet," a platform for transporting men and material for North African countries. It was a suggestion put forward by Franco Mantegazza, managing director of IDEA of Turin.

Piano's artistic course incorporates the natural universe as well as the technological which can range from a factory to a vehicle. Sophisticated eclecticism? No, the roots of this expressive pluralism are different. It is the divided self of the designer in the slow struggle to reattain wholeness. Then there is the challenge that does away with the support of a traditional stylistic repertoire and leaves open the path of inventiveness. "With every project I start from scratch. Personally, I reject terms like architectural language or expression. Style is a habit." In this challenge between himself and his raw materials, the new architect resolves his crisis of identity, each time seeking to reinvent the rules of the game.

Piano has had a fertile encounter in the automobile industry, rich in a flow of ideas at all levels. Architectural techniques are transferred to the industrial field and the techniques of the auto industry are recycled back to the architectural field. The contact with manufacturing and the entrepreneur's mentality permeates Piano's work and fixes criteria of economy into the rationalization of technological processes and containment of costs.

In the specific case of the "Flying Carpet" the starting point was exploration of new materials drawing on ferrocement technology and trying combinations of special resins. The second stage was the structural development which finally took form in the application of conventional mechanicals to a simple flat-bed truck, which can be produced using cheap technology. The result is a mobile platform, a primary vehicle convertible to any particular environment. The proposal is to manufacture the engine and transmission in Italy, and the less sophisticated parts and their assembly wherever the vehicle is needed. The whole vehicle has a load capacity of 600 kg, driver included. A simple solution to a complicated problem. Apart from the immediate goal (replacing the camel), this design aims to make the Third World as self-sufficient as possible. This is how yesterday's architect, the architect-builder, tries to measure up to today's requirements.

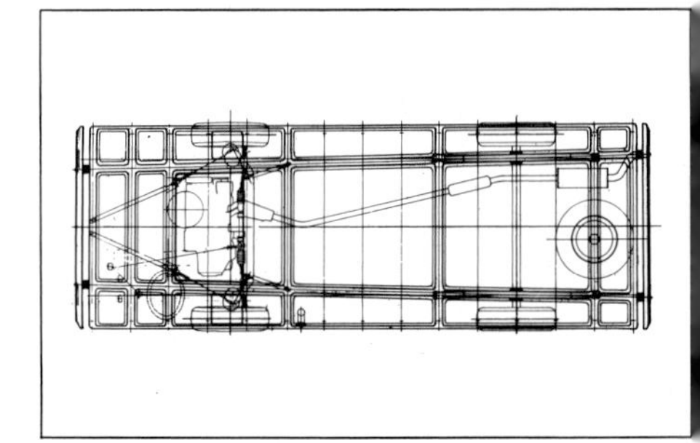

98

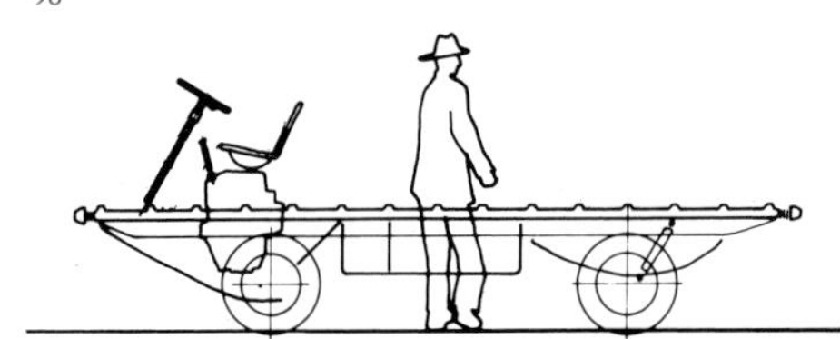

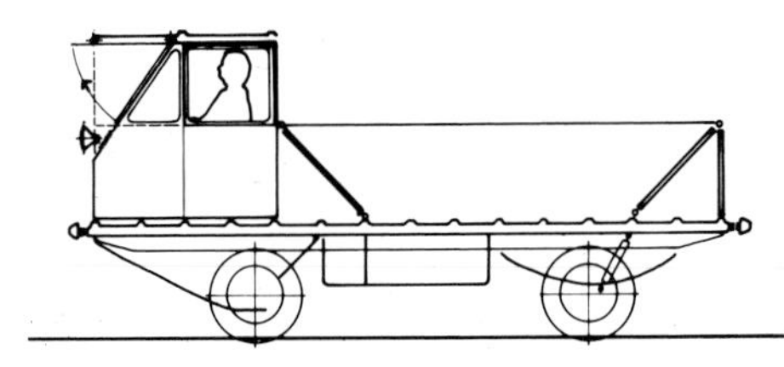

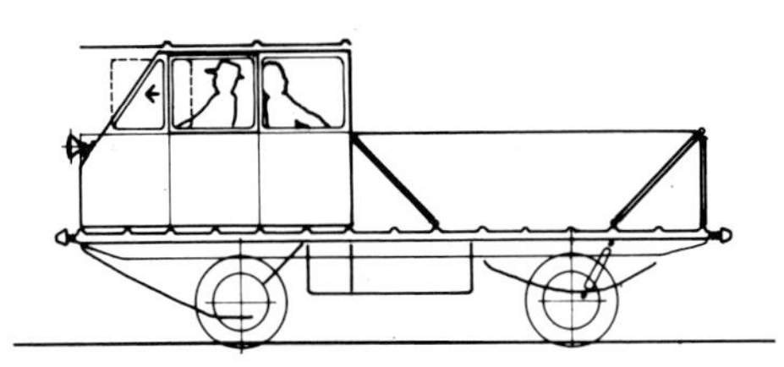

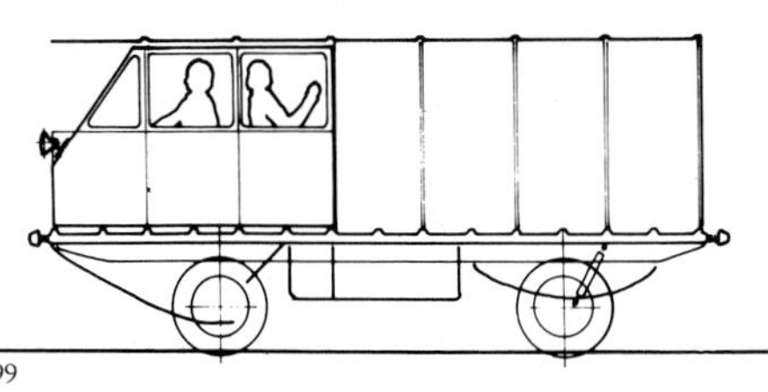

99

Sophisticated eclecticism? No, the roots of this expressive pluralism are different. It is the divided self of the designer in the slow struggle to reattain wholeness.

98. Reinforced concrete platform forming the vehicle's flatbed.

99. Different possible versions of the vehicle.

100. Scheme of the primary transport vehicle consisting of a ferrocement platform and standard mechanical components.

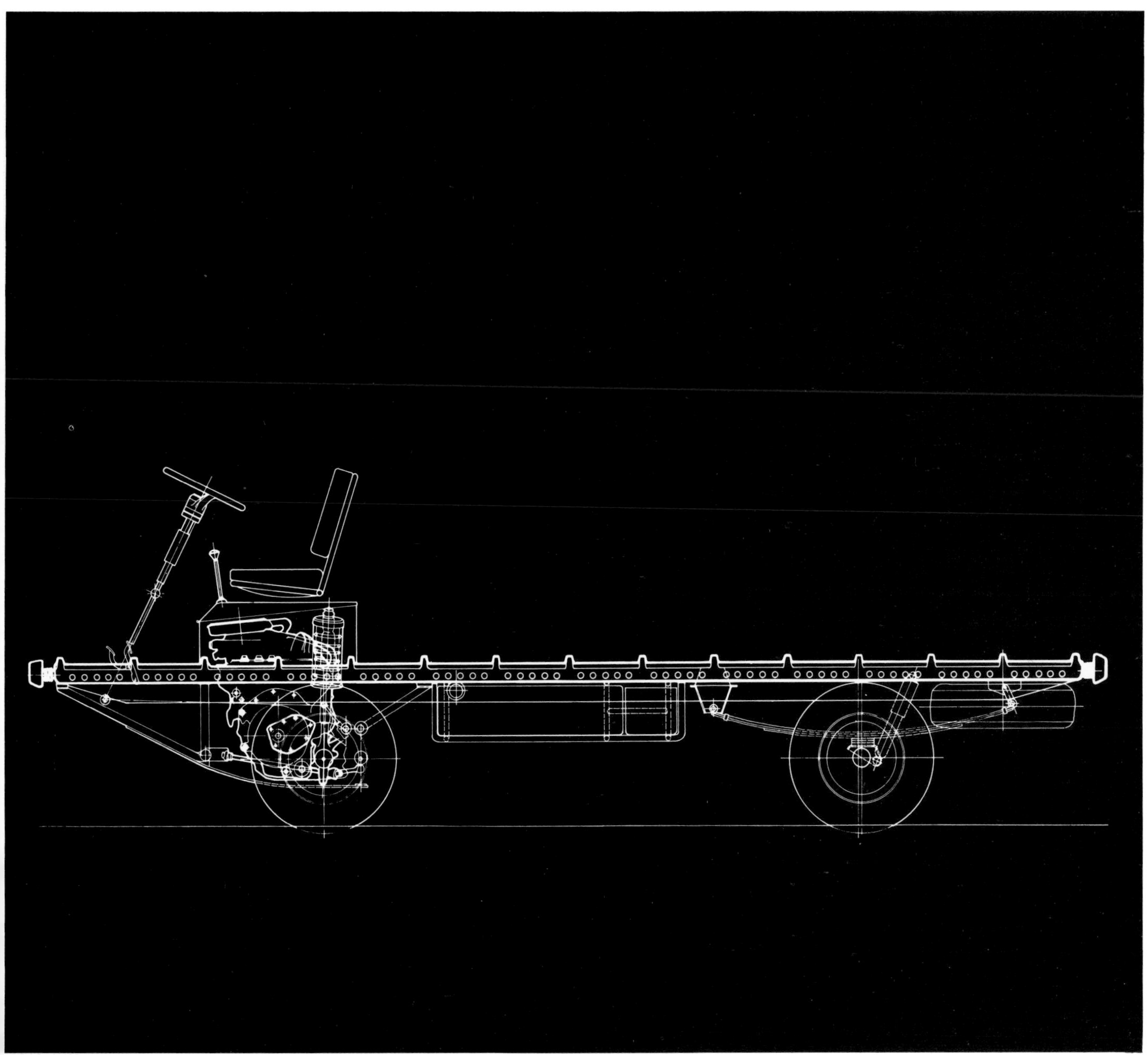

100

1979 Otranto, Italy

Neighborhood Workshop in Otranto: an experiment in urban reconstruction

The travelling workshop

Client: UNESCO (Establishment division of human and socio-cultural environments) S. Busuttil, W. Tochtermann

Architects: Piano & Rice & Associates/F.lli Dioguardi Contractors
with S. Ishida, N. Okabe, R. Verbizh, E. Donato, G. Fascioli, R. Melai, G. Picardi, R. Gaggero

Engineers: Ove Arup & Partners (P. Beckmann) IDEA Institute, Turin

with the collaboration of G. P. Cuppini, G. Gasparri, F. Marano, F. Marconi, EDITECH

with M. Fazio for the Neighborhood Workshop; G. Macchi for the films of the Radiotelevisione Italiana; R. Biondo, M. Bonino

Operational coordination and administration by G. Dioguardi

Program by Magda Arduino

101

102

"The idea underlying the Neighborhood Workshop was that while walls are a given quantity, inside and outside them it is possible to provide for a transformable space and the manner of using it. This is an educational task we have to undertake: inventing variables that can be controlled by the occupants." We wanted to reformulate architectural principles, from the process of design to the use of materials and instruments, seen in relation to the users; an architecture in use, seeking reality in the streets where there are no artificial screens to conceal the truth and you can learn what everyday needs really are.

The building workshop set up in Otranto under the sponsorship of UNESCO and the CNR (Italian National Research Council) was an experiment, lasting a mere week, yet the guiding principles questioned the nature of the architect's role.

The philosophy underlying the project is in line with the most advanced trends in European town planning: ancient town centers are not to be considered simply as cultural possessions but as a cluster of homes and services to be used for the benefit of their inhabitants. The innovatory force of the experiment is to be found in its construction approach. In this respect there are three levels of action: (1) the process of reclamation has to be carried out without the traditional "gutting" of the area and evacuation of residents towards the outlying districts; (2) active involvement of the inhabitants in the design and construction phases; (3) upgrading local crafts and trades by using new technologies, sophisticated but flexible and easy to use, conceived or adapted so as to cut costs and speed up the rate of renewal.

The Active Rehabilitation Program, devised by Magda Arduino with the collaboration of town planners, health experts, legal advisers, sociologists and local administrators came up with the solution of a cube-shaped container easily transportable on a wheeled vehicle. Protected by a cotton wrapper, the mobile unit is installed in the center of the local neighborhood. This multi-functional tool, as its deviser calls it, is subdivided into four display sections (analysis and diagnosis, information and education, open design, work and construction) each corresponding to a phase of operations.

The phase of analysis is perhaps the most stimulating aspect of the project, considering that this discipline has been neglected in the field of construction. It consists of a survey to establish the state of the decayed buildings in terms of structure, architecture and health factors, using photogrammetric electronic surveying equipment. The aim of this first phase is to carry out a thorough (structural and chemo-physical) analysis of the old dwellings, providing an X-ray photograph of the hidden face of the ancient city, with its geological stratifications, fissures, scars, extensions and infills.

The second section aims to develop an awareness of the issues involved in the rehabilitation of old town centers; it supplies information about local planning and regulations, available legislature, possible sources and means of public funding; its aim is to link the Workshop's specialists with the inhabitants of the neighborhood. This is closely bound to the third section, open planning, which informs people of the practical, technical implications of the design process by counselling on planning regulations, costs, purchase of materials through cooperatives, etc.

At this point, overinflated and hackneyed terms such as "awareness" and "participation," really fail to give a precise idea of the methods of the Otranto project and could even be misleading. "Participation can never mean abandoning design. The designer cannot abdicate from his role, because his partner in the dialogue, the user, is often uninformed and easily swayed. The architect has to look ahead and assist in the positive evolution of his mentality."

So we come to the fourth stage, work and construction. Here we have passed from diagnosis to surgical intervention. But in this case there is nothing traumatic about it; it is gentle and above all it is carried out with the help of local skilled labor and craftsmen. This is a basic feature of the Neighborhood Workshop. Maintenance of the historic town center, in Piano's view, could become the main source of employment for local craftsmen, without calculating that the rehabilitation program provides a unique chance for professional retraining and becoming familiar with advanced materials, equipment and techniques. This emerges clearly from the Otranto work site, where use was made of advanced methods of surveying, lightweight, noise and pollution-free, and unobtrusive construction instruments, mobile scaffolding, low speed electric transport modules, cableways, presses, welding-machines, etc.

Without having to evacuate people from their homes, the masonry structures are strengthened, cracks filled in, buildings re-roofed and replastered, damp eliminated, sanitary services installed. If necessary, new techniques are used, such as spraying polyurethane foam to provide insulation or soundproofing or injecting silicon resin to control damp.

Basically, the question is to halt the continuous, permanent work site, bogged down in the complex sequences which have characterized the history of the city from its medieval origins to the industrial revolution when the ancient town centers began to decay and the division between craftsmanship and urban life arose.

"Crafts are generally marginalized reduced to such

"Crafts are generally marginalized, reduced to such tasks as producing fake pillars of wrought iron, and so wasting the immense potential of techniques and knowledge of workmen who are capable of devising and creating today."

101. Shunji Ishida during preparation of a photogrammetric record using the air balloon.

102. Rainer Verbizh (with telecamera) during thermographic tests of masonry in the old city center.

103. People of Otranto.

104. Otranto old town.

105. Sample of stone prone to surface corrosion in Otranto's old city center.

103

tasks as producing fake pillars of wrought iron, and so, wasting the immense potential of techniques and knowledge of workmen who are capable of devising and creating today."

The point is to reactivate that intricate mechanism of craftsmanship. This clearly means that the Neighborhood Workshop does not complete its work in a short span of time, it is projected towards the future, progressively acquiring the properties of a self-managed workshop capable of programming its own investment cycle. Otranto, from this point of view, represents an ideal field of action: in a decayed state, the ancient center is not depopulated, indeed, it is still the nerve center of craft and commercial activities, and while it is true that living conditions are often precarious, it is likewise true that some spontaneous urban culture still manages to hold out, however submerged and demotivated it may appear.

Of course a week is not enough to restore the systems that have been decaying for a century. But at least a new path has been traced. Perhaps this is one way the architecture of "memory" can be saved: by deepening people's awareness of their needs, raising the value of craftsmanship and mastering the necessary scientific instruments.

104

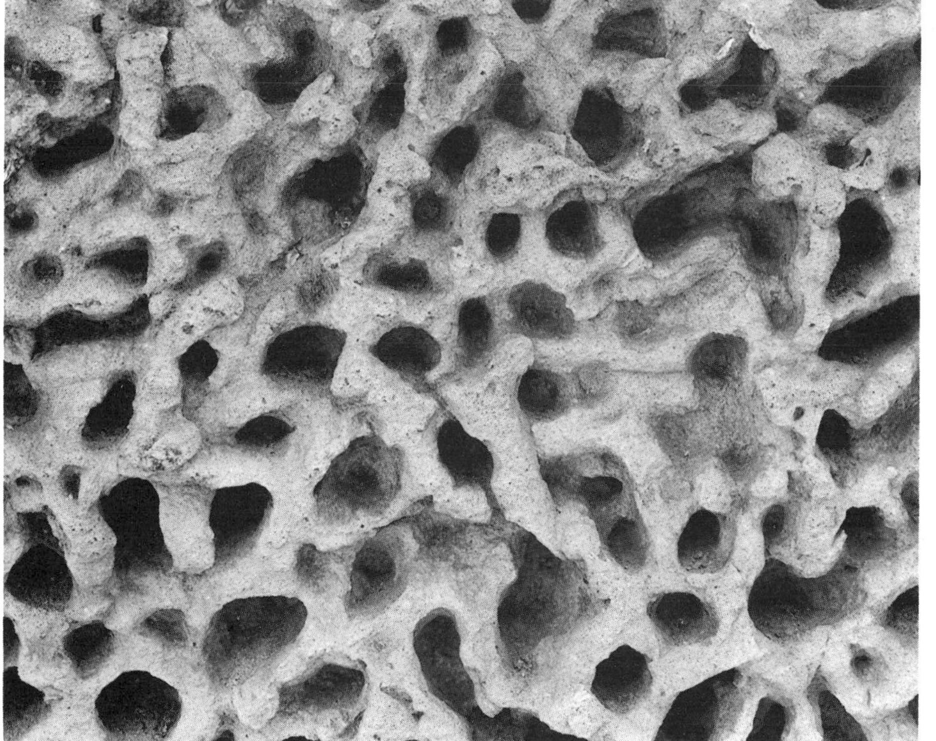

105

106-108. Mobile workshop's arrival and assembly in the square of Otranto.

109. Evening meeting around the workshop.

110. The function of the travelling workshop for restoration in ancient town centers is to work on chemophysical and structural analysis, participatory design, construction, equipment and documentation.

106

107

108

109

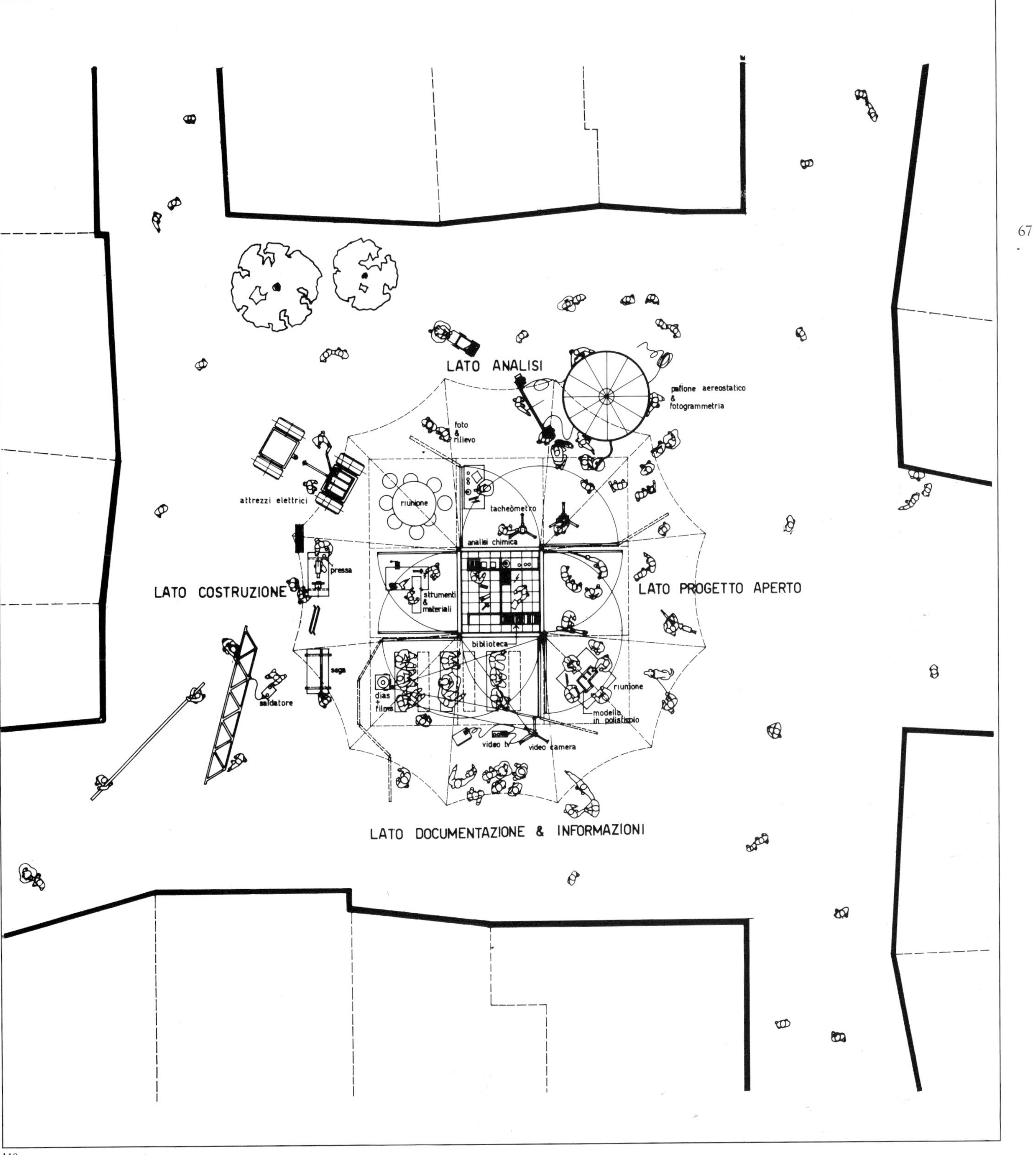
LATO ANALISI
pallone aereostatico
&
fotogrammetria
foto
&
rilievo
attrezzi elettrici
riunione
tacheòmetro
analisi chimica
pressa
LATO COSTRUZIONE
strumenti
&
materiali
LATO PROGETTO APERTO
biblioteca
sega
saldatore
dias
+
films
riunione
modello
in polistirolo
video tv
video camera
LATO DOCUMENTAZIONE & INFORMAZIONI

110

111. Diagnostic equipment of the travelling workshop for restoration of ancient city centers.

112. Preparation of an aerial photogrammetric survey balloon.

113. Photogrammetric survey apparatus.

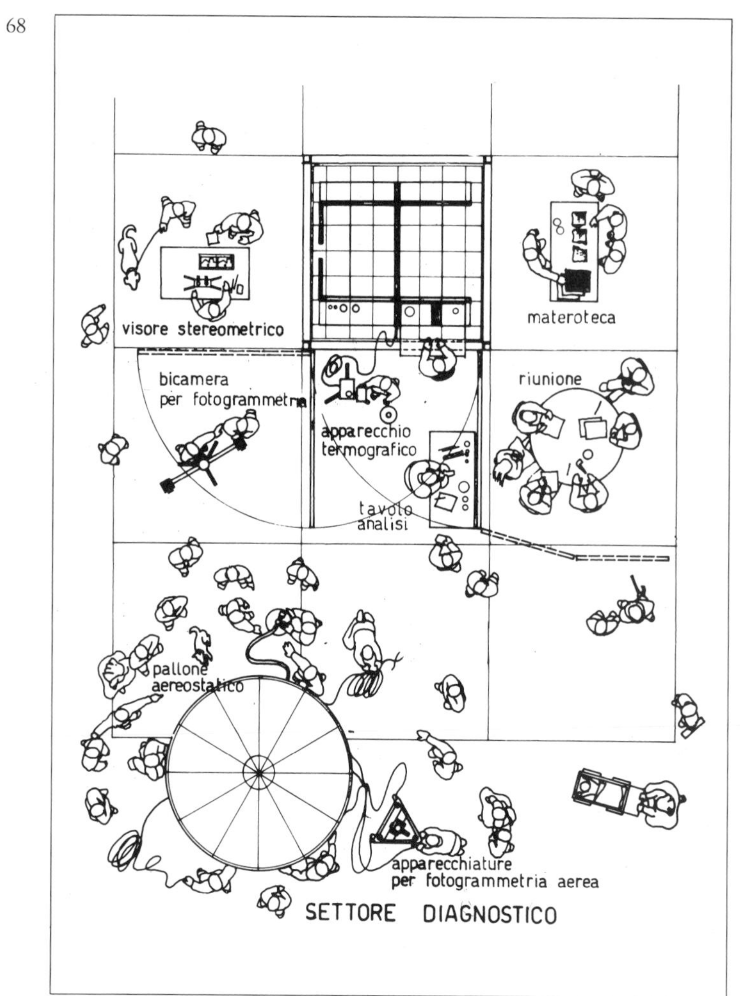

111

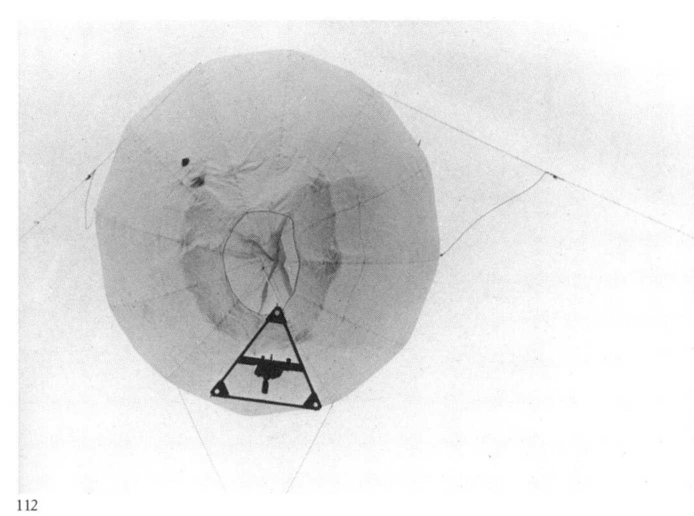

112

113

114. Plotter drawing from a photogrammetric survey.
115. Details of thermographic survey documenting composition of masonry.

116. Preparation of overhead thermographic survey.

116

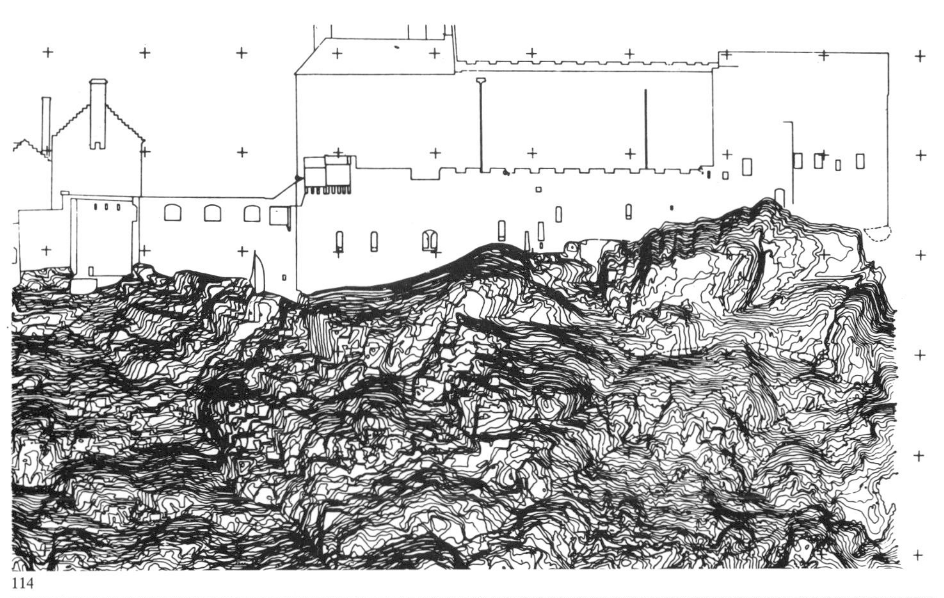
114

115

117. *Training and information sector of the travelling workshop.*

118. *Projection of documentary on Otranto's old town center in the square.*

119. *Video equipment for recording workshop operations.*

120. *Surveys of the Maroccia family's home, used for experiments in "soft" restoration.*

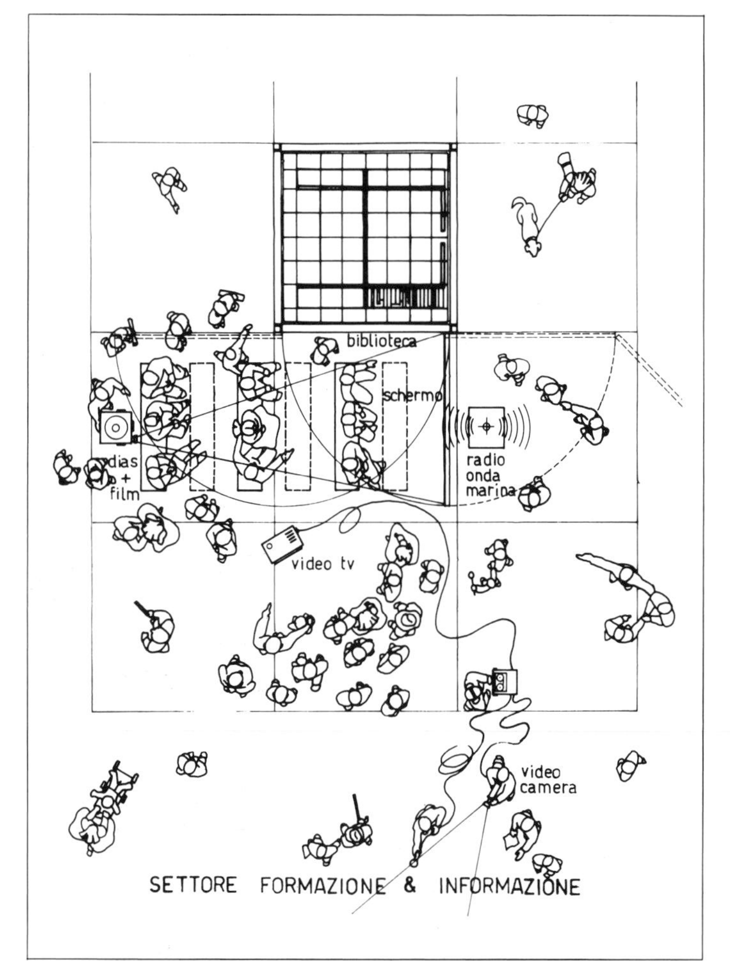

117

118

119

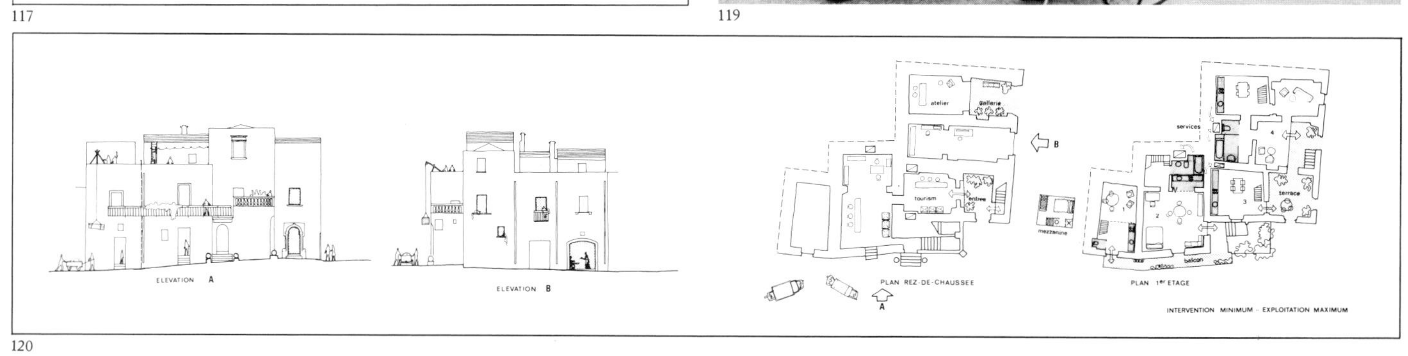

120

121. Construction and equipment sector of the travelling workshop.

122. Craftsmen preparing lightweight structural elements for restoration.

123. Spraying expanded polyurethane resin to insulate a wall.

124. Mending structural cracks.

122

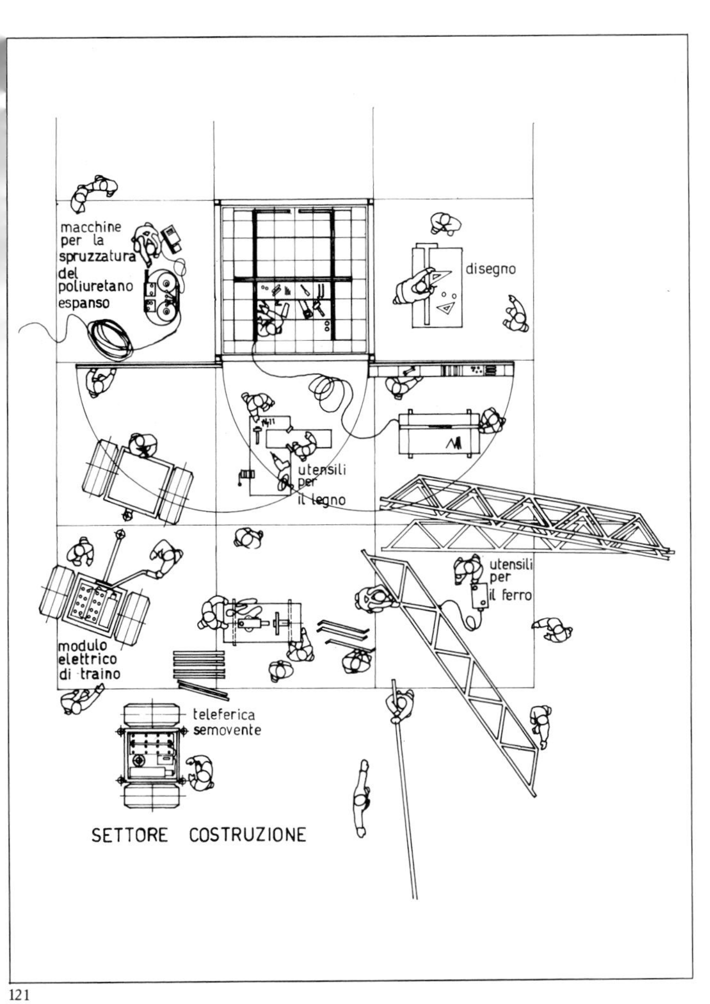

121

123

124

125. Signorina Maroccia in a room of her home before restoration.

126. The same room during light structural restoration.

127. Public meeting at the workshop.

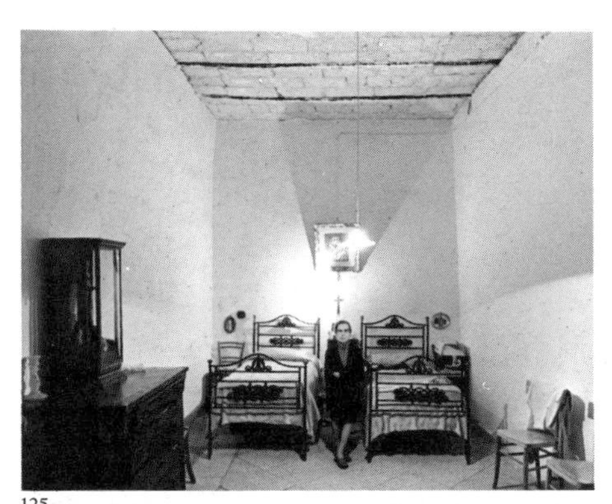

125

126

127

1982
IBM travelling exhibition

An electronic greenhouse

Client: IBM
Coordinators: G. L. Trischitta,
R. Lanterio, F. Moisset

Architects: Studio Piano/Building Workshop S.r.l.
with S. Ishida, A. Traldi, O. Di Blasi, F. Doria,
F. Marano, M. Carroll, G. Fascioli, R. Gaggero
with P. Nestler (Munich), N. Okabe (Paris),
and A. Stanton (London)

Engineers: Ove Arup &Partners
P. Rice, T. Barker, assisted by A. Guthrie
and R. Kinch
General contractor:
Calabrese Engineering S.p.A.
A. Gnoato, M. Valeriani

What surprises does the telematic future hold for us? What impact will new data processing technologies have on everyday life and the organization of work? One thing is certain that the relation between the town center and the suburbs is already changing; long-range communications will become more available and it will be less important to be in the center. Translated into town-planning, this means decentralization, revaluating the outskirts of towns, the local situation. The trend foreshadows obvious advantages, for instance, the possibility of finding a harmonious, balanced relationship with nature, but also risks such as isolation and an ever more marked division between private and collective life. This is the theme of IBM's travelling exhibition which gave the architect the task of transferring onto a spatial level the fascinating and complex theme of the electronic city.

The theme is many-sided, it ranges from seismic phenomena to pollution (i.e. whole forests controlled by sophisticated data collecting equipment), from knowledge to teaching and data processing. Ultimately the issue is the technology/nature dialectic. Piano resolves it with an evocative greenhouse, a system that encloses and relates the artificial and the organic. The great vaulted polycarbonate structure consists of a network of pyramidal elements interconnected internally and externally by a wood and aluminum element; it is to be set in a park to ensure the organic integration of architecture and landscape. "We worked on it for nine months and what resulted was an artificial typology so perfect that it evoked the rhythmical structures of nature."

The naturalistic dimension is reflected in the microelement out of which the whole is composed. The structure is a sequence of arches set one beside the other: so to speak, a gigantic earthworm; when detached, the individual pieces retain their formal properties and identity. The exhibition is conceived as a central body, with scattered fragments. "The structure is not foreign, incomprehensible not does it require heavy machinery for its erection. It is a lightweight toy. Setting it up is an almost magical gesture, automatic, calling for no special skills. Our idea is that schools of architecture and teaching institutions connected with construction should participate in mounting it." Mobility and handiwork come together in practical experiment. The "greenhouse," is a puzzle to be completed, with the finishing touches to be added depending on environment, climate and the seasons.

128

129

The "greenhouse" is a puzzle to be completed, with the finishing touches to be added depending on environment, climate and seasons.

128. Meeting with Alan Stanton, Paul Nestler, G.L. Triscitta and Roberto Lanterio.

129. Laboratory tests.

130. Section through the demountable structure.

131. Space frame system of the structural arch: the materials are polycarbonate for the transparent pyramids, wood laminate for the masts and extruded aluminum for the joints.

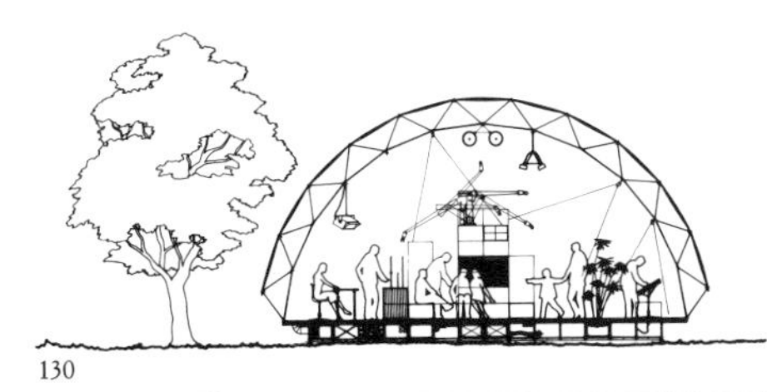

130

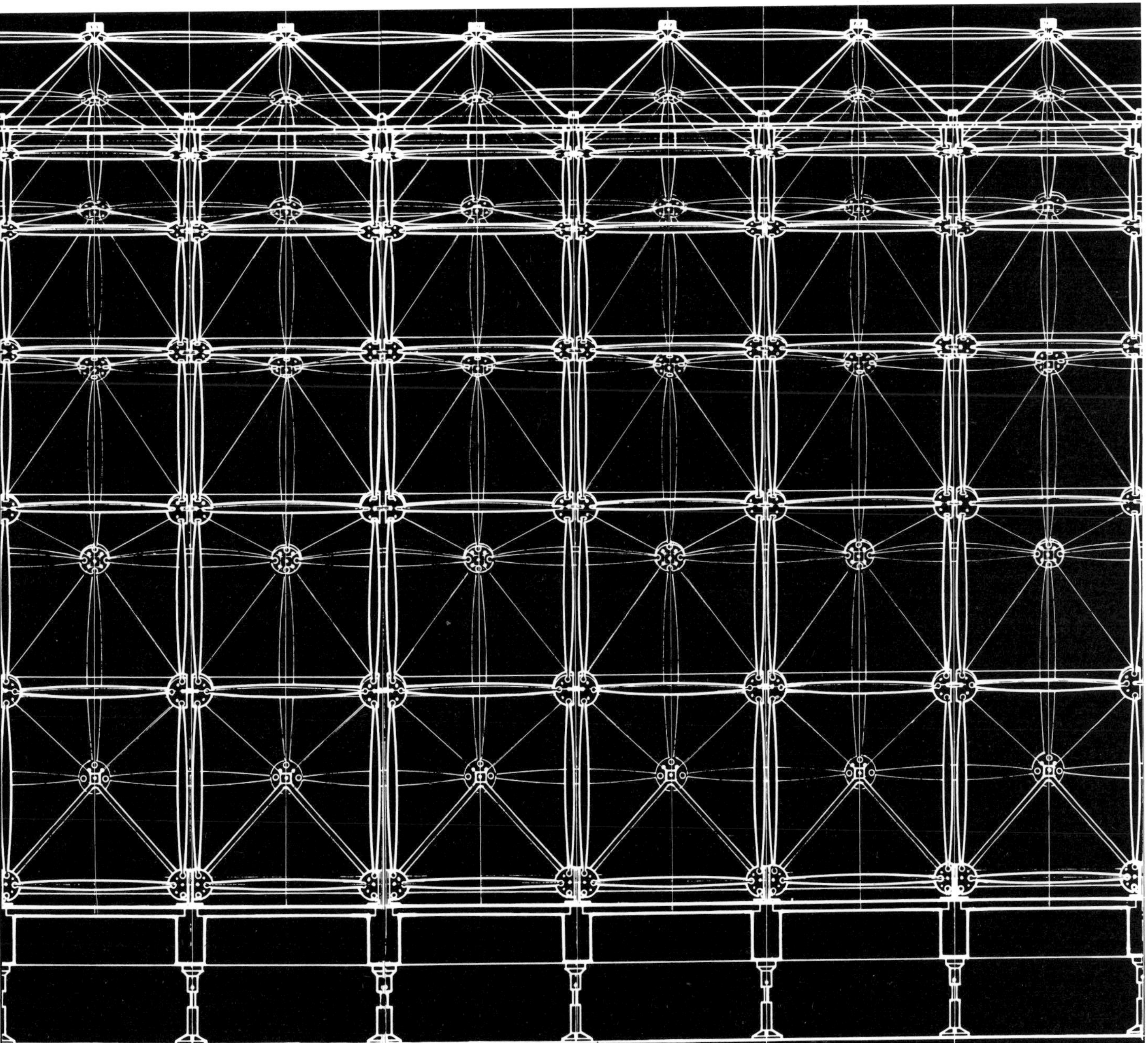

131

132. *Roof plan.*

133. *Longitudinal section.*

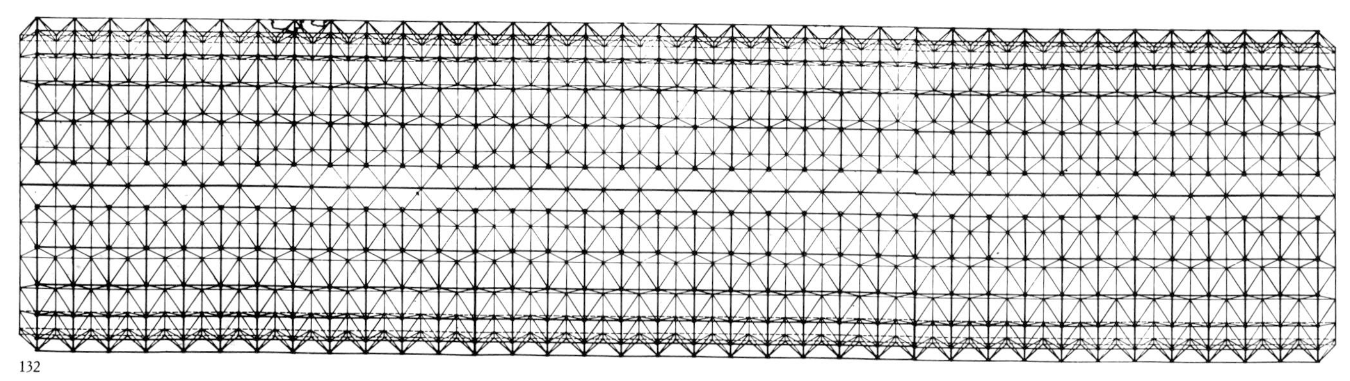
132

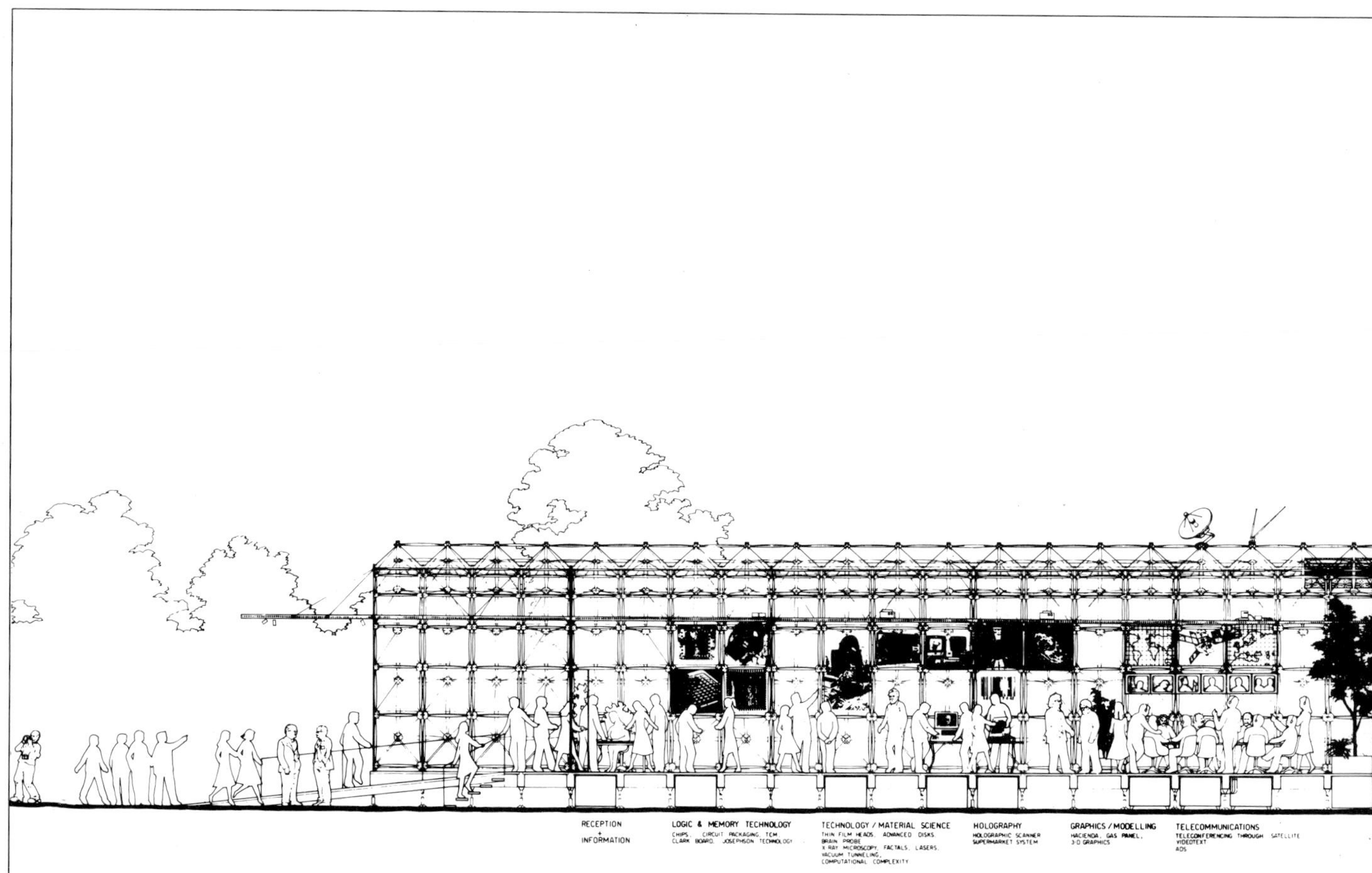

133

134. Possible localization of the travelling unit in a garden of Paris.

135. Possible localization of the travelling unit in the university quarter of Munich.

136. Possible localization of the travelling unit near the Thames, London.

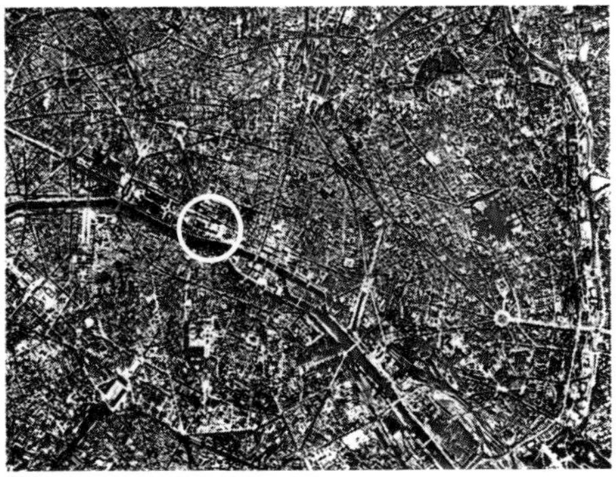

134

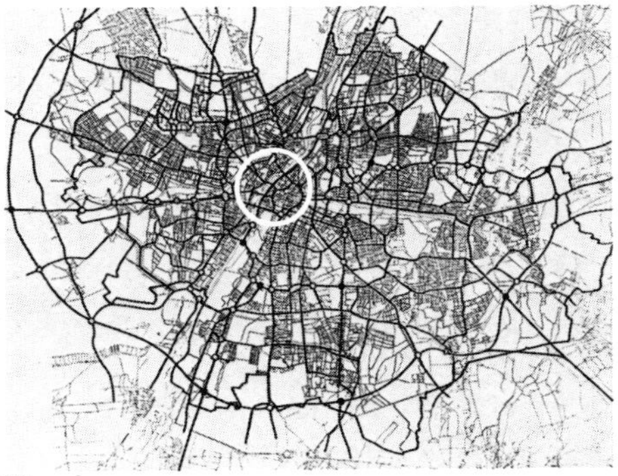

135

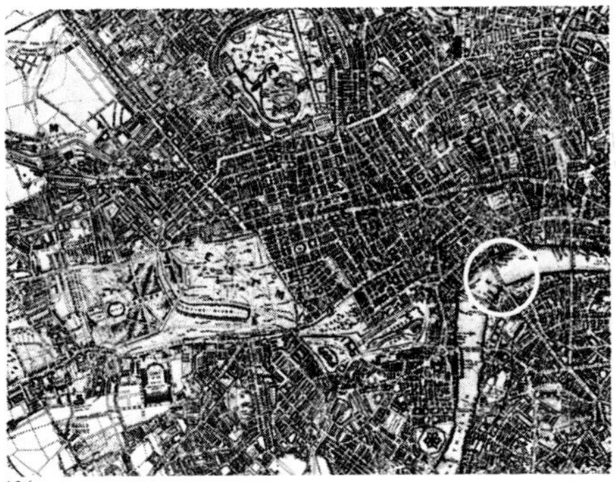

136

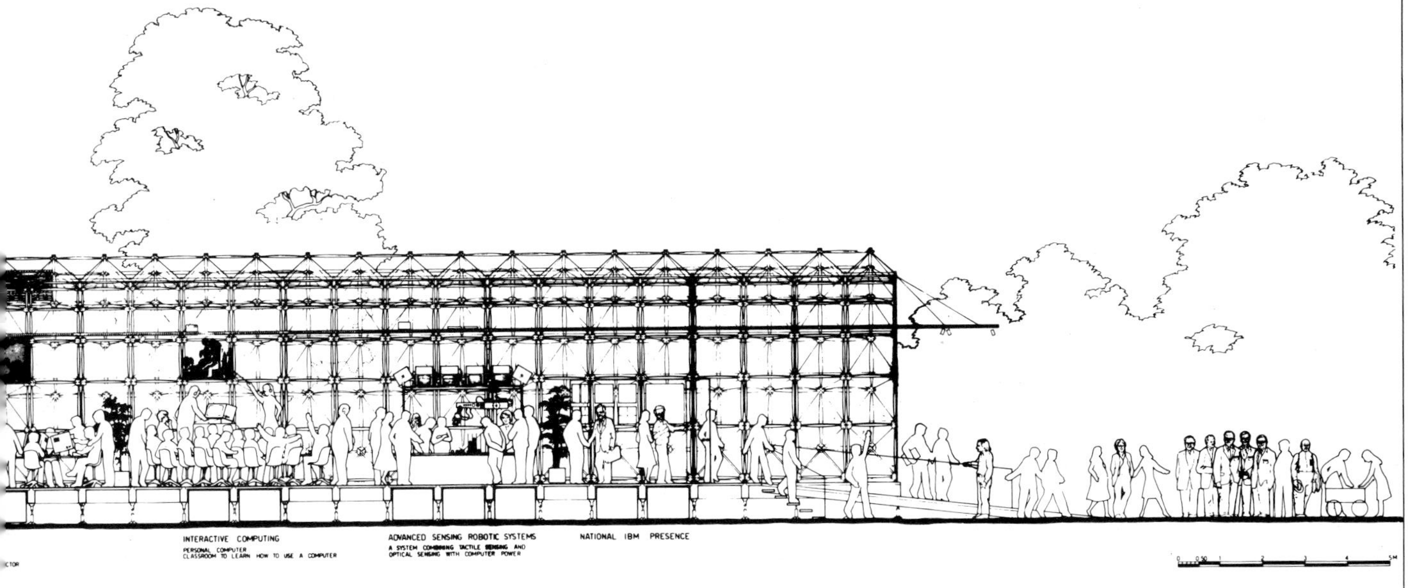

137. *Construction drawing of arch and components.*

138. *Aluminum joint.*

139. *The node made up of the polycarbonate pyramid, aluminum joint and laminated wooden spars.*

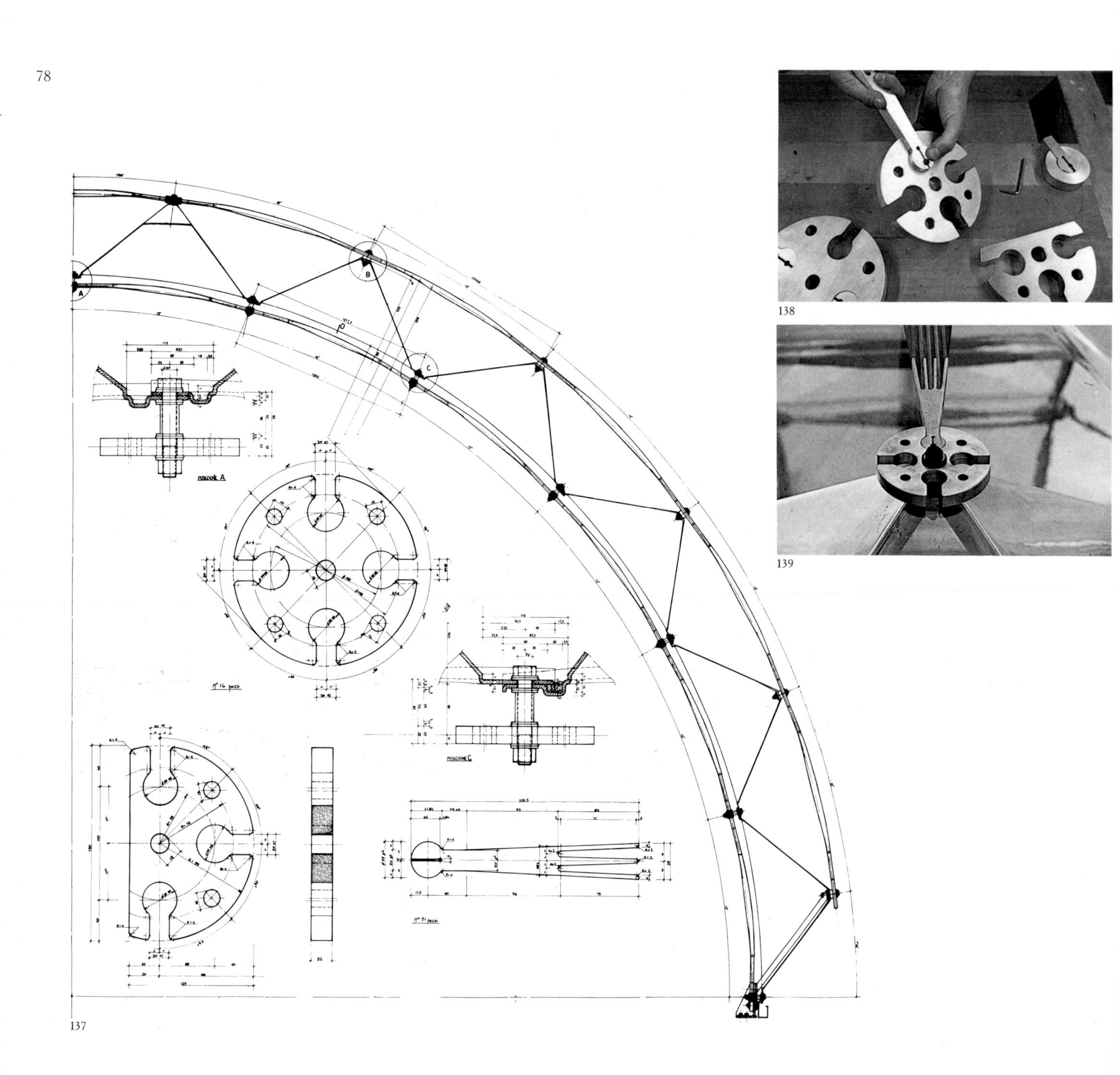

140. Prototype of the arch which is the building's basic element.

140

1968 Genoa, Italy
Industrialized construction system for a housing estate

Client: IPE - Genoa
Architects: Studio Piano
with F. Marano, O. Celadon, G. Fascioli
Engineers: SERTEC Engineering
Contractors: E. Piano Contractors

Flexible housing

The rigid parameters on area and volume laid down conditions for this residential complex, five low-rise blocks of six stories for a total of 32,000 m³. It is initially based on the principle of a complementary primary structure and a flexible interior space which can be freely manipulated. The load-bearing structure is made up of the vertical communicating towers and precompressed beam floor-slabs; the secondary structure defining the homes is cast in modular metal shutters, previously equipped with wiring and plumbing, and the assembly of prefabricated marginal fittings of Leca concrete with an external facing of plasticated grit ready for coloring. The blank walls are made up of panels, also prefabricated, insulated with a layer of expanded polyurethane and treated externally with waterproof grit rendering. Glazed walls consist of continuous window elements.

The elevator shafts and horizontal floor-slabs provide a rigid frame embedded in the ground and a fixed reference point.

Particularly significant from the functional viewpoint is the decision to raise the buildings off the ground, mainly because unusual panoramic views are obtained and also because it creates a space below for collective activities. The ground floor and basement spaces are intended to contain recreation facilities as well as the entry areas. This is a pilot experiment and suggests the resolve to interweave and fuse order, disorder, expressive freedom and functionality, qualities that reveal Piano's architecture as constantly facing live issues, open-ended, with a restless symmetry, not easily assimilated into the type categories made during these years.

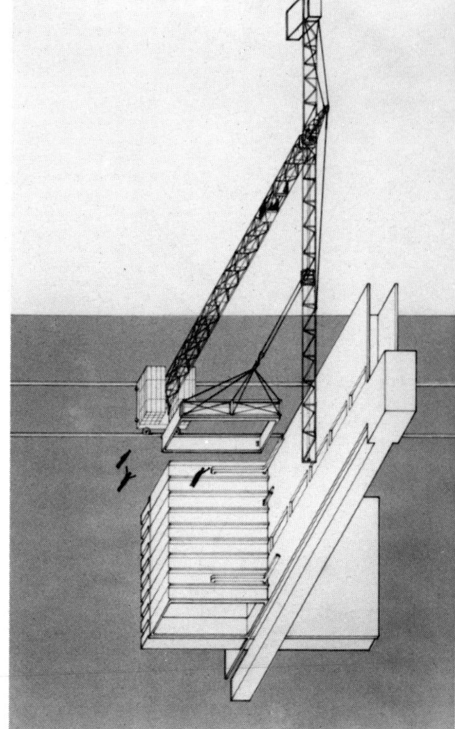

141

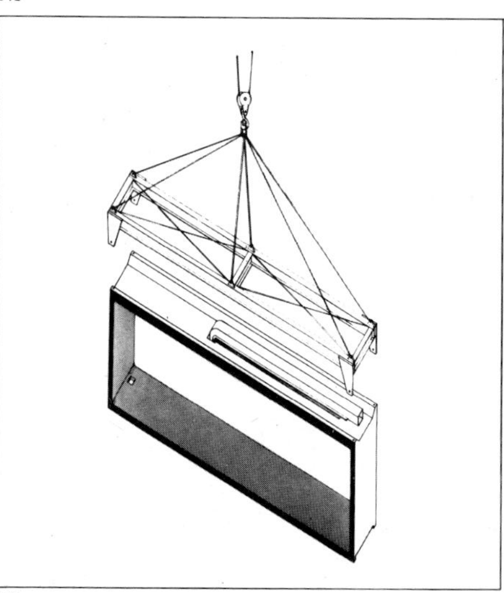

142

This is a pilot experiment and suggests the resolve to interweave and fuse order, disorder, expressive freedom and functionality.

141. Axonometric projection of the assembly of the building's basic elements.

142. Basic link element of the primary space of the house.

143. One of the buildings.

143

1968-1969 Genoa, Italy
Office workshop for the Renzo Piano studio

A flexible workshop

82

Client: R. Piano
Architects: Studio Piano
with F. Marano, G. Fascioli, T. Ferrari.
Contractors: E. Piano Contractors

This problem demystifies high technology and blends it into a setting that calls for soft technology to create a flexible, easily handled spatial arrangement. The key element of the structural layout is a steel pyramid with a rectangular base measuring 2 m by 1 m and weighing 25 kg. The ways in which this can be manipulated in horizontal and vertical combinations shapes the whole building, it functions as a load-bearing structure and an enclosure. Opaque or transparent panels are applied to the walls and roof and are interchangeable.

The organic nature of this geometrical pattern is heightened by the manner in which the light is directed from above. The roofing panels are of two-ply fiberglass; a film of gel attenuates the impact of the sunlight. This interior/exterior correlation is the main factor in giving lightness to the structural ribbing, creating effects of spatial fluency through roofing and walls. This has nothing to do with "technological trickery."

Everything is made as simple as possible and there is absolute freedom in the spatial layout. An ideal environment for an office-workshop in which there is "utmost confusion of roles and disciplines, as opposed to the subdivision of design and hence of architecture."

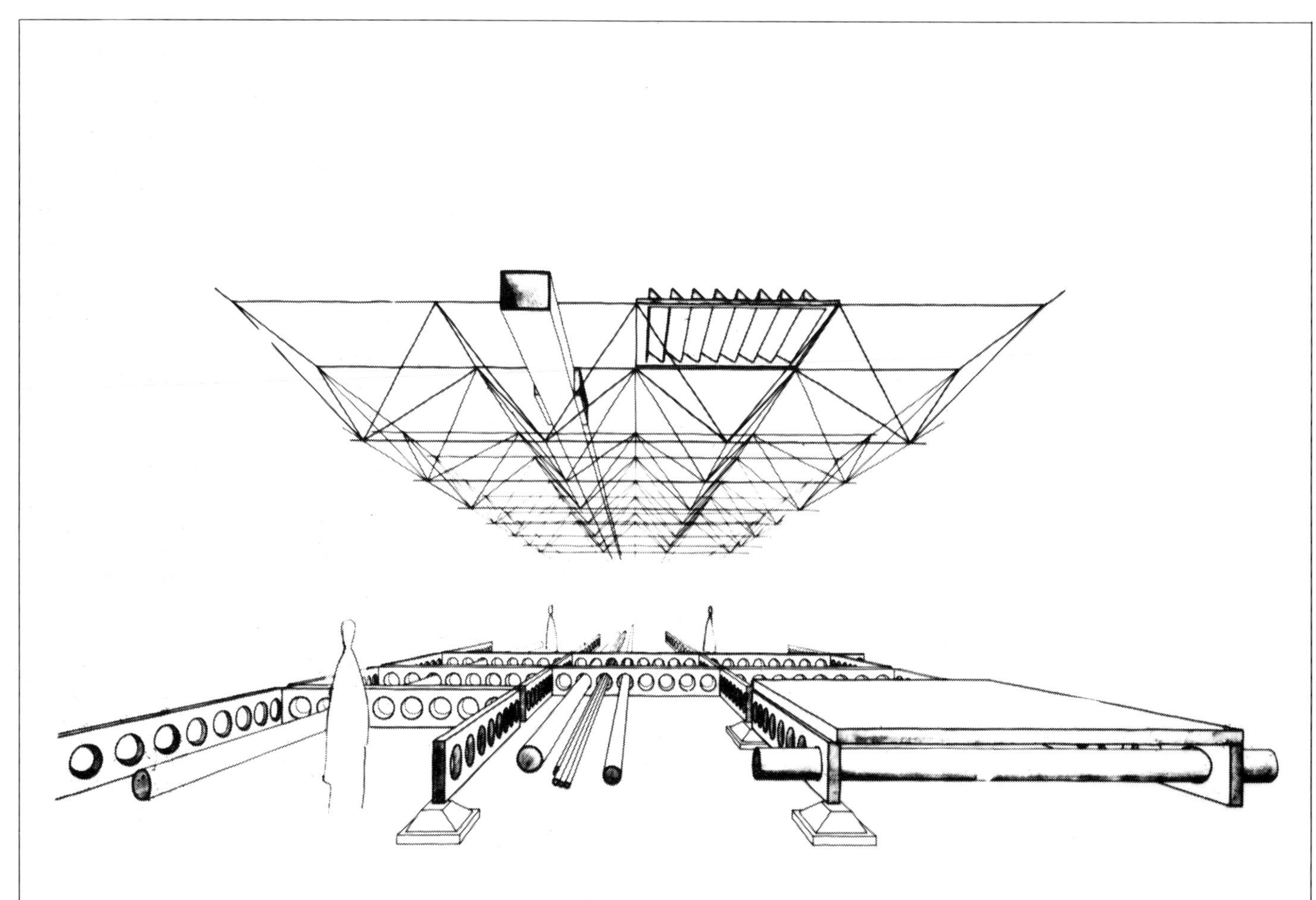

"In my workshop there is utmost confusion of roles and disciplines as opposed to the subdivision of design and hence of architecture."

144. The building's structural components: steel pyramid, translucent reinforced polyester panel and foundation.

145. Phase in assembly of pyramidal structural elements and curtain-wall panels.

146. Pyramidal elements during transport and storage.

145

146

147

148

147. Assembly of curtain-wall.
148. Lightweight concrete curtain-wall elements.

149. Detail of system of façade and door and window frames.

149

150. Assembly of a translucent roofing element: the element only transmits light from the north to the interior.

151. The "organic" texture of the roofing panels screens light from north and south.

152. View inside the factory; the natural lighting falls exclusively from above.

150

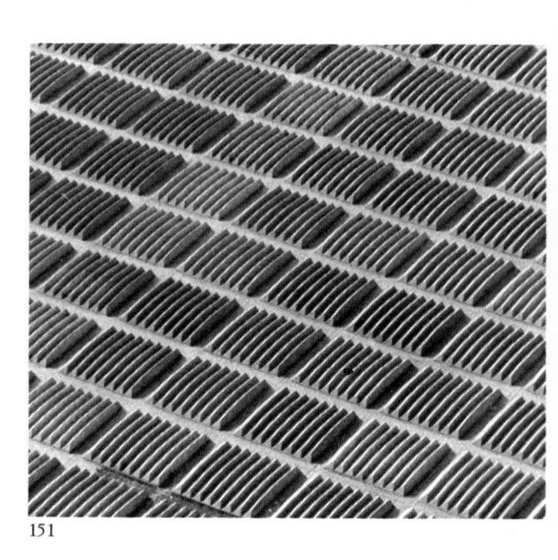

151

152

1969 Garonne, Alessandria, Italy
Open plan home

Architects: Studio Piano
with F. Marano, G. Fascioli, T. Ferrari
Contractors: E. Piano Contractors

The roof's the thing

This is a house reduced to the essential, almost elementary: a platform that acts as an umbrella and an open space underneath, no dividing walls, no physical barriers. Static space? Random space? The designer contests this interpretation. "Walls are not the only way of segmenting space. Soft elements can be used to make interiors dynamic: light, air, wind, color, sound, etc." From this point of view, the experimental home at Garonne, simple though it is, foreshadows the spatial modulations of far more complex projects like the Beaubourg, the Menil Collection in Houston or the "Exhibition Machine" in Milan.

The main element in the building is its roof: a pyramidal wooden framework, light and easily handled, supported on a steel base; the roofing and walls are made of panels. The nature of the spatial layout allows plenty of scope for introducing variations: the layout secures a wide range of inner divisions and movement of the supporting elements. All this is achieved without sophisticated technical equipment: the various components can easily be assembled by the occupant, and it is the occupant who will decide how to divide up the interior, imparting a dynamic impulse to the whole — making it live. In a nutshell, one of Piano's most strongly held architectural principles is evolution. Behind the screen of a conventional house type, with its box-like appearance, lies something completely different, extraneous to the formalistic architectural tradition. "I think that neither a home nor any facility can indulge in the luxury of being unchangeable. Evolution is something which I feel is indispensable. It is only ignored for bureaucratic reasons or for reasons of taking responsibility for the final result."

A home, in other words, is anything but a finished product to be handed over complete to the client. It is "zero hour," something still to be created.

153

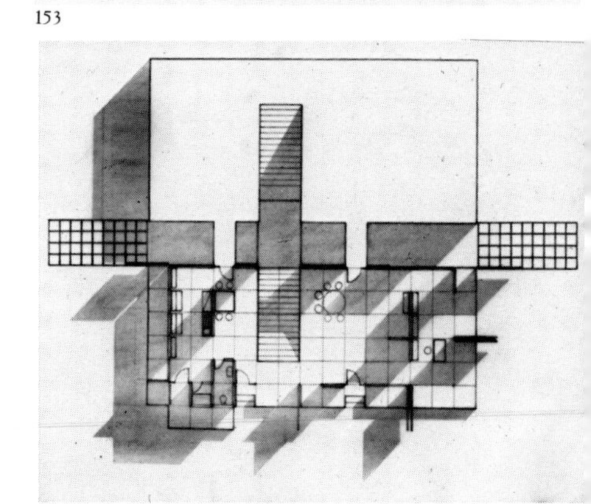

154

"I think that neither a home nor any facility can indulge in the luxury of being unchangeable. Evolution is something which I feel is indispensable. It is only ignored for bureaucratic reasons or for reasons of taking responsibility for the final result."

153. Model of the basic wood structural element for the roof.

154. Open plan of the home under the flat roof.

155. Detail of the roof space frame: elements functioning under compression are made of wood while those subject to tensile stresses are steel.

156. The house under construction.

155

156

1971-1973 Novedrate, Como, Italy
B & B Italy office building

A suspended structure

Client: B & B Italy, S.p.A., Como
Architects: Studio Piano & Rogers
with C. Brüllmann, S. Cereda, G. Fascioli
Engineer: F. Marano

The little office building at the entrance to the B&B Italy factory presents an intensity of chromatic effects and a display of its plant engineering and equipment, transmitting a feeling of vivacity, suggesting an ironical or, at least, demystifying attitude. It is a double roof on a box-like volume; a constructional solution (inspired by the intermediate barn-roof space) that secures a twofold objective: (1) deployment of air-conditioning and service ducts outside the box; (2) creation of an efficient heat exchanger that circulates air in the cavity between the two roofs and cooling the extrados of the inner volume, so reducing the work of the air-conditioning system in summer. The interior is open, a large space which can be laid out freely, divided up, reduced or expanded as required. Everything is functional and movable, walls, lights, electric sockets, switches. Even the outer frame is an extensible screen, made up of poles: by increasing the number of doorways of welded tubular steel, it is possible to extend the container as desired. The box has another unusual feature: it is suspended from a delicate trellis structure constituting the outer envelope.

The evocative chromatic variations, open plan and suspended space are all features that taken together give the Novedrate building a suggestion of the futuristic, the acrobatic, looking ahead to the stellar tones of the Beaubourg. The designer is not trying to heighten the contrast between the technological landscape and the natural environment. On the contrary, the lightness and transparency of the envelope attempt a link-up, a merging of two worlds which so rarely communicate with each other, technology and nature, interior and exterior.

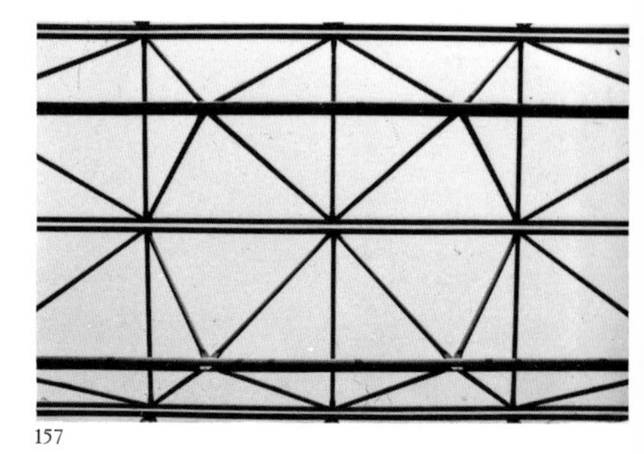

157

The chromatic variations, open plan and suspended space are all features that give the Novedrate building a suggestion of the futuristic, the acrobatic, looking ahead to the stellar tones of the Beaubourg.

157. Detail of metal structure.

158. Structure of a truss.

159. Assembly of trusses with a clear span of about 30 m.

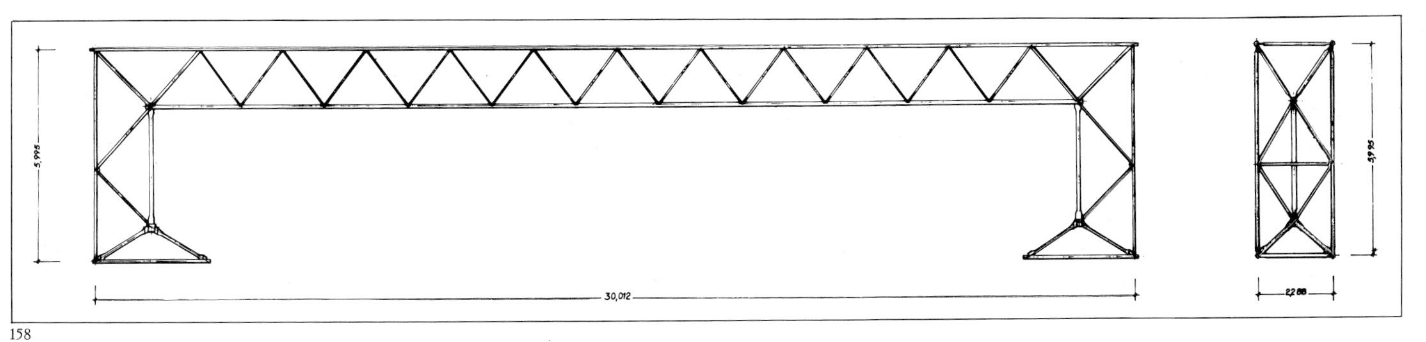

158

159

160, 161. Exterior of the building.
162. Detail of joint.

160

161

162

163. Construction details.

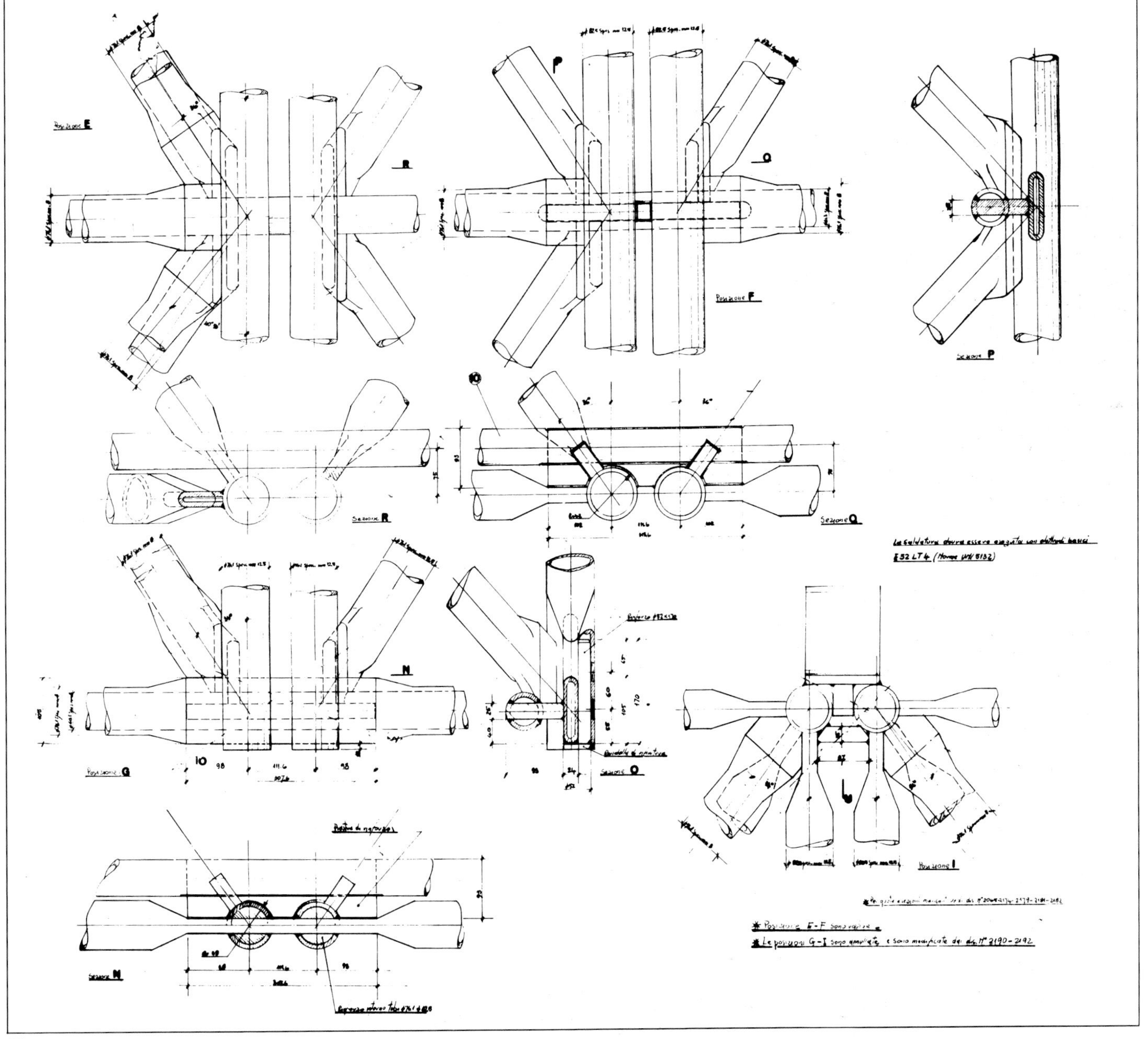

163

164. Detail of façade to the north and garden.

165. Construction details

164

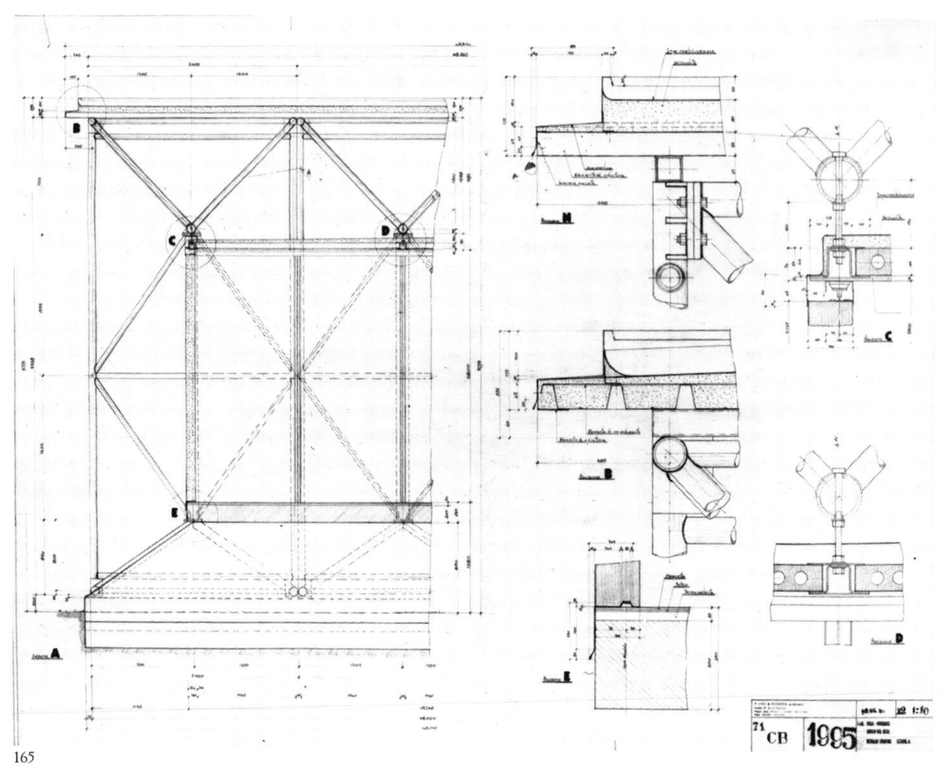

165

166. Catwalk linking office block to production areas.

166

167. Longitudinal section of the building.

168. East side of building with distribution of air-conditioning and other plant.

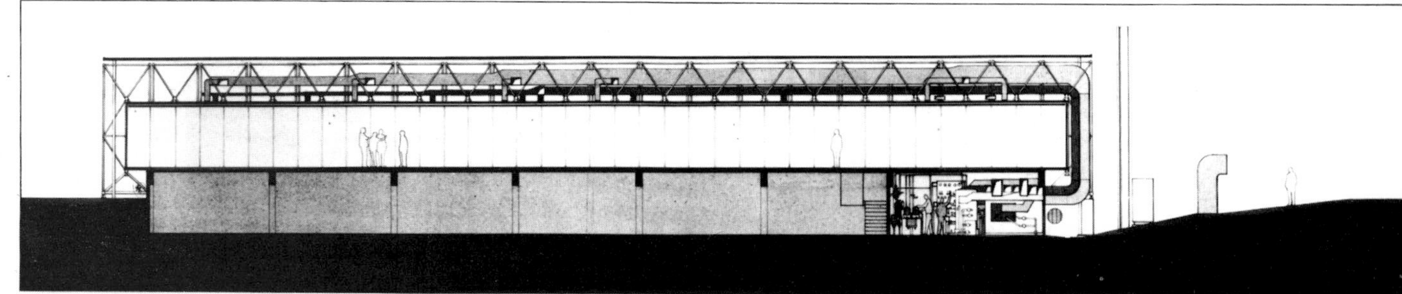

167

168

169. Plan of the inner ceiling and roof: this space provides summer and winter ventilation and contains all the building's plants.

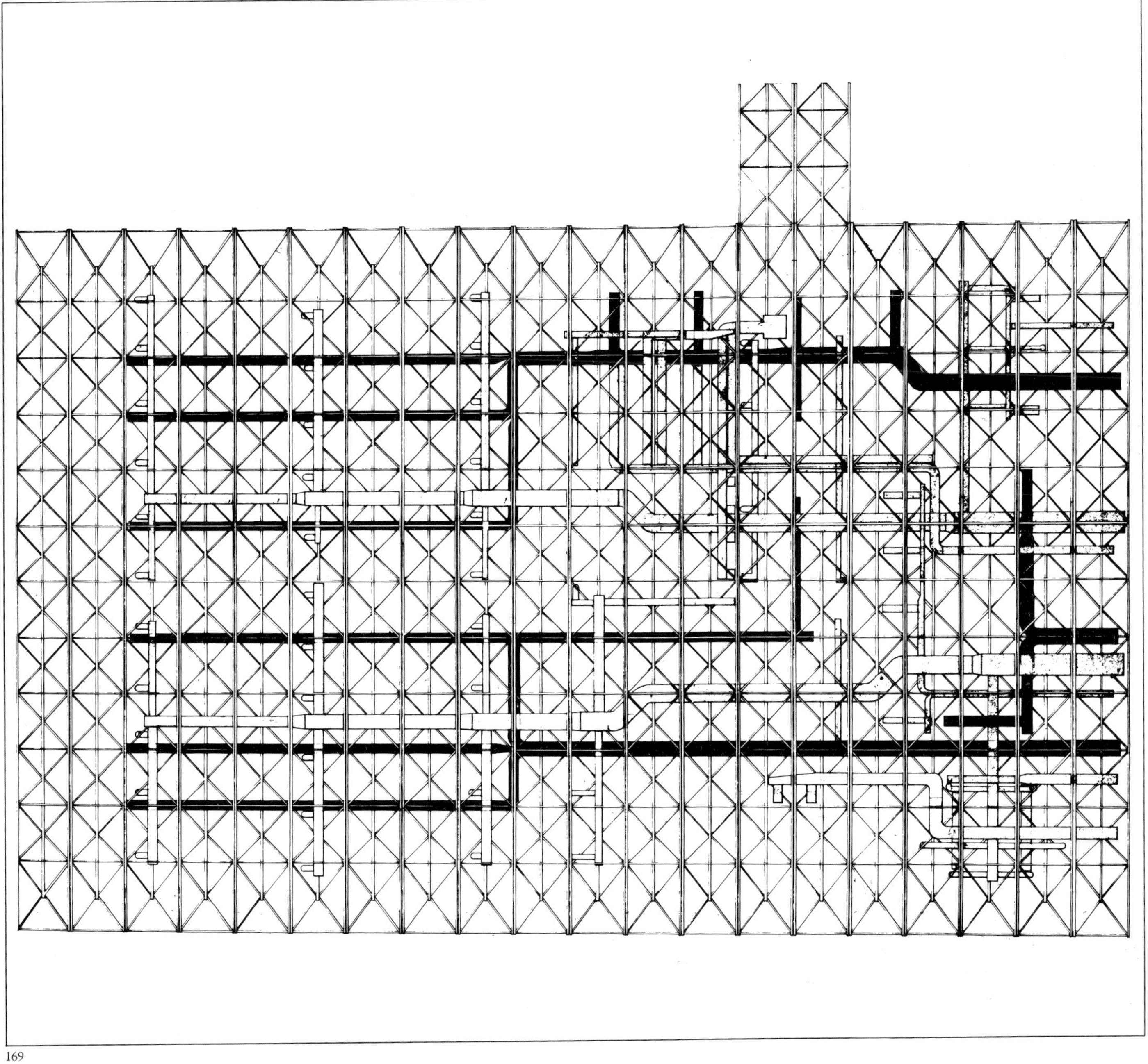

169

1972-1974 Cusago, Milan, Italy
One-family homes

The industrial home

Clients: Lucci, Giannotti, Simi, Pepe

Architects: Studio Piano & Rogers
with C. Brüllmann, R. Luccardini, G. Fascioli, and the collaboration of R. and S. Lucci

Engineer: F. Marano

What is a house? A machine, an industrially produced dwelling cell, a territory, or a space to be used as one likes? One thing is certain, constraints of different kinds (technical and legal, economic and psychological) now confine the house inside a rigid unchangeable cage which no longer reflects the needs, tastes and culture of the individual. Even simplicity and purity of form often merely camouflage the aim of cheap and rapid construction. The problem is whether there exists a realistic, feasible way of giving the occupant responsibility for his home. Piano reveals his plan for adjustable housing in this design: a capsule without divisions in which the articulation of space is effected by the furnishings and not by walls nor pillars. The building's flexibility stimulates a creative response in the occupant participating in its arrangement.

From outside the four one-family homes look identical. But inside the open plan suggests different and personalized layouts for everyday living. The whole point is to create a culture of the home. It is not enough to limit the operation to interior decoration — which is only marginal — it has to go further and affect the structures, modify the vocabulary of housing. "If the occupant cannot alter his living space, then he cannot put down roots in it either. Since he cannot make it his own, he manipulates objects, perhaps through associated mythologies: false style."

The proposal is provocative but essentially mediatory; reformist but not revolutionary. The description chosen is of "industrial housing," but the concept of mass production does not imply here that the spatial layout is rigid. All that is needed is a standardized enclosure, an outer shell plus, of course, the roof. Here the latter consists of double roofing: a series of metal elements sheathed in plastic and, underneath it, separated by a beam grid, a double layer of steel sheeting lined internally with expanded polyurethane.

The side walls are of masonry; the front and back walls, set in about two meters from the roof line, are extensively glazed with Glasal panels, half fixed and half sliding. We have small factory sheds, flexible and brightly lit, perfectly integrated into their setting.

To create a culture of the home, it is not enough to limit the operation to interior decoration: it has to go further and affect the structures, modify the vocabulary of housing.

170. Section and plan of the houses.

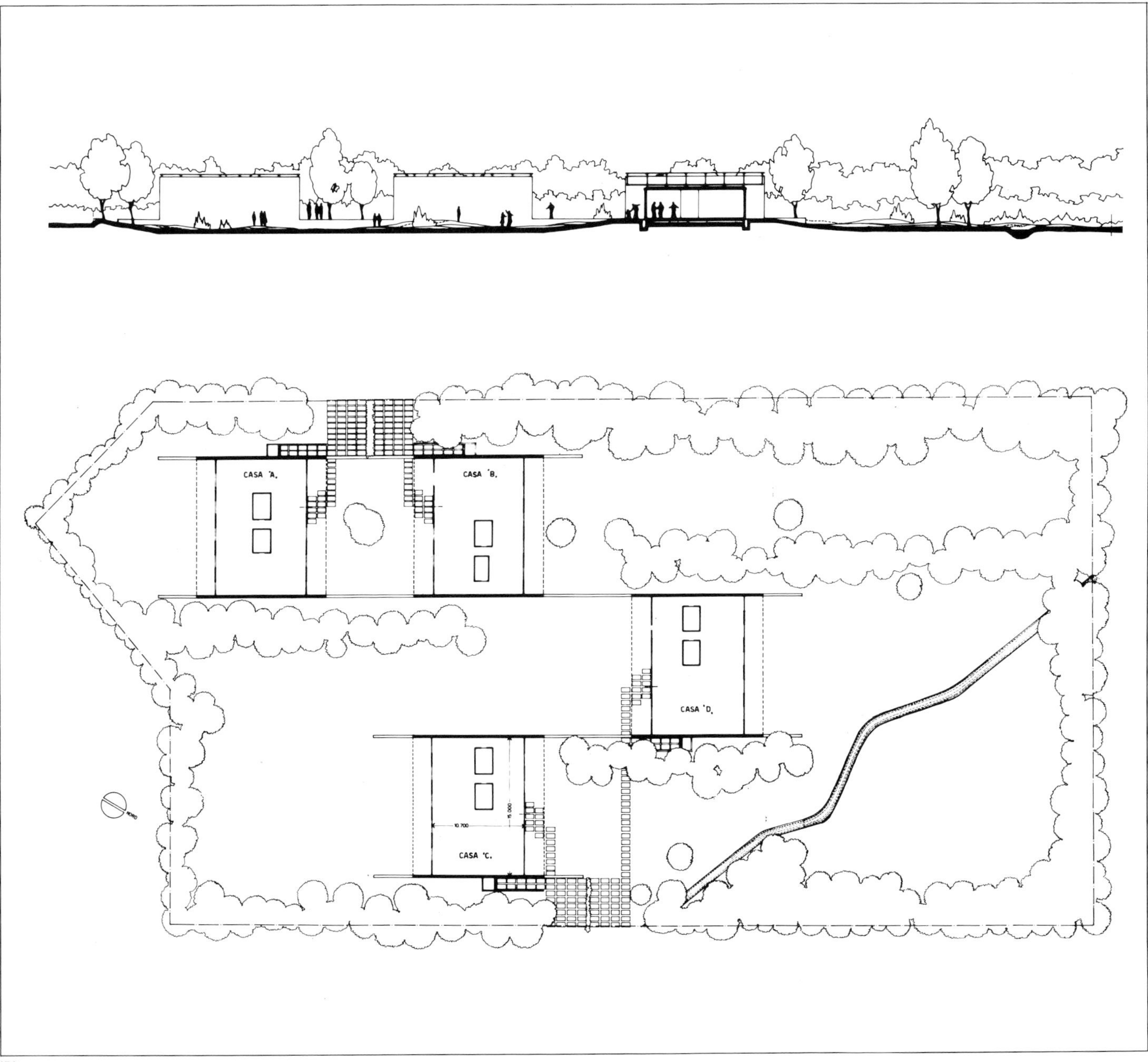

170

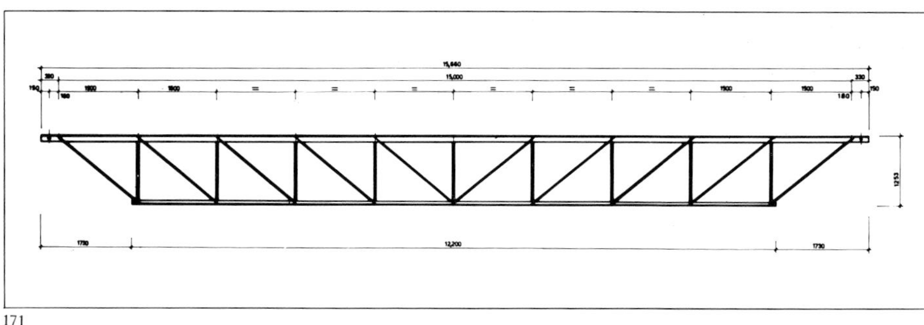

171

172

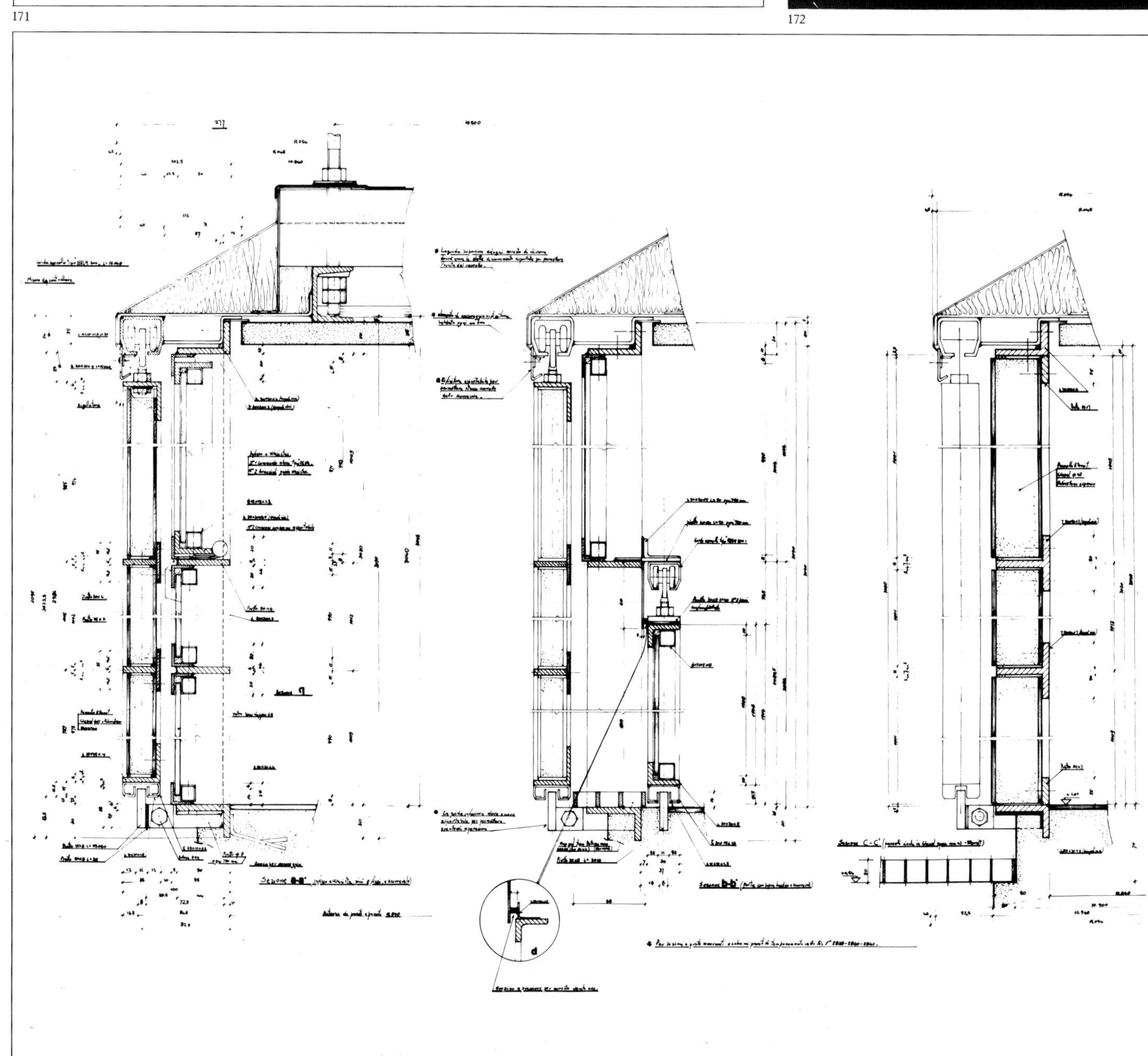

173

171. One of the roof beams. The clear span is 15 m.
172. Assembly of the roof beams.
173. Construction details of façades.

174. Façade of one of the houses: the space between roof and inner ceiling allows passage of air and is important for summer ventilation.

174

175. *Section and plan of basic design.*

176, 177. *Interiors of a home designed and executed by the occupants.*

178. *View onto garden.*

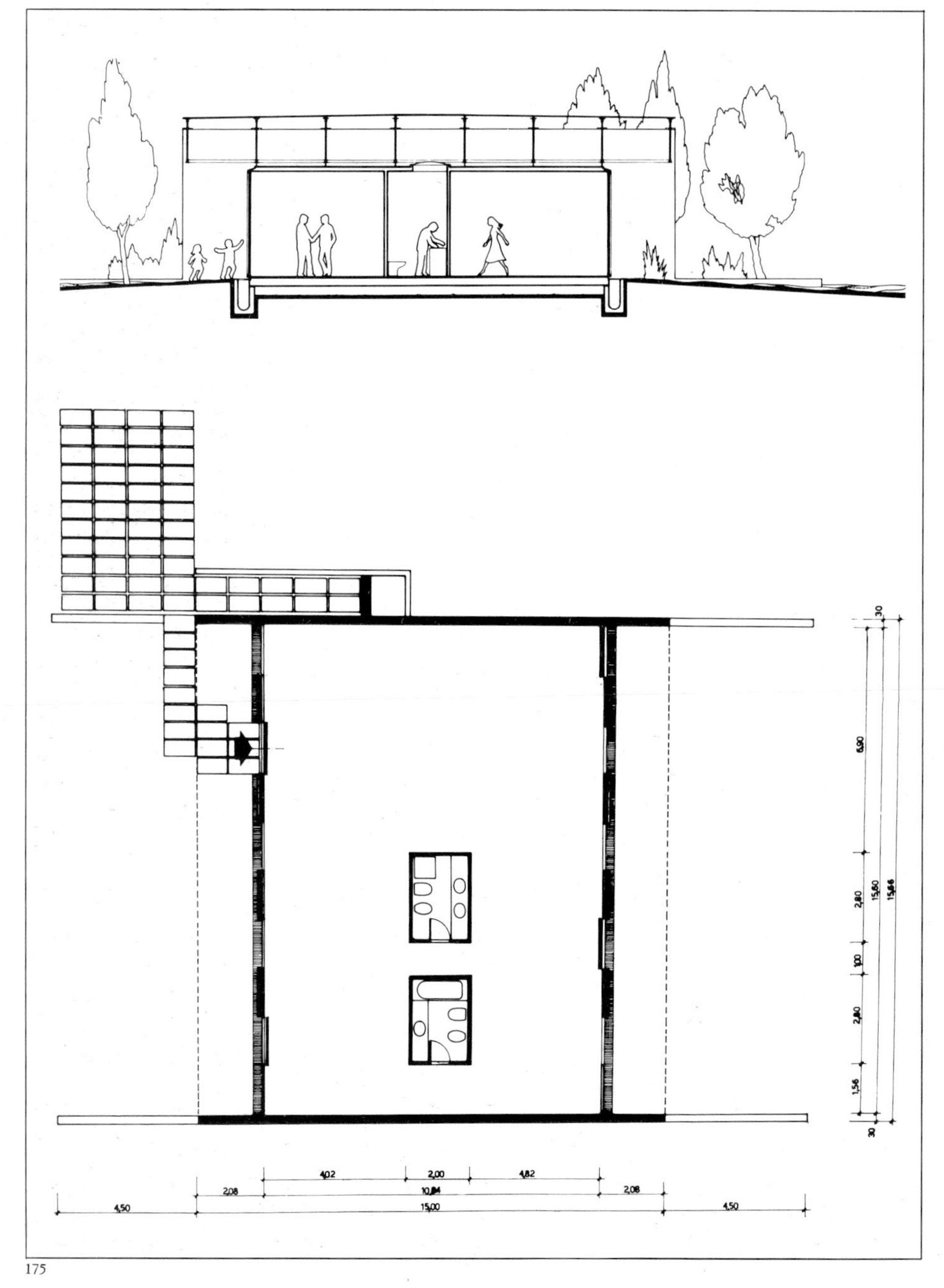

175

176

177

1978 Perugia, Italy
Industrialized construction system for evolving-type homes

Client: Vibrocemento Perugia S.p.A., Perugia
Coordinator: Engineer R. Jascone
Architects: Piano & Rice & Associates
S. Ishida, N. Okabe
with E. Donato, G. Picardi
Engineers: P. Rice assisted by F. Marano, H. Bardsley, with the collaboration of Vibrocemento Perugia
Client: Commune of Corciano
Architects: Piano & Rice & Associates
S. Ishida, N. Okabe, L. Custer, architects responsible
with E. Donato, G. Picardi, O. Di Blasi and G. Fascioli
Engineers: P. Rice assisted by H. Bardsley, F. Marano with the collaboration of Edilcooper, RPA Associati, Vibrocemento Perugia
Director of works: L. Custer
with F. Marano

Inventing an apartment

A dwelling space is not an absolute, irreversible dimension. This is the principle underlying the "EH" project submitted to the AIP competition in Friuli and subsequently developed for large scale application to a medium density estate in Corciano near Perugia. With this system, the apartments are the result of the combination of a primary space built by specialists whose job is to provide the technical essentials — structural solidity, seismic resistance, insulation and soundproofing — and a secondary space, the interior (on two levels) which is equipped and transformed by the occupants themselves.

The basic element in the prototype house is a three-dimensional U-shaped structure of reinforced concrete. The occupants can organize the interior of the box-like enclosure by manipulating lightweight beams and panel flooring. Assembly operations are made easy by self-stabilizing structures and standardization of the additional components. One detail expresses the building's flexibility: the living space can be varied from approximately 50 m² to 120 m² simply by moving window surfaces and intermediate floor panels. On paper it looks very simple; in reality the impact is more complex. "The expansion of the State into housing," says Piano, "is undeniably a social advance, but at the same time it displays features of a welfare mentality, it diminishes the sense of responsibility, it acts as a demotivating factor. Of course at Corciano the people made their contribution at the design level but it is also true that in certain cases what was movable ended up as immovable; a bed or a wardrobe blocked evolution." This experience clarified the misunderstanding over participation: it is difficult to allow the occupants indiscriminate freedom of action. Choices have to be guided, directed, protected from the pressures of advertising. Only in this way it is possible to reach the goal of active and direct control of the home.

In this sense the architect's role is, as ever, decisive. There is no question of reviving the techniques of Romantic or traditionalist spontaneity, or do-it-yourself methods, but of experimenting with new equipment, new working tools, since only soft technologies can come within the grasp of the occupants. From this arises the need for a neighborhood workshop enabling investments to be spread over a certain length of time and the evolving village to be continually rearranged. The workshop is part of the primary structure (itself reduced in cost) and the contractor sets it up in the neighborhood. Subsequently it becomes the basis for the maintenance system.

This project indicates one possible way to escape the ever-present constraints of mass society. The danger is to see the house as a fixed container, a service to be accepted passively instead of a mirror of oneself and one's personal culture, a "den" shaped by the individual himself.

179

180

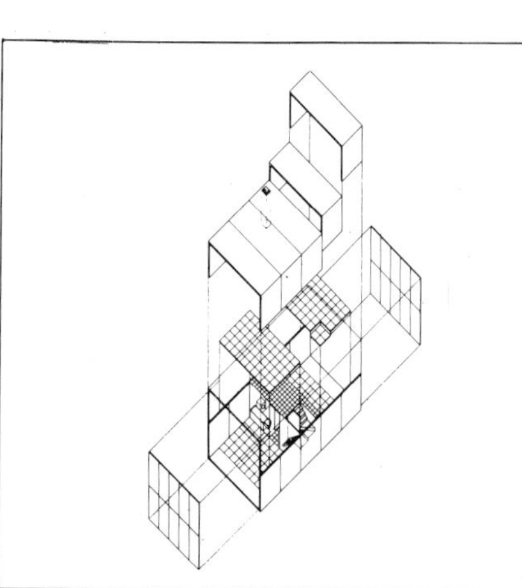

181

"The expansion of the State into housing is undeniably a social advance, but at the same time it displays a welfare mentality, it diminishes the sense of responsibility, it acts as a demotivating factor."

179. House-type typical of Friuli.

180. Basic construction module: width 6 m, height 6 m.

181. Axonometric of a home consisting of a fixed external enclosure capable of securing structural solidity, seismic resistance, and evolving inner space.

182-184. Assembly of two structural elements forming the primary enclosure.

185. Assembly with construction organized in line.

182

183

184

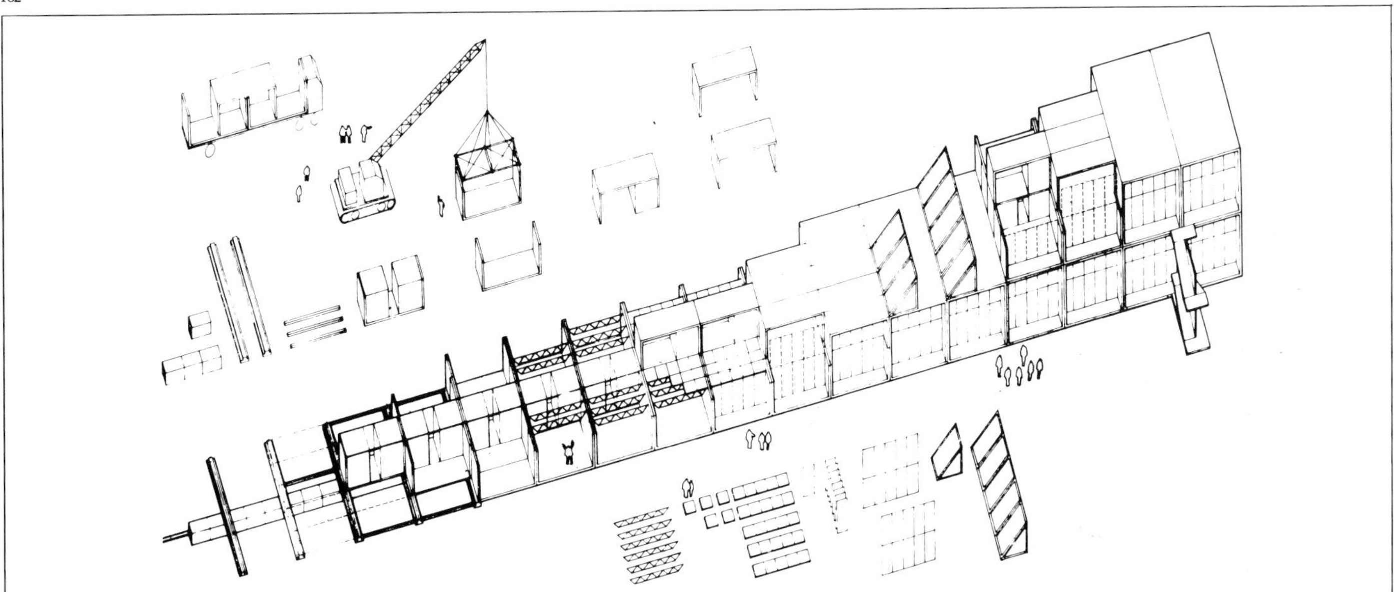

185

186. Mounting a lightweight beam within a primary space to create a second level inside.

187. Mounting intermediate lightweight floor panels.

186

187

188. *Schemes of interior with scope for extension from 56 m² to 131 m² of living space. This increase can be made available without touching the primary structures.*

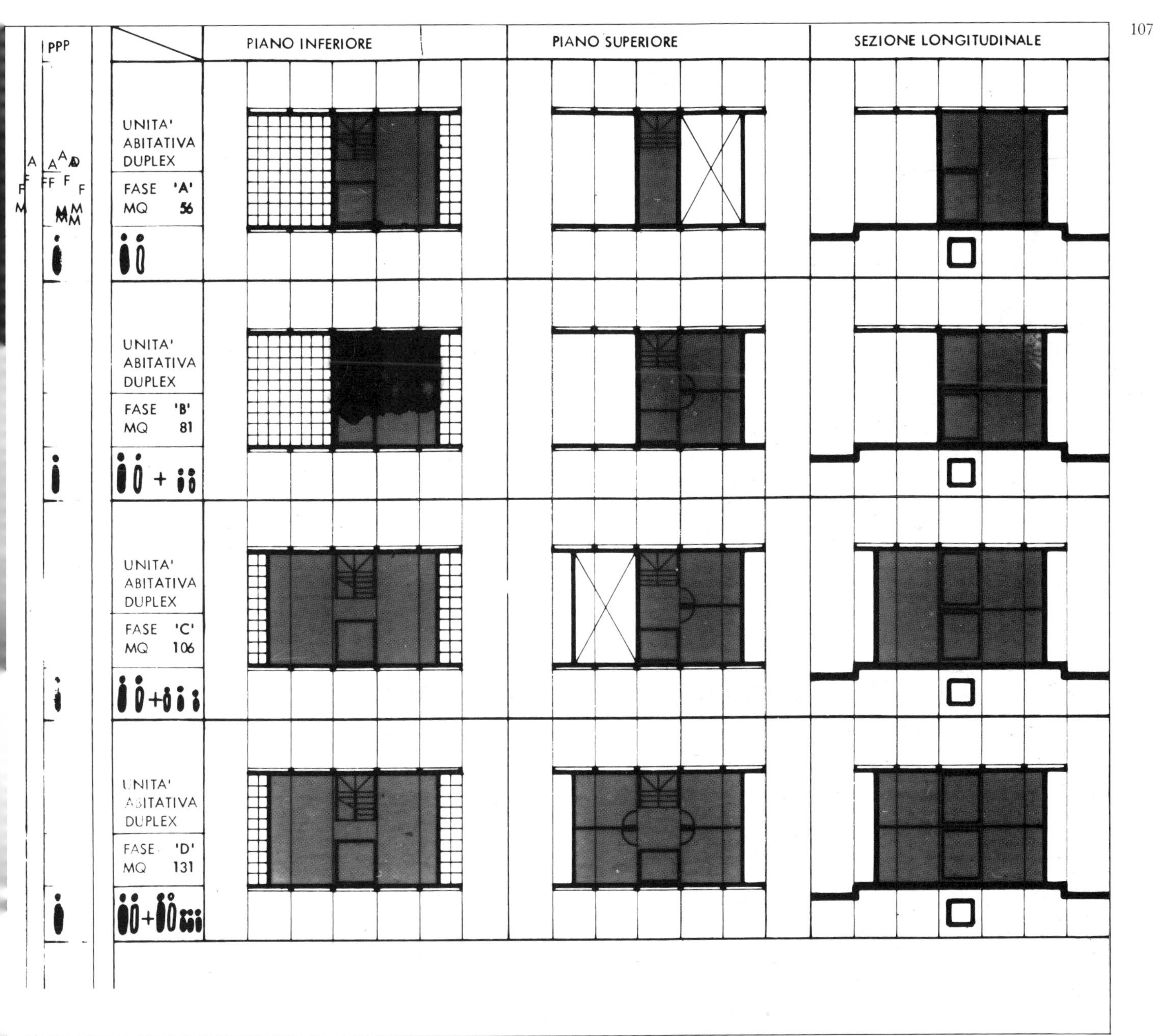

188

189

189. *Plan of the Corciano estate near Perugia designed for pilot scheme of the Evolving House.*

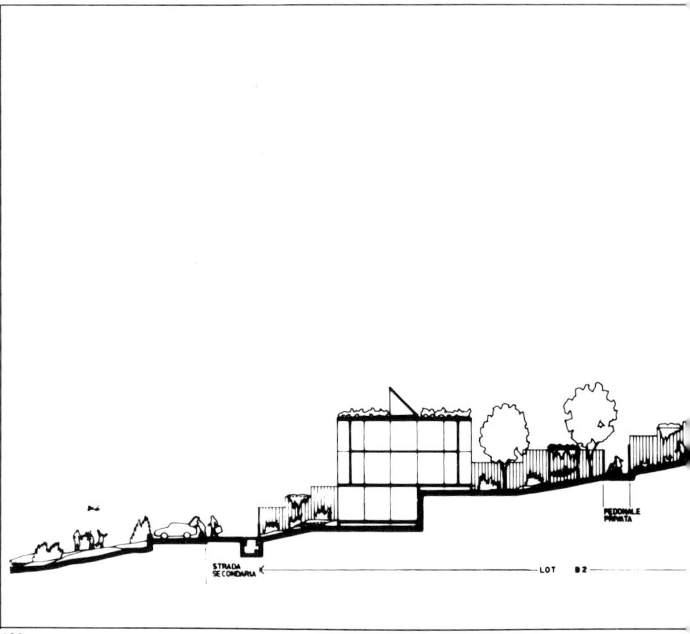

190

190. *Section of Corciano pilot estate.*

191

191. *Elevation of the estate on central street: all the homes are duplex with a height of 6 m.*

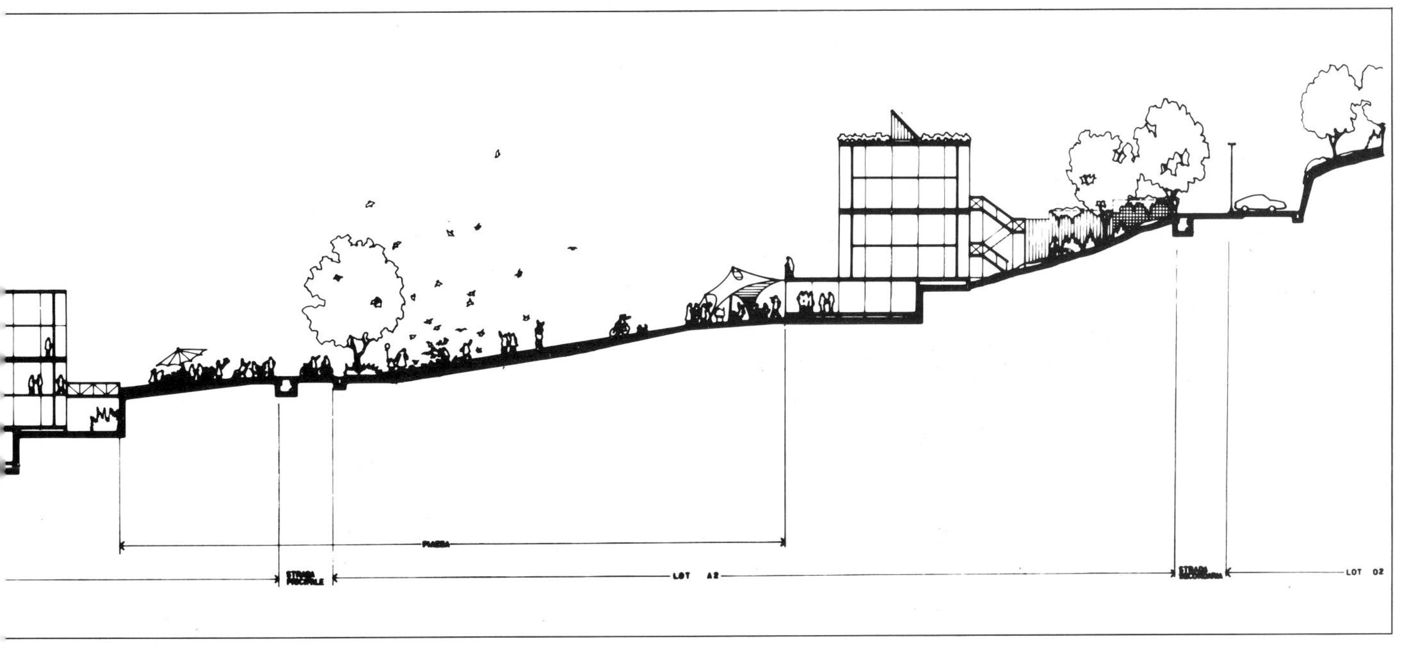
LOT A2
LOT 02

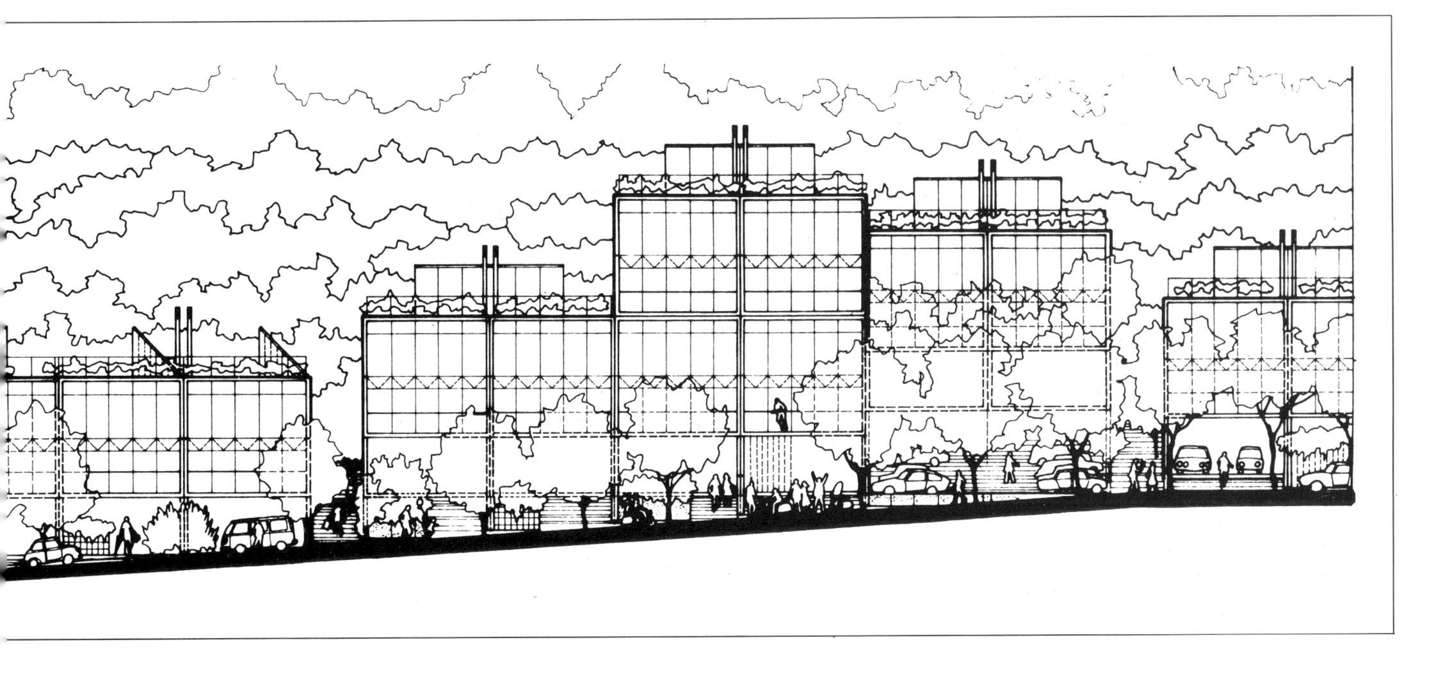

192. *Work sheet of one of the inhabitants of the estate.*

3C

RP/mb

Nome

Professione di Lei disoccupata ragioniera

Professione di Lui metalmeccanico

Composizione famiglia 4 adulti (nonna + madre + coppia)

Disponibilità finanziaria al di là del finanziamento di 24.000.000 ~ 2-3 ~~000.000~~

Lavori eseguibili successivamente:

3^ camera solo solaio (subito) struttura finitura dopo

2^ servizio completató dopo intanto solo allacc.

caminetto e impianto ~~elettrico~~ RISCALDAMENTO. impto

terrazza attrezzata

pitture o tappezzeria niente tappezzeria pitture da solo

pavimenti farseli fare (amico rev.)

strutture leggere da giardino —

solette intermedie leggere pannelli da solo

mobili da solo (indipendente)

Che tipo di lavoro ritengono di ~~poter~~ ~~fare~~ da soli

pittura da solo

piastrellatura no

tappezzeria —

montaggio sanitari e idraulica semplice primo no secondo si

saldatura e carpenteria leggera si

falegnameria leggera no

muratura leggera (getti di calcestruzzo) zio

impianto elettrico zio

Varie: importante struttura grosso
imp. risc. gasolio indispens.
int. generale per risc. solare

Genova, 21/9/1979

192

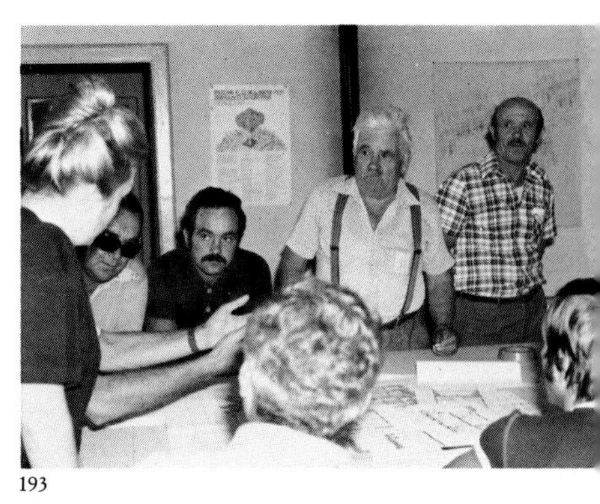

193. *Meeting with inhabitants to organize their task of completing some of the fittings.*

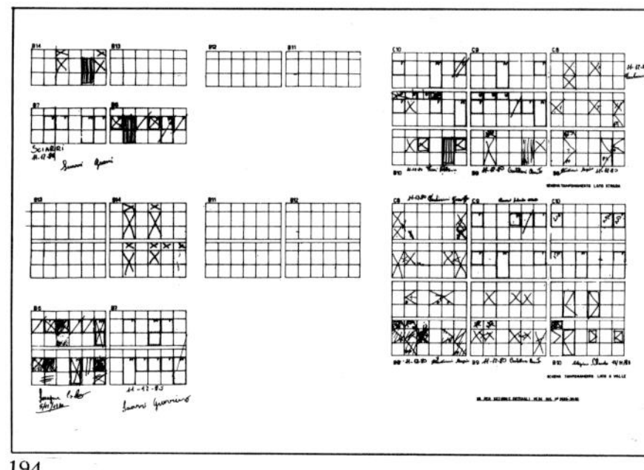

194. *Schemes of façades worked out with the inhabitants.*

195. Plan of the neighborhood workshop which will supply materials and tools for arrangement of the interiors and control of modifications to living spaces.

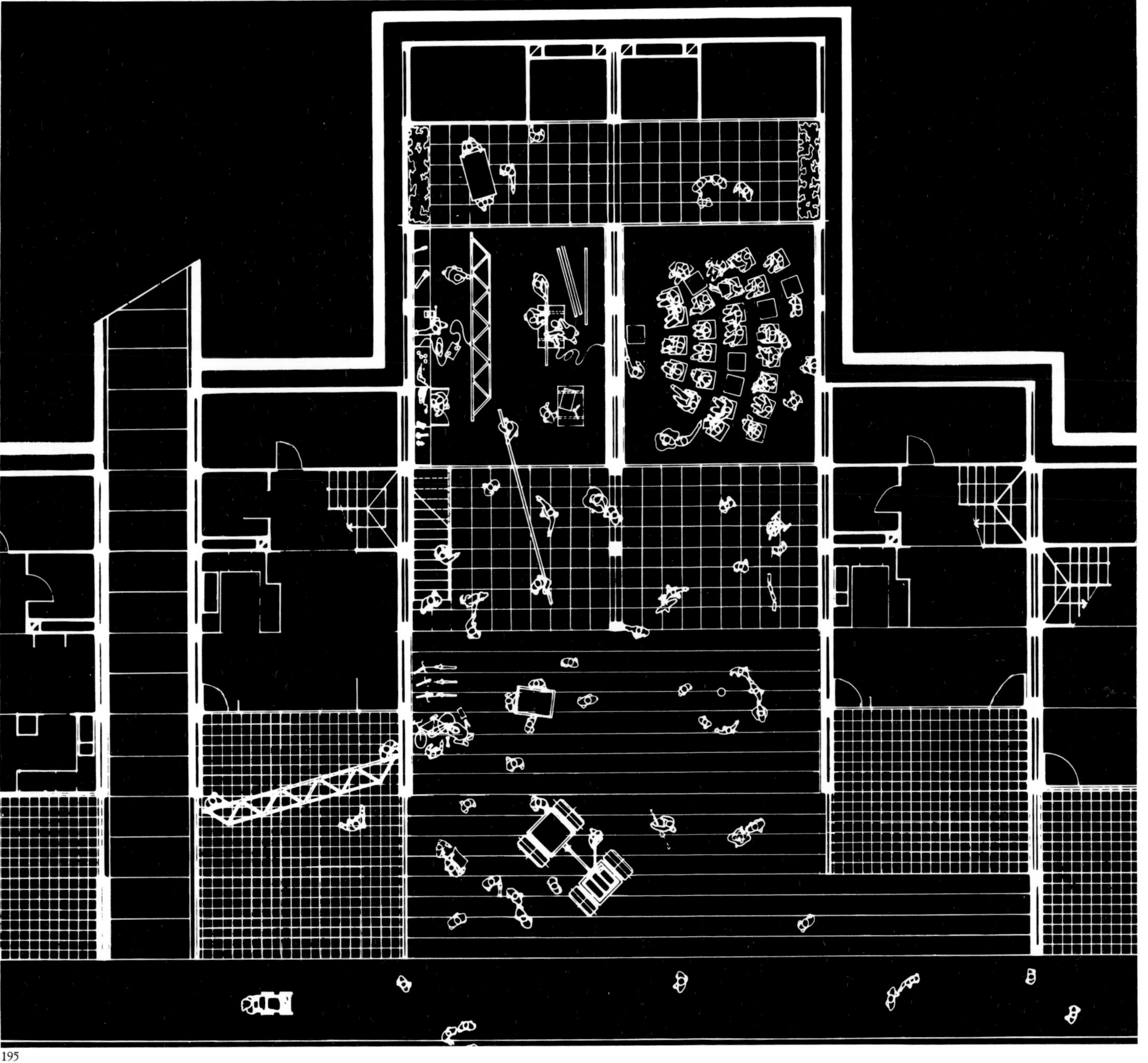

195

196. View of construction site.

197. Partial view of construction work.

198. Axonometric of the estate. The façades of the housing look onto a private space on the road and a private space fronting onto gardens.

196

197

198

1980 Milan, Italy
Exhibition complex

The exhibition machine

Client: Nidosa - Gruppo Cabassi

Architects: Studio Piano/Building Workshop S.r.l. with S. Ishida, F. Doria, E. Frigerio, A. Traldi, F. Marano, G. Trebbi (coordinators) assisted by M. Carroll, O. Di Blasi, E. Miola, G. Fascioli, R. Gaggero

Film documentation: M. Arduino, M. Bonino, S. Battini

Engineers: Ove Arup & Partners
P. Rice, T. Barker, assisted by N. Noble and A. Guthrie, C. Giambelli, D. Zucchi

Consultants: Italian Promoservice (exhibition services)
B. Richards (transport)
G. Lund (technical services)
APT (fire prevention and security)

199

Imagine an urban microcosm, a miniaturized city spread out beneath the shelter of an immense canopy; a roofing that suggests some of Frei Otto's fantastic designs, with its spaces protected by soaring membranes, translucent veils stretching as far as the eye can see. This is the exhibition city: a great chrysalis-roof of 12,000 pyramidal elements in reinforced concrete suspended over an area of 200,000 m^2. A concept both simple and complex, "because it is beneath this roof that an environment that is impalpable in architecture, air and light begins to take shape. The problem is to simplify the structural idea, otherwise an architect's desire to occupy the center of the stage, to indulge in gestures, could well exhaust all the space, shutting the door to creative contributions from other disciplines."

The design for the integrative focus of the Milan Trade Fair is conceived as a specialized instrument, a "machine for exhibiting." The trade fair in the electronic era is no longer a festival, a great market with a romantic aura, but an instrument of trade which has to comply with definite criteria of flexibility in organization and plant engineering. Internally the building is subdivided into eight pavilions. Access to the exhibition area is by means of a central covered concourse 600 m long and 48 m wide. The concourse and exhibition spaces are placed at the same level and have independent entrances so that there are multiple possibilities for mounting exhibitions, either one big fair including all the eight pavilions or else a number of smaller displays articulated separately.

The single level solution has advantages for the public (shorter distances to walk, easily controlled flow of visitors, simplicity of orientation) and also for the exhibitors (reduction of change-over times). The great rectilinear concourse is virtually the backbone of the building: a clear point of reference (all the services are laid out along its path) but also an enchanting piece of stage-setting, a Crystal Palace, an emotive environment made up of light, sunshine, water, natural views and artificial breezes ("air pulsations") with all the qualities of outdoors yet also those of a covered space, protected from the cold and heat, where one can move around freely whatever the weather is like outside. Distances are reduced by mechanized pedestrian conveyors overhead and converging on the center.

Inside, under the great technological sky, people move around in a controlled microclimate; each area will have different levels of energy consumption. "The trade fair structure is like an immense apartment in that every room has different uses that need to be continually varied."

Ducts, plants and services are placed in the loft space between ceiling and roof; on the roof 56 minipower plants are coordinated by a single computer to supply ventilation and air-conditioning throughout the volume, balancing consumption in the different sectors. Here everything is mobile, flexible, evolving: the pavilions can be altered in height (from 10 m to 13 m), surfaces can be changed, the "islands" containing restaurants, information offices and so on, can be shifted around. The principle of this trade-fair-happening is efficiency plus spectacle. "A fair that is also a performance has to have a clear, immediately recognizable character that will remain impressed on people's minds." These two concerns are interwoven into its decentralized layout: the "exhibition machine" is envisaged as set within a huge natural extra-urban frame (of a million square meters). This organic relationship is necessary for functional reasons, since this center for the trade fair cannot exist without a "lung" to dispel the effects of a great concentration of traffic around it (vast car-parks, rapid access systems); and also for ecological reasons since a commercial structure needs a surrounding green belt, perhaps even an artificial lake, to foster a soothing, enjoyable perception of the scenario. It synthesizes outdoors and indoors, of urban and rural spaces, an operation typical of the "frugal society" in which construction research is carried to industrial production (mathematical procedures based on the computer and experimental controls, giving rise to prototypes in scale and testing them in laboratory conditions) with the aim of economizing on materials and equipment and so cutting costs. This is a constant feature of Piano's design achievement, a gravitational field where past and future converge and are harmonized.

It is beneath this roof that an environment that is impalpable in architecture, air and light begins to take shape. The problem is to simplify the structural idea, otherwise an architect's desire to occupy the center of the stage, to indulge in gestures, could well exhaust all the space.

199. Work model for a structural module 24 m x 24 m, made up of 36 prefabricated pyramids.

200. Study model.

201. Study model for the lower structural node.

200

201

202. *Scheme of movement of the public within the building.*

203. *Scale comparison with St. Peter's in Rome.*

204. *Section of the building along the central concourse.*

205. *General plan with parking and external areas: the exhibition machine requires an external area equal to at least 5 times the size of the roofed area.*

206. *General plan of the building. Roofed surface area 200,000 m² with eight independent exhibition pavilions.*

ENTRATA NORD
ENTRATE SOPRALEVATE
ENTRATA SUD
INGRESSI
0 8 24 48 M

202

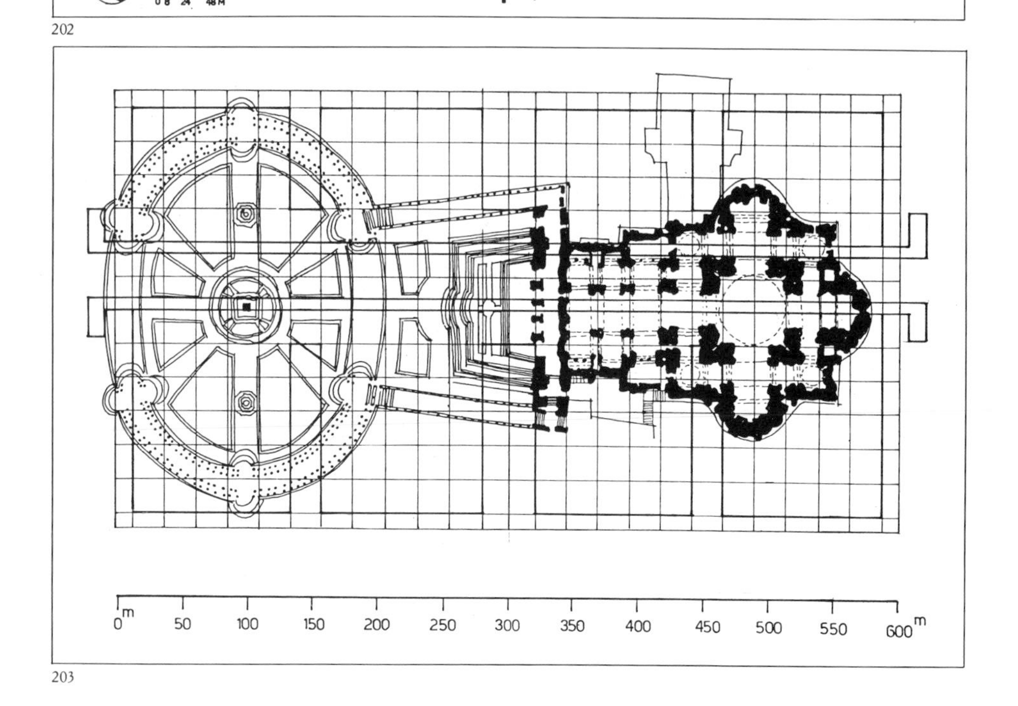

203

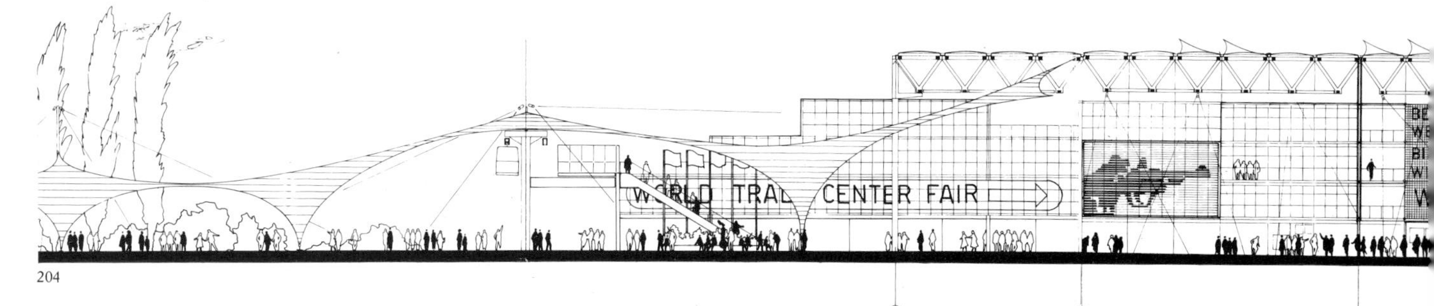

204

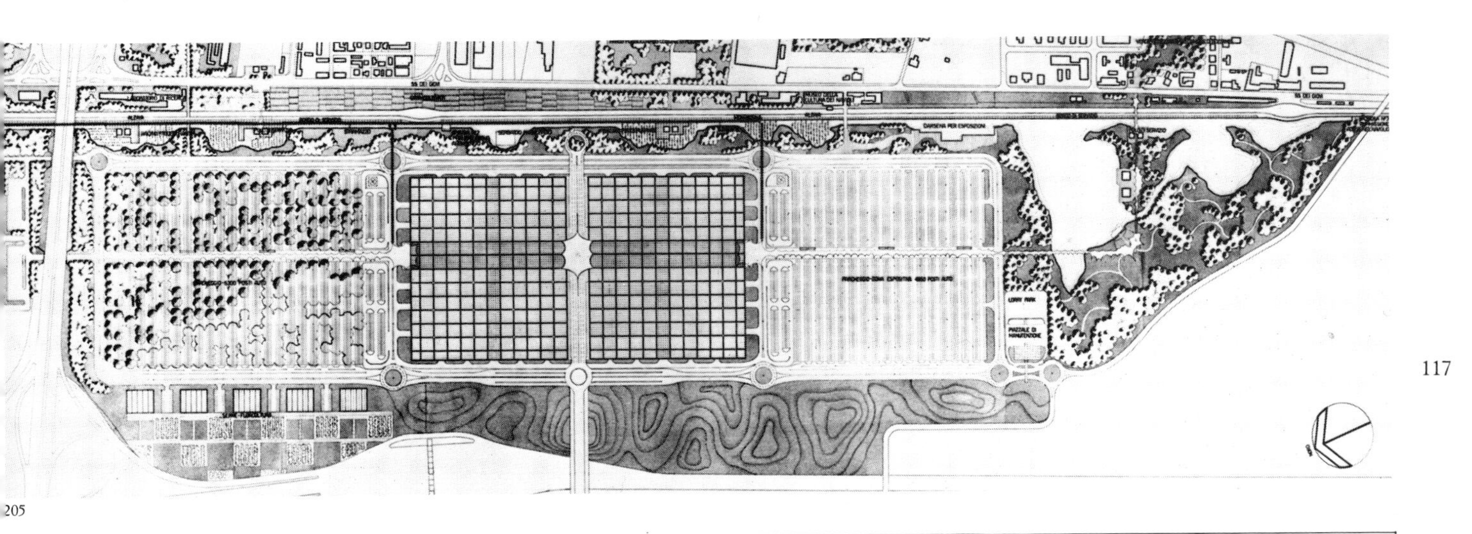

205

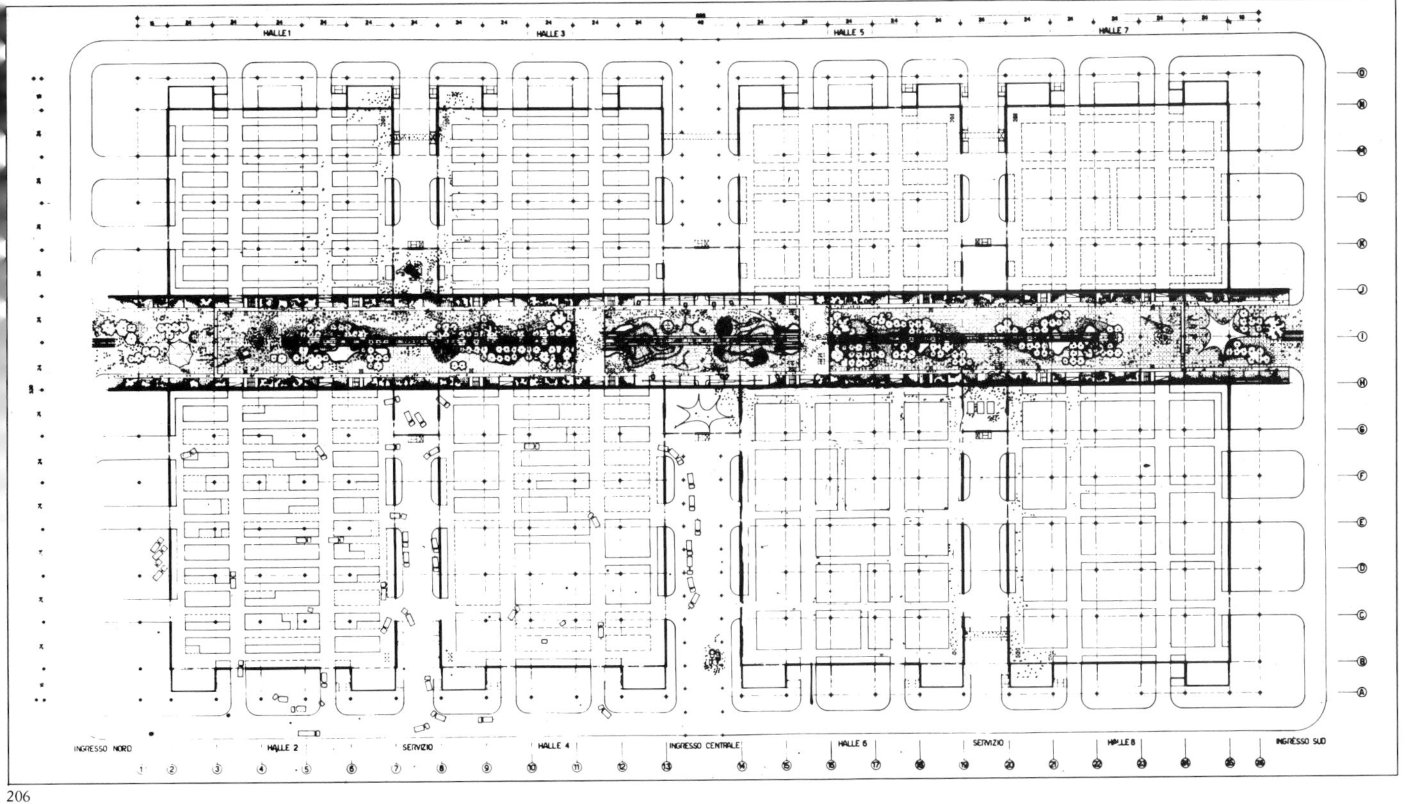
HALLE 1
HALLE 3
HALLE 5
HALLE 7
INGRESSO NORD
HALLE 2
SERVIZIO
HALLE 4
INGRESSO CENTRALE
HALLE 6
SERVIZIO
HALLE 8
INGRESSO SUD

206

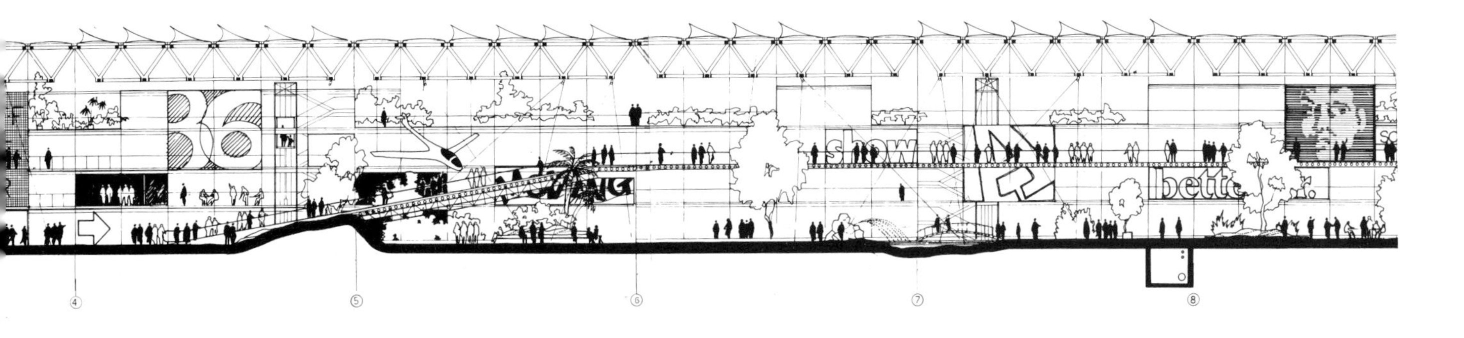
show

207. Study of penetration of natural light into the concourse.

208. Diagram of computer-controlled plant, energy consumption and data supply.

209. Ventilation and air-conditioning plants for the concourse to create "air pulsation" and natural climate control.

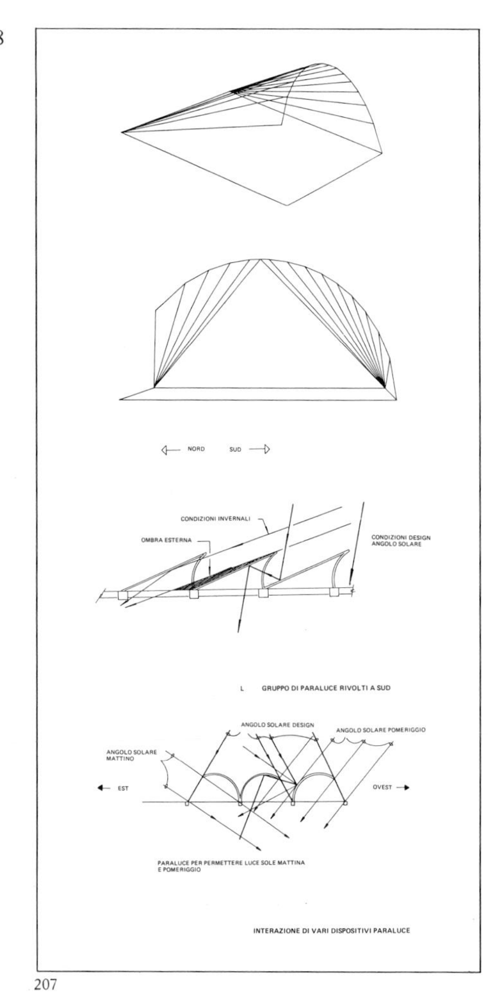

207

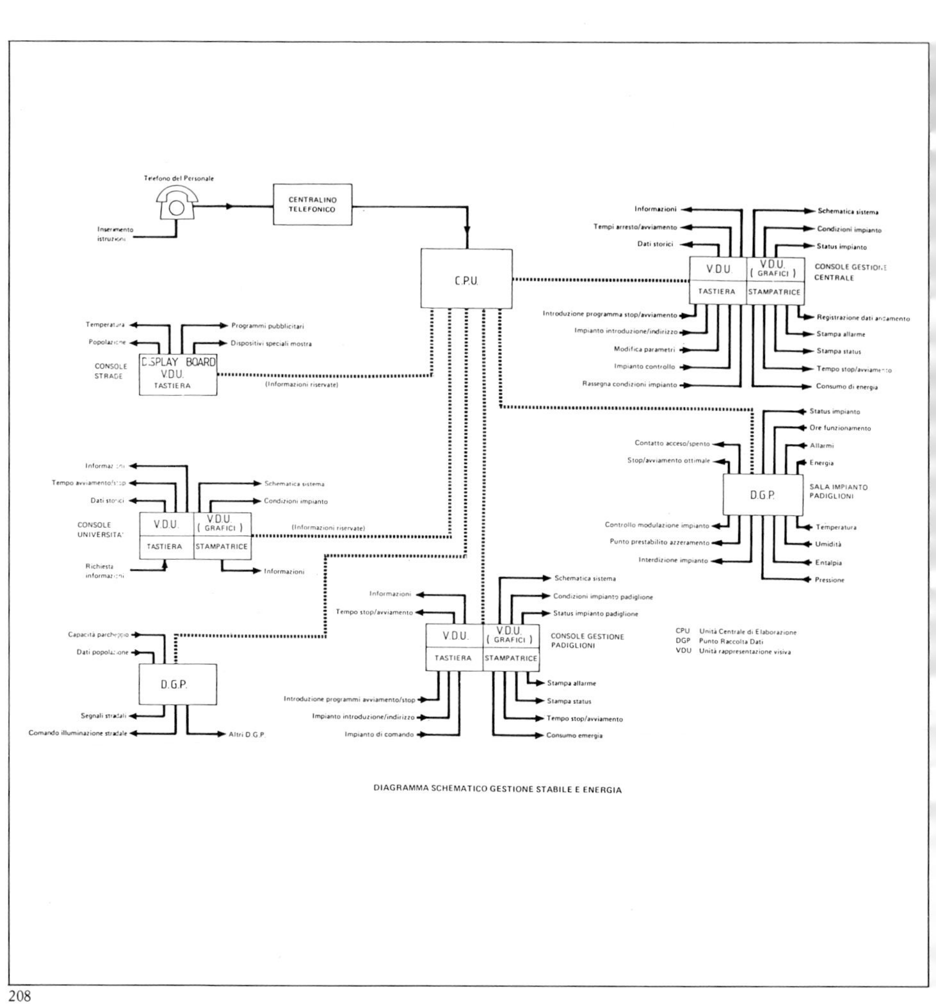

208

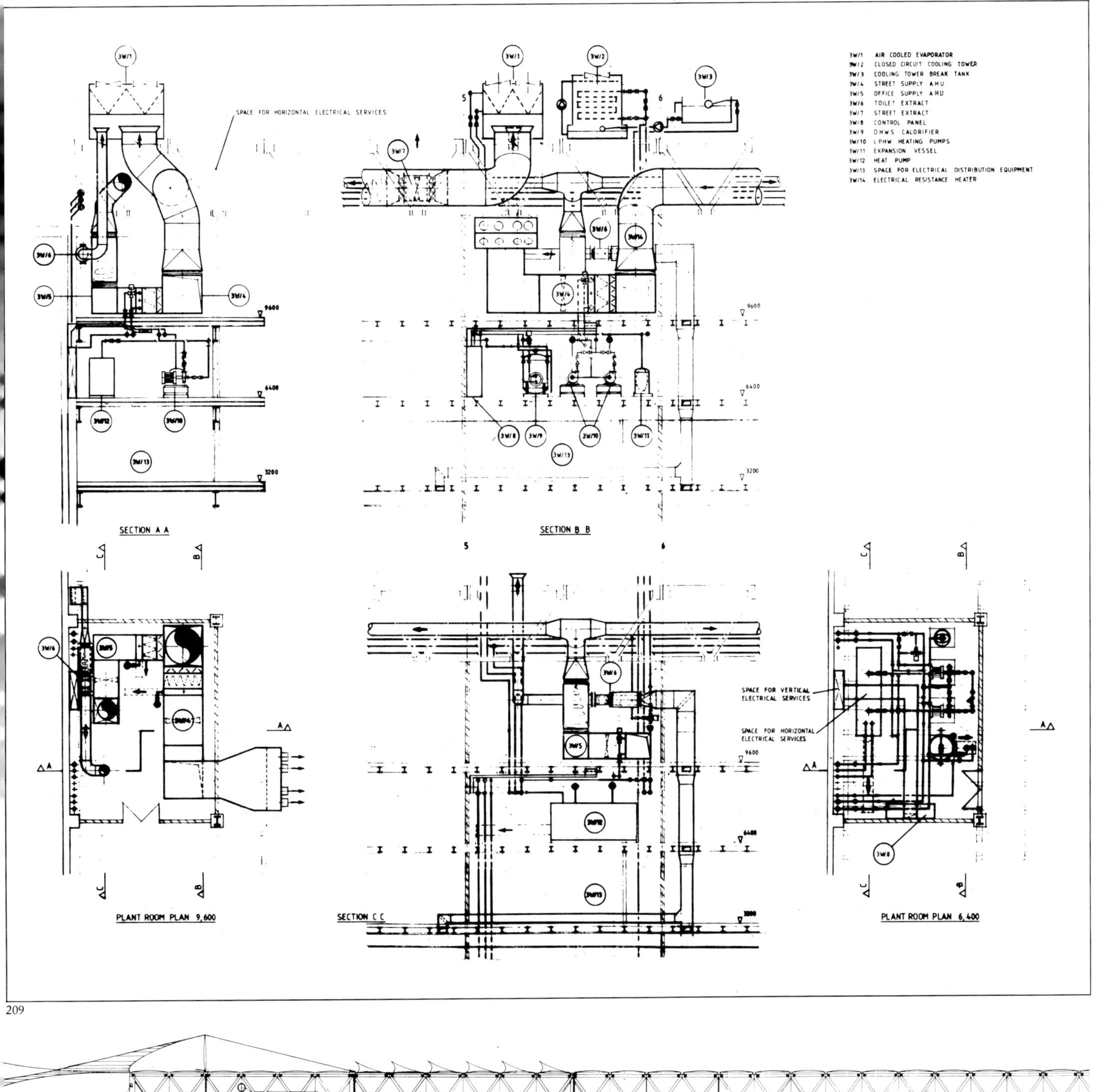

3W/1 AIR COOLED EVAPORATOR
3W/2 CLOSED CIRCUIT COOLING TOWER
3W/3 COOLING TOWER BREAK TANK
3W/4 STREET SUPPLY A.H.U
3W/5 OFFICE SUPPLY A.H.U
3W/6 TOILET EXTRACT
3W/7 STREET EXTRACT
3W/8 CONTROL PANEL
3W/9 DHWS CALORIFIER
3W/10 LPHW HEATING PUMPS
3W/11 EXPANSION VESSEL
3W/12 HEAT PUMP
3W/13 SPACE FOR ELECTRICAL DISTRIBUTION EQUIPMENT
3W/14 ELECTRICAL RESISTANCE HEATER
SPACE FOR HORIZONTAL ELECTRICAL SERVICES
9600
6400
3200
SECTION A A
SECTION B B
5
6
PLANT ROOM PLAN 9,600
SECTION C C
SPACE FOR VERTICAL ELECTRICAL SERVICES
SPACE FOR HORIZONTAL ELECTRICAL SERVICES
PLANT ROOM PLAN 6,400

209

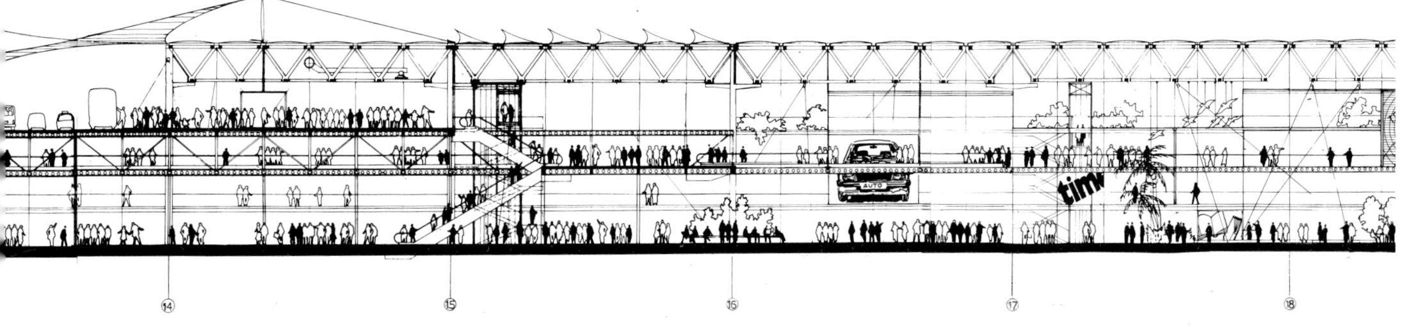

AUTO
tim
14
15
16
17
18

210. Catalogue of basic elements making up the "machine."

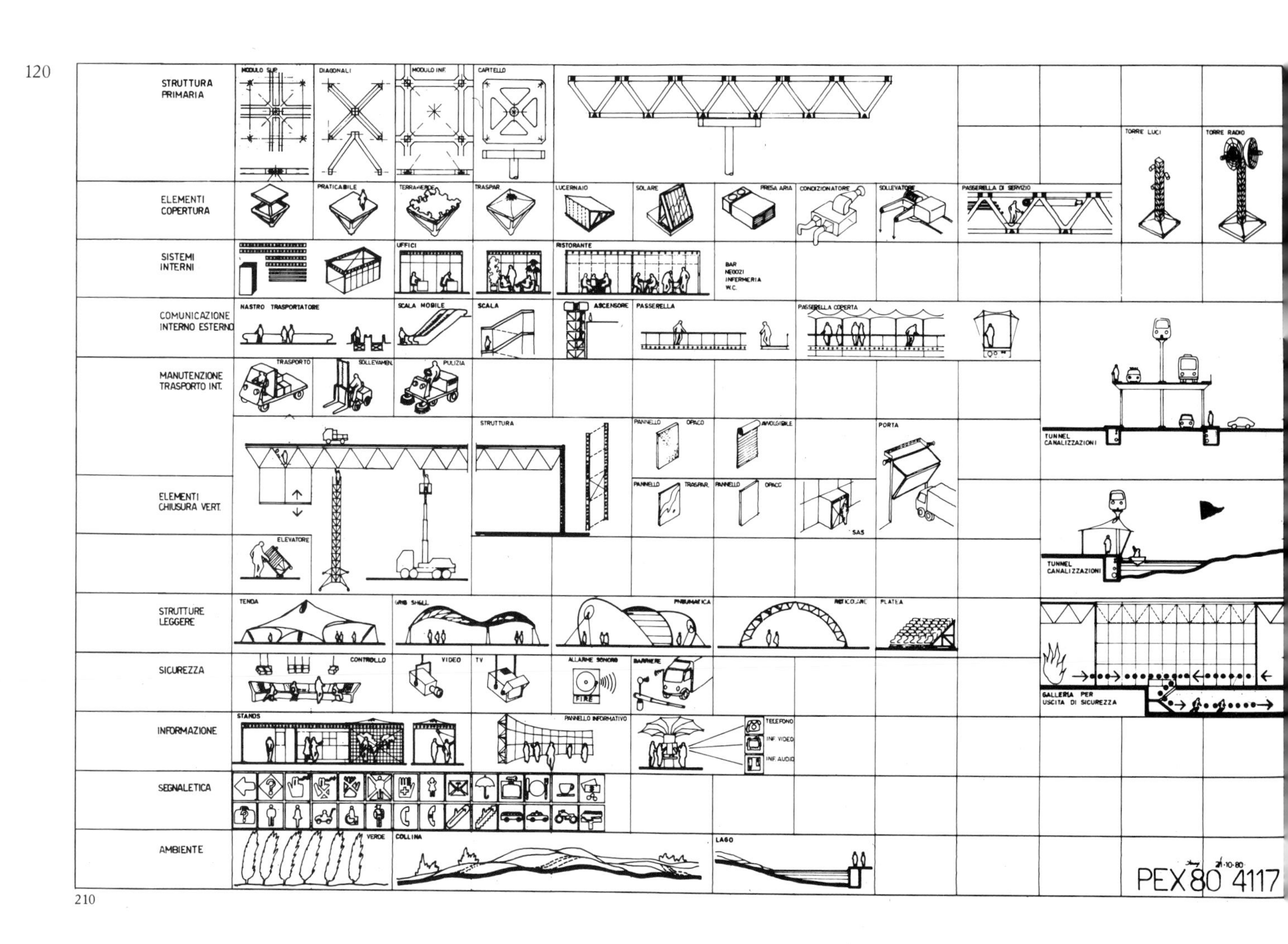

210

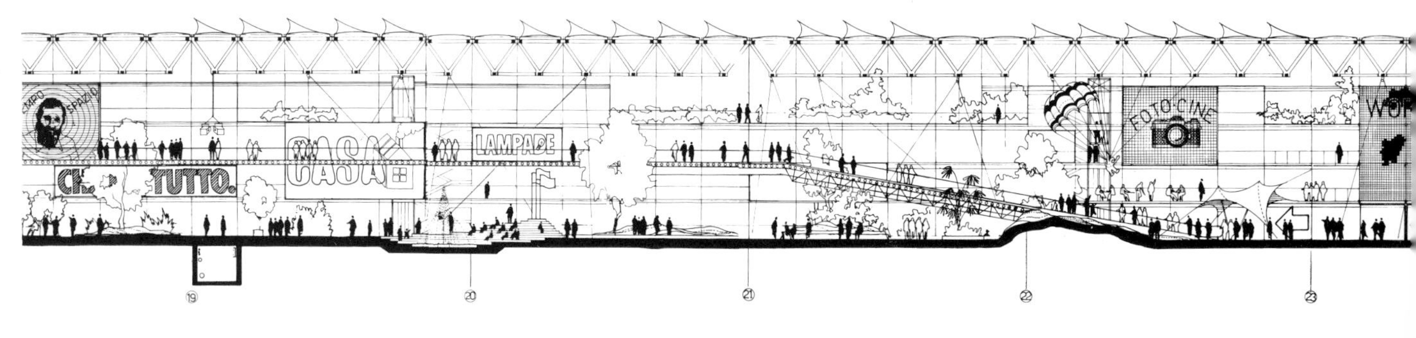

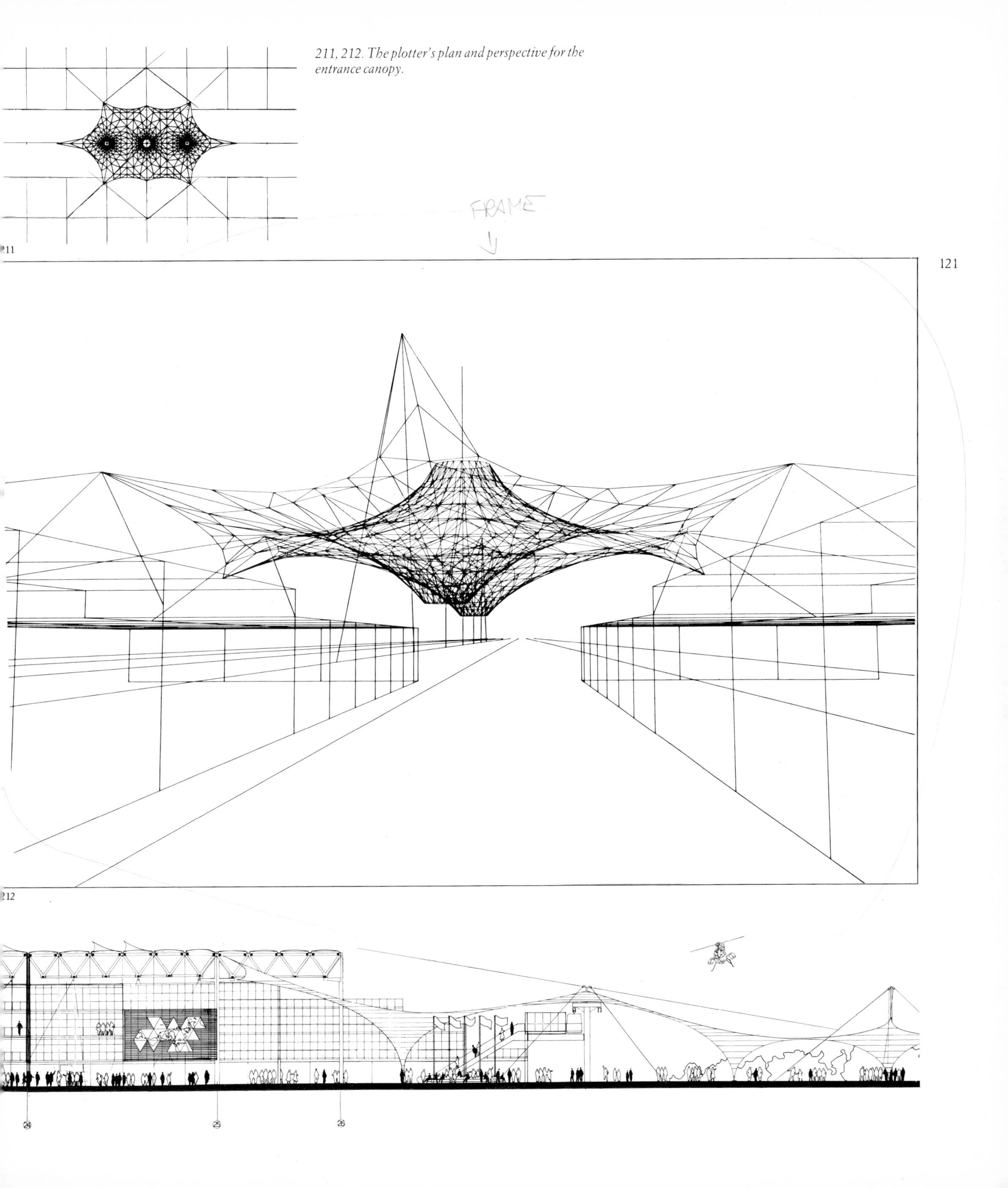

211, 212. The plotter's plan and perspective for the entrance canopy.

213. *Model of upper joint connecting pyramids.*

214. *Computer diagram for analysis of stress on different sections of the node.*

215. *Drawing of 24 m x 24 m structural module.*

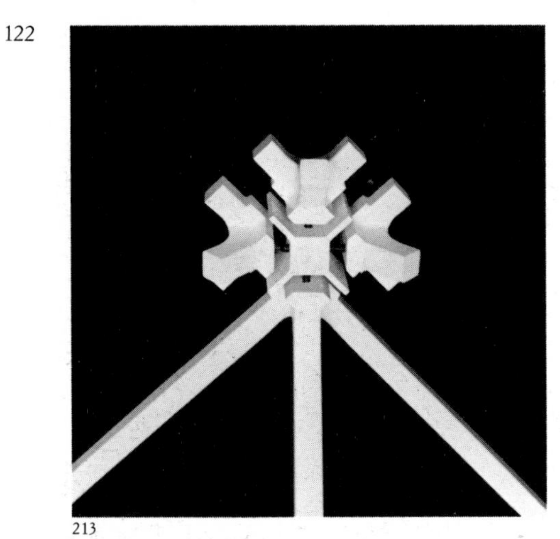
213

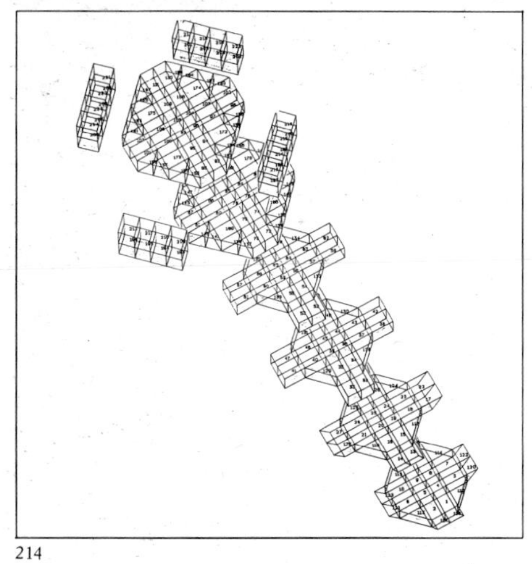
214

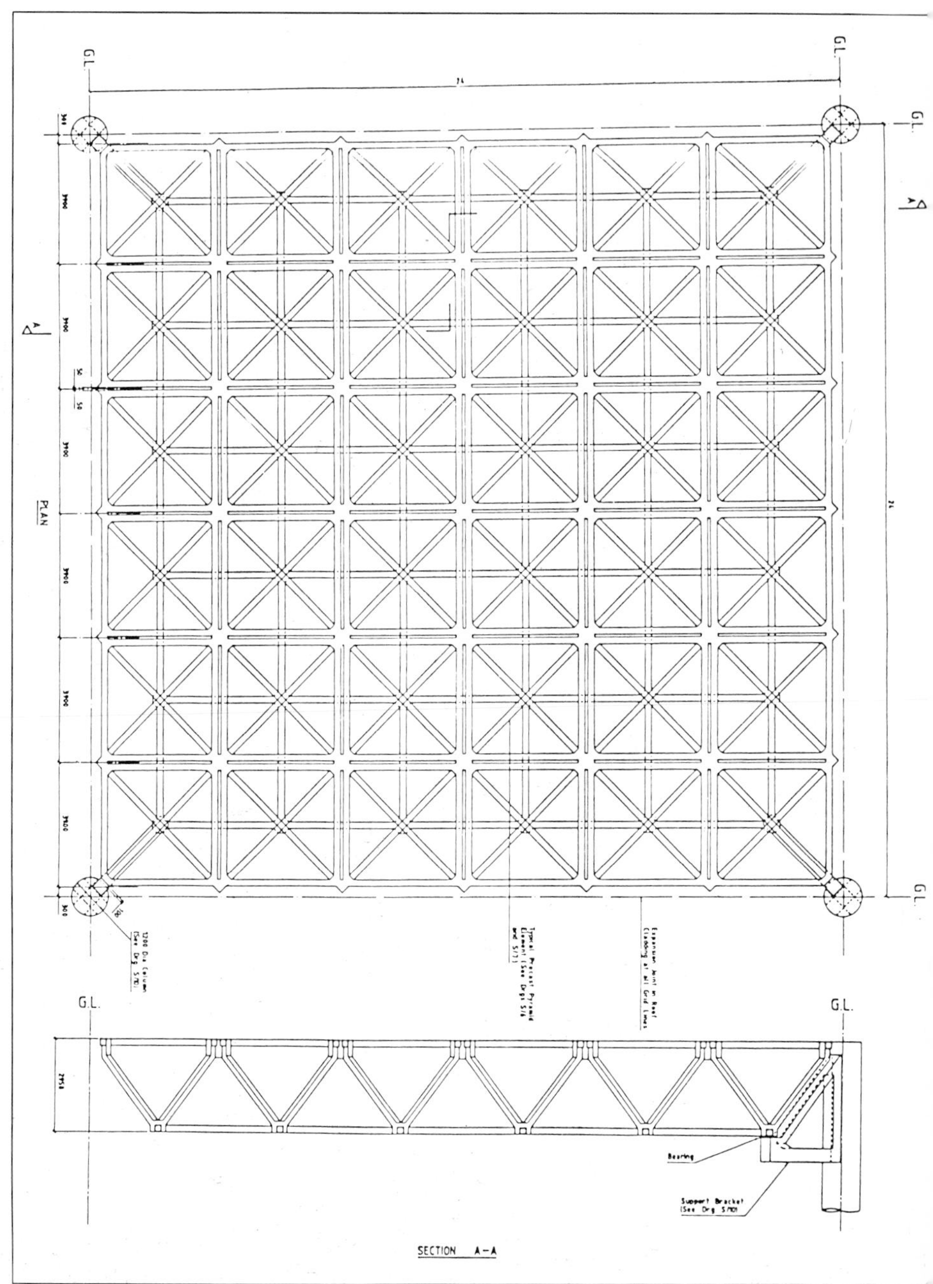

215

216. *Section of the service area intended for the layout of plant and maintenance.*

217. *Construction drawing for the basic pyramidal element to be cast in a metal die and produced in a single operation.*

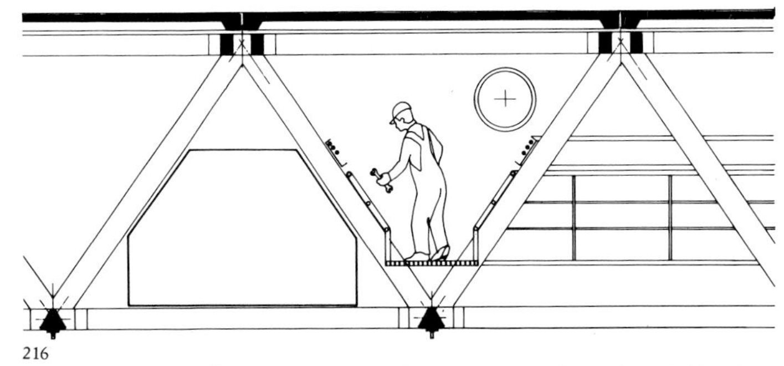

216

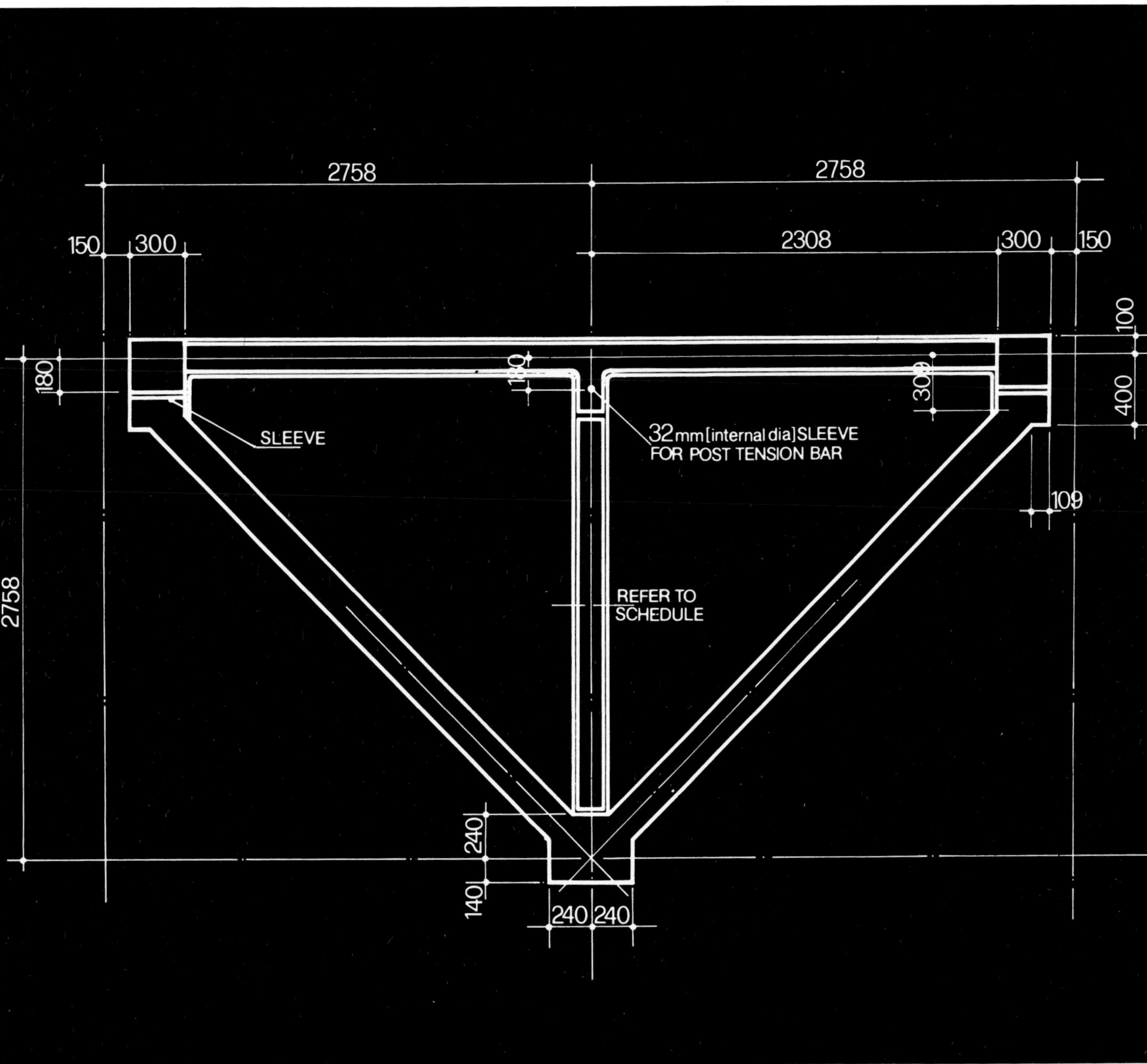

217

218. *Cross section of the internal "street."*

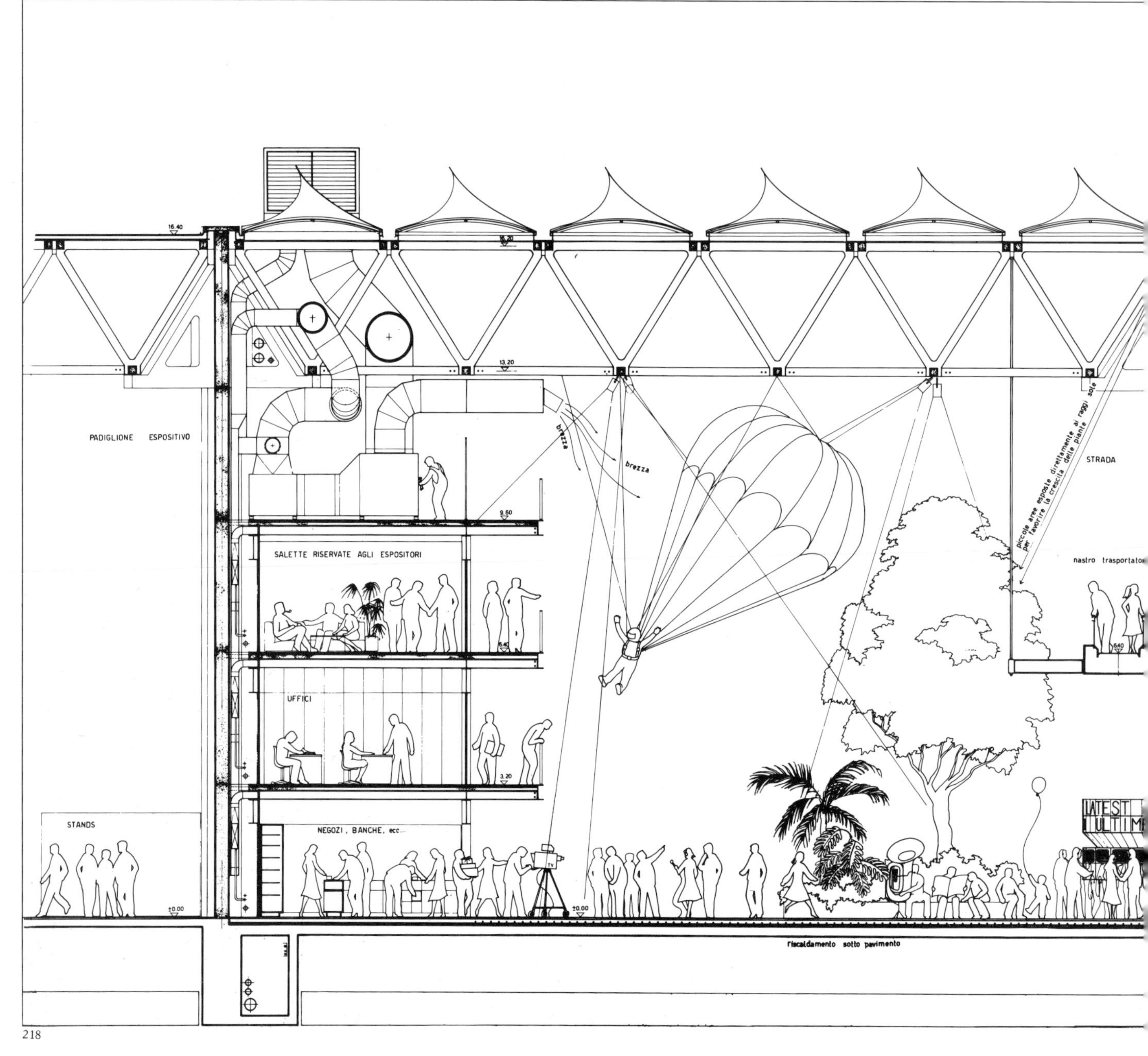

218

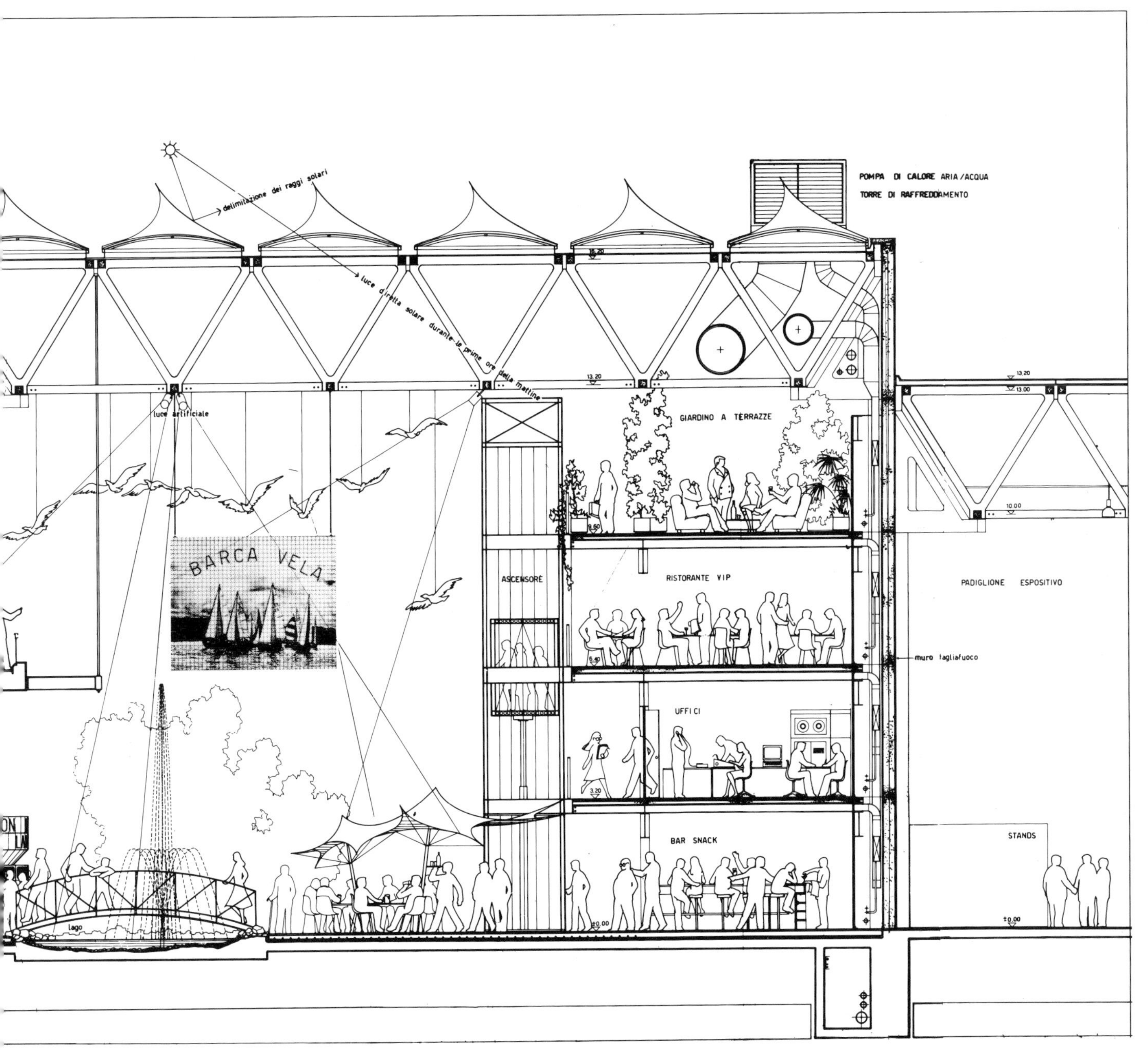

POMPA DI CALORE ARIA/ACQUA
TORRE DI RAFFREDDAMENTO
delimitazione dei raggi solari
luce diretta solare durante le prime ore della mattina
luce artificiale
GIARDINO A TERRAZZE
ASCENSORE
RISTORANTE VIP
PADIGLIONE ESPOSITIVO
muro tagliafuoco
UFFICI
BAR SNACK
STANDS
BARCA VELA
lago

1971-1977 Paris, France
Georges Pompidou cultural center

Client: Ministry of Cultural Affairs and Ministry of National Education, Paris
Architects: Studio Piano & Rogers
Design team: Renzo Piano and Richard Rogers; G.F. Franchini (competition, program, interiors); W. Zbinden with H. Bysaeth, J. Lohse, P. Merz, P. Dupont (substructure and mechanical services); L. Abbott with S. Ishida, H. Naruse, H. Takahashi (superstructure and mechanical services); E. Holt (façades and galleries); A. Stanton with M. Dowd, R. Verbizh (internal/external systems, audiovisual system for piazza); C. Brüllmann (environment and scenographic space); B. Plattner (coordination and site supervision); M. Davies with N. Okabe, K. Rupard, J. Sircus (IRCAM); J. Young with F. Barat, H. Diebold, J. Fendard, J.Huc, H. Schlegel (interiors); B. Merello, F. Marano (participation in the first phase of design); F. Gouinguenet, C. Spielmann, C. Valensi (secretarial)
Engineers: Ove Arup & Partners
Design Team: P. Rice, L. Grut, R. Peirce (structure); T. Barker (plant engineering); M. Espinosa (cost control)
Contractors: GTM - Grands Travaux de Marseille; J. Thaury (job engineer) with: Krupp, Mont-a-Mousson, Pohlig (structures); CFEM (façades); Otis (elevators and escalators); Voyer (secondary structures); Industrielle de Chauffage, Saunier Duval (heating installations)

219

220

A ship in Paris

An unidentified object from outer space lands in the heart of Ville Lumière: it is the Centre Pompidou, a futuristic macrostructure, fully equipped with special effects, looking like a set lifted from *Star Wars*. Controversy immediately bursts, why translate culture into the language of high-tech? What is the point of grafting a science fiction machine onto the urban fabric? Why emphasize technology without bothering to connect it organically with the environmental setting? Now, ten years after, the cultural center created by Piano and Rogers (winners, together with the engineering firm of Ove Arup & Partners, of the international competition held in 1971) is still under fire from formalist critics.

What exactly is this remarkable piece of gadgetry — or rather, what was it meant to be in the minds of its designers? A hymn to industrial production perhaps? "No, not at all," explains its co-designer. "First of all it is not a triumphant building. In fact, I would say it displays a certain sense of humor: one might even call it a joke. Far from being a triumph of technology, the Beaubourg is not even an industrial building. If anything, it is a gigantic piece of craftsmanship, made by hand, bit by bit, a great prototype. There is the relish for the polemical, the provocative, the sending up of the accepted idea of a museum and what it is meant to be. At the start of the seventies we were at a crossroad, we had to choose between two different concepts of culture: either institutional, esoteric, intimidating, or something unofficial, open and accessible to the general public. We opted for the latter."

Ideological heresy goes hand in hand with the subversion of formal dogmas. To leave the interior clear, the mechanical services and plant have been spun round the outside of the building. The various means of access (lifts, escalators, horizontal galleries) are hung around the load-bearing structure so that the flow of visitors is channeled, totally transparent, placed to dominate the urban panorama and provide a view of the spectacle of the building itself. Evolution is the distinguishing feature of the building's geography, nothing is rigid, immutable; the container is flexible, adaptable through the use of "soft" mechanisms, articulated so that it can be adapted to rapid developments in information systems and communications.

Each of the five stories is made up of a spatial enclosure measuring 50 m x 170 m with an open plan and which can be equipped for any type of activity, the various structural systems are relatively independent; plant and layouts are separate and can be expanded or diminished as required. Even the system of movement of visitors can be completely dismantled and readapted to new needs via mechanical connections with the primary structural grid. A place open to every blowing wind, as Piano describes it. The building integrates many functions, from the public library to the museum of modern art, from travelling exhibitions to services of documentation and research, from cinema to theater, from music to industrial design.

Though the Beaux-Arts critics may hate it, this container-tool has sunk its roots deep into the urban setting. People have assimilated the shock and become familiar with the mechanical monster, its gadgetry, its mobile walkways. Much the same thing happened with the Eiffel Tower. The fact remains that now the public is flocking to the Centre Pompidou (an average of 25,000 visitors per day) and using it like an amusement park. Decoding it is immediate, elementary. "The building is a diagram. People read it in a flash. Its 'viscera' are on the outside, you see it all, understand the way people get around it, its lifts and escalators."

The whole fantastic gadget stimulates curiosity, acts as a magnet, a crowd-puller, a catalyst, and in so doing reactivates the relationship with its urban context. It may not mimic its urban setting but it does bring it to life. The pedestrian area around the building (specified by the designers themselves) completes the work, acting as the interface with the rest of the city. Street and building form a continuous and homogeneous space: they penetrate and shape each other. The plaza is the venue for unprogrammed, spontaneous activities, and in this regard it is an offshoot of the cultural workshop, interpreting it and reinforcing its popular quality, rather like some fantastic transposition of Speakers' Corner in Hyde Park.

Can Piano and Rogers be said to have pulled off their gamble? Only up to a point. Piano has his moments of soul-searching. "What I oppose is the use of the Beaubourg by the public: a type of use that is superficial, uneducated, consumer-minded. This risk is, of course, implicit in the concept of mass-culture itself. But above all I contest the bureaucratic, centralized administration of the center, which contradicts the principle of participation underlying the whole project.

One thing, however, can be said with certainty, the Beaubourg is a place open and comprehensible to everyone." Perhaps this is why its off-beat architecture has become an object of imitation. "This is the most negative side of it. It is ridiculous to try and transfer the Beaubourg somewhere else in time and space. The fact that it is becoming a functional or even a formal architectural model is tragic and absurd. If anything is worth copying, it is the design procedure, the scientific approach, the technical research. What its immensity conceals is craftsmanship. We designed everything, right down to the smallest screw."

It is ridiculous to try and transfer the Beaubourg somewhere else in time and space. The fact that it is becoming a functional or even a formal architectural model is tragic and absurd.

219. Press conference with Robert Bordaz, president of the Etablissements Publics, and Richard Rogers.

220. Gianfranco Franchini, one of the Beaubourg team.

221. The team of architects at the site in 1973.

222. Site of the Centre Georges Pompidou, in the center of Paris.

221

This is the key to interpreting the construction process. After much arm-twisting, Piano and Rogers succeeded in obtaining a special contract from their client on the basis of complete control over the design's execution, including site work. The architects thus became responsible for budget and deadlines (the former with a margin of 12%, the latter with a margin of two months). This was ratified by a ministerial decree which is a historical landmark, the beginning of a reformed system of design in France.

These were years of gruelling work, studded with technical and bureaucratic problems. The construction process proceeded along two parallel lines: the first, on the site, with excavations, the laying of the foundations and construction of the four floors below ground level; the second, in the workshop, consisted in the prefabrication of the parts to be mounted above ground level. A tremendous fuss was stirred up by the architects' decision to get around the inflated costs of French companies by having the steel lattice beams cast at the old Krupp works in Essen. Controversy ran high until Pompidou himself authorized the contract to go abroad with a special permit.

"The arrival of the trusses from Germany," Piano recalls, "was a nocturnal ritual. Each would be loaded on two lorries — a lorry at each end of the truss — and brought to the site along a prearranged route. Because of their weight (110 tons) the sewers even had to be reinforced at some points."

The whole story of the Beaubourg was like a long voyage to the sources of architectural creation, with occasional forays into a computerized future. Then finally the great ship reached port, safely within the deadlines and cost margins of the contract. Today you can see it, anchored in the ancient center of Paris, ready to sail off once more in defiance of imitators and the culture bureaucrats. It is a symbol, even more than that, it is alive.

222

223. Model for the 1971 competition.

223

224

224. The Beaubourg: rightly or wrongly, it is now one of the symbols of Paris.

225. View of the building from tower of Notre-Dame.

226. Exterior.

227. View of service façade of the building from one of the streets of the old Marais.

228. Montmartre seen from the Beaubourg.

225

226

227

228

229. Aerial view.

229

230-232. The Centre Georges Pompidou is completed by a 4-hectare pedestrian precinct.

230

231

232

233. View of the public reading room of the Beaubourg.

234. Children's library.
235. The library's audio-visual service.
236. View from inside onto the square.

237. Catwalk and escalator.

233

234

235

236

237

238. *Elevation of the building in its final version.*
239. *Final model of the building.*

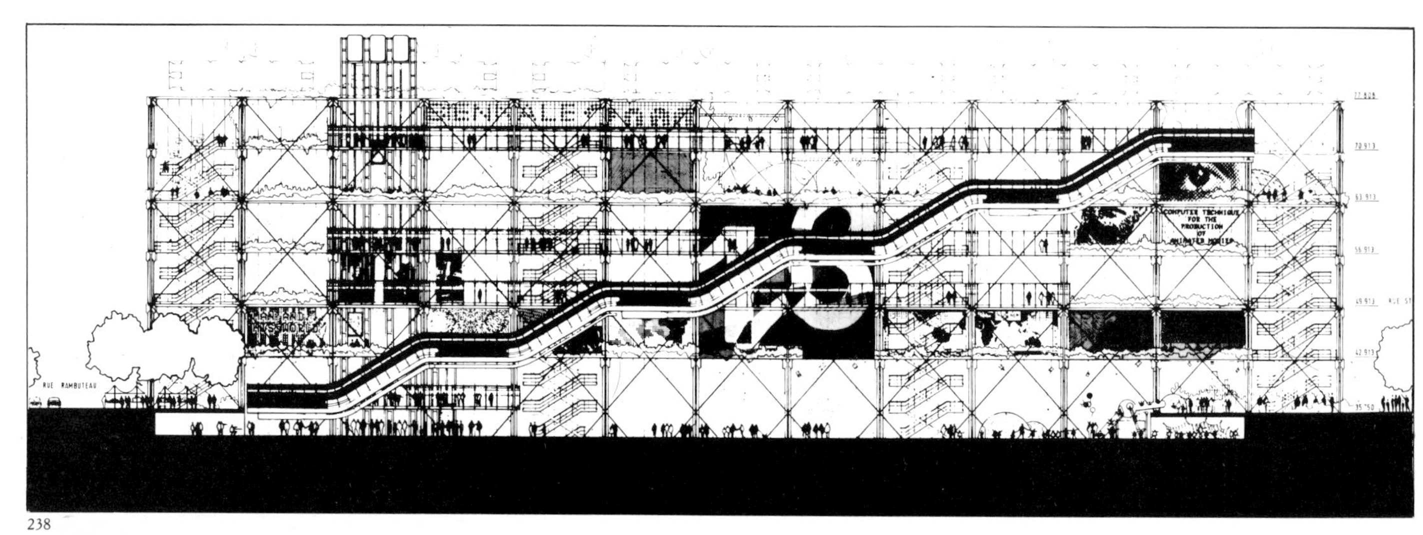

238

239

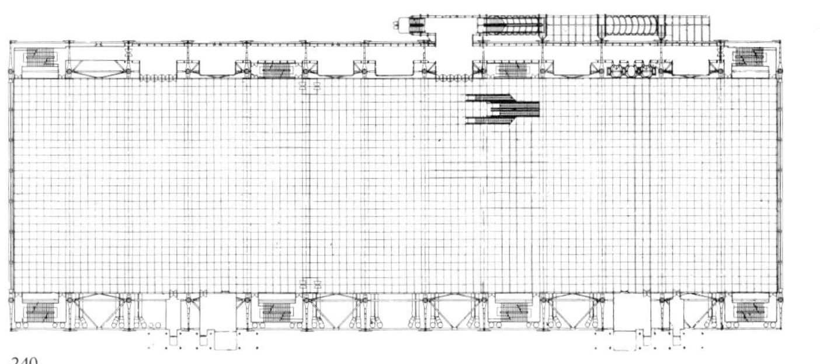
240

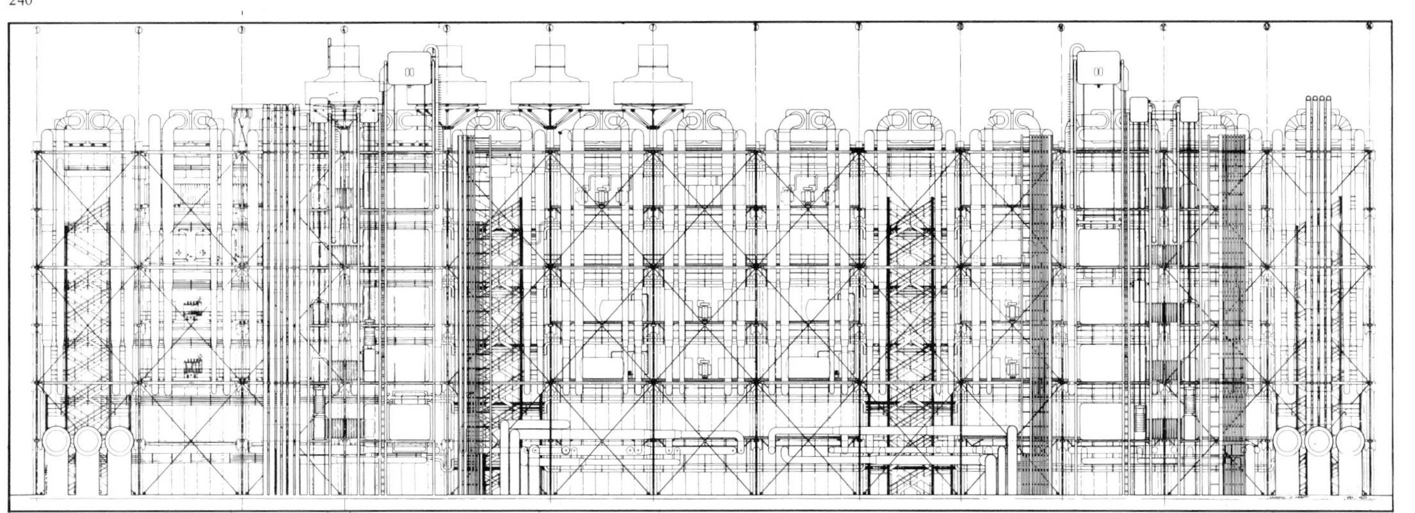
241

242

240. Standard floor plan.
241. Elevation on Rue du Renard.
242. Model of the service façade.

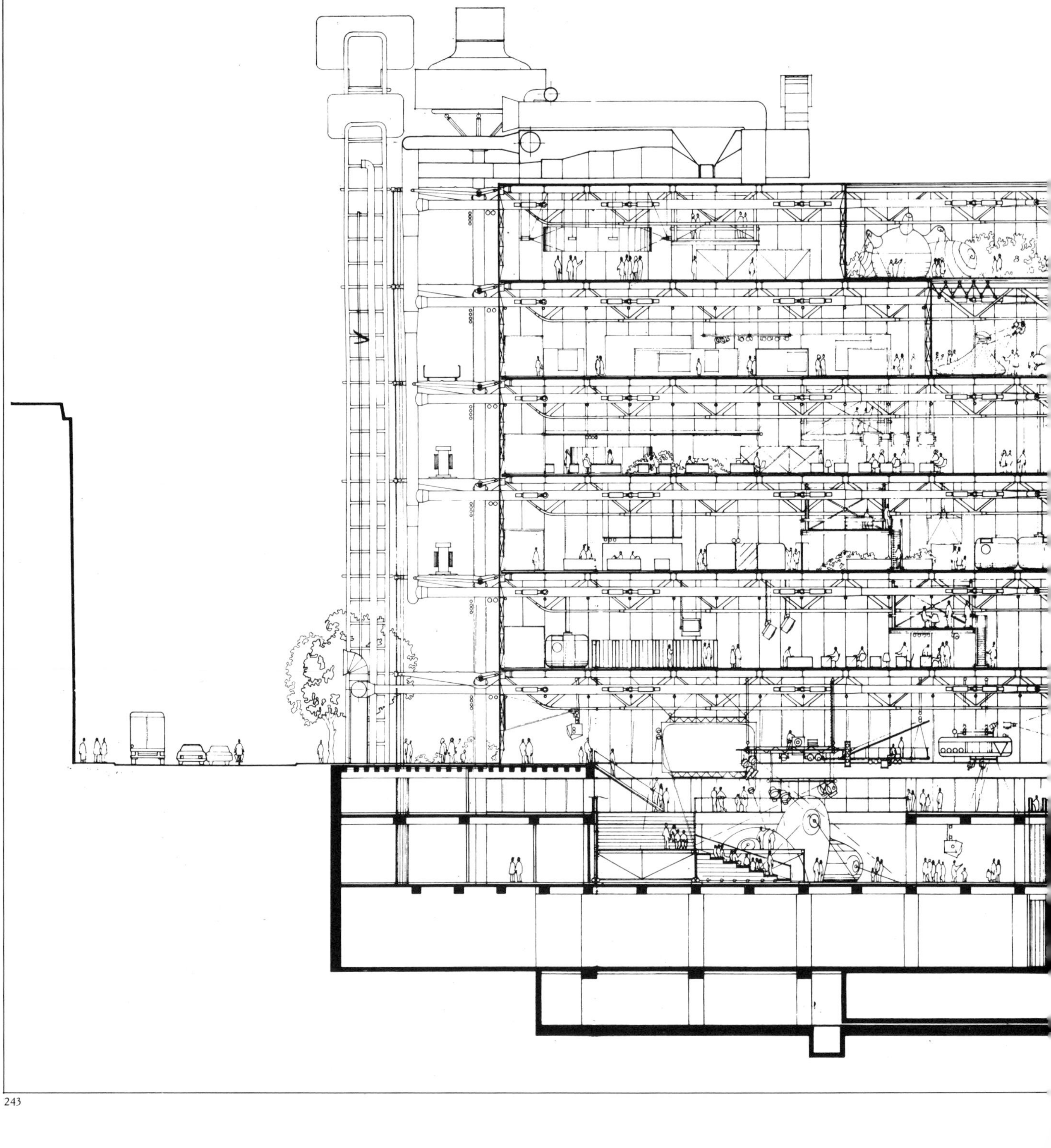

243. *Cross section of the building.*

243

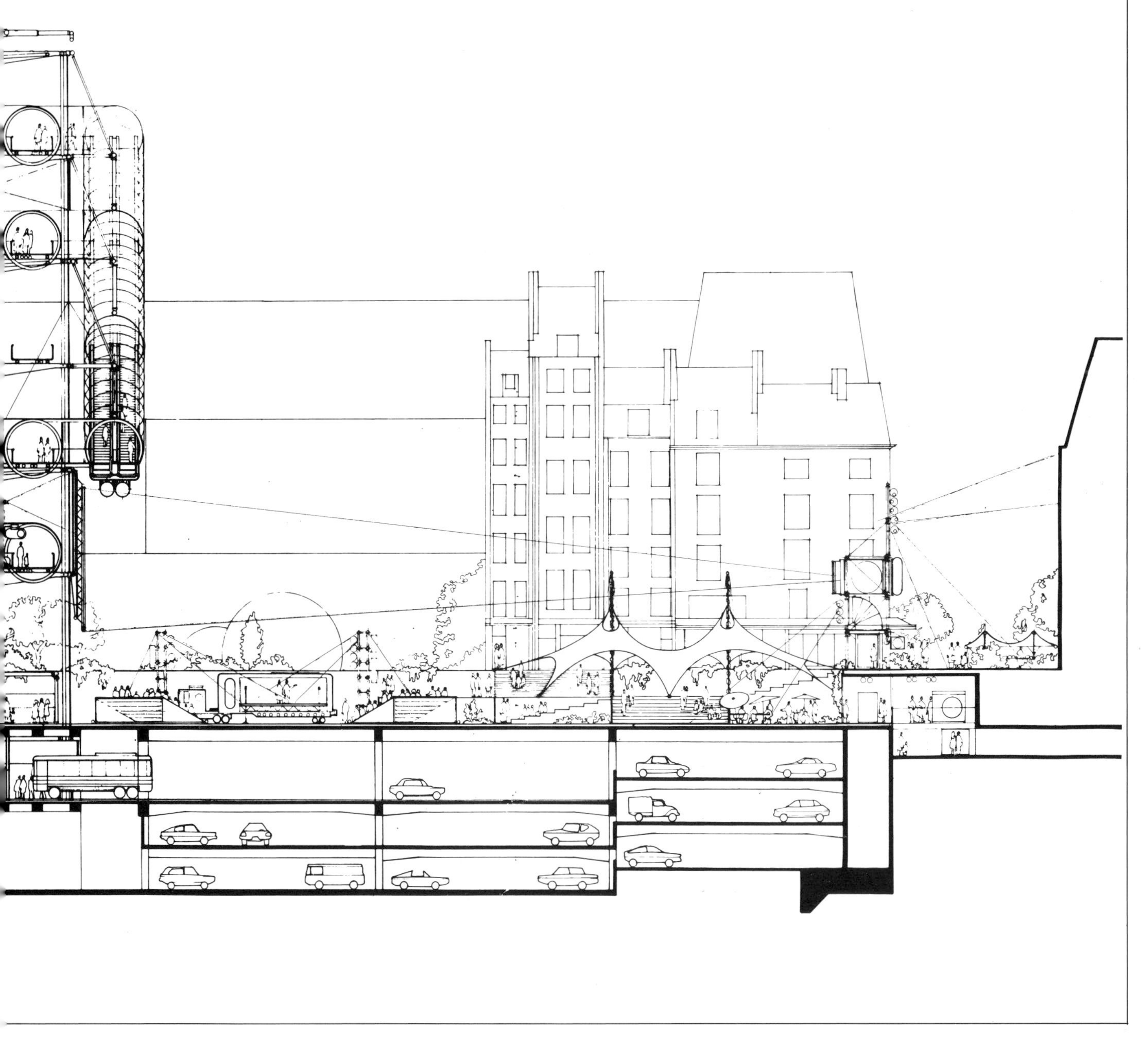

244. Connection of hinge which permits movement between beam and column.

245. Heads of the Gerber beams immediately after casting.

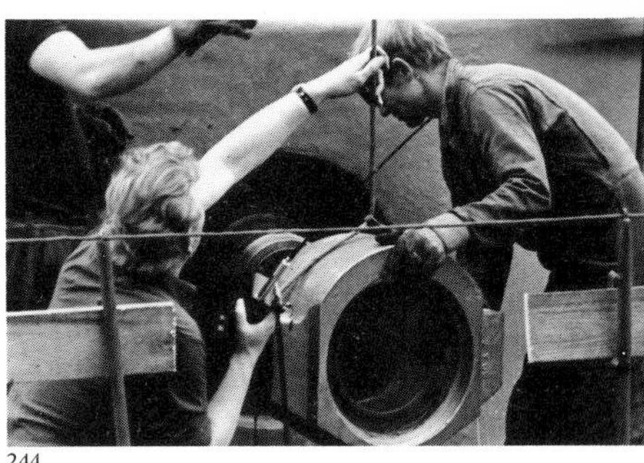

244

245

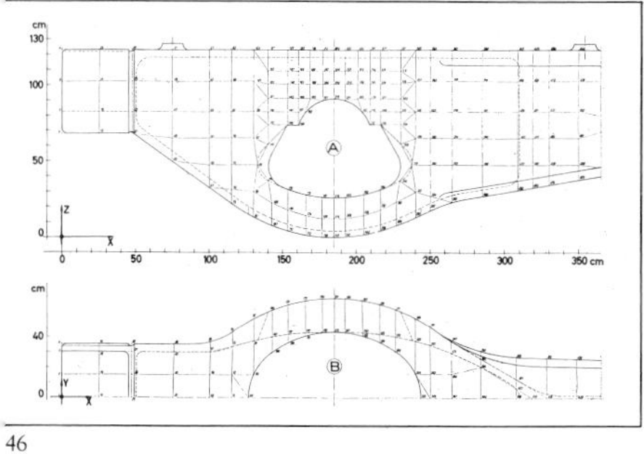

46

246. *Plotter diagram of the main stress area of a "Gerberette."*

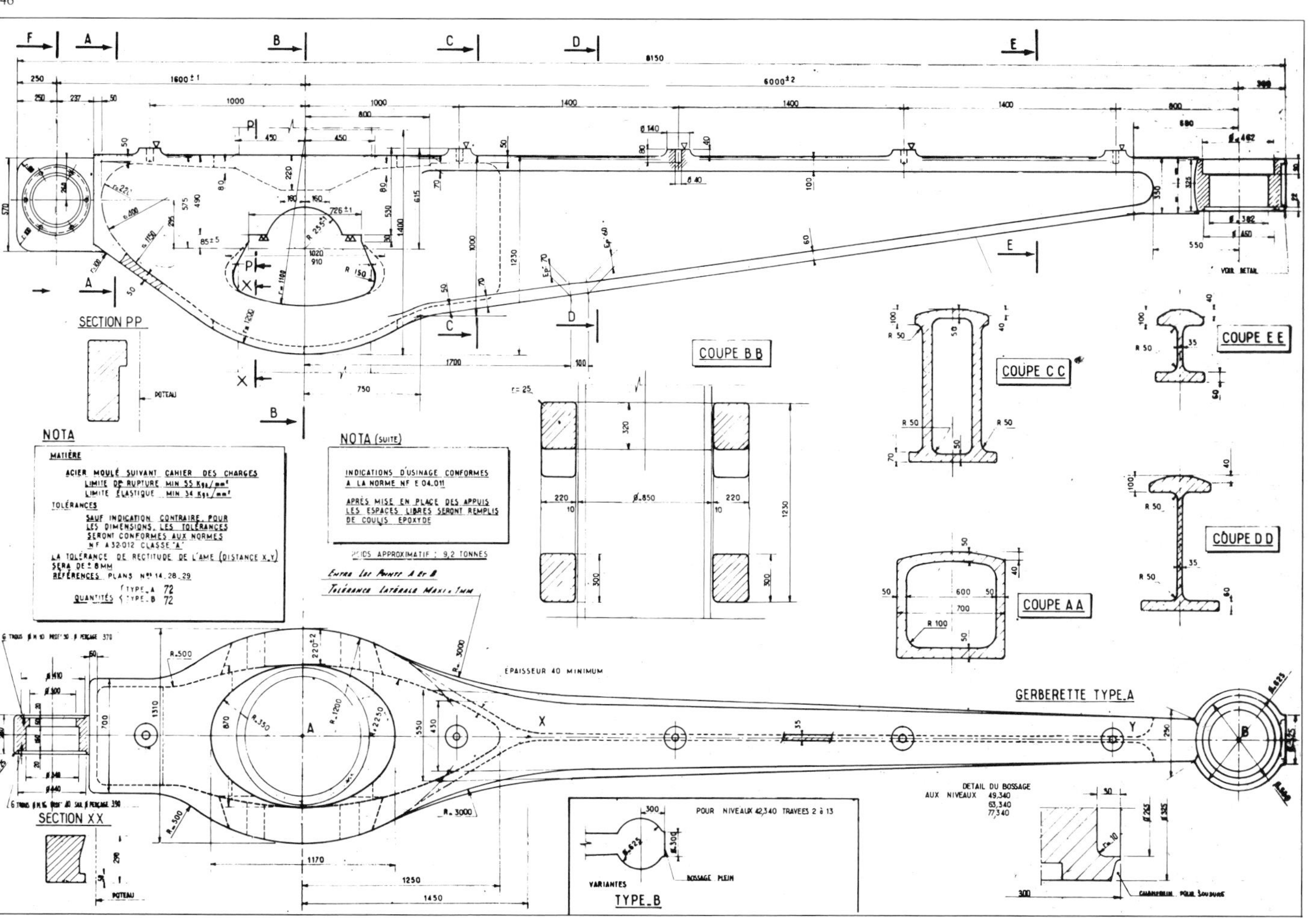

247

247. *Engineering design of the "Gerberette:" a single casting of 11 tons of steel.*

248-250. Mounting a prefabricated truss (length 48 m and weight 75 tons). Mounting each of these elements was remarkably quick, thanks to the accuracy of the assembly systems planned.

248

249

250

251. Section through the visitors' circulation system on the façade.
252. One of the terraces facing west.

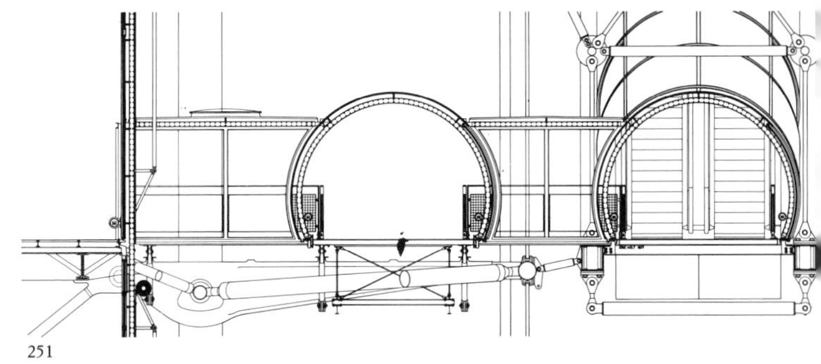

251

252

253. Structural detail of the node between horizontal and vertical booms and diagonal braces.

253

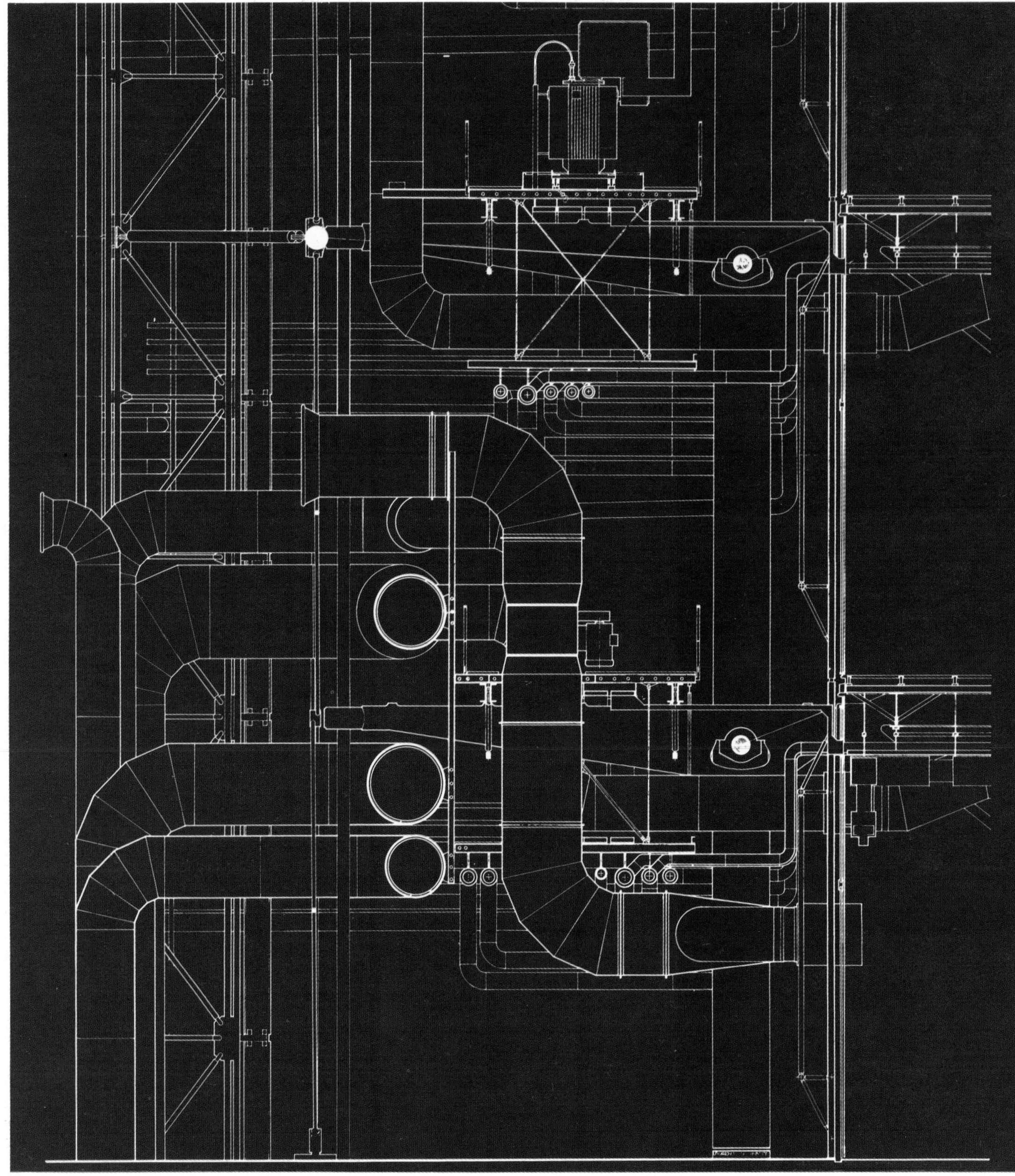

254

254. Section through the ventilation and air-conditioning system on the ground floor.
255. Partial elevation of the services façade.

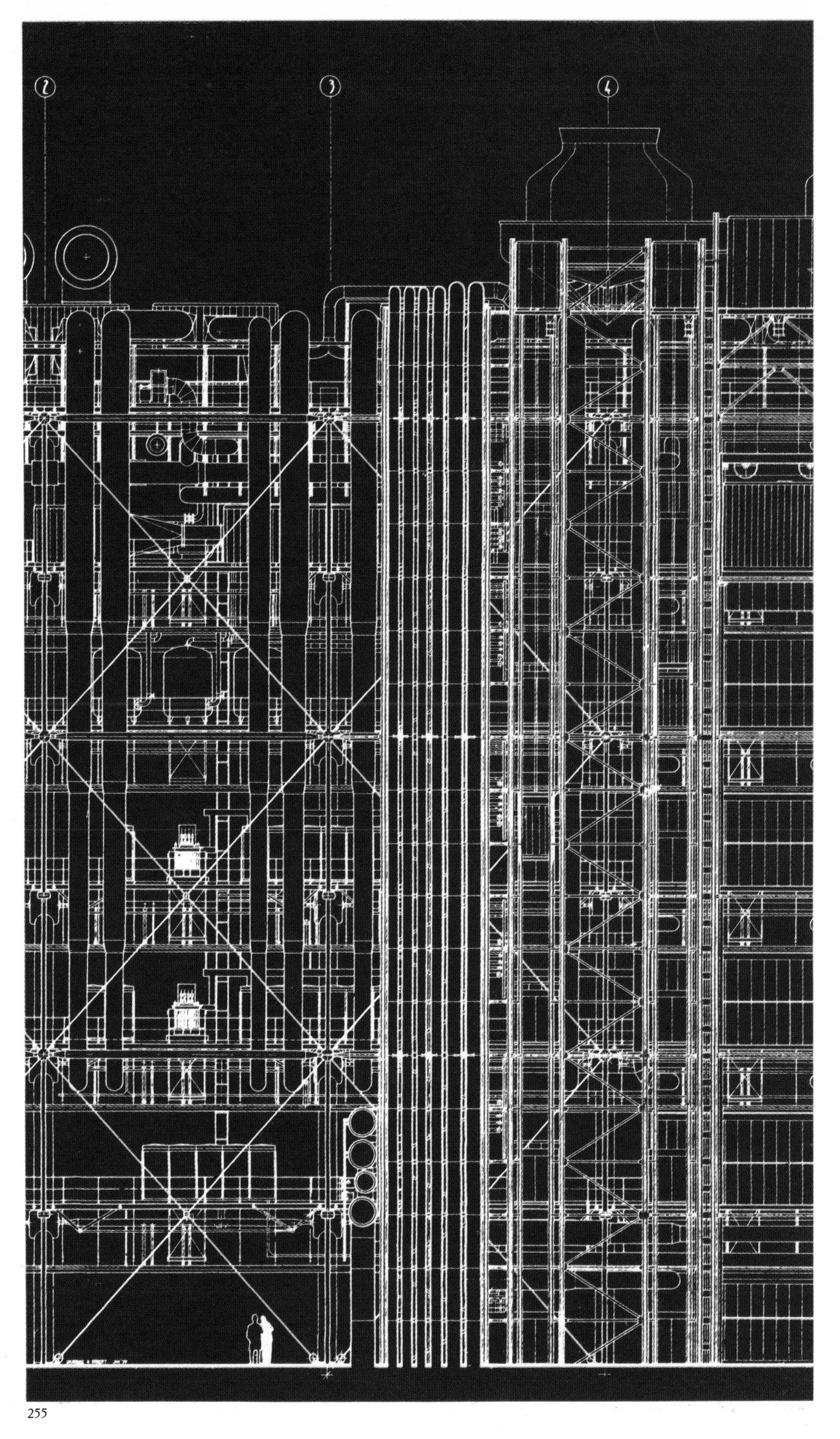

255

1973-1977 Paris, France

IRCAM: Institute for Research and Coordination in Acoustics and Music

Architecture and music

Client: IRCAM, Paris

Architects: Studio Piano & Rogers with M. Davies, N. Okabe, K. Rupard, J. Sircus, W. Zbinden

Engineers: Ove Arup & Partners

Acoustic consultant: V. Peutz

Scenographic consultant: G.C. François

"The scientific approach may seem schematic but it must be turned into operational practice, because it is now clear that creativity over the last sixty years has shifted from the arts to the sciences." It is in science that the paths of architecture and contemporary music intersect. Just as Piano anchors architectural activity to objective parameters, Luciano Berio eludes the random and the gratuitous through mathematical exploration of music. The encounter between the two worlds is inevitable. Hence the Institut de Recherche et Coordination Acoustique/Musique (IRCAM): a building that entails interdisciplinary team-work and at the same time is its virtual symbol. At IRCAM scientists and musicians collaborate as equals in the achievement of a common goal — to abolish the boundary line that separates art and science, research and creation.

It is an adventurous journey through unexplored territories: acoustics, physics, psycho-acoustics, electronics, informatics, neuro-physiology, psychology, linguistics and sociology. By definition IRCAM is not a single studio or even a series of studios but a "cluster of means and techniques necessary for musical exploration." The institute is articulated into five sections: instrumental and vocal, electro-acoustics (under the direction of Luciano Berio until 1980), computing and synthesis, general acoustics and pedagogics. Pierre Boulez is director of the institute.

It is clear that to establish a new system of relationships between musicians and researchers, between creators, musical works and the public, it is necessary to formulate new spatial hypotheses. It is equally clear that the new hypotheses have to be verified constantly with those directly involved: musicians and sound engineers. This is the concept which has produced IRCAM, "a musical instrument on an urban scale," the outcome of interdisciplinary and international research.

To improve acoustics Piano and Rogers designed a subterranean edifice between the Beaubourg (of which IRCAM constitutes one department) and the church of Saint Merri. The roof is at street level; the interior comprises studios and workshops plus an experimental concert hall intended for use either for scientific research or listening to music as required. Above all, there is one dominant feature that especially distinguishes this hall, the largest available in IRCAM: its high degree of flexibility. The reason is easily understood, different types of communication with the public (maximum size of audience at "projections" is 400 persons) or research into a new musical dimension can be made possible only by variation of aural and visual factors, involving of spatial layout, acoustics, lighting, etc.

How to meet these needs? Piano and Rogers invented a polyvalent variable volume possible because of a movable ceiling, floor and walls. By modifying the position of each of these elements (and the relative materials), the dimensions of the space and hence the quality of its acoustics varies. In addition, the projection auditorium is a sealed compartment, independent of the building's primary structure, completely isolated from what is above and around it.

Acoustic combinations are multiple, from high to low frequencies, from chamber music to cathedral compositions, and likewise the spatial relation possible between the sources of sound and the audience. In this sense, according to Victor Peutz IRCAM's sound consultant, the chamber does not constitute "a given space to which the user has to adapt himself but, on the contrary, a space which is user, music or experience-oriented."

There is also an echo-free chamber, a reverberation chamber, suspended studios, control chambers and computers. IRCAM is a musical oasis set in the lower depths of Paris where nothing, not even air-conditioning and security systems (consisting of fireproofed and soundproofed materials) can disturb the atmosphere of concentration. But it is not an island cut off from urban life. Just above the ceiling is the plaza, with people coming and going, a space for outdoor concerts. It is a different, more scientific, more intense and communicative mode of living culture. It is, moreover, an experiment destined to remain unique. "In other fields, such as lighting, you can work to scale. You can construct a 1:10 scale model to check what is going to happen when you transfer to full scale. But in acoustics you always have to work to scale. This is the reason why we have created variable acoustics, depending on the kind of music or effect you are after. In the past, composers worked on the basis of given acoustics; they knew beforehand that their music was going to be performed in a certain church and adapted their tones accordingly."

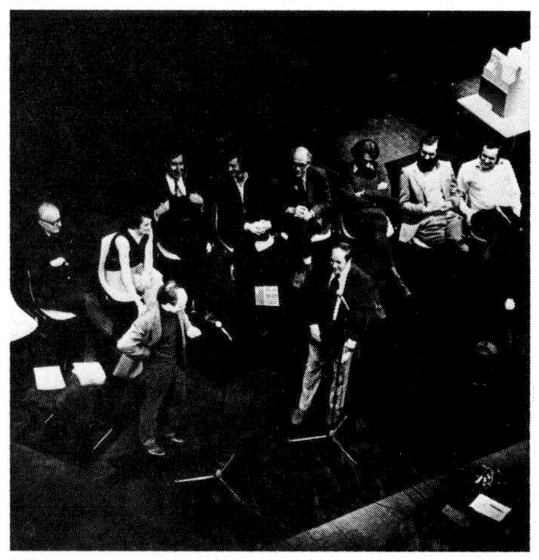

256

IRCAM is a musical oasis set in the lower depths of Paris where nothing, not even air-conditioning and security systems can disturb the atmosphere of concentration. But it is not an island cut off from urban life.

256. Press conference at the Théâtre de la Ville in Paris, with Pierre Boulez, Luciano Berio, Robert Bordaz and the complete IRCAM team.

257. View of work site during excavation: the building is underground to reduce problems of acoustic insulation and provides an unobstructed view of the church of Saint Merri in the background.

257

258. Plan of the first underground level: (1) acoustic projection room, (2) recording room, (3) public area, (4) research offices. The entire lower band is assigned to specialist research areas.

259. Cross section through the projection auditorium: in the background, Saint Merri.

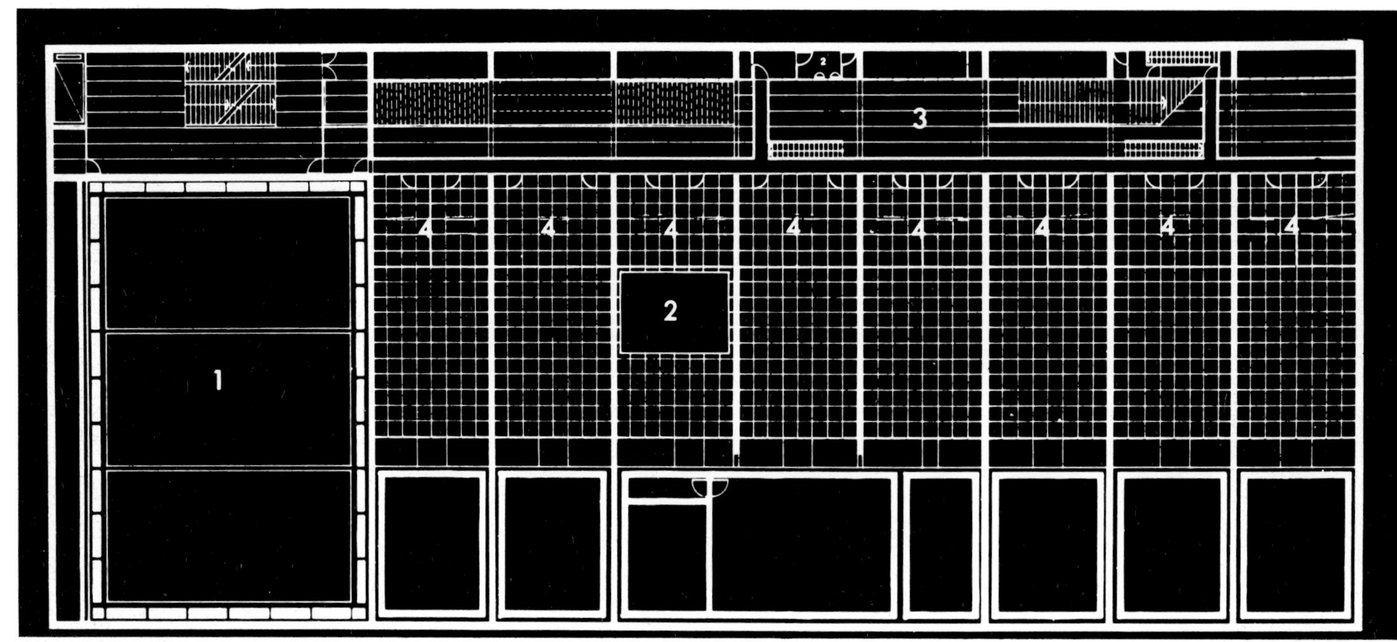

258

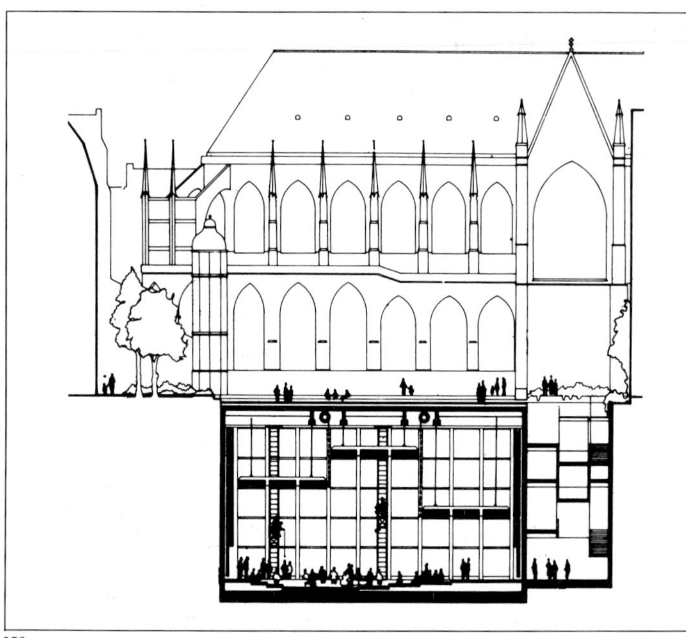

259

?60. *Longitudinal sections of the building. Top: section through the specialist area. Bottom: section through the public access area.*

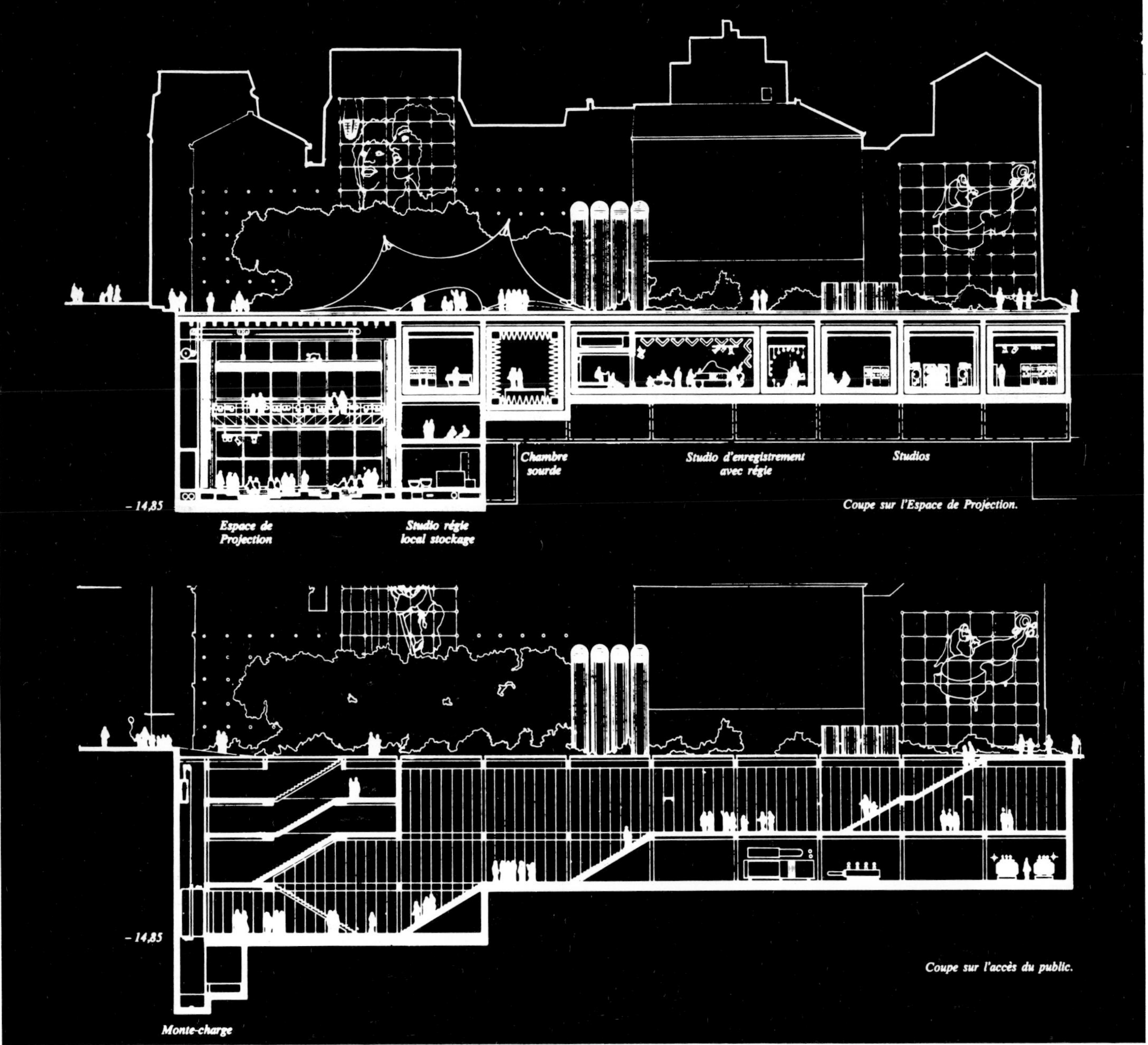

260

261. Entrance area of the building.
262. Peppino Di Giugno at work on a synthesizer.
263. Interior of musical research chamber.

261

262

263

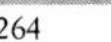
264

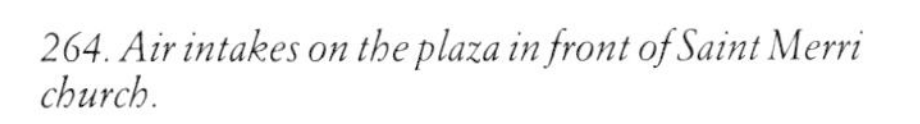
264. Air intakes on the plaza in front of Saint Merri church.

265. The plaza in front of Saint Merri, which is above the IRCAM building.

265

266. Section of the acoustic projection room in one of the possible layouts.

267. Diagram of reverberation times.

268. Reverberation consists of a multitude of reflections with decreasing intensity in time.

269. Detail of one of the wall elements of the flexible acoustics chamber: the surface can be varied from a highly absorbent to a highly reflective finish and other intermediate conditions.

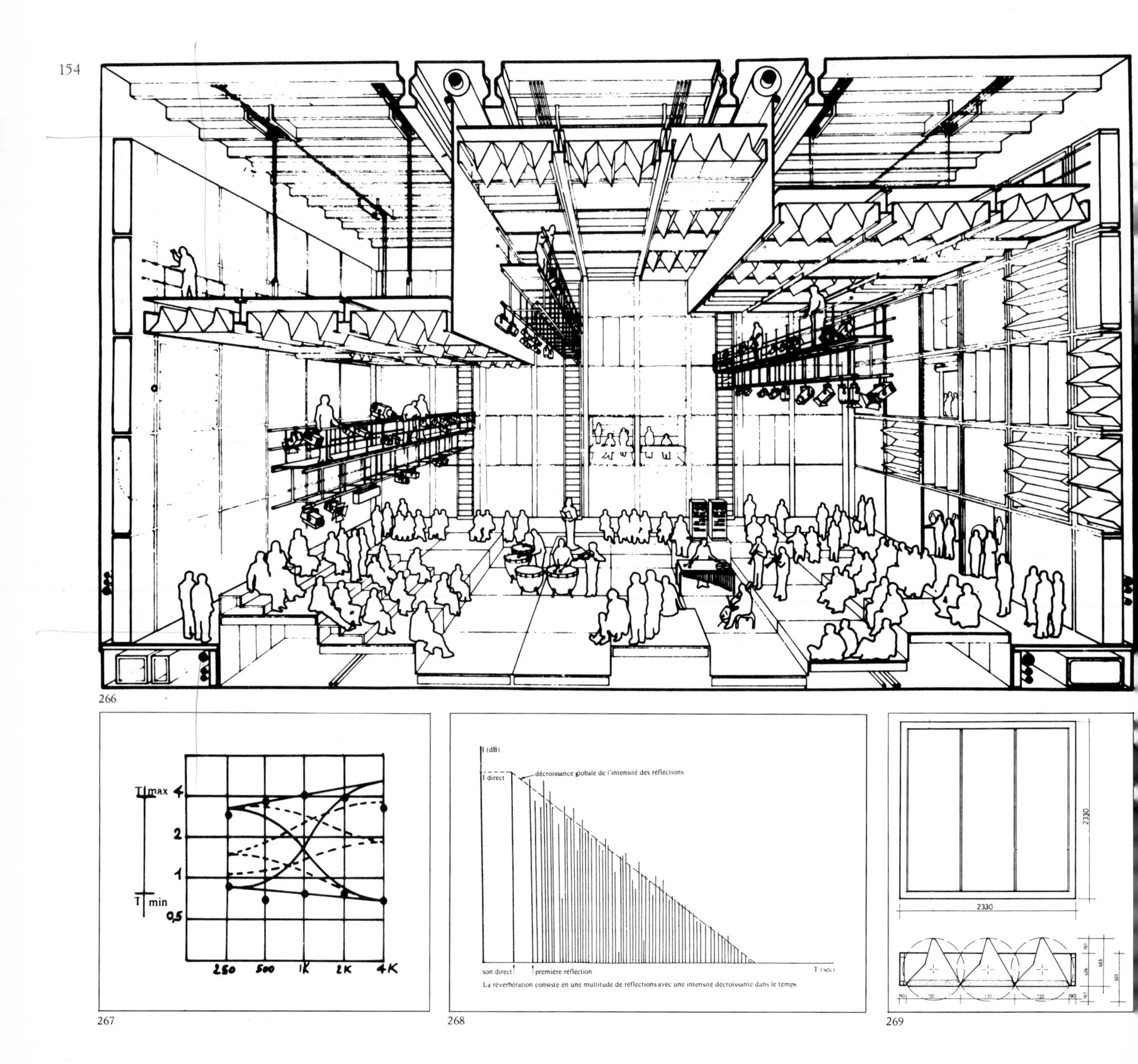

270. The acoustics projection chamber is a large-scale musical instrument: inside this chamber it is possible to modify sound reverberation time from 0.6 to 6 seconds.

270

1981-1983 Houston, Texas USA
The Menil Collection

Client: Menil Foundation
Mme D. De Menil, president; W. Hopps, director; P. Winkler, associate director

Architects: Piano & Fitzgerald Architects, Genoa-Houston, with S. Ishida, assisted by M. Carroll, F. Doria, C. Süsstrunk, B. Plattner; project director, P. Kelly, assisted by L. Turner, E. Huckaby, M. Downs

Engineers: Ove Arup & Partners
P. Rice, T. Barker, assisted by N. Noble and A. Guthrie with Gentry Haynes & Whaley and Galewsky & Johnston, structures and fluids; R. Jensen, fire-protection; E. Brown, security; E.G. Lowry, contractors

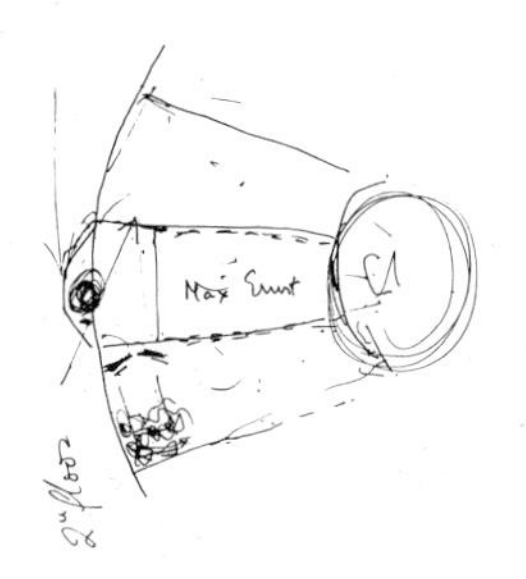

271

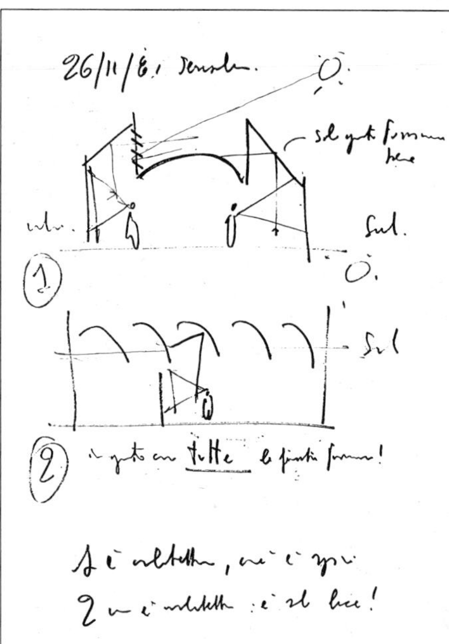

272

In the atelier of light

"In Paris the task was to demystify the idea of the museum, to negate its institutionalism, break down the barriers between culture and the public. In Texas the concept was the exact opposite. In an immense territory, devoid of cultural landmarks, the problem was to confer to the museum the ritual which is one of its attributes." We are at the opposite pole to the Beaubourg. The design for the premises to house the Menil Collection, destined to become one of the main cultural landmarks in Texas, is an act of exorcism of the spirit of Beaubourg: the spectacular Parisian machine is spirited away and the journey undertaken, with frontiersman-like zeal, towards an antithetical goal.

In Paris the contact with the public soon proved skin-deep, consumer-minded, rarely deeply emotive; but here an attempt is made to reestablish "the right to enjoy works of art," by creating an oasis of peace in the heart of a throbbing metropolis. Everything in the Houston design contributes to the creation of an atmosphere of almost religious concentration, a soft technology modelled on physical reality, a relation with the setting that avoids contrasts and seeks to establish a dialogue, a harmonious rapport. Above all it is light that has the crucial role.

"The first step was a trip to Israel planned by Dominique De Menil. An absurd journey north of Tel Aviv to visit a tiny museum in a kibbutz. Yet it was there that the idea she was nursing took on mature form, to make light the key theme of the Houston museum. One of the architect's tasks is to interpret the existing elements of the environment but also the desires of the client, two sets of requirements which have the same value for me."

Light is thus the protagonist, but how is it used specifically in the Texan context? The construction of a museum entrusts its aesthetic message to the rediscovery of natural light. Artificial lighting is lifeless, it dulls the fascination of the work of art offering a static perception of it. What is needed is a formula that will rekindle the dynamism of natural light. A living, dramatic light, enhanced precisely because of its evolving qualities. "There is no sense in trying to control natural light to obtain a flat dimension. The work of art has to modify its relation with light each time a cloud sails by or the sun suddenly comes out or when dusk begins to fall."

The problem has to be resolved on an aesthetic level but even before that on the technological and scientific level. The direct entry of the sun's rays is harmful to works of art, so the aim is to provide diffused natural light in the exhibition rooms without losing a sense of the changing conditions of the outside. Thus, the design course was laid out from the very beginning: practical scientific research combined with theoretical scientific research. On the empirical level we produced the solar machine especially built to study the relevant physical phenomena (the behavior of light at different latitudes, multiple refraction, protection against ultraviolet rays, etc.); we used the computer to work out the mathematics of relations between outdoor and indoor light. This complex inquiry resulted in the definition of a basic structural element, the "leaf" (made of 25 mm ferrocement): 300 of these form the roofing platform and act as a light filter and a thermic screen.

Every single element in this intricate mechanism is devised to transmit the impression of a serene, reflective setting, intimately home-like. The quality of the lighting varies, muted in some zones and stronger in others, dilating or contracting. The longitudinal backbone of the design, the 150 m central promenade, evokes a meditative atmosphere, a domestic interior rather than that of a cultural institution: here visitors can sit and talk, consult books or video documents related to the center's activities. The exterior tropical gardens along the street create evocative effects and heighten the sense of continuity with the organic dimension (already present in the "leaf" element of the structure). In this way the space ceases to be inert or uniform, and becomes elusive, shifting, mirroring the live spaces of inner landscapes.

Another factor aids in lightening what could otherwise be called "museum stress," the feeling of cultural saturation. This is achieved by not exhibiting all the works in the Menil Collection, ten thousand pieces hitherto scattered between Houston, New York and Paris, the most precious collection of African art and one of the most precious collections of Symbolist art in the world. The visitor will be able to admire between twenty and thirty works at any one time, while facilities such as television monitors or other information sources will enable the works to be seen in a historical and technical context. Meanwhile the other masterpieces will be preserved in perfect conditions of security and climate control in the Treasure House, a chamber suspended over the main building. At frequent intervals the works will be rotated, with those on exhibit being returned to storage — where they will be available to scholars for study purposes — while another group of works will be exhibited at the People House. This system of rotation further guarantees that the works will not suffer from prolonged exposure to potentially damaging light.

In this way a gentle reconciliation becomes possible between opposites: ancient and modern, everyday and exceptional, technical innovation and preservation. Indeed, one of the essential qualities of this museum is its fluid connection and interaction

"There is no sense in trying to control natural light to obtain a flat dimension. The work af art has to modify its relation with light each time a cloud sails by or the sun suddenly comes out or when dusk begins to fall."

271. Sketch by Dominique De Menil for the functioning of the Treasure House.

272. First studies sketched with Dominique De Menil in Israel, November 1981.

273. Location of the project in the urban fabric of Houston, rigorously organized along the north-south and east-west axes.

274. Aerial view of the site.

with the environment. It is not a question of formal camouflage. The museum is itself a piece of the city, a fragment of the environment. It is constructed on a "domestic" scale, spacious but not monumental; its glazing and timber walls evoke the historical consciousness of Texas in a physical sense (including a park and a certain number of small houses already existing on the urban grid) and also structurally (by referring to the balloon-frame technique used by the pioneers of the Wild West).

It is not so much a museum as an atelier or even a home, where everything — materials, construction techniques, spatial dimensions, even the system of illumination — deliberately moves away from the institutional model. "Here culture," as a critic writes, "needs a ritual gesture, a serene initiation; for quite simply there is hardly any history around it. So nothing scintillating but a serene object, yet one that is extremely effective and equally carefully researched."

The result is anti-Beaubourg, it revives the museum tradition and updates it, goes beyond it. Piano has not abandoned his line of response. Behind his rejection of artificial lighting there is a clear polemical purpose. Houston is the petroleum capital, the realm of affluence and energy waste. Raising the banner of solar energy in these parts is a challenge. A challenge is likewise implicit in the choice of horizontality against the backdrop of a vertical metropolis.

273

274

275. Work session in the Genoa studio with Peter Rice.

276. Work session in Houston with Dominique De Menil.

277. Work session with Tom Barker in Houston.

278. Full-scale mock-up of an exhibition room to study on the true latitude of Houston experimental results obtained previously on 1:10 scale models using theoretical-mathematical analysis.

275

277

276

278

279. General plan of the museum: in the center the inner promenade; the professional area of workshops and conservation is to the south, the public exhibition area is to the north.

280. General scheme of the building in relation to reception of sunlight and ventilation.

281. General principle of distribution of air-conditioning in exhibition rooms, workshops and Treasure House, above.

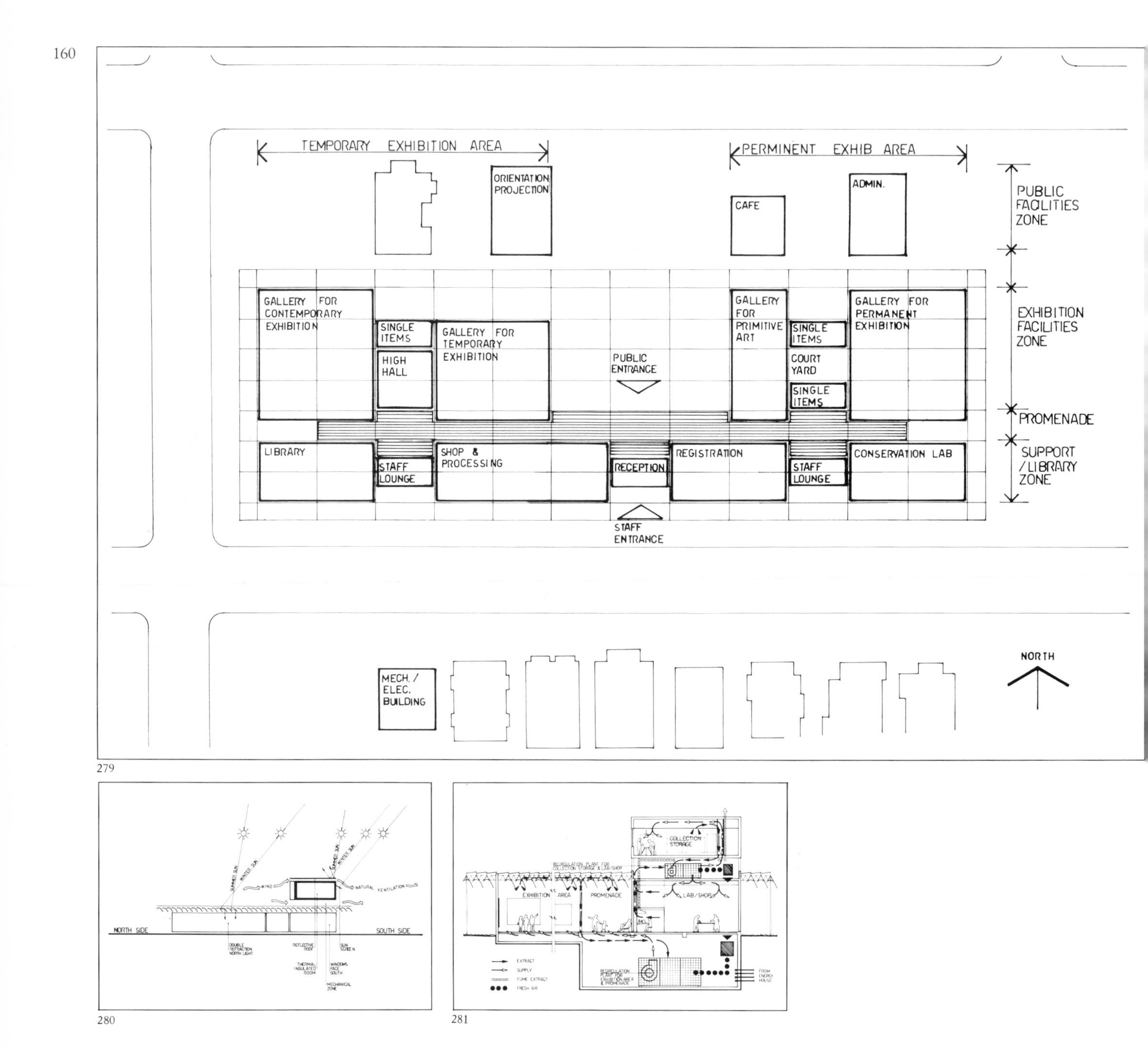

279

280

281

282

282. One of the surrounding houses; the grouping of houses will be retained and organized with complementary activities to constitute the Village Museum.

283. General plan: the adjacent houses will be used for activities complementing the museum.

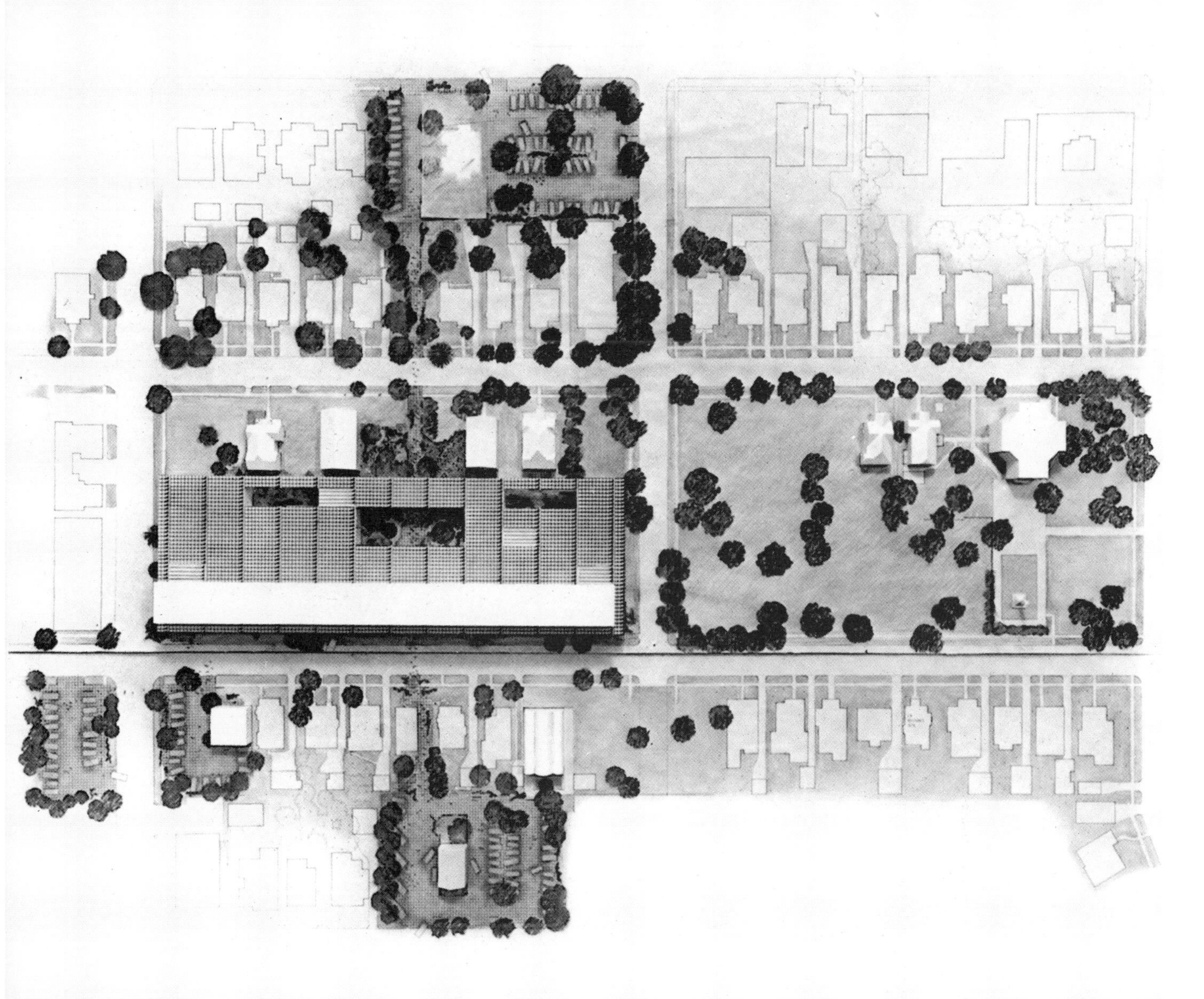

283

284

285

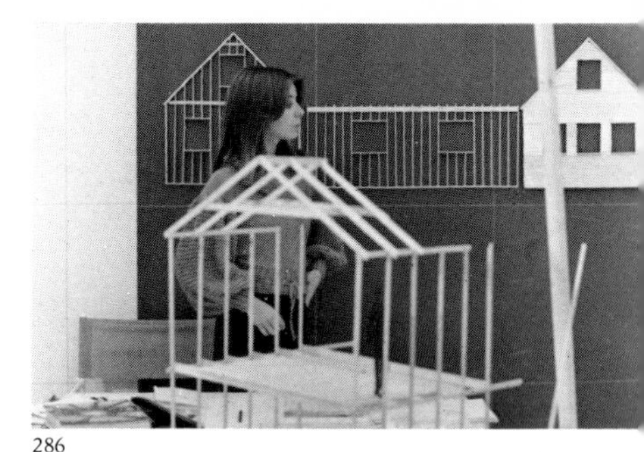

286

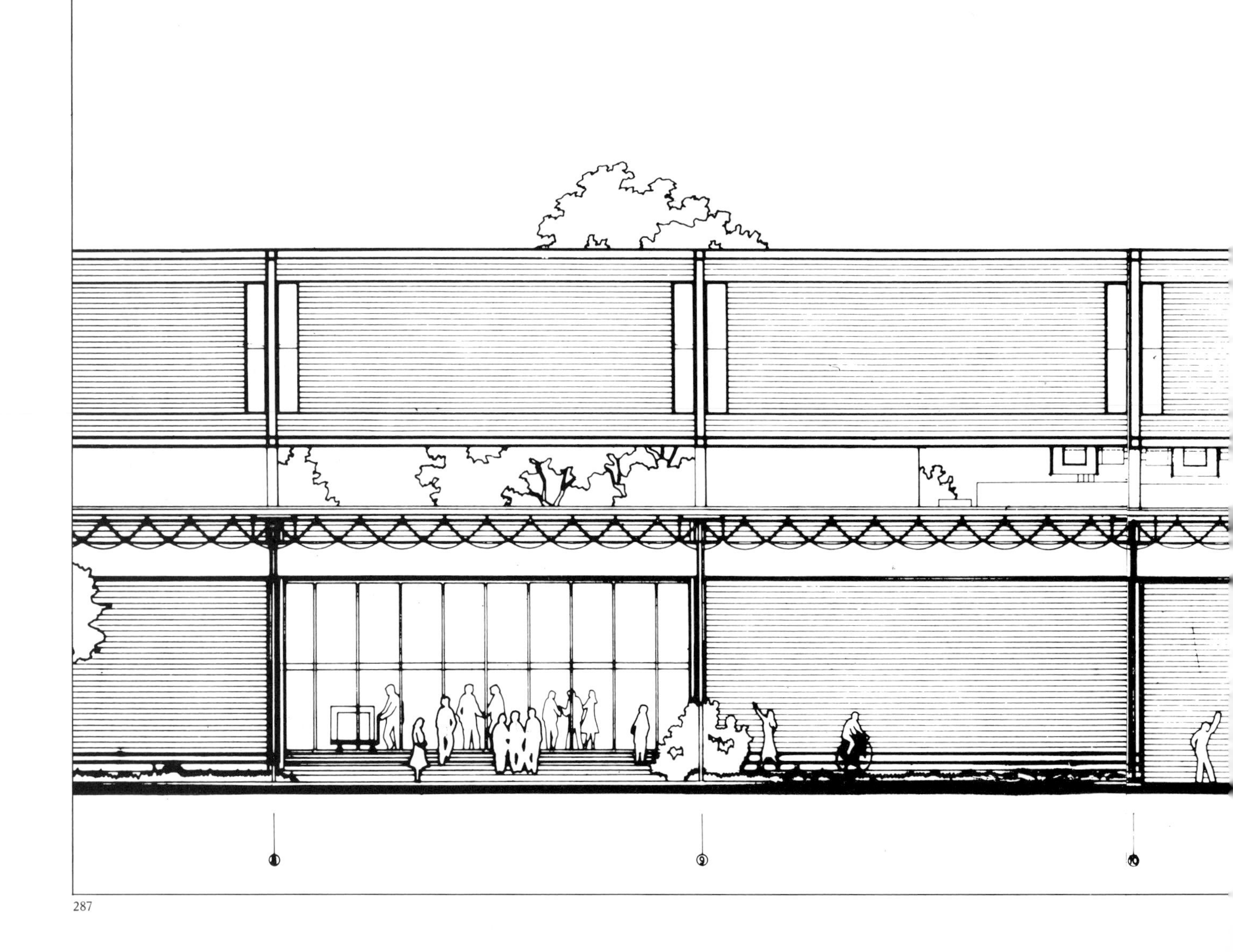

287

284. Detail of traditional façade.

285. Study of detail of the façade of the new museum to house the Menil Collection.

286. Studio-made TV program on construction of the balloon frame; this system is characterized by extreme simplification of assembly and minimal use of tools.

287. Partial view of south side.

288. Standard platform framing construction scheme; this developed from the old pioneering balloon-frame system.

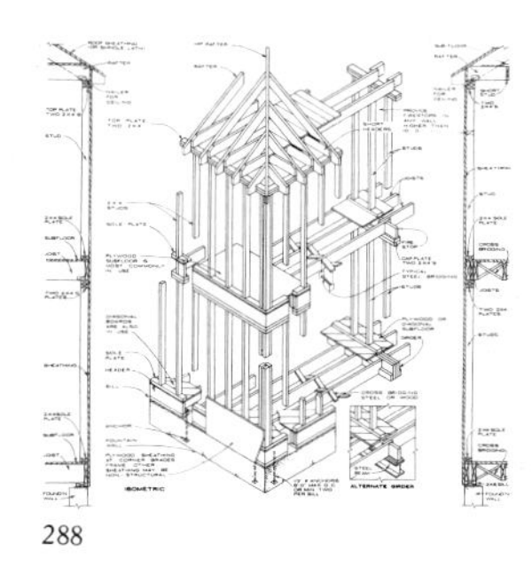

288

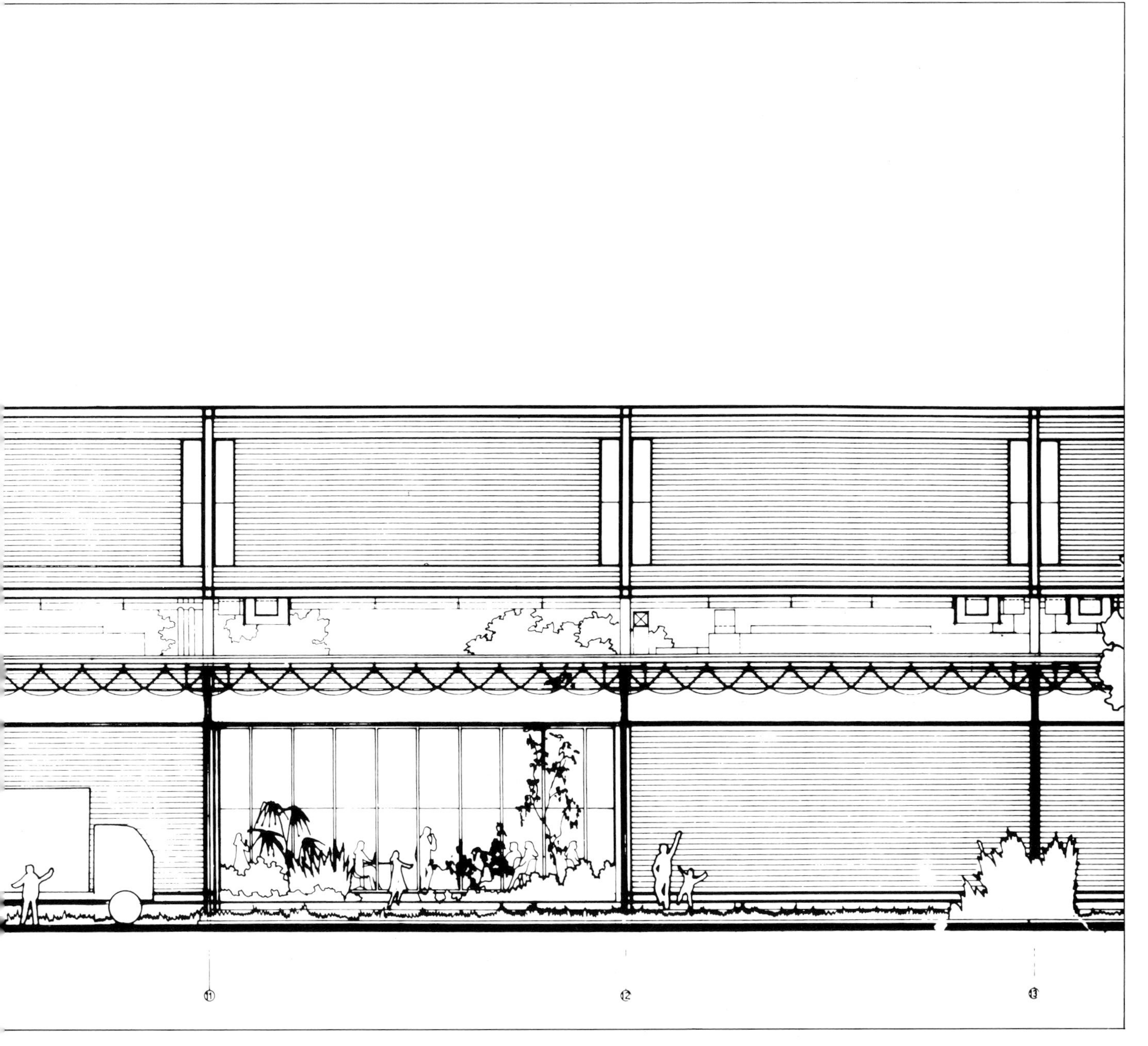

289. *Final plan: on the right the permanent exhibition zone, on the left the temporary exhibition area.*

290. *Elevation of south side on Branard Street.*

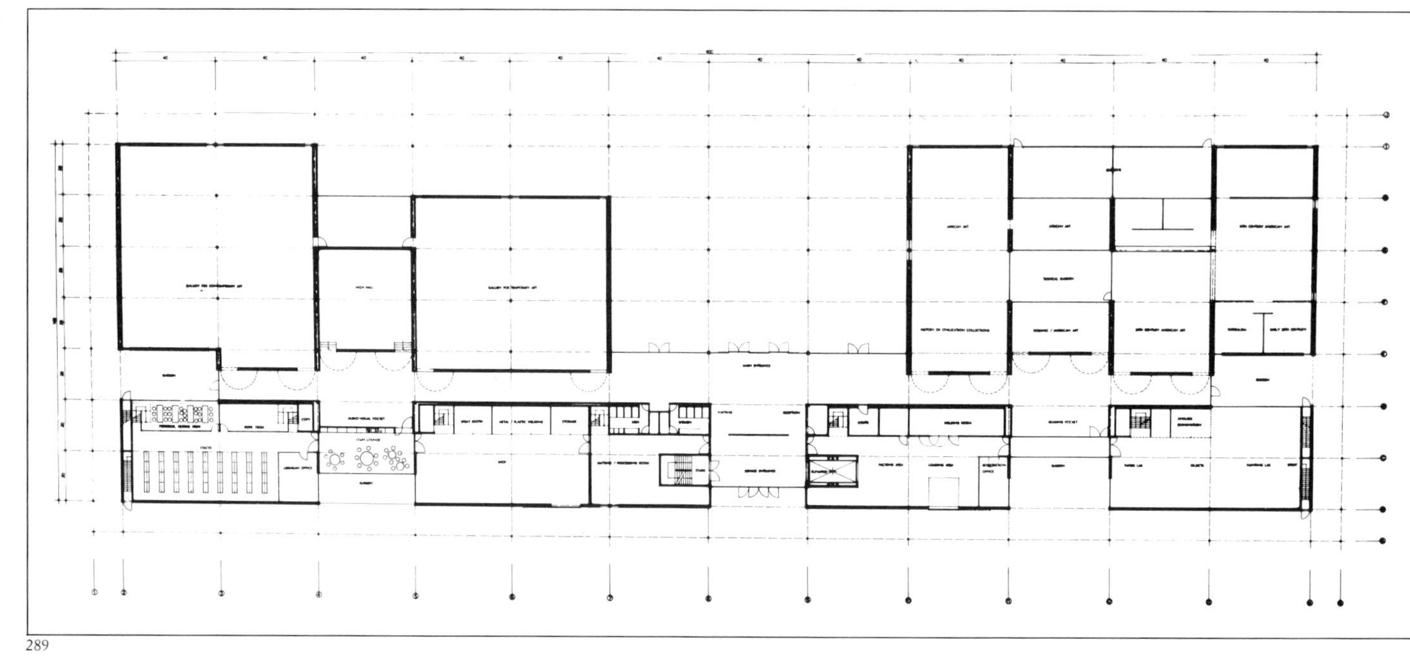

289

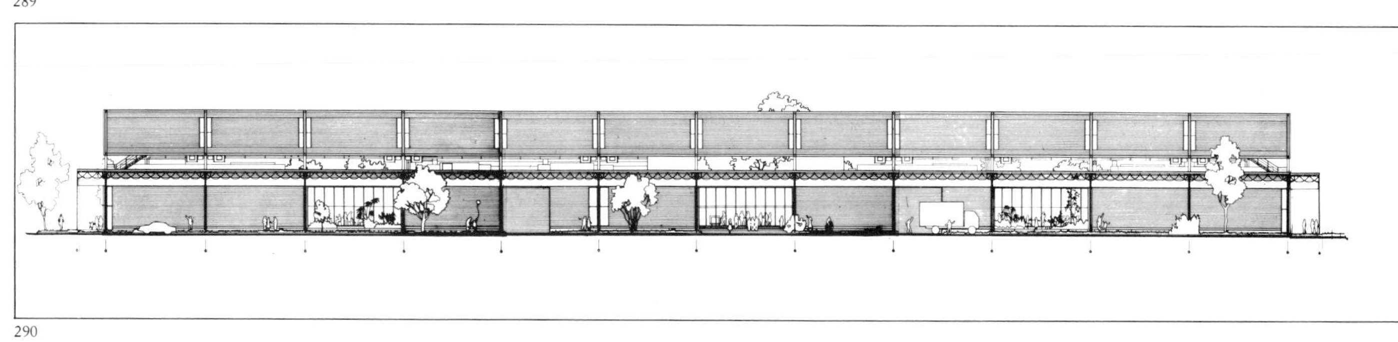

290

291. *Sections through* (a) *exhibition area,* (b) *entrance area and* (c) *elevation on Mandell Street*.

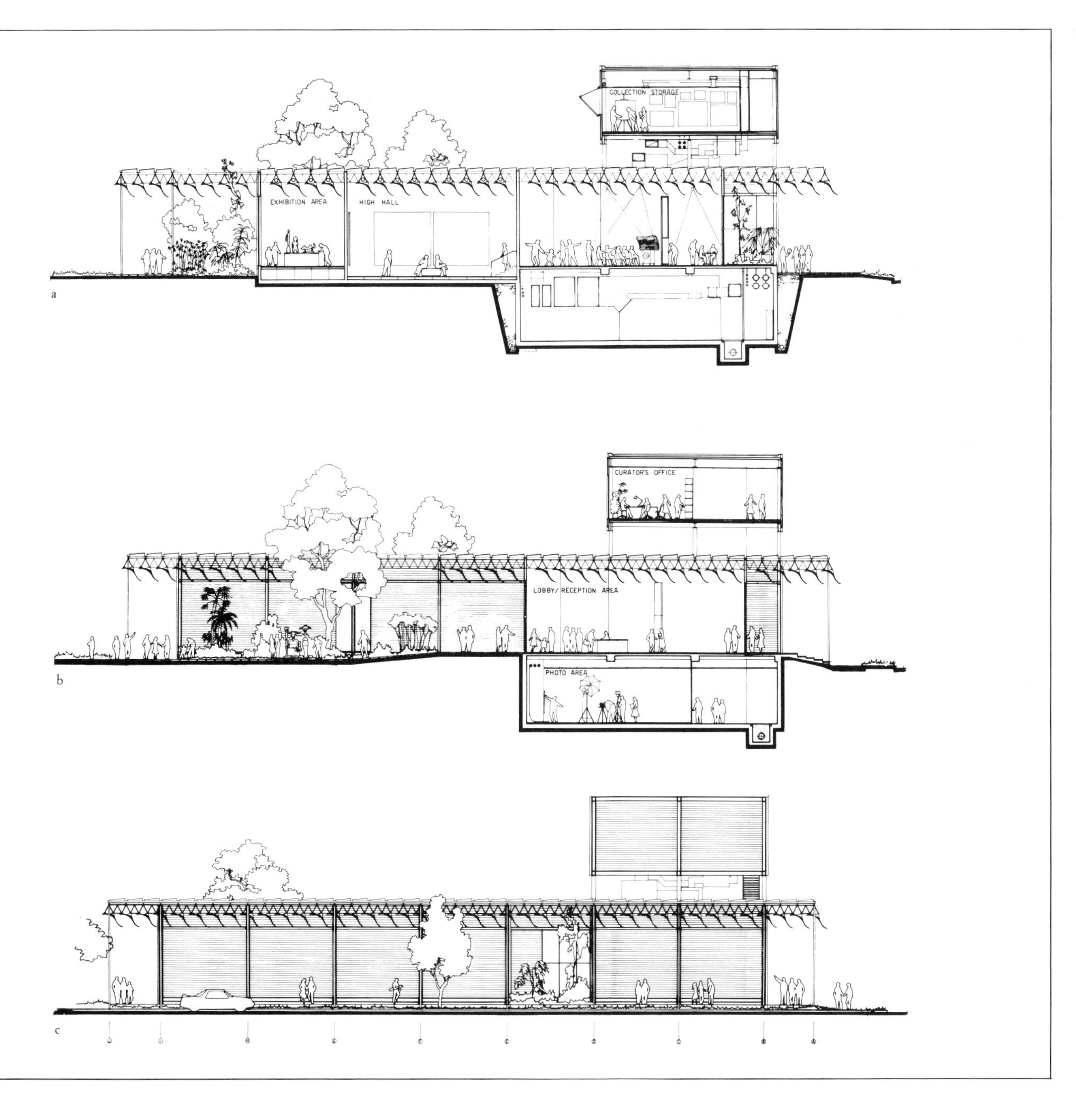

291

292. *Simplified solar machine constructed in the Genoa studio to reproduce Houston sunlight conditions.*

293. *At work on a 1:10 scale model in the Genoa studio.*

294. *Measuring levels of natural illumination at different heights in a model.*

295. *Early scheme for construction of ferrocement leaf.*

296. *Chart of sunlight conditions in Houston.*

297. *Partial section through exhibition room: at the top the system of multiple refraction for natural lighting; at bottom the double flooring for ventilation and air-conditioning.*

292

293

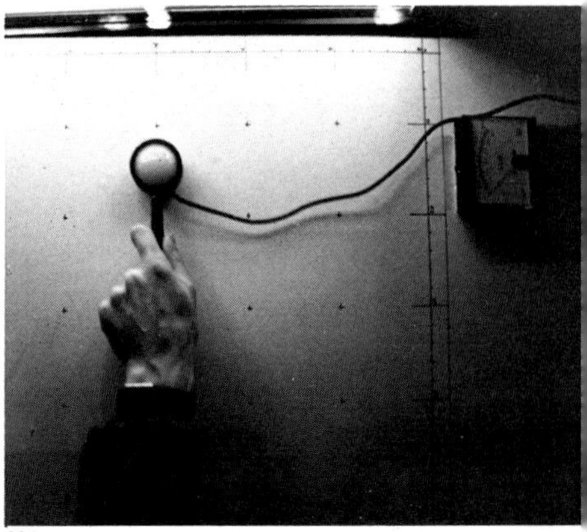

294

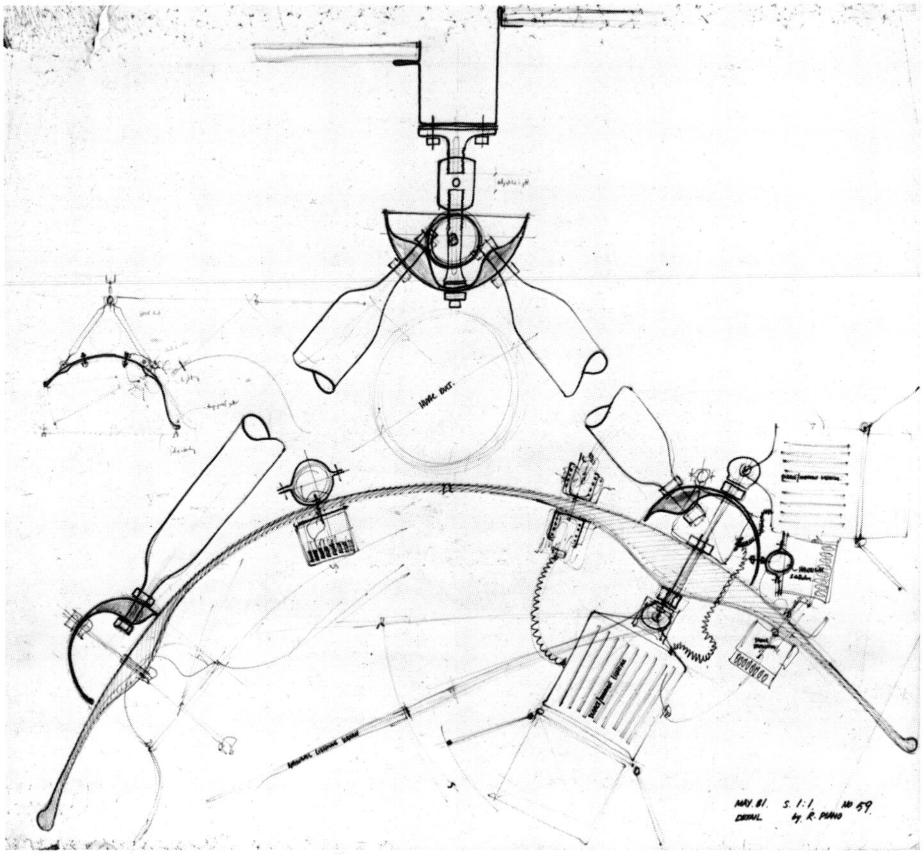

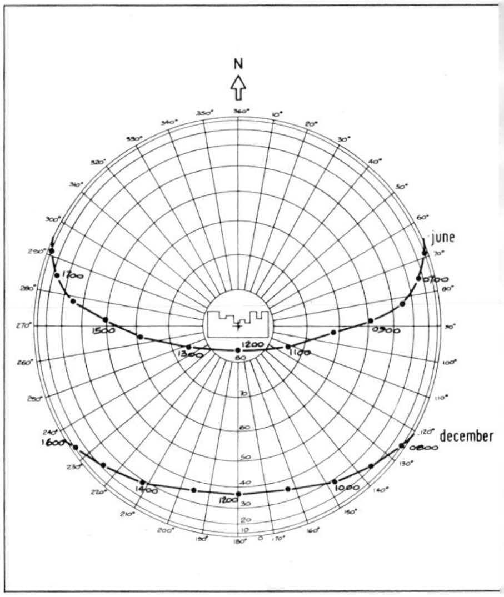

296

295

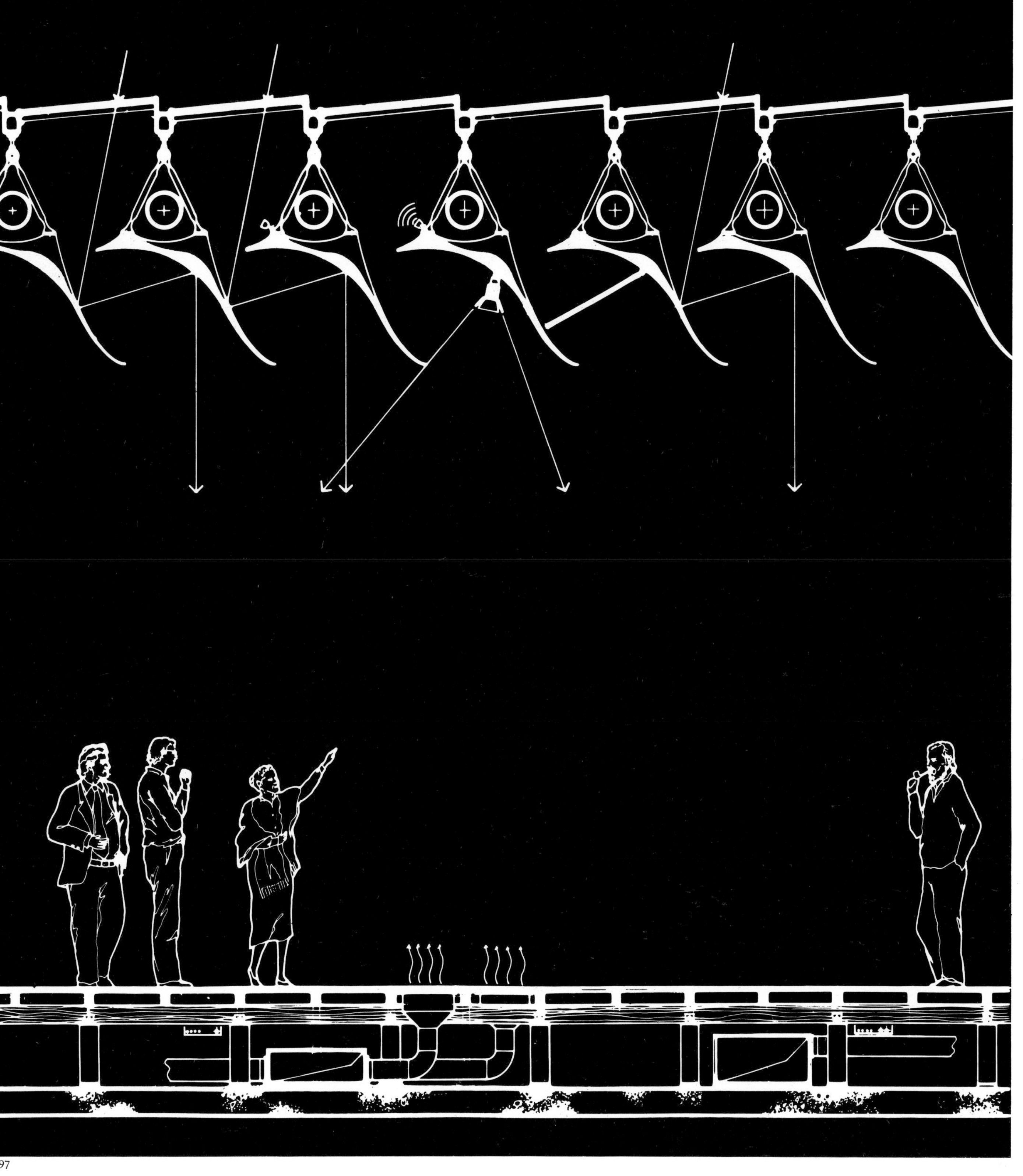
297

298. Construction of ferrocement leaf.

299,300. Assembly of the upper node of the cast-steel structure.

301. Plotter pattern with geometrical modifications of the leaf under load stress.

302. Construction scheme of structural system of roofing: below, the ferrocement leaf; above, the cast-steel beam.

303. Test prototype of part of the roofing beam: the ferrocement leaf and rigid beam work together to create a 12 m free span.

298

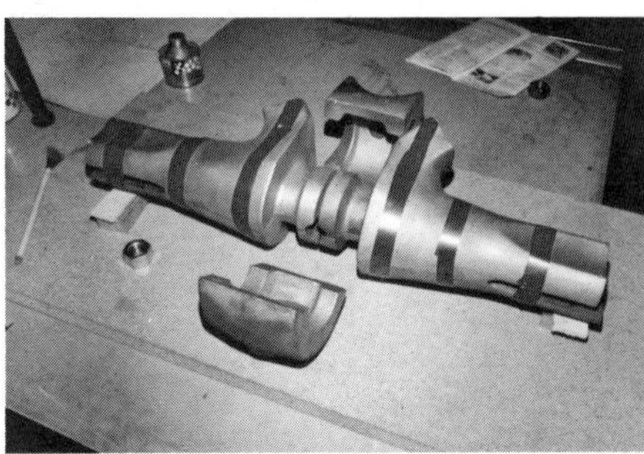

299

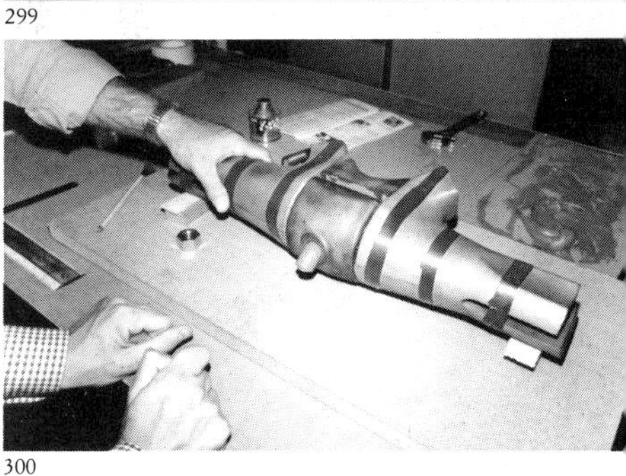

300

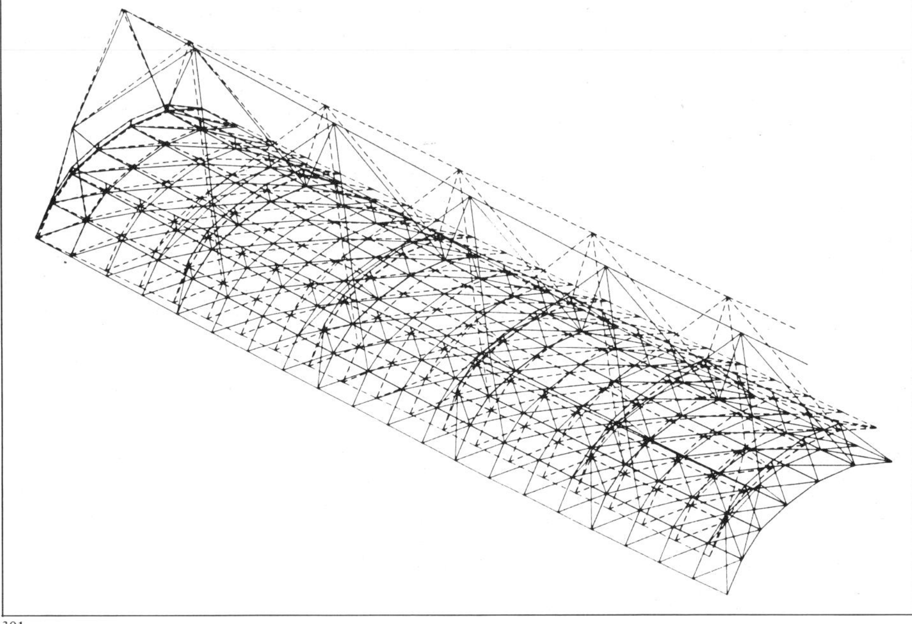

301

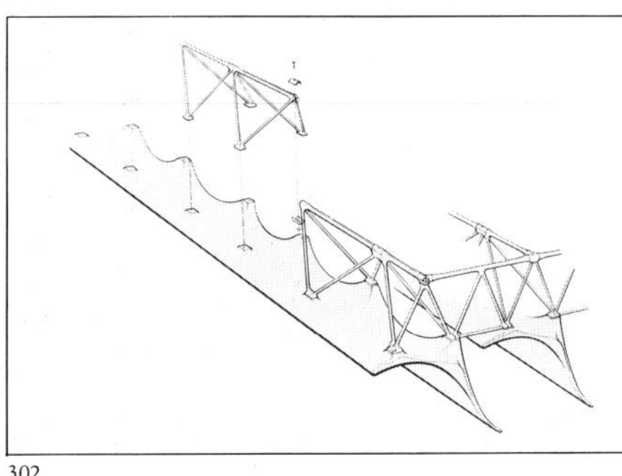

302

303

1982 Turin, Italy
Reuse of the Palazzo a Vela for the Alexander Calder retrospective

The cathedral of shadow

170 Client: Commune of Turin, Toro Insurance
Curator: G. Carandente
Architects: Studio Piano/Building Workshop S.r.l. with S. Ishida, O. Di Blasi, E. Frigerio, P. Terbüchte, F. Marano, A. Traldi
Engineers: Ove Arup & Partners
Lighting: P. Castiglioni
Graphics: P. Cerri

The craftsman of technology interprets the craftsman of sculpture, the poet-constructor whose mobiles hover in space evoking and reinventing, simply and humorously, the civilization of the machine, its mutable mechanisms, its frenzied movement. The occasion came about for the first complete retrospective of the great American artist's work, directed by Giovanni Carandente and to be mounted by Renzo Piano in the Palazzo a Vela, a gigantic hangar 120 m long and 30 m wide.

It was an event of international scope and offered another occasion to transgress the rules of aesthetic handling, but not a dramatic transgression. "The intention is polemical: to eliminate the architect's tendency to put himself at the center of the stage. We want to transform the exhibition into a festive occasion with the public at its center. The architect keeps a low profile in the wings." This justifies the choice of the Palazzo a Vela: a multifunctional space, not museum-like and hence not esoteric, psychologically very approachable. The philosophy is the same as with the Beaubourg: art is not a domain reserved for a restricted circle of initiates, but a leisurely activity, a colorful spectacle, an open-house party. If the philosophical premise is simple, its execution is original, a sign that the pleasure of branching out adventurously, leaving the trodden path, is still there.

Entering the building is like stepping into a dream. As soon as the visitor steps over the threshold he is drawn into a microcosm, a great interior wrapped in semi-darkness. In the glimmering half-light float the 400 works (mobile sculptures, paintings, drawings, tapestries, jewels, toys, tools, bronzes, wood objects), onto which are focused the only lights in the vast pavilion. The sensation is of moving in a Gothic interior, through arcane and silent spaces of a cathedral. But this is no more than a sensation, for all is vague, insubstantial, illusory, on the point of slipping away into unknown depths. You move through a dimension of reverie, until, in the deep shadow, a focal point emerges, an illuminated island in the center of the room where three stabiles project upwards and a single mobile projects downwards. The rest of the works of art are radially arranged about a large bay cut out of the darkness along a route which follows a chronological ordering of the pieces, from the center outwards, finally emerging into the park and lakeside where the great stabiles are displayed. Here the route comes to an end, a long journey through oneiric space.

"The idea is to rediscover two different emotional stages. A collective emotion bound up with the image of the cathedral in its half-light, and an individual emotion created by the personal response to the works of art. We achieved this aim by segmenting the exhibition space with white free-standing screens, seats, benches; like little oases, coves appearing out of the sea of shadows. Everything sails through the darkness: this is why we also planned a sophisticated system of cables in which supports are almost non-existent." A fantastic and magical setting for the art of Calder and at the same time a key to its interpretation.

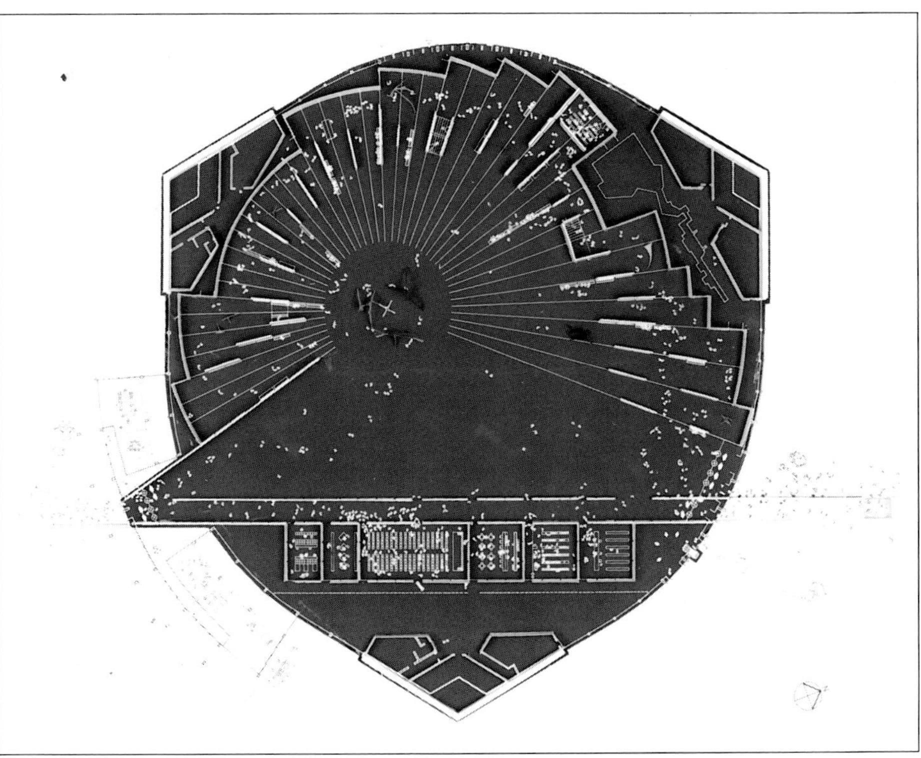

305

The sensation is of moving in a Gothic interior, through arcane and silent spaces of a cathedral. But this is no more than a sensation, for all is vague, insubstantial, illusory, on the point of slipping away into unknown depths.

304. "Sandy" Calder.

305. Zenithal view of model of Palazzo a Vela with the exhibition layout.

306. Elements in the exhibition system.

306

1980 Burano, Italy

Design for restructuring the island of Burano

Client: Commune of Venice

Architects: Piano & Rice & Associates with the collaboration of P.H. Chombard de Lauwe, S. Ishida, University of Venice and coordination of the Fondazione Tre Oci, G. Macchi and A. Macchi assisted by H. Bardsley, M. Calvi, L. Custer, C. Teoldi

Program by Magda Arduino

The roots of the lagoon

In an extremely heterogeneous cultural world, divided between humanism and technology, economics and science, intellectualism and industry, Piano's architecture attempts to act as a factor of continuity, a point of interaction, opposed to all the barriers, divisions and elements of separation. The Neighborhood Workshop on Burano (set up in collaboration with Peter Rice, Magda Arduino and Paul H. Chombard de Lauwe) continues this work of recomposition. "We have carried out research and interviews with old artisans to discover the techniques once used in maintenance work. We have to create a bridge between the ancient memory and the technology of today. It would be wrong to take up a rigid position in relation to the past. Why give up the advantages of technology?"

On the issue of ancient town centers, Piano rejects the either/or approach, the irreducible dichotomy between the destructiveness of reconstruction and the safety of completely freezing and protecting the old, which leads to stagnation. Technological knowledge offers the key to revitalizing the city of the past but only if using a certain discretion in employing the sophisticated resources of the post-industrial era. Indiscriminate use of them would snap the umbilical cord that links us with our roots, the symbols of history. It could have harmful effects in certain cases. An example would be to replace the old wooden window frames with new ones in aluminum, altering the relation between full and empty volumes, breaking up the elements of the urban landscape. In the same way, the use of cement rendering instead of the old system of whitewash is often counter-productive. The old whitewash rendering needs regular maintenance but it is much more hygienic; cement rendering does not allow the damp to "breathe" (the moisture is laden with salts), and while cement lasts longer it tends to come away all at once.

Hence the need for soft technologies and mobile instruments to heal the ailments of the ancient city without producing traumas, dissonance, demolition operations. The question is not to reject the new out of prejudice but rather to distinguish between cases where it is acceptable and others where it should be avoided. "Aluminum window frames, for instance, are not just a question of formal design but also a functional requirement: they completely exclude drafts. Our approach has rather been to ask ourselves how to interpret the double-glazed window, perhaps with an aluminum frame, in terms that are culturally correct for Burano."

But a bridge has also to be built between technology and society, between architect and user. "My feeling is that the architect is no longer able to interpret, to know the true needs of people. The Neighborhood Workshop attempts to establish a circuit linking a project with its users, in a setting that is not invented but real. Usually everything gets screened out by the system. We are trying to get rid of this screening process which is artificial and harmful." The theme of participation, with its misunderstandings and pitfalls, comes into play again on Burano. It is no accident that the architect at the service of the community should work in close collaboration with Chombard de Lauwe, the "sociologist of aspirations." Architecture is outside studies, it is in the streets and on construction sites, amid the inhabitants of the lagoon, in direct contact with the everyday and the useful. The fundamental point is to look to the future. Never yield to the temptations of demagogy, the group mentality. The demand has to be interpreted and at the same time directed, piloted. One has to intuit the general trends, what lies ahead, people's aspirations. "Chombard de Lauwe always stresses the capacity aspirations have of taking on the strength and weight. The only way to avoid distortions is to find certain limits, certain thresholds to guarantee a reversibility of decisions affecting design and construction, but above all to activate a process of learning, to stimulate developments over the long term." Only in this way can participation function and become valuable in dealing with the perennial problem of Venice.

Connecting never means simply giving way, accepting compromise. The Neighborhood Workshop is a terminal, an instrument of diagnosis which makes it possible to photograph stones, survey physical situations, but it is also a way of structuring participation to shed light on social situations which often show signs of deterioration. It is natural that rehabilitation should often involve deviations from the norm. This is precisely the task of the new architect: "Not to obey anyone — indeed, to disobey and if necessary to transgress."

307

"We have to create a bridge between the ancient memory and the technology of today. It would be wrong to take up a rigid position in relation to the past. Why give up the advantages of technology?"

307. Seminar organized by the Tre Oci Foundation, coordinator Giulio Macchi.

308. A typical Burano façade.

309. Aerial view of the island of Burano.

308

309

310. Section through the Neighborhood Workshop established in existing structures and outdoors.

311. Replacing wooden roof-frame with reinforced concrete.

312. View of Burano.

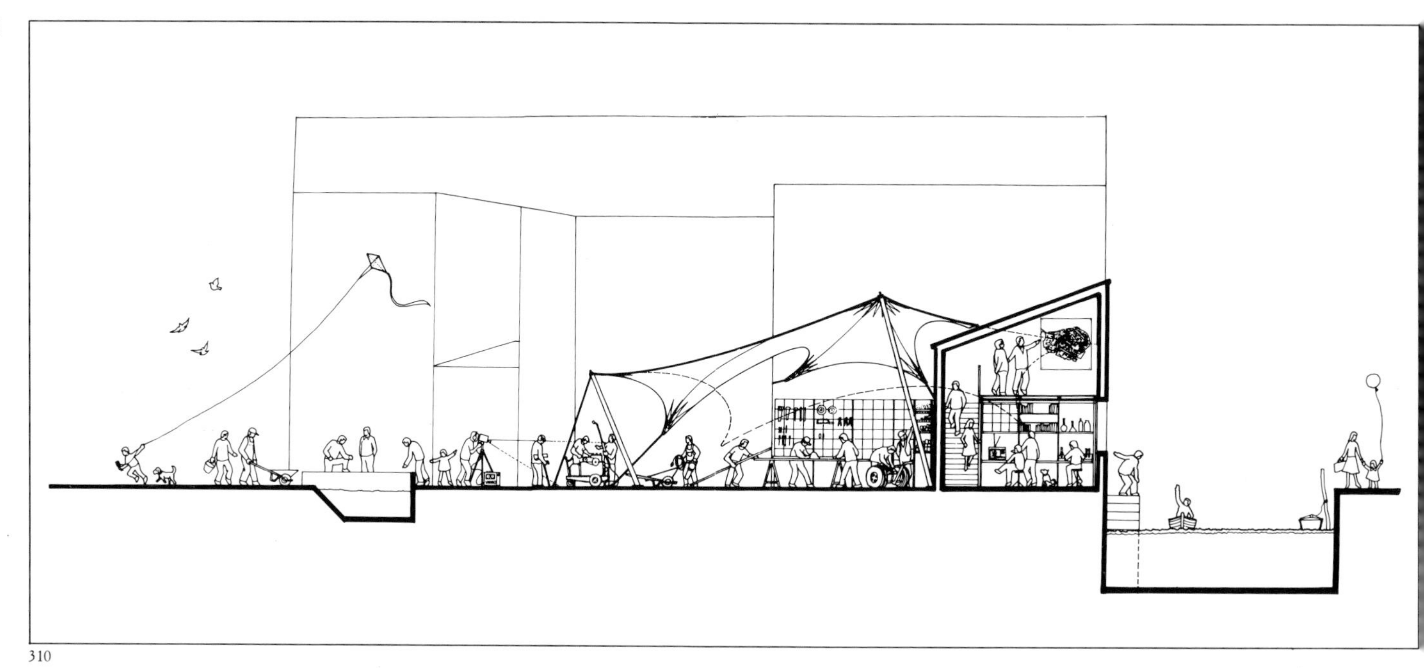

310

311

312

313. *Ferroconcrete reinforcement of first floor completed without demolishing wooden beams.*

314. *Layout of relationship between Neighborhood Workshop and property belonging to the Commune of Venice, chosen to test the Workshop maintenance system.*

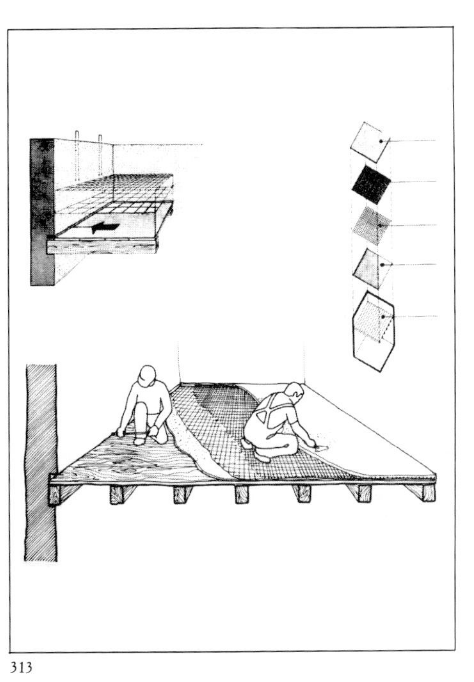
313

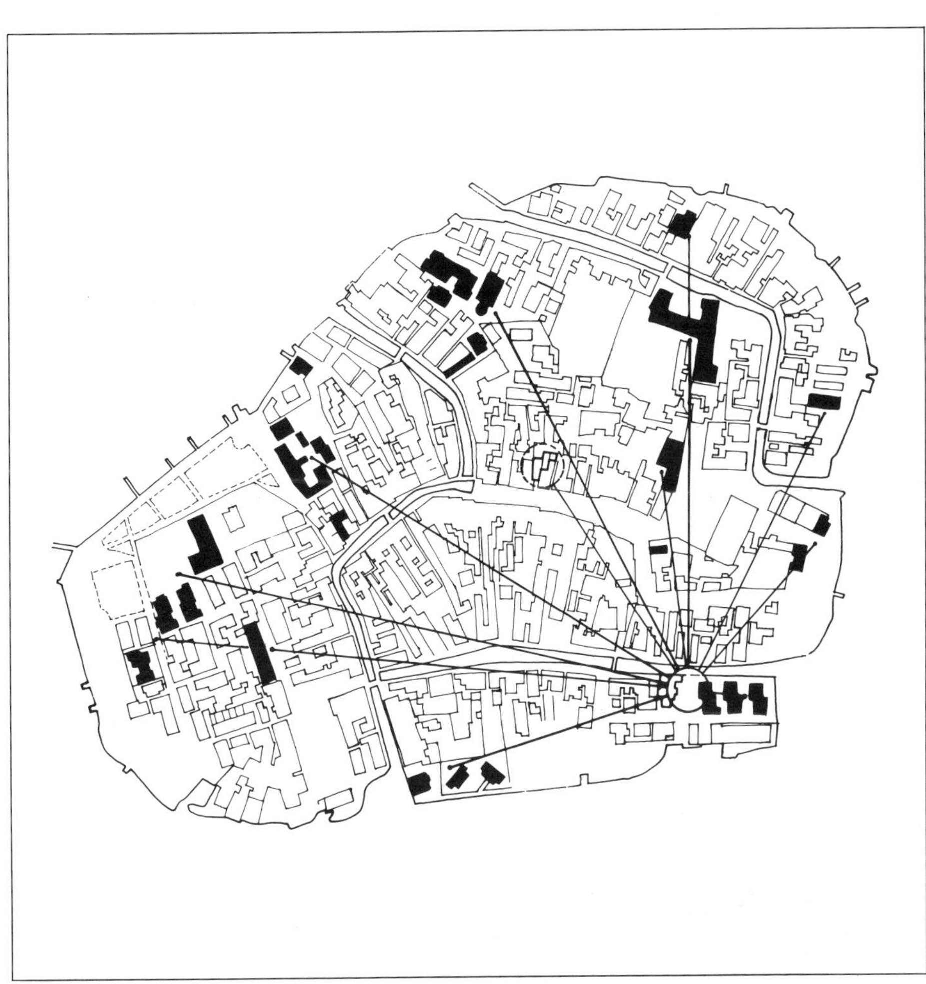
314

1981 Genoa, Italy
Renewing the old Quartiere del Molo

Protecting without demolishing

Client: Commune of Genoa

Architects: Studio Piano/Building Workshop S.r.l.
S. Ishida, A. Traldi
with R. Ruocco, F. Icardi, F. Marano, A. Bianchi, E. Frigerio
with the collaboration of R. Melai, E. Miola
and for planning aspects
V. Podestà, G. Amadeo of Tekne Planning
with consultancy of F. Pagano

Program by Magda Arduino

315

The Molo is a district which began to be uninhabitable by building speculation as long ago as the 17th and 18th centuries, resulting in deteriorating health conditions and lighting. Yet it was once an important center in Genoa, still one of the most fascinating but most decayed in all Europe. This was the area entrusted to Piano's staff within the municipality's comprehensive rehabilitation program for the old town. The Quartiere del Molo is structurally sound; it has shops, warehouses, workshops and other commercial activities connected with the sea. In the 13th century it was established as a depôt for the port area. Grain, salt and other goods were stored in large buildings, true silos, which still many centuries later retain interest and spatial dynamism. Hence the simplicity and clarity of the general layout.

The plan is structured in three phases: (1) intervention on the urban scale – this phase involves connections between the district and the rest of the city; (2) intervention on the district scale, aiming to identify services required and a reorganization of traffic; (3) intervention in four blocks envisaging rehabilitation of about 50 homes, construction of a concert hall and a nursery school. The last of these is a pilot project aiming to show that the rehabilitation project can be carried out without evacuating the inhabitants by combining appropriate technological instruments and upgrading of the skilled work-force of local craftsmen. No upheavals and demolition, but an improvement in living conditions while retaining memories, structures and building types based on the principle that the ancient town center is an indivisible union of stones and people.

There is, however, one big obstacle to overcome: the Molo district is a mosaic of roofs and terraces, a maze of *carruggi* (alleys) immersed in gloom, hemmed in by damp unhealthy buildings of seven or eight stories, without elevators and with steep staircases. The sun never penetrates. How is this to be renewed? By knocking down the 19th century upper stories? This would be too traumatic, eliminating the finest part of these buildings, the top. A more rational planning concept seems to be to layer their use, with the lower stories kept for commerce and tertiary services, the middle part for homes and the top section for collective services.

All that has to be done is to tilt everything upwards, where there is sunshine and air: schools and social services on the rooftops with a panoramic view of the sea, hanging gardens, vertical transport mechanisms projected to the outside, gangways and pedestrian malls crossing the alleys in transparent tubes, mirror surfaces to catch the light, etc. It is both a technical and an aesthetic problem: how to provide street blocks with service facilities without compromising the spatial quality. The solution adopted for the elevators is an indication of this approach: three poles of vertical movement outside the buildings to avoid interfering with the stairwells and having to close up the central shaft, which would cut off both air and natural lighting.

Scientific research provides essential support for the rehabilitation operation but without severing the links with the area's historical past in supplying both lighting and ventilation. Inclined surfaces, for instance, were previously used in the past to bring light in through the windows; the rays falling from above were deflected into the interior. The idea of having mirrors on the rooftops merely translates this tradition into present-day scientific terms. The idea goes beyond just trapping the sunlight: light is reflected deep into the alleys by a double-refraction system, creating bands of light that heighten the spatial dimension, the geometrical complexity of these maze-like passages.

The same is true of the natural ventilation provided by solar chimneys: a tube is installed on the rooftops, it is made of glass with a black central body through which the air passes, the flue draws well because of the difference in temperature between the air above and the air below, i.e. the natural movement of air caused by heating the air above with a refractive element, a Pyrex tube. "An extremely simple principle, the greenhouse effect, but one that gives first-rate practical results. It also re-establishes the presence of the old chimney-pots on the rooftops, next to the TV aerials."

Another stimulating feature in this reinterpretation by the Studio Piano is the proposed reuse of historical structures for cultural activities. The salt deposit enclosures, for instance, with buttresses designed to resist strong lateral thrusts of the sea (with the drying of the salt), possesses excellent acoustics and could easily be adapted to a concert hall, either as auditorium or museum (understood, of course, in Piano's characteristic terms as a structure for participatory activity rather than a place of reference). The whole complex could be combined with commercial activities by setting up shops in Vico Malatti, the Molo's backbone, which has gradually lost its original function as the main center of marine craftsmanship.

Nostalgia is out of the question. The plan, far from being regressive, tries to connect old and new and does not overlook practical considerations. In this regard, the plan supplies definite instructions for the means and timing of the project to deal with the various financial and legal issues involved in the whole operation. The operation itself is envisaged as involving cooperation between public and private capital. The municipality would have to shoulder the *nclined surfaces, for instance, were previously used in ᵓe past to bring light in through the windows; the rays alling from above were deflected into the interior. The lea of having mirrors on the rooftops merely translates his tradition into present-day scientific terms.*

315. Aerial view of the old Molo district in Genoa, with the salt and grain deposits of the ancient port.

316. Standard survey sheet systematically completed for all homes in the project area.

317. Plan of the Molo district showing spaces for salt and grain silos.

318. Old plan of Genoa showing the Molo at "G" and the old port of Mandraccio.

319. View over the roofs of the Molo district: the ideal place for the neighborhood's collective services.

320. One of the alleys of the Molo at the beginning of this century. The proportions of the streets were initially correct. When the buildings were extended upwards as a result of speculation there was a deterioration of health conditions.

osts of certain basic works (vertical communications, angways, schools on the rooftops, etc.), which would rigger off the process of restructuring and ubsequently would be administered by small roprietors. No coercion would be involved, there vould be no obligation from the private sector to ollow a fixed course of action; the plan will merely lay own certain parameters with which conversions hould comply.

Here the district's past is preserved without ecourse to freezing the urban organism. Piano's esson seems to be that it is possible to intervene in the ncient town centers provided the systems and ometimes even the instruments of rehabilitation are edesigned at the same time. It is in this sense that revious methods of organization are unsuited to the hysical and structural reality of old town centers. What is needed is a flexible operational approach, ne-tuned, capable of dealing with each case based n its own merits and above all of interpreting the arying needs of the true protagonists of the ehabilitation project, the inhabitants of the district.

317

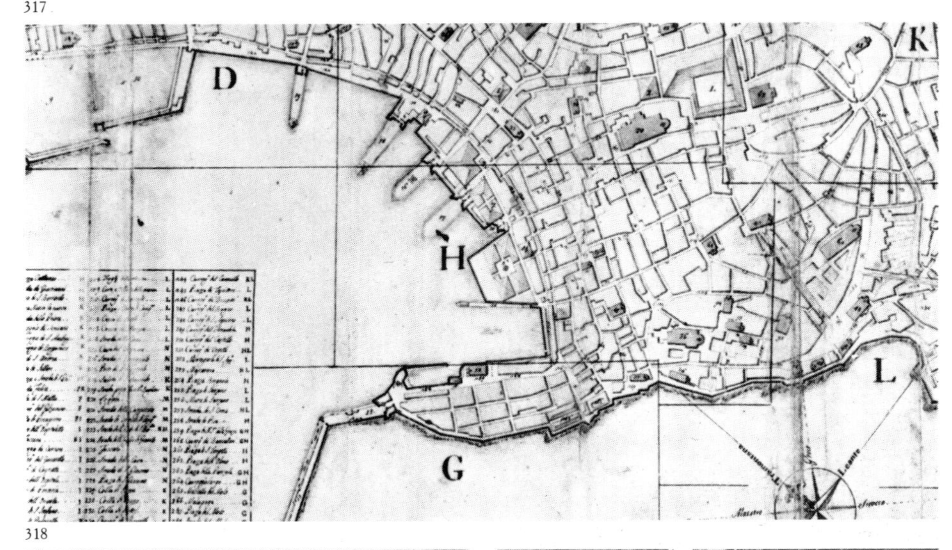

318

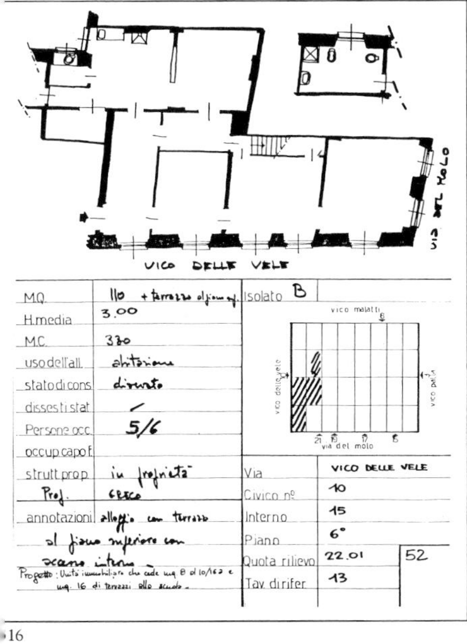

MQ.	110 + terrazzo al piano sup.	Isolato	B
H.media	3.00		
M.C.	330		
uso dell'all.	abitazione		
stato di cons.	discreto		
dissesti stat.	/		
Persone occ.	5/6		
occup. capo f.			
strutt. prop.	in proprietà	Via	VICO DELLE VELE
Prof.	GRECO	Civico nº	10
annotazioni	alloggio con terrazzo al piano superiore con accesso interno.	Interno	15
		Piano	6°
		Quota rilievo	22.01
Progetto: Unità immobiliare che cede mq. 8 al 10/16? e mq. 16 di terrazzi alla scuola.		Tav. di rifer.	13

52

16

319

320

321. Section of the pilot block for an experimental project site. The ground and first floors, unfit for occupation for health reasons, are intended for commercial and tertiary services. The central part of the building is designated for homes and the top section, including rooftops, for collective services such as a nursery school, day care centers and public spaces.

322. Plan of the pilot block; this displays various significant features of Genoa's old town center.

323. Plan of rooftops, top story and the block as location of a nursery school and day care center.

324. Reflecting panels used historically in Genoa to divert light from above into the homes on the lower stories.

325. The old system of reflection from above but using mirrors and more sophisticated technologies was adopted in the project, involving careful study of methods of light reflection.

326. Experiment in the Genoa workshop on the solar chimney for natural ventilation.

327. Example of use of the rooftop in Genoa for overhead passages.

328. View of the model of arrangement of rooftops.

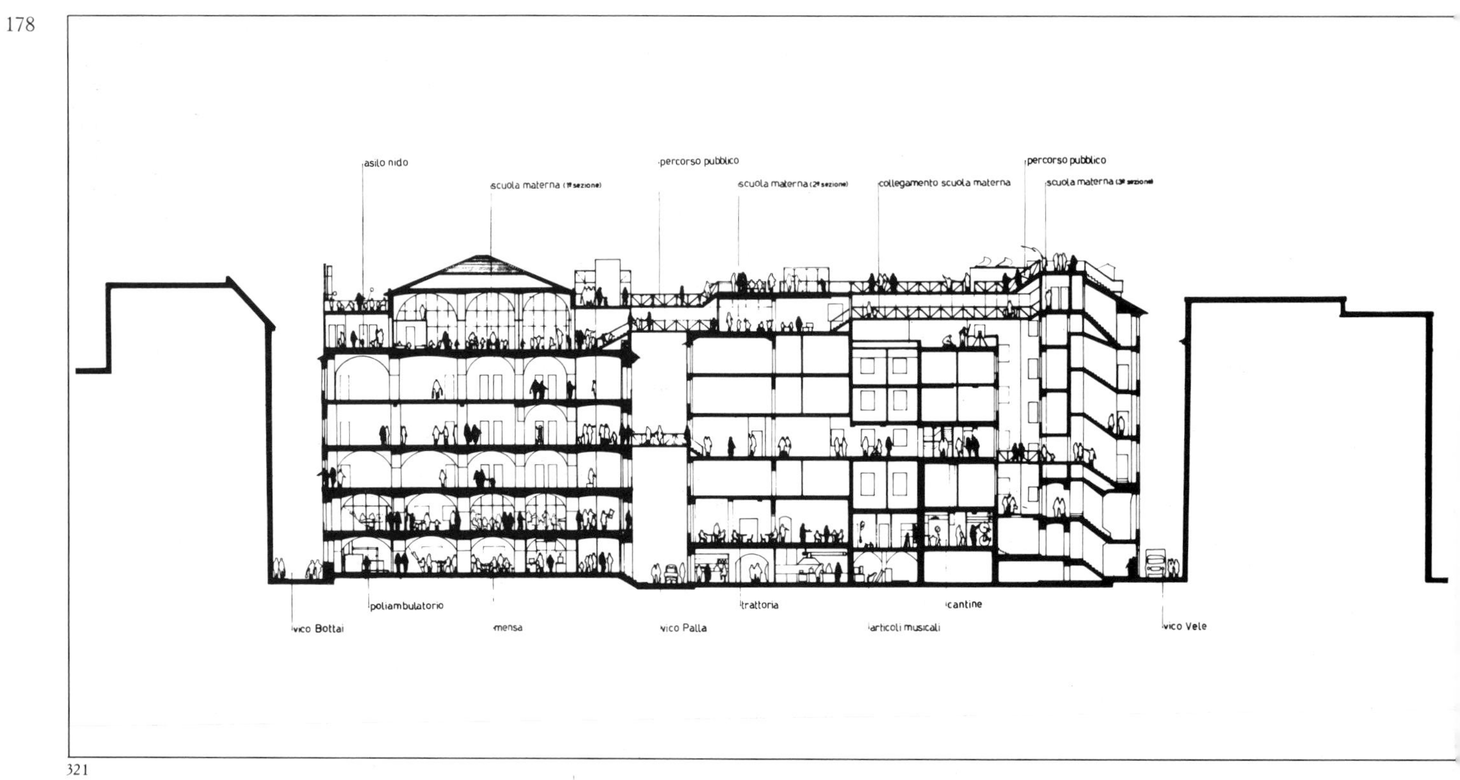

321

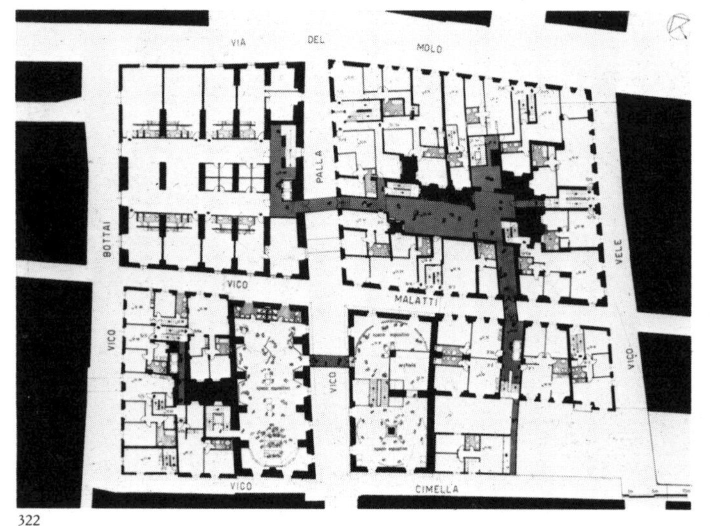

322

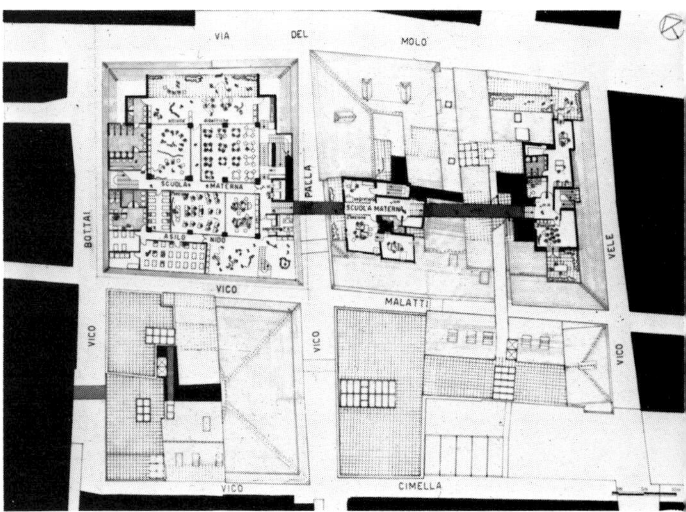

323

324

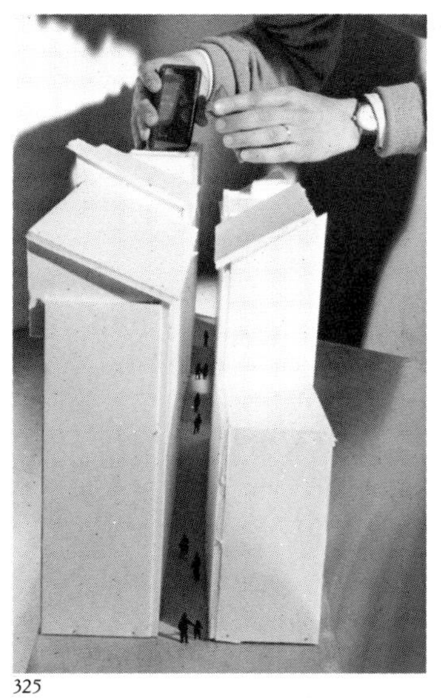

325

326

327

328

1981-1984, Montrouge, Paris, France
Urban conversion of the Schlumberger works

Client: Compteurs Montrouge (Groupe Schlumberger Ltd.)
Coordinators: A. Vincent, assisted by R. Lafon and G. Messand
Architects: Atelier Piano with N. Okabe, B. Plattner, M. Dowd, architects in charge assisted by S. Ishida, T. Hartman, J.F. Schmit, J. Lohse, G. Saint-Jean
Technical engineers: GEC
Landscaping: A. Chemetoff

329

Living restoration

The opportunity for Piano to advance his knowledge of industrial past and technological culture came about when he was offered the reconversion project for the Schlumberger works in Montrouge, near Paris: eight hectares in all, covered by an old manufacturing plant to be transformed into workshops and research centers. "In practice we have to negotiate the changeover from lathes to computers: a stimulating experience. The chairman of the company asked me when we started out not to completely obliterate the basis of the company's original activities in the process of modernization. The fact is that when we began to concern ourselves with the company's premises we ended up having to deal with its organization, starting from the container we ended up with the content."

The theme is not a new one. The reorganization of industrial complexes that originally grew up within the city's walls has been one of the leitmotifs of European town planning in recent years. The margin for manoeuver has also shrunk in appearance at least. This conversion is a question of retrieval not of building from scratch. The problem is how to link the past with the company's future, assisting the delicate process of transition from the electromechanical era to the electronic by carefully calculated architectural intervention. To begin, the solid early 20th century buildings have been left standing, except for one located at the center which will be razed to make way for an enclosed space, patterned after the great Parisian squares (Place de la Concorde, Place des Vosges, Place Vendôme, etc.) and destined to stimulate socialization among the company's staff.

This layout with a central square provides a stimulus for a silent revolution. Volumes and materials remain unchanged, yet rehabilitation goes beyond a simple face-lifting exercise. In reality, behind the old façades — symbolizing the site's industrial function and history — lies the changing structural pattern. Under the square, in the recesses of the hillside there is a parking area for a thousand vehicles, sports center, multi-purpose hall for meetings and shows, a restaurant, maintenance installations, etc. The monumentalism of the machine age is matched by a "non-architecture" that changes the substance while the form is left virtually intact.

The closed spatial system becomes in its turn the connective tissue of the various buildings facing onto the square. Schlumbergers are among the world's leading manufacturers of measuring instruments; the company is a multinational company with a mosaic of affiliated firms each with premises more or less differentiated from the central block. Hence the need to establish a structural identity without altering the character of the individual units. This link is reinforced by the insertion of collective services and recreation spaces along the concourse: a sports center, assembly room, show rooms, a restaurant, travel agencies, banks, shops, post offices, a health clinic. "An industrial forum," as Schlumberger defines the new complex.

Cohesion is the key, integrating the site with the city, the industrial past with the electronic future, satellite companies with the parent company. But the relationships do not end here, there is also the need to attune technology to the natural landscape. This problem is resolved through a harmonious, non-traumatic graft: an urban park (created by Alexander Chemetoff), subdivided into four sections surrounding the old buildings. The park area breaks up the structural grid and forms internal areas of green. "Construction has often meant the death of nature, obliterating it. So whenever I'm tackling a rehabilitation project I tend to do the opposite, to favor nature against the city. Only at this point it is a new kind of nature, constructed, not fake natural. At Montrouge the internal court is spotted with objects belonging to Schlumberger's output. It is an adaptation of a craft workshop where the products are set outside on display. The theme of nature is fascinating: it is sure to be one of the great themes of the immediate future."

Imperceptibly the automatized environment merges with the physical environment. With the passing of the seasons the forms of the plants will change, as will the colors, sounds, scents hovering in the air. Sinuous elastic membranes and catwalks over the water evoke the idea of a harmonious synthesis between old and new, all this within a cheerful framework intended to mask a sense of melancholy and sterility that inevitably hangs over factories from the pioneering age of industrialism.

From the container to the content: the rearrangement of the external setting, the office planning and the complete renewal of the interiors will profoundly affect the organization of work. Staircases, elevators, windows, garden spaces and other changes will make working conditions more comfortable and at the same time meet certain functional necessities, avoiding fragmentation and increasing efficiency. This all demonstrates how at the moment of execution the architect's sphere of action widened out, and suggests that renewal of the obsolescent, far from being hampered by restrictions can open up new horizons to artistic practice. This can be done without recourse to the obvious solution of demolition and mass evacuations. "Rehabilitation goes on simultaneously with the evolution of a social and productive reality. At Montrouge two thousand people carry on with their work at the same time that the contractors are busy with the conversion. One has continually to match the needs of construction with

Rehabilitation can provide an opportunity for facing fundamental architectural subjects throughout history: building onto what already exists. When redesigning the historic city it is important not to denature the architecture of the past but, more humbly, to limit oneself to bringing out the continuity with tomorrow's architecture.

329. Bernard Plattner at work on the tensile structure covering the central "Forum."

330. The Compteurs factory, Montrouge, 1924.

331. The industrial complex built early in the 20th century as it was before the current renovation.

332. Products of Schlumberger's Montrouge factory: they are all systems connected with measurement, from meters for gas, water and electricity consumption to methods of measuring the presence of petroleum in the ground.

330

those of production, restoration on a living body, not industrial archeology. I should add that we are witnessing some interesting developments. When work began a year ago, people were detached from the project. Now they are involved, they have taken it over. Parallel to the metamorphosis of the walls and masonry there has been a change in the people."

Rehabilitation can provide an opportunity for facing fundamental architectural subjects throughout history: building onto what already exists. When redesigning the historic city it is important not to denature the architecture of the past but, more humbly, to limit oneself to bringing out the continuity with tomorrow's architecture. Any kind of separation would be artificial, a pathological symptom. "What is more," an American critic has observed, "the costs of this humane approach are lower than those of a conventional dictatorial solution."

331

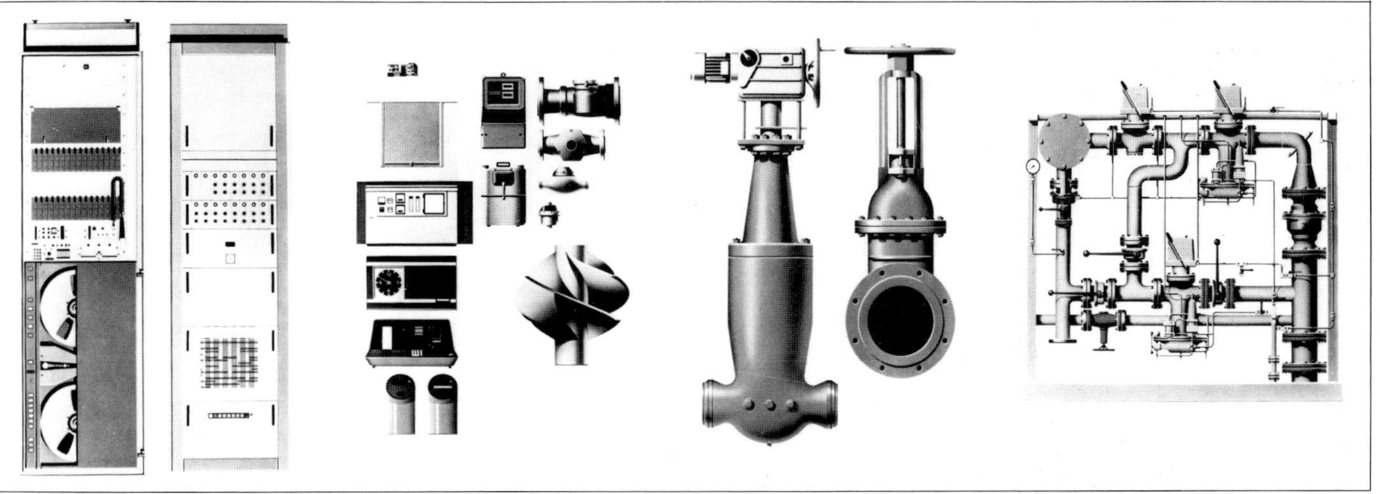

332

333. Early sketches for the central park and Forum of collective services shared by all the companies in the group.

334. Shed roofing of the buildings for heavy engineering.

335. Parisian squares laid out on the principle of closed urban spaces: internal garden at the Schlumberger complex, enclosed by the (a) *preserved industrial buildings,* (b) *Place des Vosges,* (c) *Place Vendôme* (d) *Place de la Concorde.*

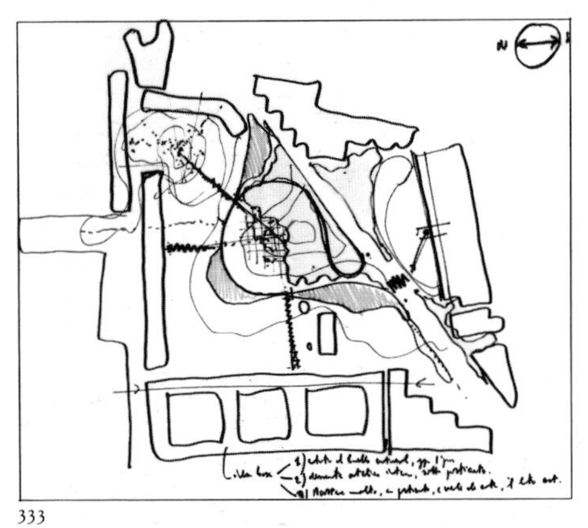

333

334

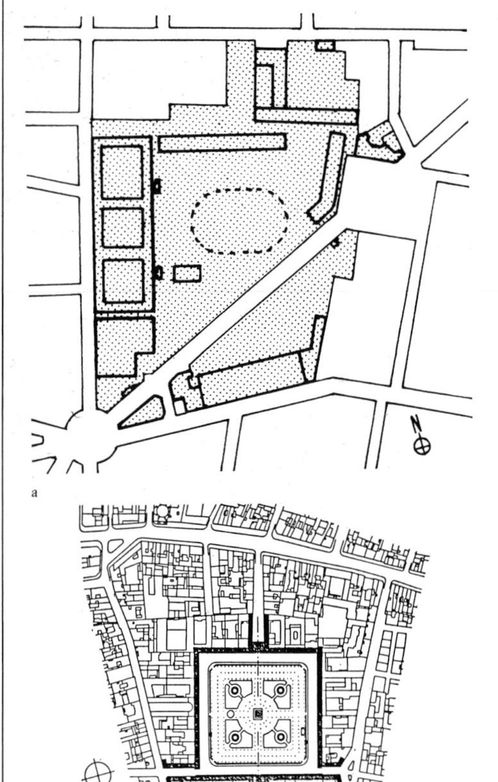

a

b

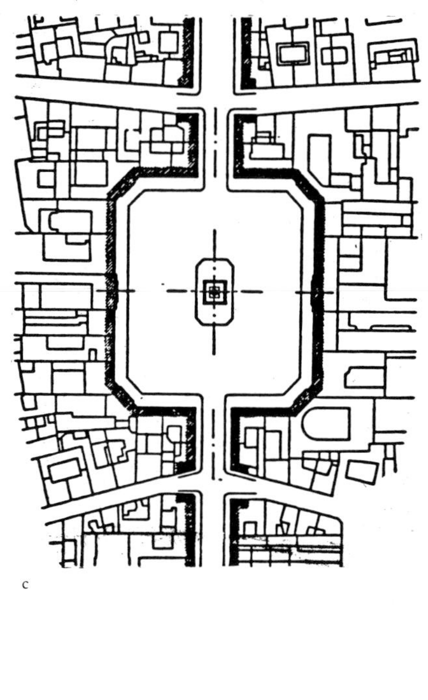

c

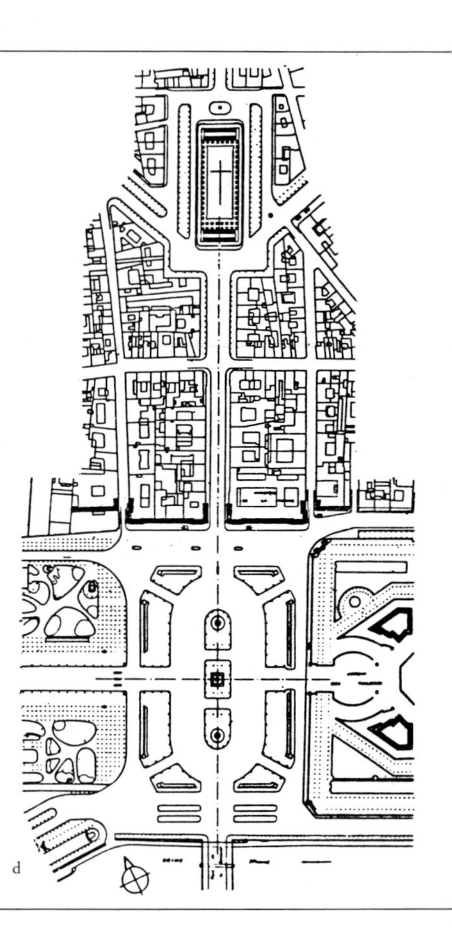

d

335

336. Brickwork making use of rejects of industrial production as raw material.
337. Detail of façade.

336

337

338. Longitudinal and cross sections of the garden, showing the bordering industrial buildings and the great central hill with parking for 900 vehicles, post office, travel agency, bar, restaurant, gymnasium, conference rooms, meeting rooms, exhibition rooms.

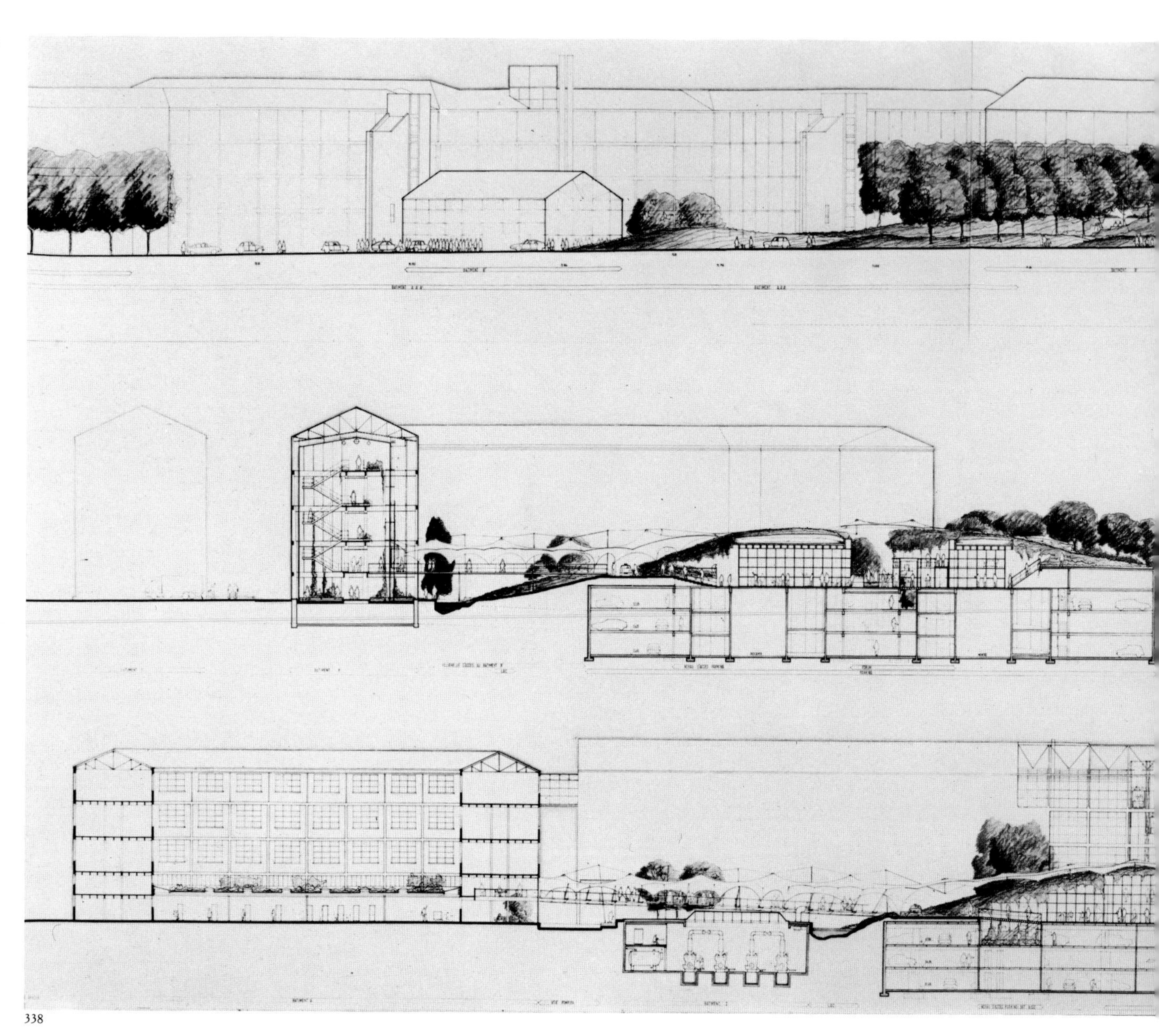

338

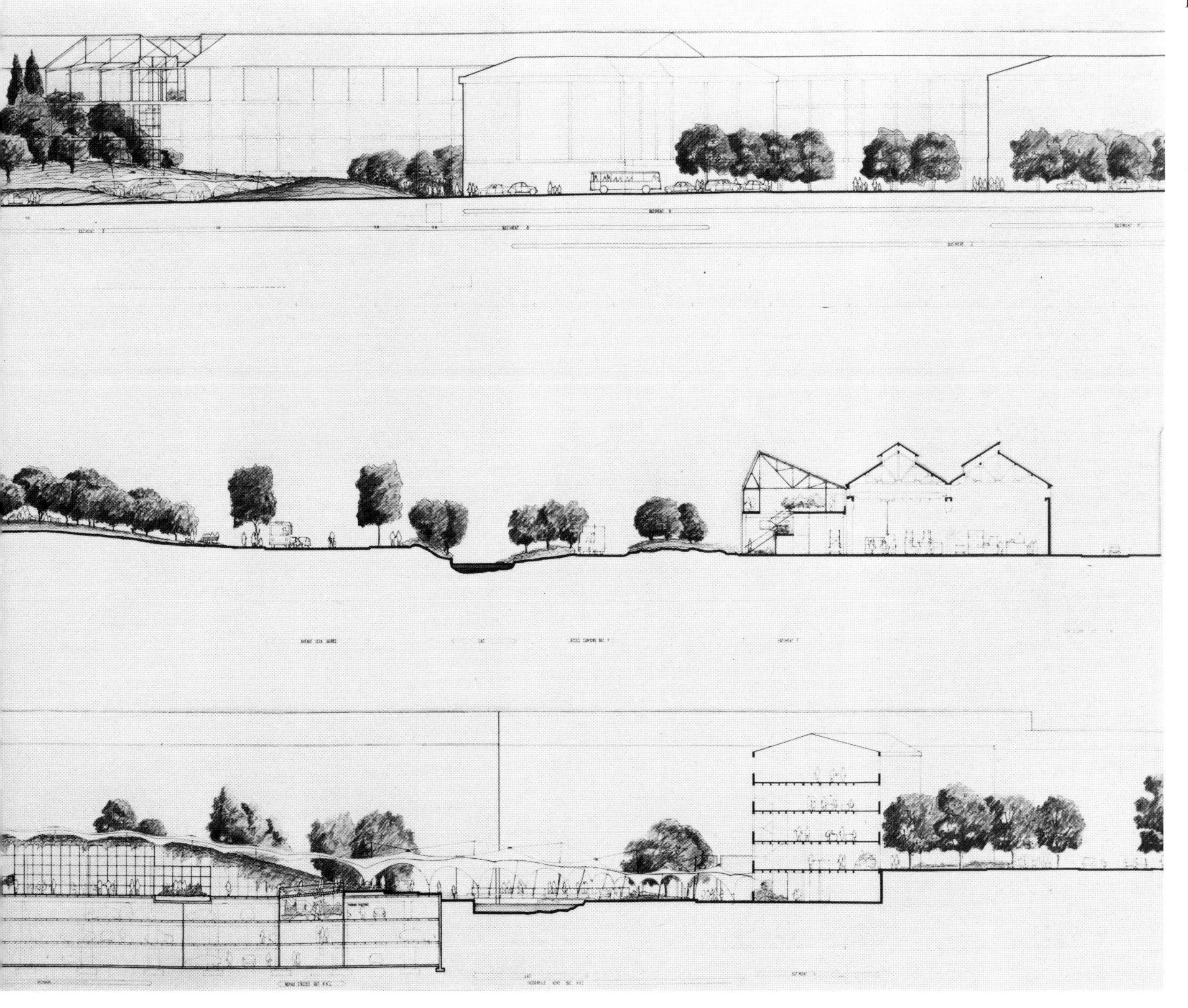

339. The garden reproduced in colors appropriate to the four seasons: (a) *spring,* (b) *summer,* (c) *autumn,* (d) *winter.*

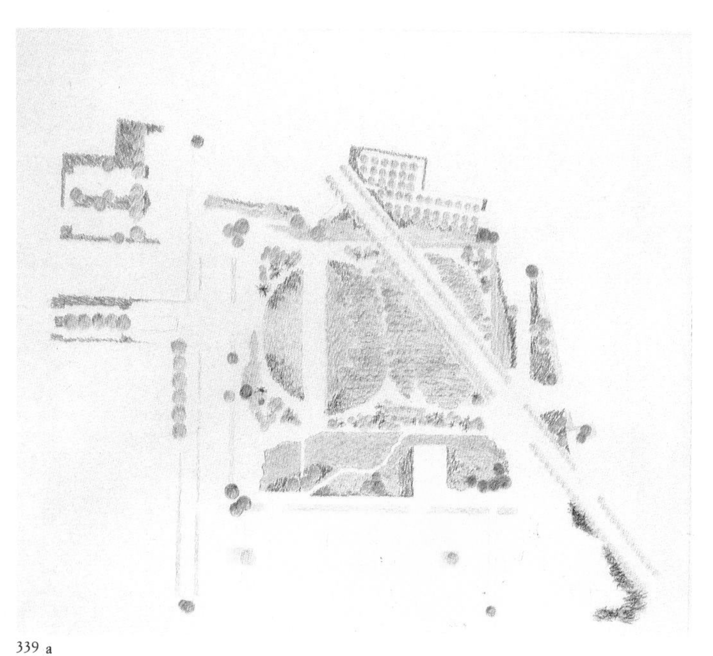

339 a

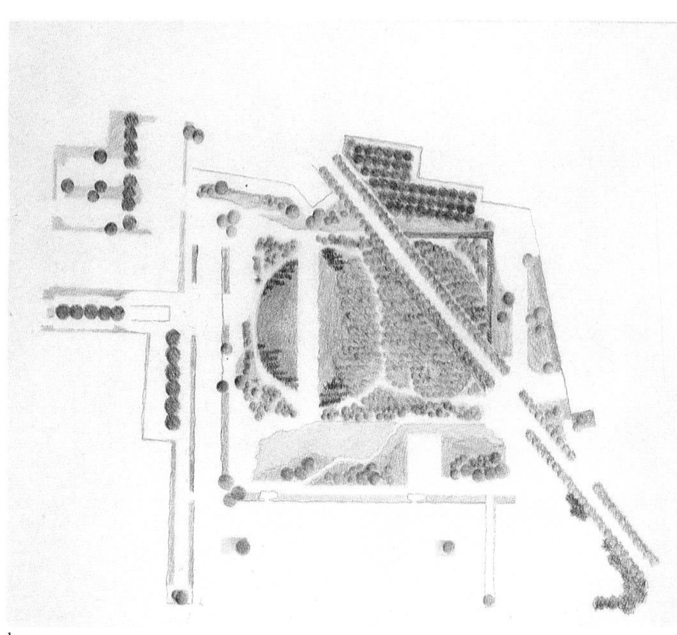

b

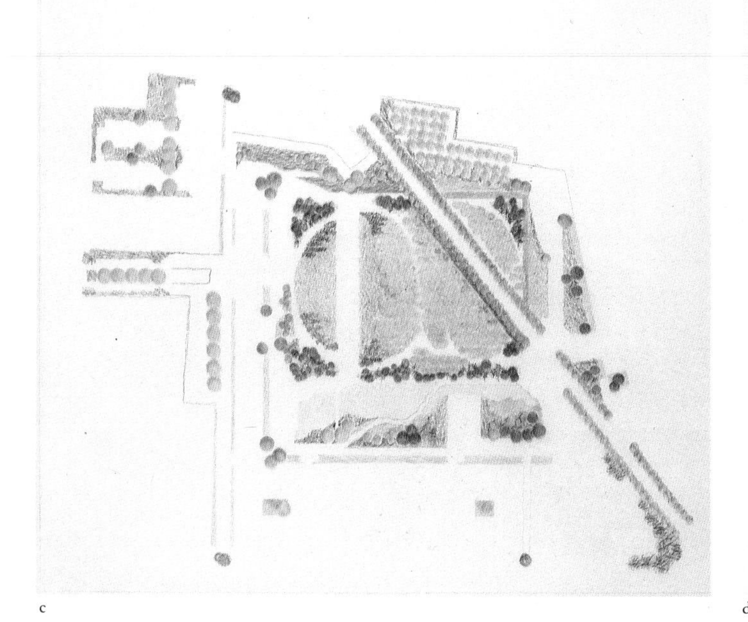

c

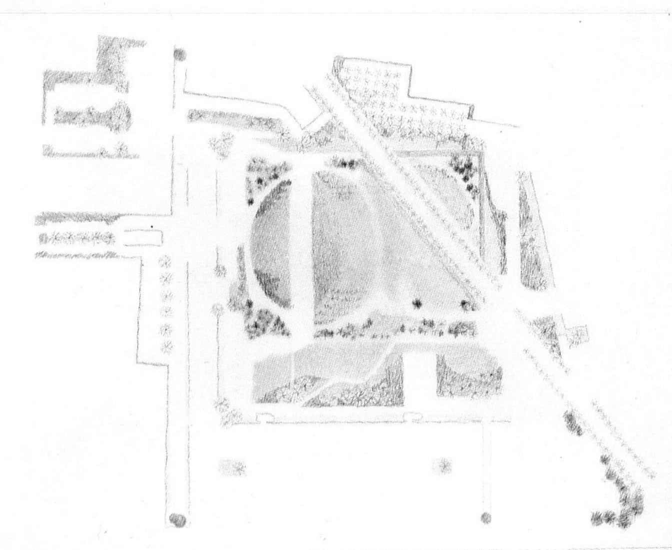

d

340. *Study of the coloring of plants and nature during the four seasons.*

341. *Studies of relationship between the garden and buildings bordering it:* (a) *street-block,* (b) *street,* (c) *lakeside,* (d) *courtyards.*

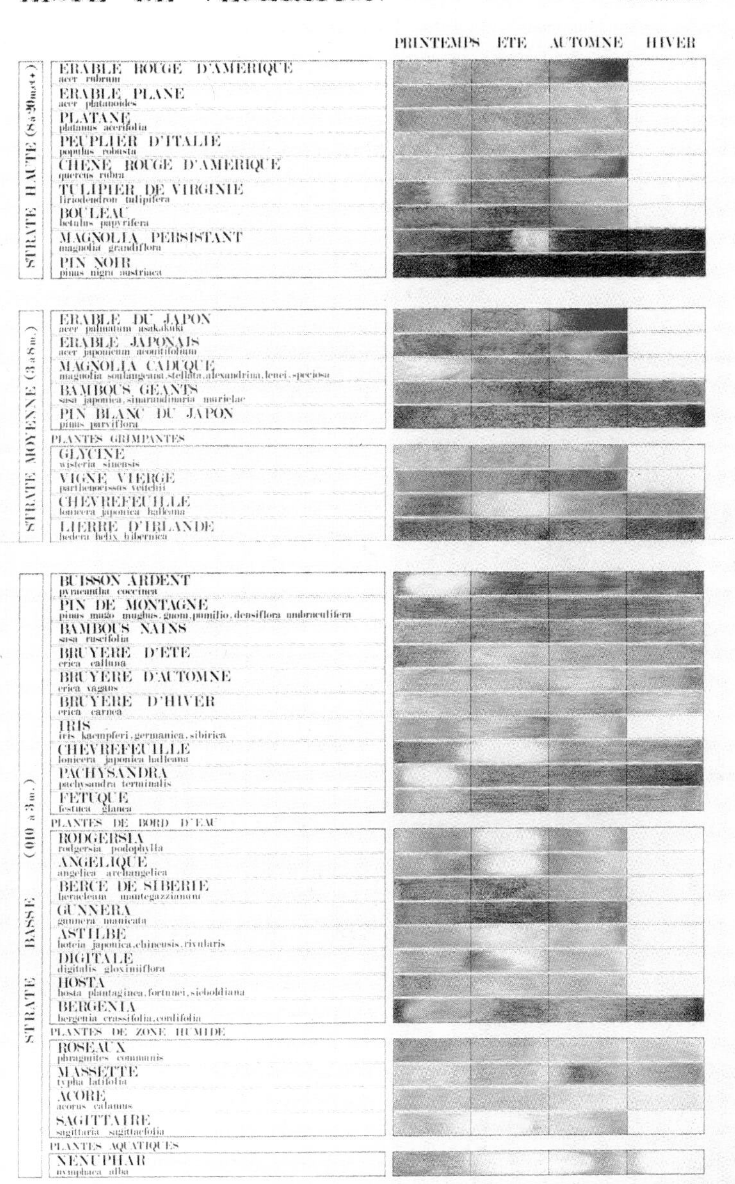

340

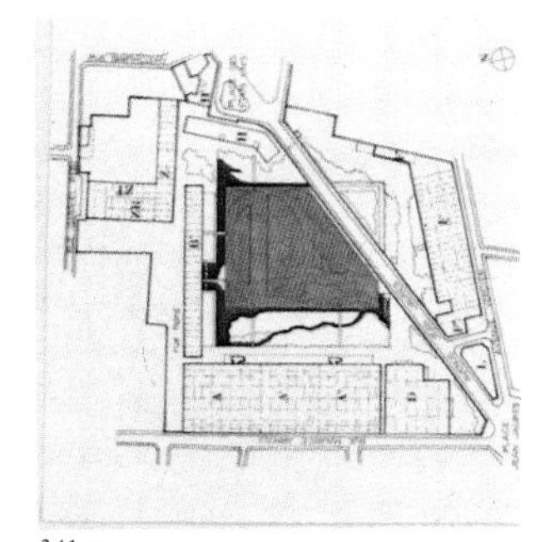

341 a

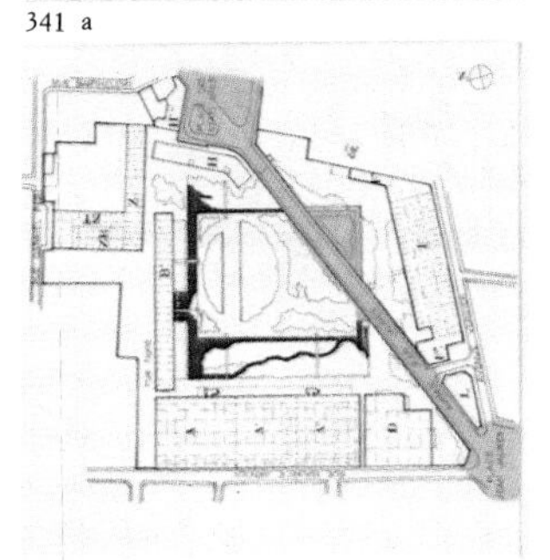

b

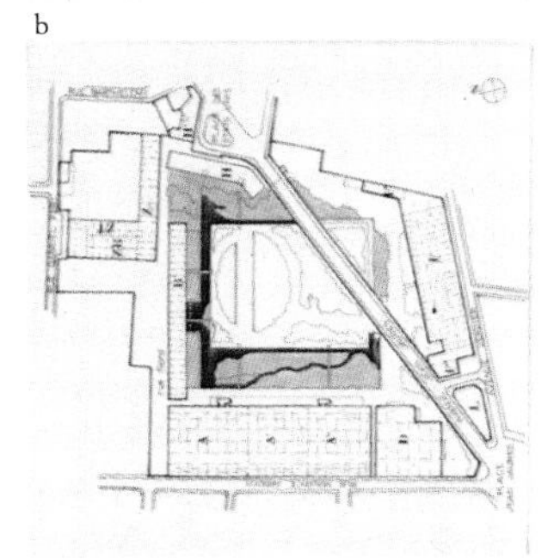

c

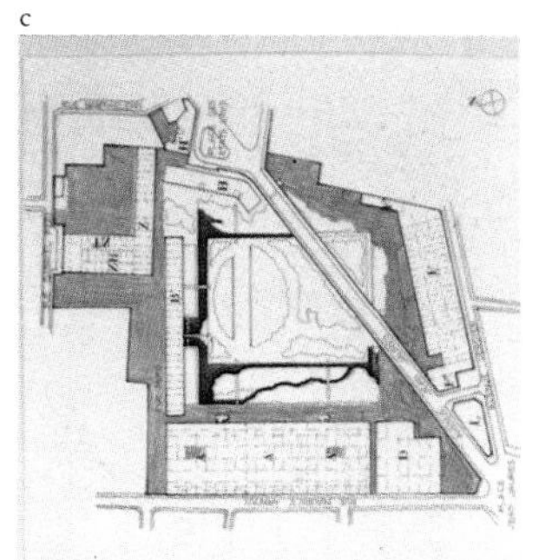

d

342. Longitudinal sections through the street: this space is lit from above through the translucent teflon structure. It constitutes a sheltered outdoor space.

343. Section of the hill transversing to the street: the latter provides access for the public, employees and research workers to the various facilities of the underground car park.

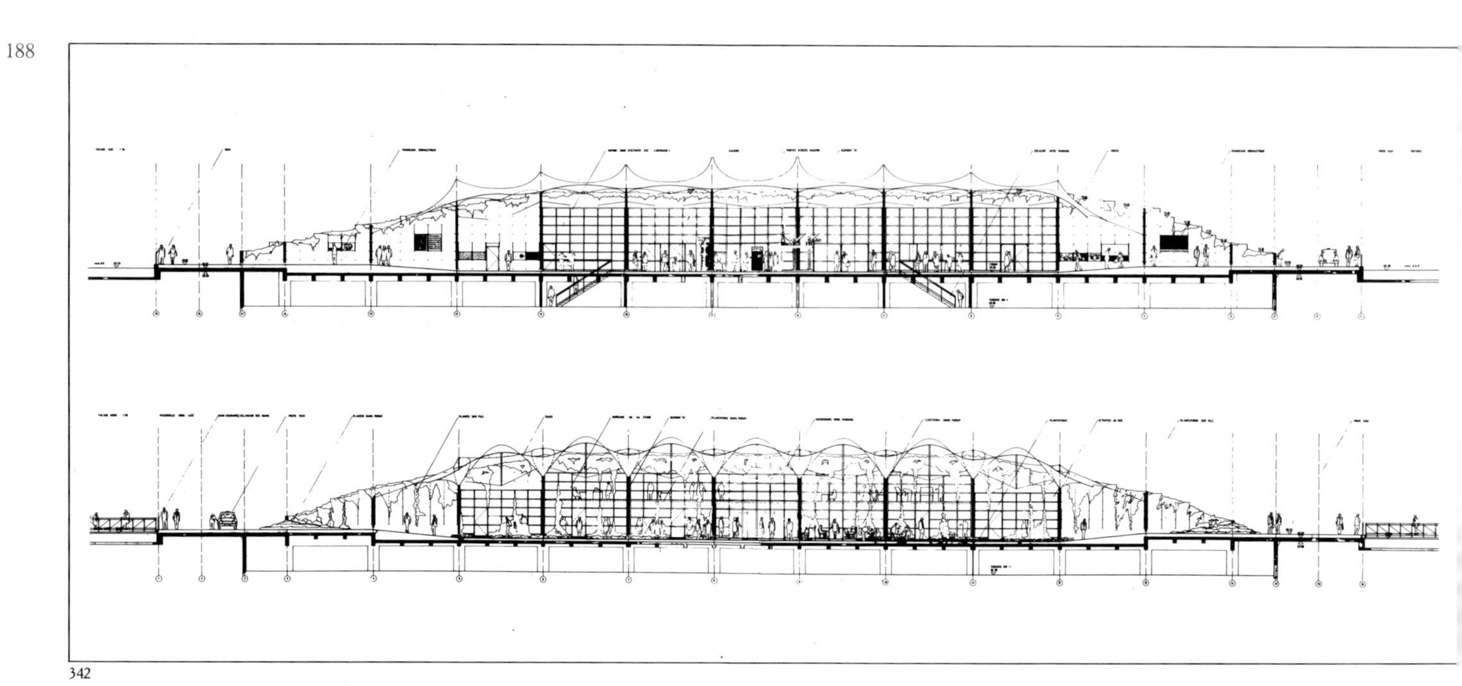

342

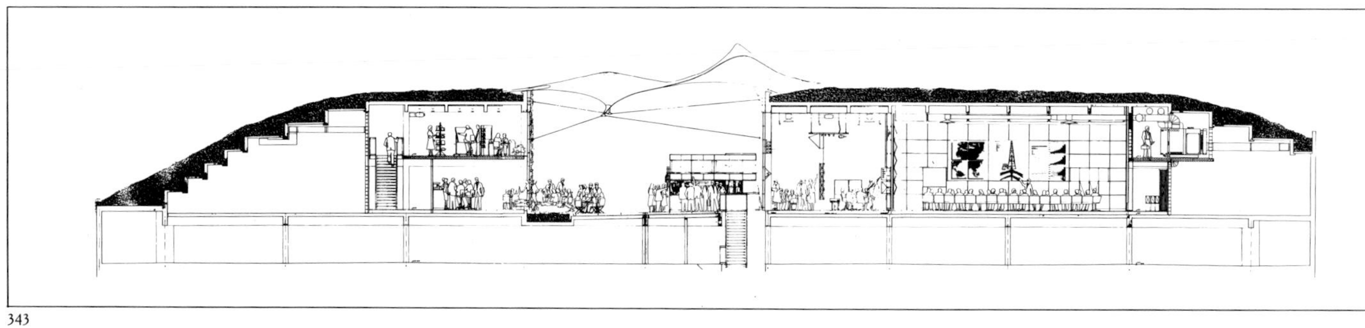

343

344. Plan of activities contained by the hill.

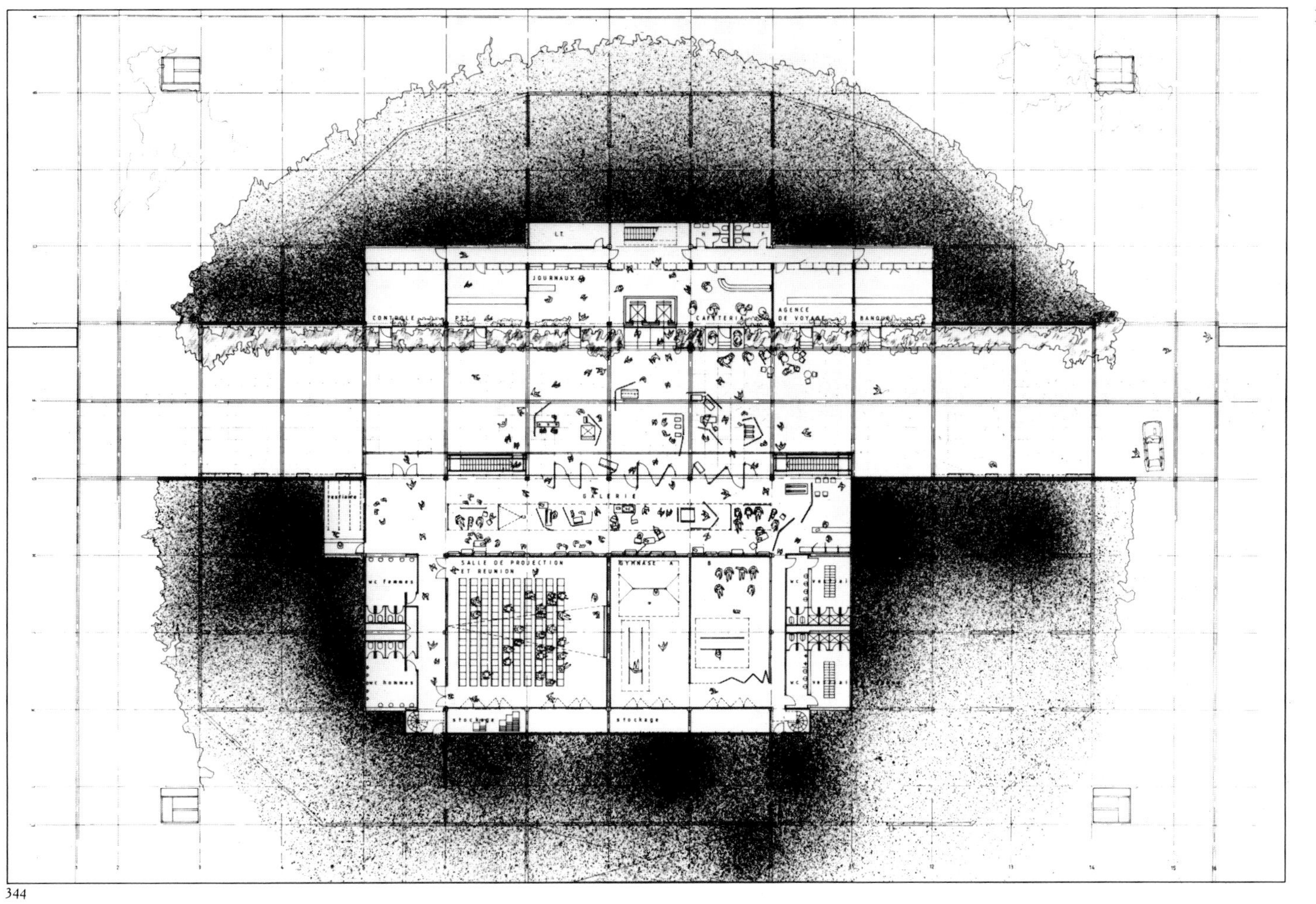

344

345. Elevation of the south façade, north of the garden.

346. Interior of the offices: the central area is for service activities and contains all the data processing and electronic equipment.

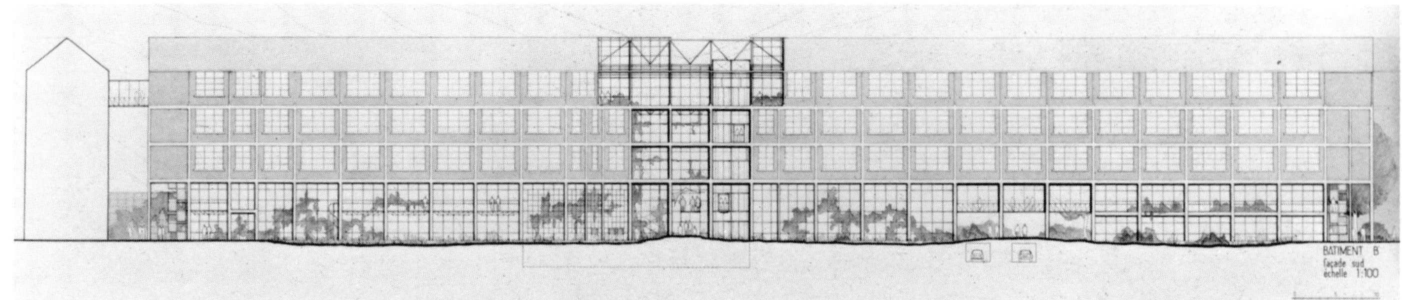

345

346

347. *Section through the access node of one of the big linear buildings.*

348. *Construction detail of the external glazing system.*

349. *Photo of the site during construction of the central access node: a great vertical greenhouse by which the quality of the garden is related to the building's interior.*

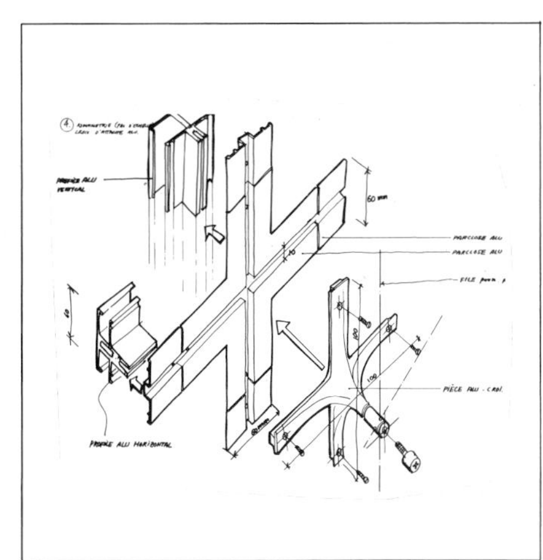

348

349

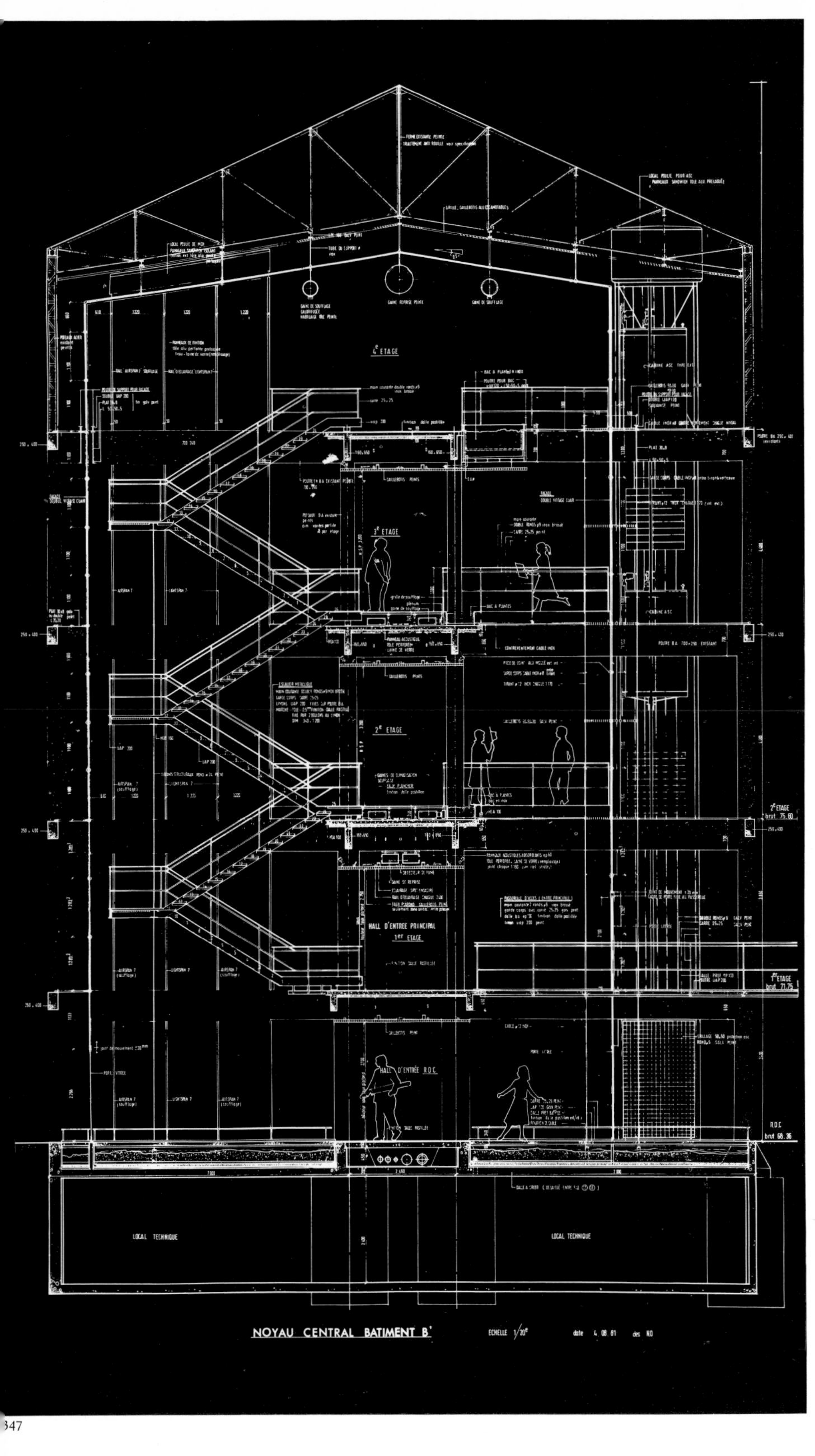

347

350. Detail of a rooflight after conversion of the spaces to laboratories and offices.
351. View at night.

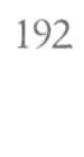

350

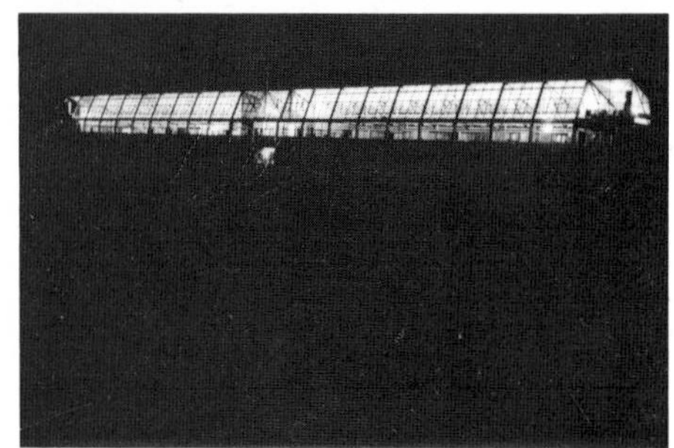

351

52. *View of internal space of offices and laboratories.*
53. *Conditions before renovation work.*

352

353

1980-1982 Bari, Italy
Neighborhood Workshop for local maintenance

194 Client: F.lli Dioguardi Contractors, Bari

Architects and Engineers: Studio Piano/Building Workshop S.r.l. and F.lli Dioguardi Contractors with N. Costantino, S. Pietrogrande, G. Ferracuti, S. Ishida, F. Marano, E. Frigerio, E. Donato, G. Fascioli, C. Teoldi, SES Engineering, L. Malgieri assisted by A. Alto, G. Amendola

Program by Magda Arduino

City maintenance

Zero growth in the city means a new awareness in urban planning philosophy and hence new operative responses. In Italy building is at a standstill and over half of the existing housing was built before 1950. It is not hard to imagine what this implies: the relation between decay and renovation no longer affects old city centers but generally extends to the existing housing stock. Too many recent buildings require substantial repair work and maintenance to ensure a proper level of habitability. How can this be taken care of? Certainly a new technical and entrepreneurial structure will have to be invented, that can be decentralized and which possesses adequate scientific skills to reduce the traumatic effects of "hard-nosed" approaches to reconstruction, such as the often permanent evacuation of inhabitants during maintenance work and the difficulties of economizing.

The Neighborhood Workshop, after the experiment in Otranto's historic town center, has entered a new spatio-temporal dimension. This happened in Bari in a newly constructed district, Japigia, where the mobile unit was installed. The project involved intervention on two levels, one contingent, the other projected towards the future. On the one hand there was the need to adapt the new prefabricated homes built by the client F.lli Dioguardi, to the highest levels of habitability, and on the other an attempt was made to provide the district with a thriving center for progressive renovation operations through involvement of the local inhabitants.

The truly innovatory aspect of the project was the close cooperation with Gianfranco Dioguardi, managing director of the firm of building contractors and lecturer in Industrial Economics and Company Organization at the University of Bari. This was a significant step forward. The solution to the problem of urban decay calls for a reformulation of the way architecture is realized and also a rethinking of the operative logic of the building trade. Without such a change, the philosophy of reuse will remain on the level of previous intentions. "What was at stake in Bari," explains Gianfranco Dioguardi, "was a new concept of the building firm, one that should occur directly in the firm's general organization that participates in the lives of the users of its product, that implements the techniques of feed-back, returning information to the inhabitants in the attempt to administer the building process and the product in the best possible way."

The Neighborhood Workshop becomes, in Dioguardi's own definition, "the city's maintenance firm," an operative reality which, without restricting its managerial, technological and scientific scope, projects itself outwards and accepts the contribution of craft workers. Indeed, actually stimulating their skills and bringing them back into the productive processes. Piano and Dioguardi's objectives converge. If the aim is to cut the costs of urban renewal in economic and, above all, human terms, then local craftsmen will have to be re-equipped, provided with up-to-date, effective and easy to use instruments previously all too often manipulated and mystified by the building industry and "pure technicians."

In this way the "community architect" becomes allied with the "new building manager." This is inevitable. "There is no use," says Piano, "in asking the occupants what they want. The answer will not come from them but from the mass media speaking through them. Even if you wanted to psychoanalyze them there just is not the time. What we have to do is to get them involved in 'our' (our/their) workshop. Otherwise the technological commitment is hollow. At the same time, a Neighborhood Workshop that did not have notable innovations in organization, equipment and techniques of intervention would be completely useless." The architect and the contractor share responsibility for the maintenance workshop. Here in Bari, moreover, the agreement was drawn up at the beginning of the design process. The new Japigia works were conceived according to avant-garde principles of construction so that the issues of rehabilitation could be taken further than preventive care and aim to favor reappropriation of the dwellings (constructed to a standard prefabricated typology using industrialized methods) by the occupants themselves. The occupants participate actively in the creation and renovation of their habitat. At the same time, participation has to be understood within clearly defined boundaries. "I do not believe in participation as an intellectual phase at the start of the process, because the type of information that people receive has already been manipulated at its source, falsified by conventional models. But what does interest me is the capacity to respond to real needs, to supply the instruments of awareness and, if possible, of future modification."

354

A new technical and entrepreneurial structure will have to be invented that can be decentralized and which possesses adequate scientific skills to reduce the traumatic effects of "hard-nosed" approaches to reconstruction.

354. Meeting with Giandomenico Amendola, Attilio Alto, Gianfranco Dioguardi and Enrico Frigerio.

355. Aerial view of the Quartiere Japigia; in the background, the city of Bari.

356. Early sketches.

357. Elevation of the building with external canopy sheltering outdoor activities.

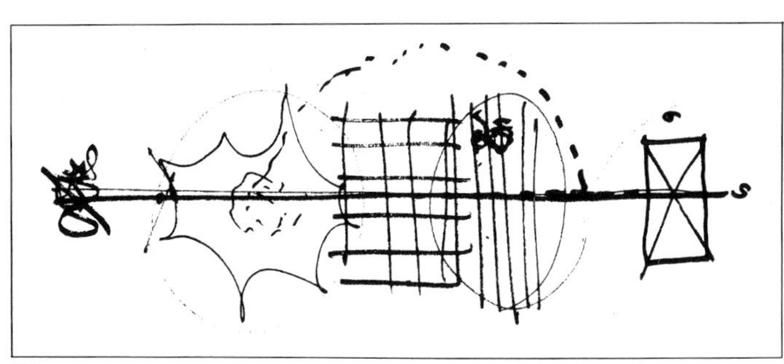
356

355

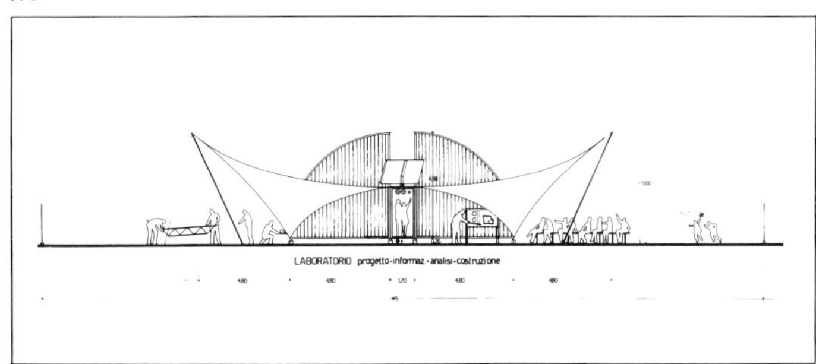

357

358. *Longitudinal elevation of the Workshop.*

359. *Plan of Workshop.*

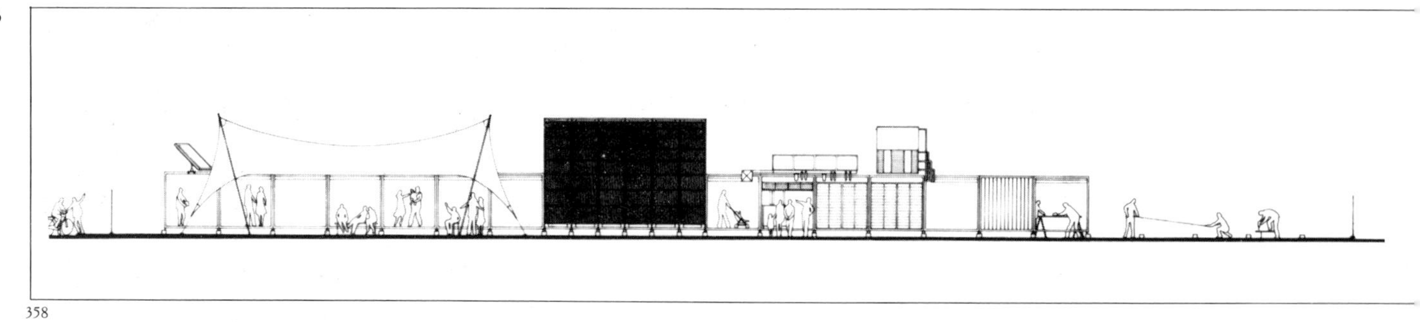

358

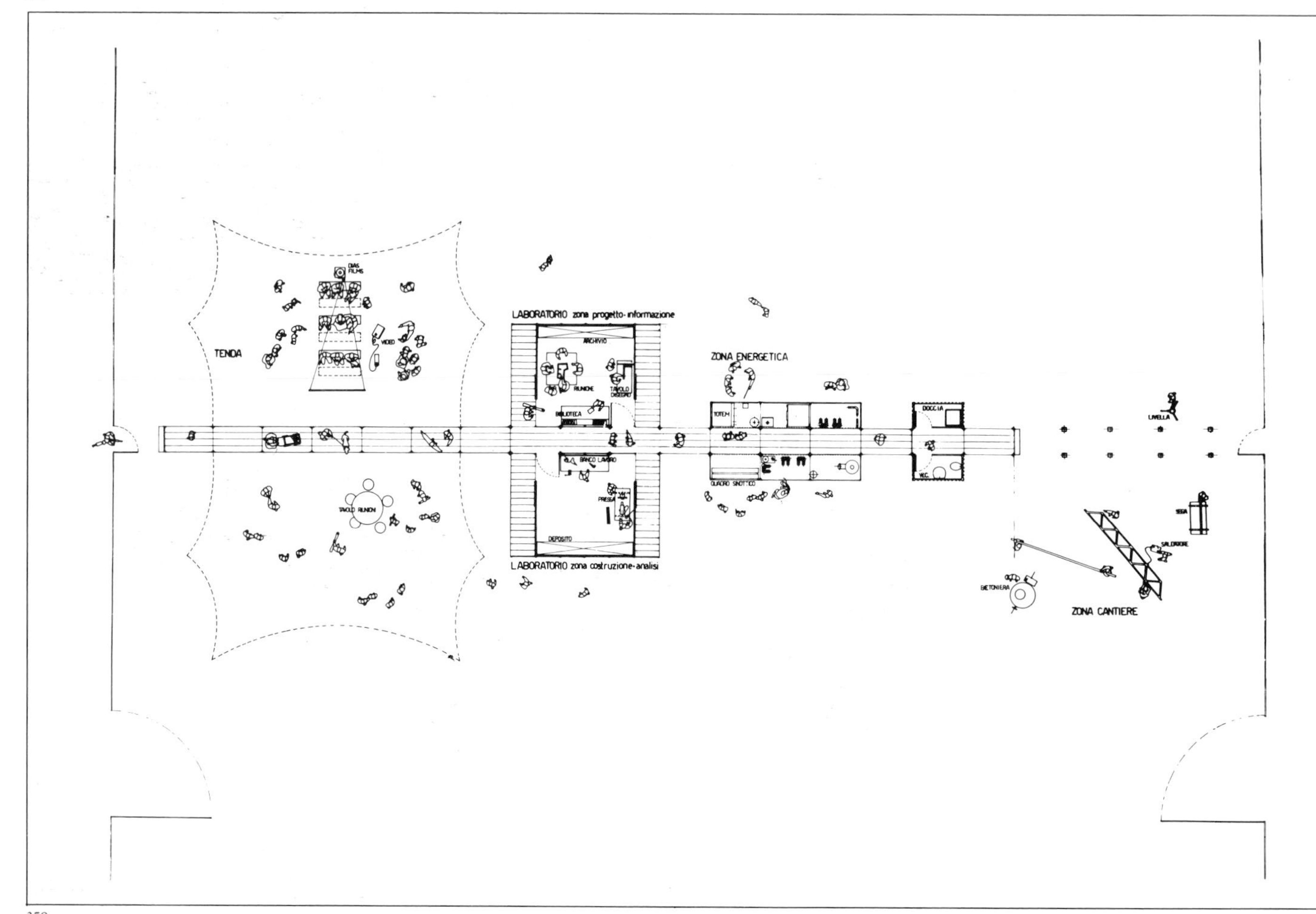

359

360. View of the completed Workshop. The canopies protect a space for the community's use.

360

361. Work meeting.

362. Partial view of an existing façade.

363. Plan for maintenance of the buildings' energy supplies: the scientific approach underlies this kind of planning.

361

362

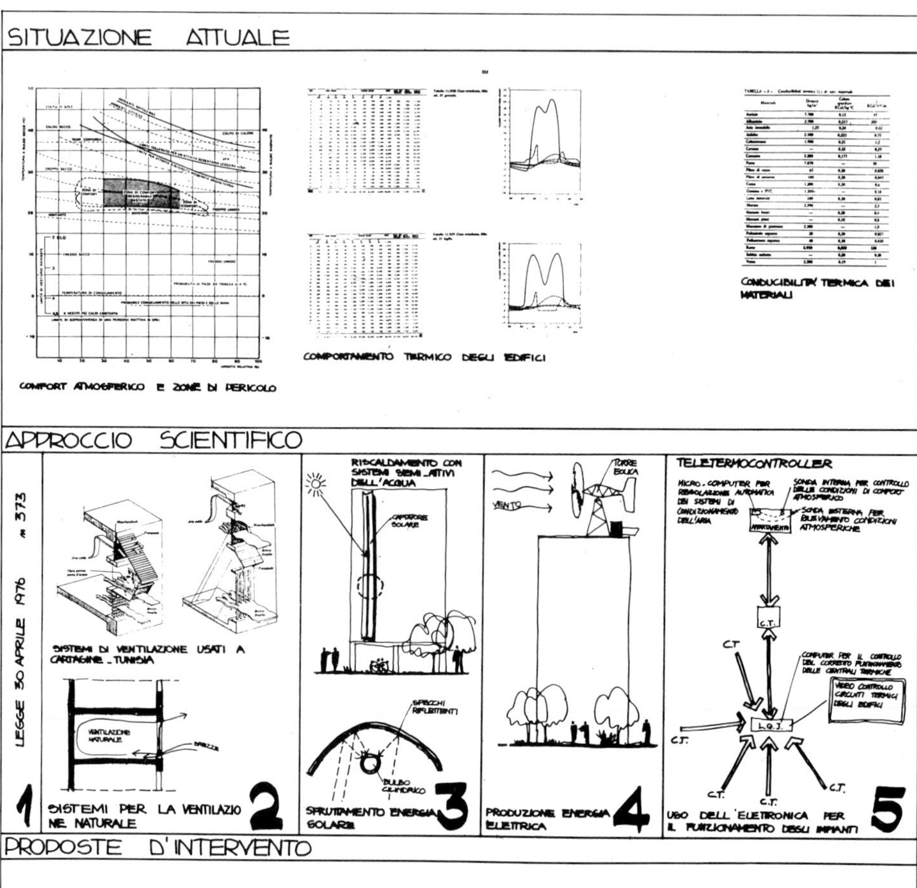

363

364, 365. *The documentation of experience, dialogue and communication is one of the Workshop's educational functions.*

366. *View of an area to be shared.*

367. *Experimental maintenance work.*

368. *Section of an experimental evolving home-type being tried out at the Workshop: it is to be used for various tests related to natural climate control and heating.*

369. *Plan of one of the experiments with housing types.*

364

365

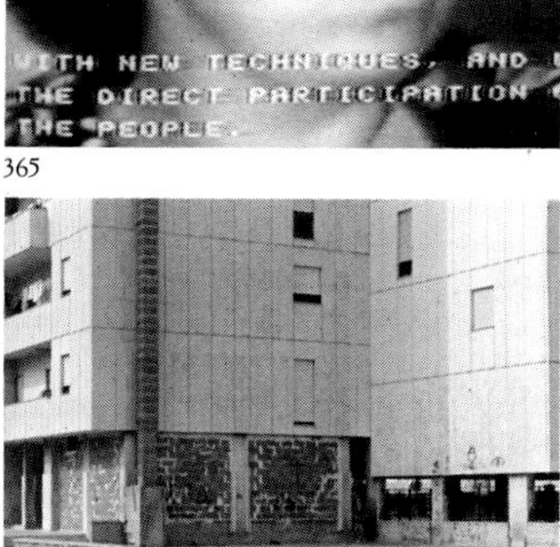

366

367

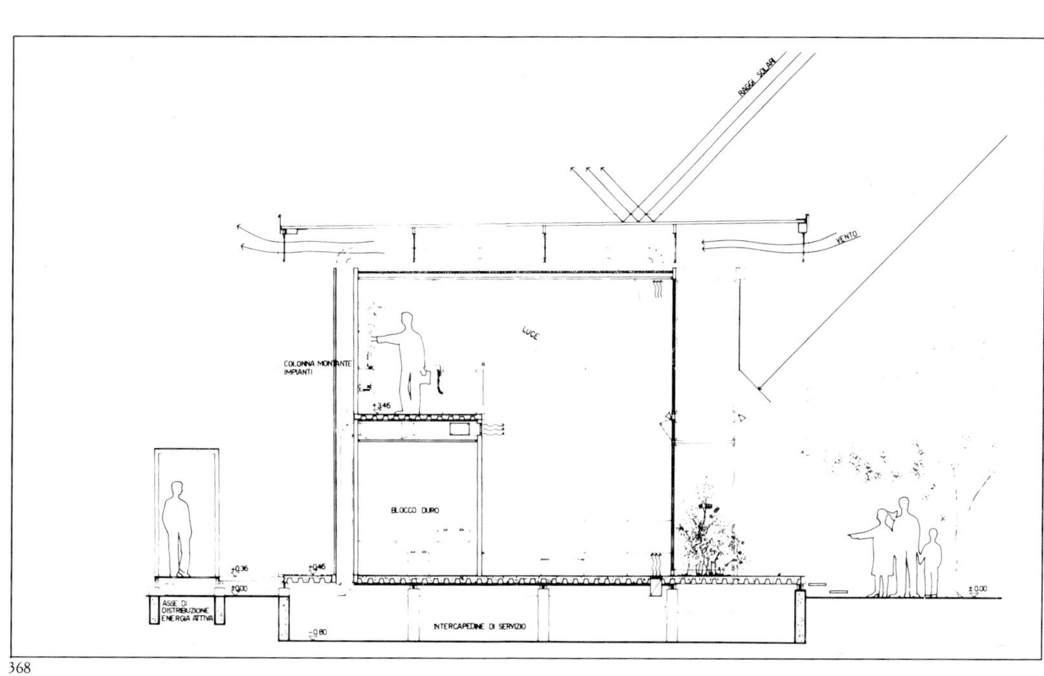

368

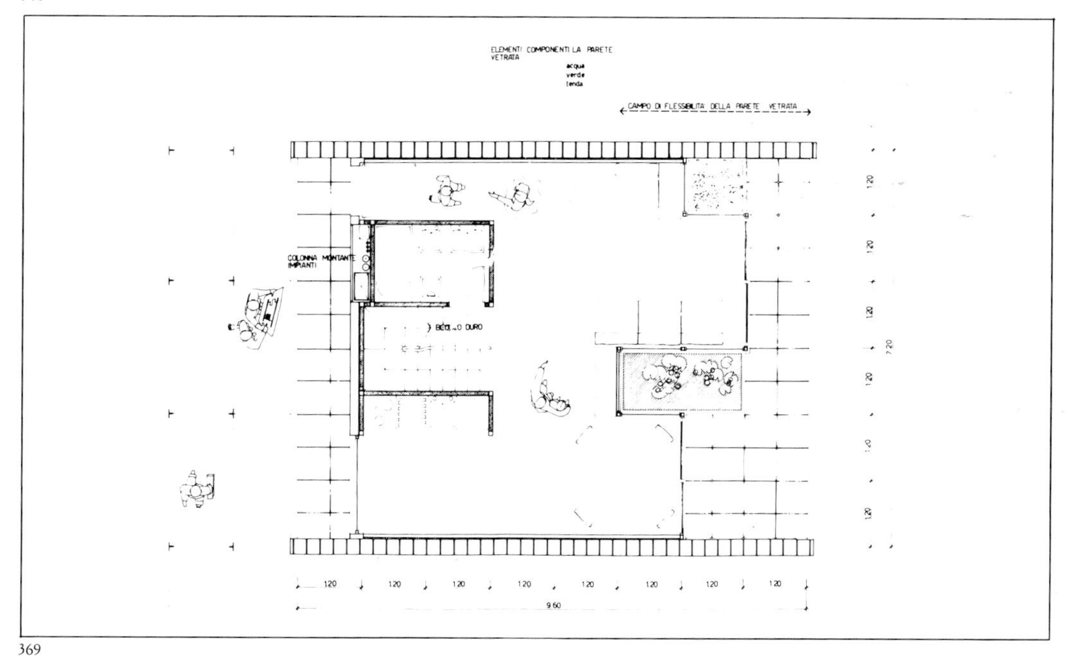

369

1981 Turin, Italy
Restructuring a street block in the ancient city center

Work as culture

Client: Commune of Turin (Housing Department)
Architects: Studio Piano/Building Workshop S.r.l. with S. Ishida, F. Marano, R. Ruocco, E. Frigerio and F. Icardi
Program by Magda Arduino

From the welfare model to the active approach, Piano has realized a broad range of work. As an architect he reflects a concern with the revaluation of interior space: how to transform the home into an environment made to the measure of man. The impact with the urban reality deepens the issues but the terms of the equation are unchanged. "It is only by reappropriating space that one can appreciate the quality of living. By living through the process of construction yourself, you avoid waste, stopping consumerism and effectively distinguishing between fundamental factors and the superfluous, marginal ones. The occupant then accepts a level of finish and fittings which he would never accept as a client of the welfare state. The Neighborhood Workshop evades the hegemony of the bourgeois model and also of transforming work into culture."

Turin, with its pronounced flair for craftsmanship and manufacturing traditions is the ideal terrain for implementation of a soft technology to the building site. The project moves along the same lines as the "EH" scheme, devised for the new, adapting it to the old. The conversion plan is articulated in two separate phases. In the primary phase the professional structure (a contractor) will carry out the work requiring specialists and heavyweight equipment, the insulation and soundproofing of the apartments, creation of collective spaces and services on the ground floor, energy retrieval, use of advanced electronic data-processing systems (Videotel, Videolento, Telemedicina), retrieval of solid wastes and, finally, preparation of a sample house to provide training for the future occupants.

Once the structures have been rehabilitated, the second phase begins: the inhabitants, who have been moved during the first phase, will finish the work on their homes. In exchange for this work, the Commune of Turin, owner of the properties, will make rent cuts and extensions of leases. During the self-build operations, the occupants can count on help from the Neighborhood Workshop, which will provide technical advice, store materials, tools and control costs.

The details of the project envisage restructuring a pilot street block bounded by Via Stampatori, Vicolo Santa Maria and Via Barbaroux. The aim is to relate the different structures of the complex to one another harmoniously and integrate the complex as a whole with its urban setting. Obstacles will be demolished, thoroughfares laid out for public use, and provision made for garden areas and places where people can meet. The Neighborhood Workshop, on the ground floor between the two courtyards, forms the backbone of the entire residential block and itself acts as a physical link (because of its strategic position) and also as a social one (through contacts between the people who come for training and advice).

"Living the future in an old neighborhood" is the slogan that sums up the planning approach: a 'third way' which is neither building from scratch nor formal, museum-type restoration. In this sense, rehabilitation of the old is meant to renew a dimension of urban life, both internally and externally in touch with the times. A process of growth that is inextricably bound up with a qualitative breakthrough in the individual and social patterns of behavior on the part of the inhabitants. "Because of the absence of information, the legislative, technical and administrative have dimininished the occupants' responsibilities and turned them into passive clients, lacking control over their own homes. A new way of living necessarily implies a new type of occupant. The home is not just a social service but an autonomous and responsive space."

Authentic, active participation is in its turn dependent on the dissemination and understanding of the techniques needed to transform the housing system. Hence the need to redefine the urban construction process. A new generation of technologies, materials and equipment is easily available on the market: one merely has either to select or, possibly, reinvent them relating each to a new context. At this point the occupant's participation is no longer limited to simple face-lifting operations, but will affect flooring, plumbing and sanitary equipment, tiling, painting, etc. This can be taken even further when one realizes that the interiors of the homes are so structured as to give wide scope for evolution.

The Turin project (together with the Molo Vecchio project in Genoa) constitutes a new and perfected model of micro-site-engineering. No alternative formulas seem at present relevant to the problem of renewing old residential neighborhoods. "The ancient city centers represent a complex, lacerated, fragmented reality in social, legal and economic terms. Construction site megastructures have no use here. What is needed is a microstructure operating on a local scale. The self-build inhabitant is the grass-roots reality of site-engineering, followed by the craftsman, then the small building contractor. Once you get beyond this scale, everything gets more cumbersome."

"It is only by reappropriating space that one can appreciate the quality of living. By living through the process of construction yourself, you avoid waste, stopping consumerism and effectively distinguishing between fundamental factors and the superfluous ones."

370, 371. Views of the building earmarked for the experiment in rehabilitation.

370

371

372. Plan of the building with two inner courtyards typical of housing in Turin; the building's central axis will house the Neighborhood Workshop on the ground floor.

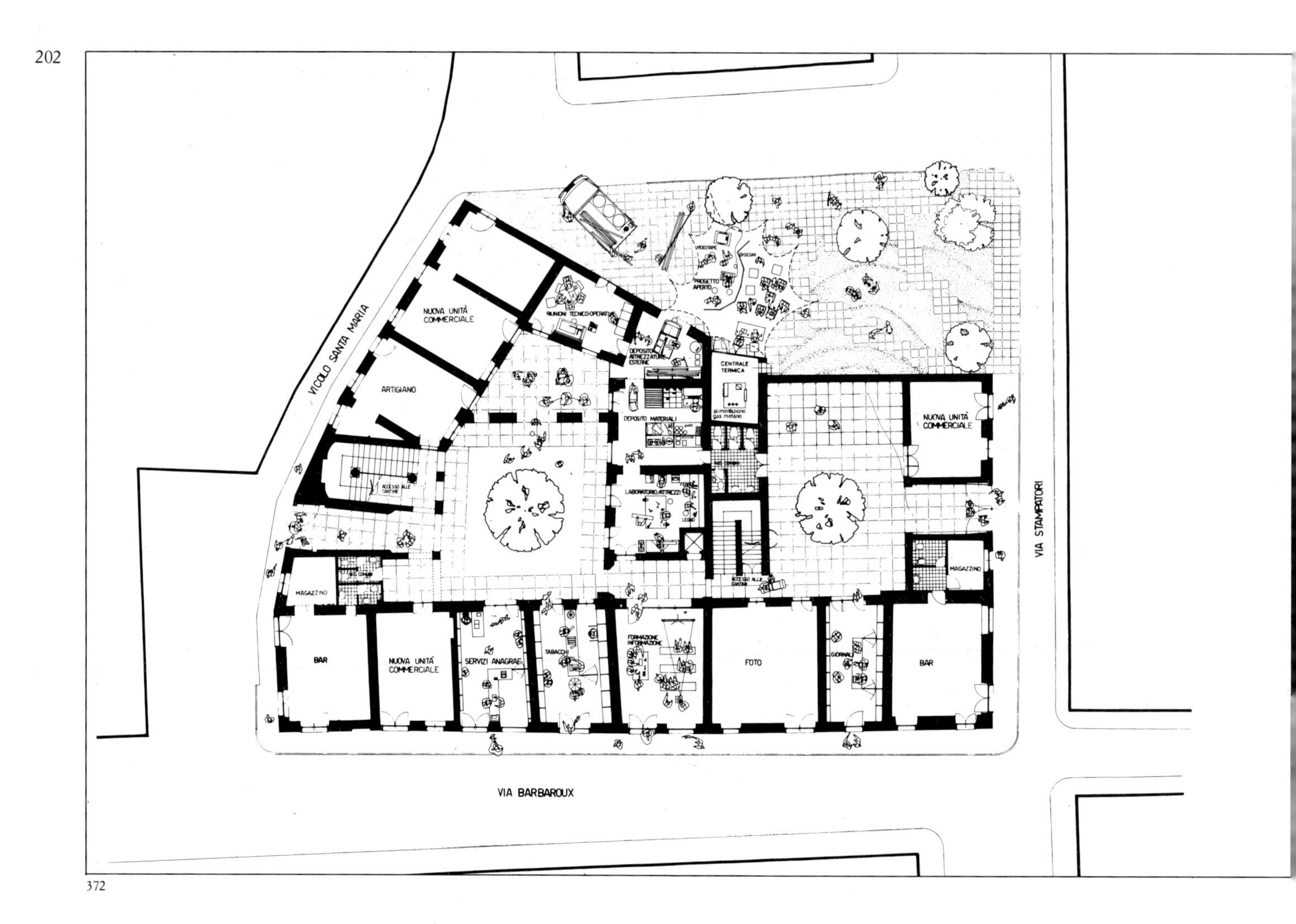

372

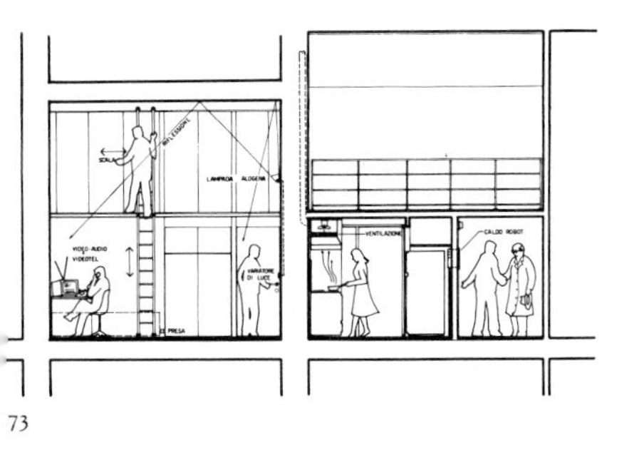

73

373. *Section of a home: the primary space consists of the existing masonry load-bearing walls while the interior arrangements can be designed and modified as the occupants desire, with the aid of the Neighborhood Workshop.*

374. *Section of the building through the axis of the Neighborhood Workshop.*

375. *Section of street-block between Via Stampatori and Vicolo Santa Maria.*

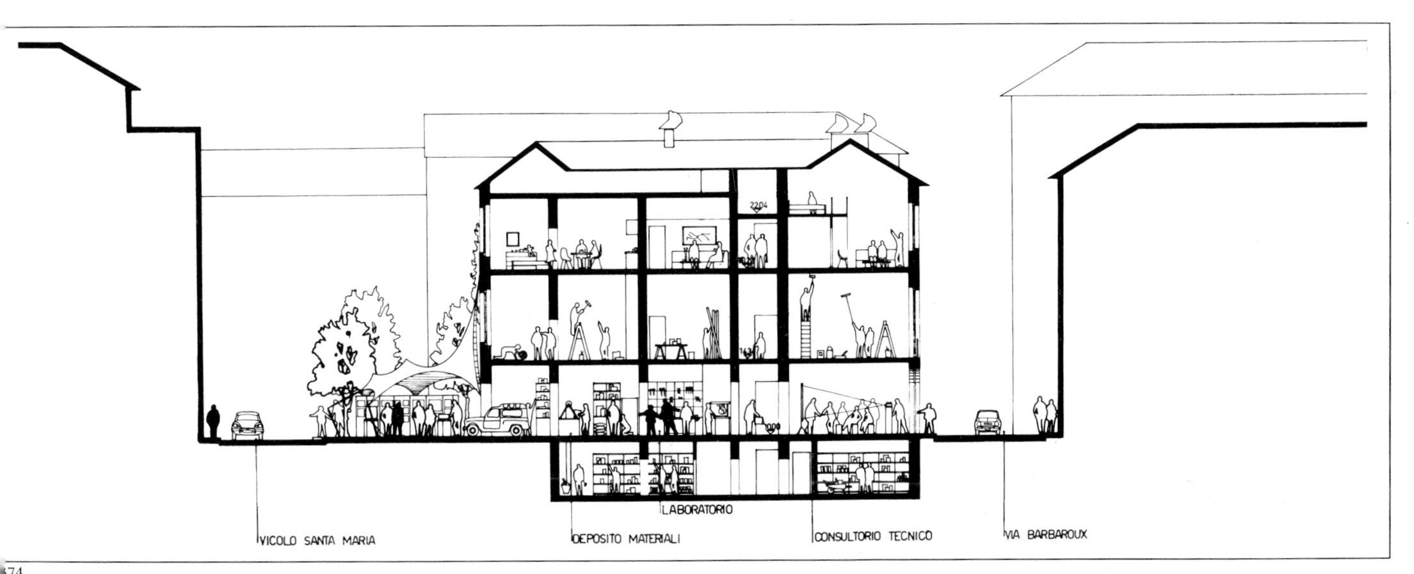

374

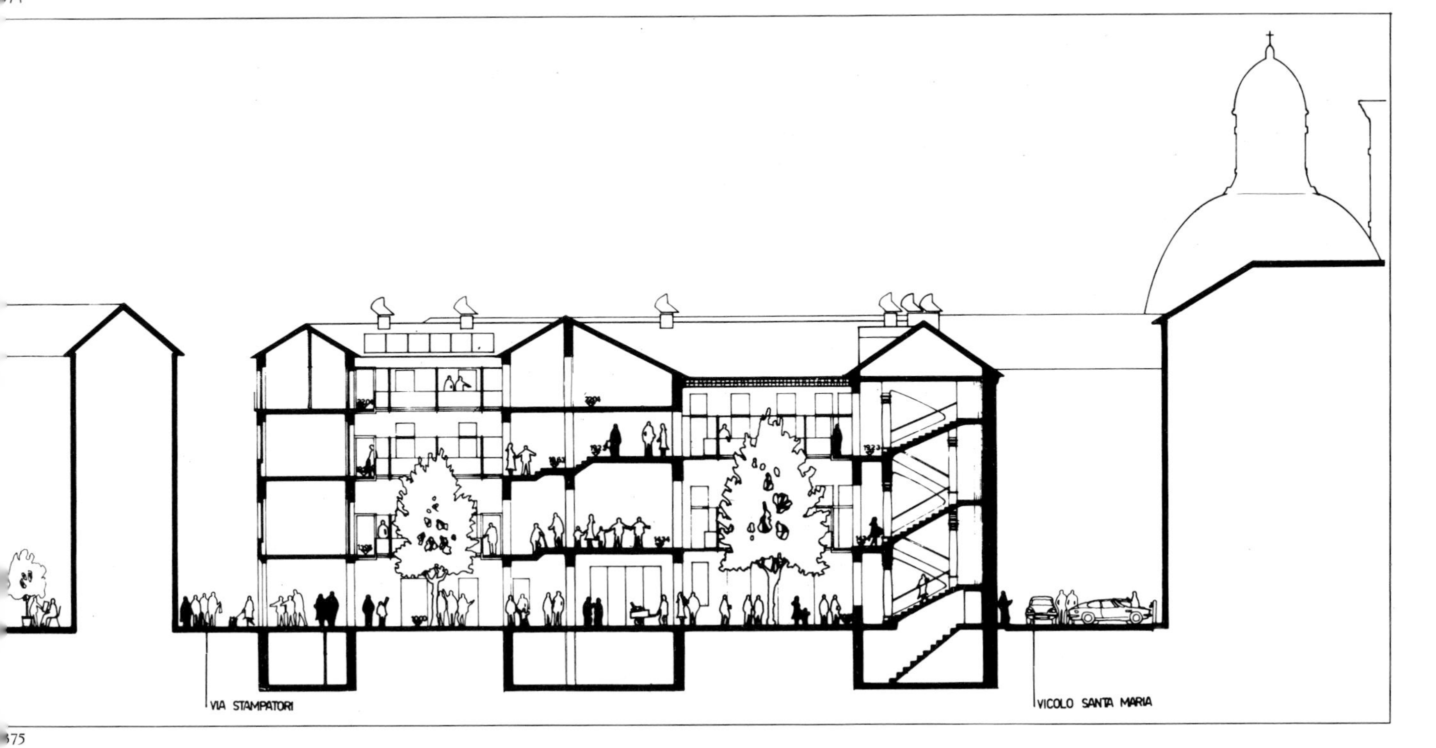

375

1981-1983 Reggio Emilia, Italy
Building for the Banca Agricola Commerciale, Automobile Club Italiano and collective services

Healing the city

Client: Banca Agricola Commerciale
Coordinator: S. Ferretti

Architects: Studio Piano/Building Workshop S.r.l. with S. Ishida, A. Traldi, F. Doria, E. Donato, F. Marano, C. Süsstrunk

Engineer: A. Rossi

From Genoa to Reggio Emilia: the long backward journey through the symbols of the historic city continues. Here, too, the idea of preservation takes concrete form in the plan of a line of services to support the ancient structure. The only way left to save the historic city centers is to equip the immediately adjoining areas with collective facilities (starting with underground car parks to reduce traffic). So in Reggio Emilia the plan envisages construction of a building block incorporating a bank (the Banca Agricola Commerciale), the Automobile Club, a shopping center, a conference room, a sports and cultural center and, of course, a sizeable car park. The attachment of the new volumes is achieved in structural harmony with the continuity of the old town: a continuity which, in the case of Genoa, was embodied in the sea and here is in the spatial pattern of buildings with their internal courtyards, reproduced and expanded on the formal level by the line of services.

The system of interaction has not, at any rate, been entrusted to a web of verbal quotations. A street-corridor, a pedestrian mall, describes a long path from the "deterrent" car park to the city center. It is precisely this "suspension bridge" that evokes the idea of the courtyard and gives it dynamic life. Similarly, an element modelled in ceramic specially designed for this building recalls another distinctive feature of the city's past — the use of brick.

This is not the theatrical break with the past nor a nostalgic retreat into the urban past but a realistic attempt to respond to the present needs of the modern city while matching the parameters of the ancient town. In this way the city becomes a homogeneous organism. This homogeneity should also be reflected on the microcosmic level. For instance, the building is created out of the combination of a simplified base structure and a metal grid to which you can affix illuminated signs, notices, glass or ceramic panels, and so forth. "Complexity has to be embodied as richness, not complication."

376

377

378

This is not the theatrical break with the past nor a nostalgic retreat into the urban past but a realistic attempt to respond to the present needs of the modern city. In this way the city becomes a homogeneous organism.

376. Plan of the ancient city center; at bottom left, the area to be used for services, with car park, bank structures, conference rooms and halls for performances.

377,378. Reggio Emilia, details and materials of the city.

379. General plan.

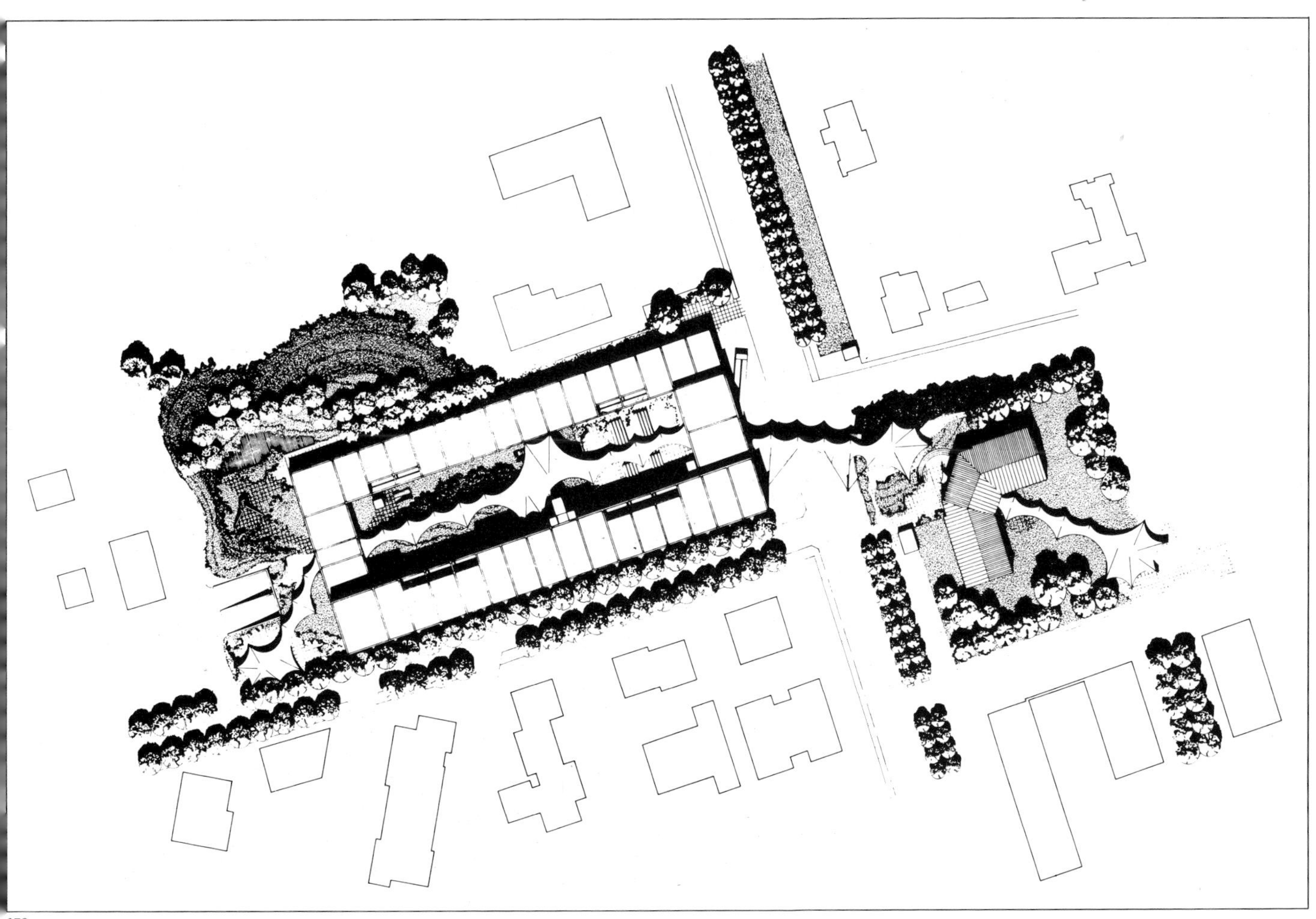

379

380. Detail of an elevation and section with integration of services in the building; the main use of these floors is for data processing for the Banca Agricola Commerciale.

381. Longitudinal section of the mixed-use building: the building type with enclosed inner courtyard, typical of Reggio Emilia, is retained.

382. Attachment of elements added to the primary structure.

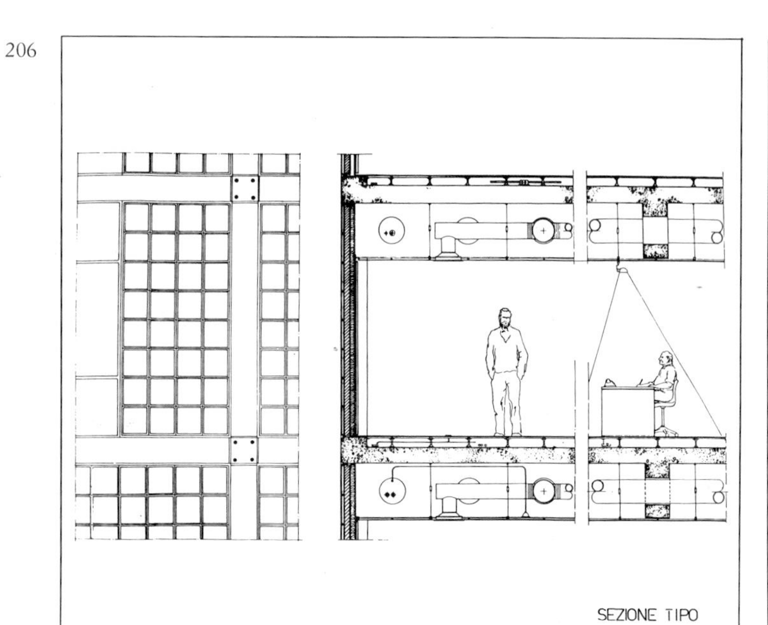

380

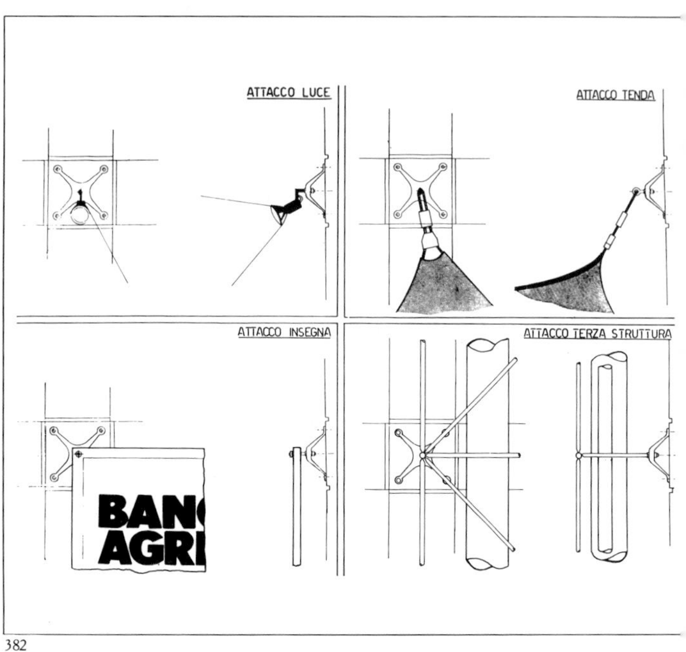

382

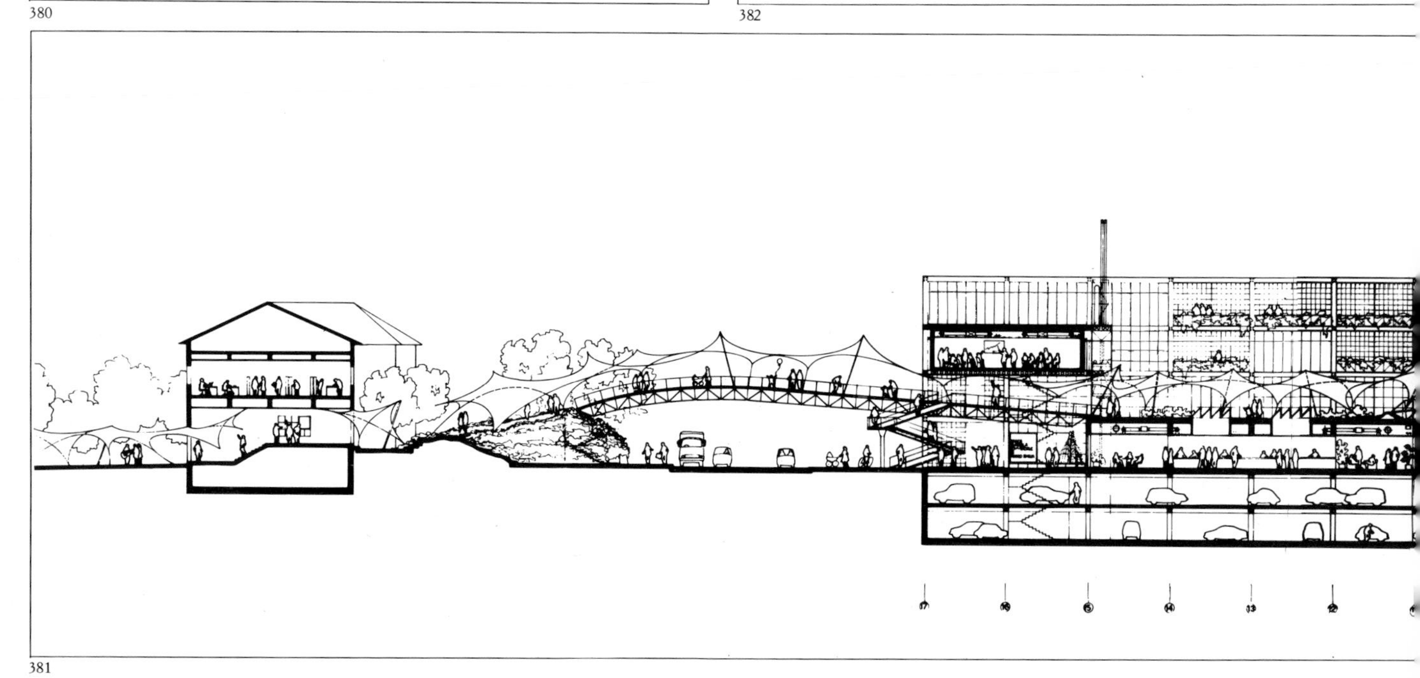

381

383. *Cross section of the multi-use building.*

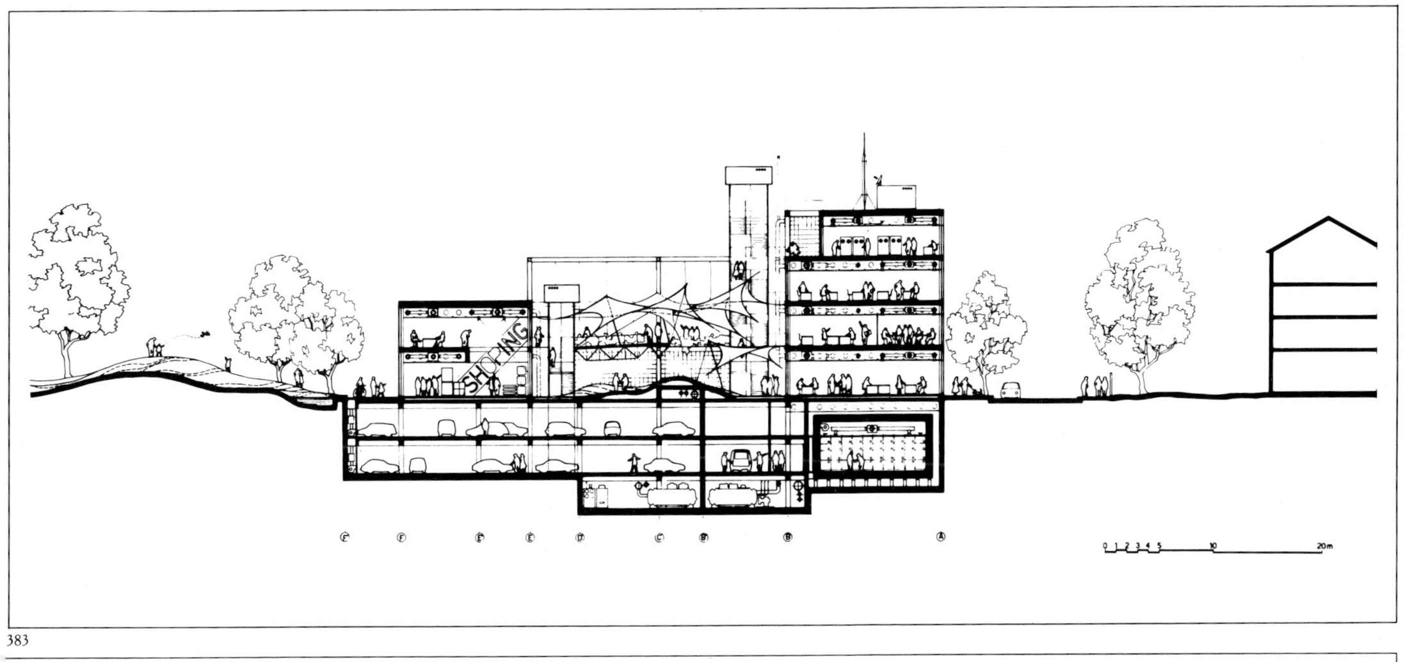

383

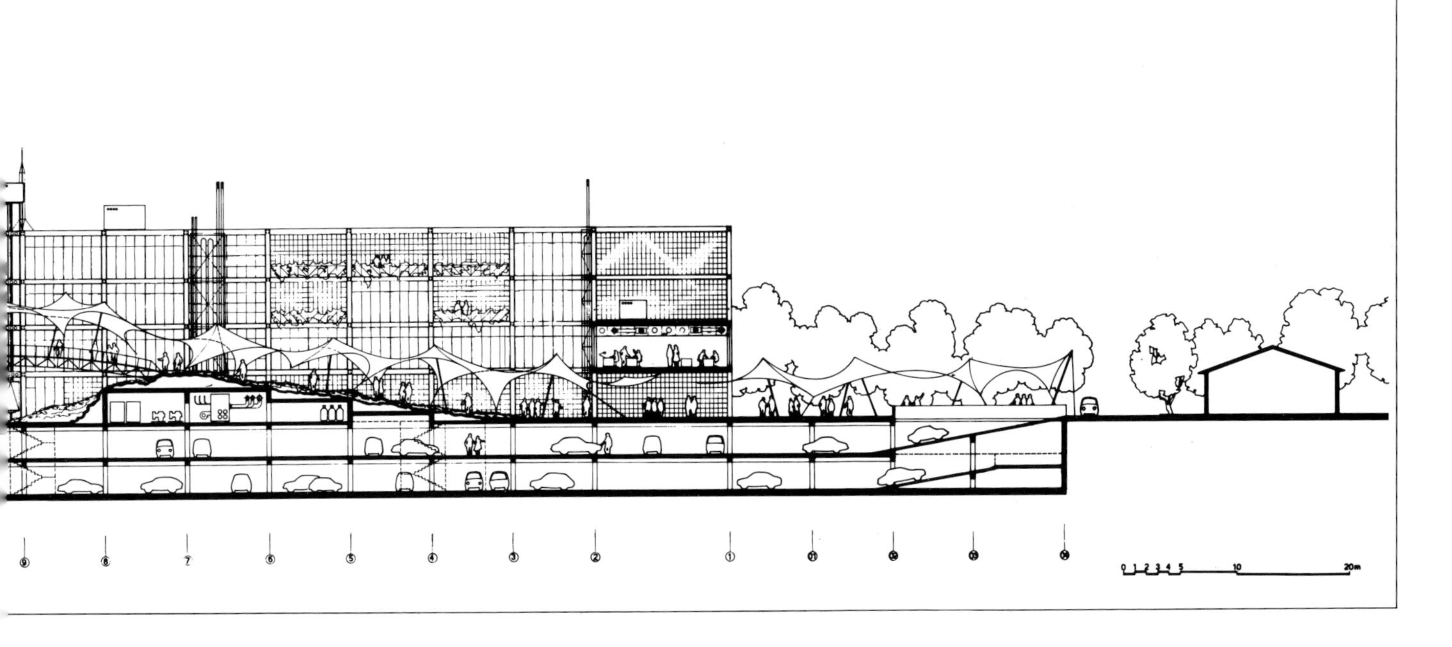

1981 Berlin, West Germany
IBA design for extending the Nationalgalerie and housing

Client: IBA, Berlin

Architects: Studio Piano/Building Workshop S.r.l.
S. Ishida, C. Süsstrunk, architects in charge
with F. Doria, N. Okabe, A. Traldi, M. Carroll

The everyday and the exceptional

Berlin is a city of emergencies, torn apart, disintegrated by the landscape of war, where the architectural object exists in isolation, enclosed in its lonely space. The problem in Berlin is one of reassembling the city, sewing it together again, establishing a rhythmical rapport between the scattered fragments of the urban landscape. The plan for the extension of the Nationalgalerie and construction of 50 apartments (an entry submitted, by invitation of the IBA, to the competition on the theme of "Living in the City") had as its objective to provide an example of connective tissue that would create a connection between the new and the existing scene (Mies van der Rohe's Nationalgalerie and James Stirling's design), harmonizing the everyday facts of living with the exceptional ones of culture.

The main obstacle to overcome is the fact that the two key elements in the urban whole (habitat and culture) have different purposes and requirements. While the housing cluster has to receive the maximum of light and achieve the maximum of spatial simplification, the museum has to screen sunlight (to protect the works of art) and aim at the minimum of spatial simplification. It is thus clear that definition of the form must come to terms with the technological problem of distribution of the sources of light. An element of continuity has to be invented, capable of meeting opposite requirements; this means typological and structural flexibility.

A shell system satisfies these requirements, provided it has the appropriate formal adjustments and the orientation is properly handled. The proposal is: (1) for the residential units, double curved ferrocement roofing with insulation in the center; oriented towards the sun to allow for light penetration; (2) for the museum, ferrocement roofing slightly undulated and oriented to protect the interior spaces from direct sunlight. This structural link allows the fragments of the urban jigsaw puzzle to join together again and a close relation is established. An invisible thread connects not just the two units but also the new and the existing, the Nationalgalerie, whose platform base is prolonged until it runs into the residential structure which, in its turn, projects towards the museum by a system of descending terraces. The everyday is blended with the exceptional. "It is only through this kind of combination that you can bring the city to life. The urban structure cannot be built up out of specialized units (residential, commercial, cultural, recreational, etc.), otherwise you end up with something that is, by its very constitution, the opposite of what a city ought to be: a mixture. Wherever this has happened, as in London or New York, it is always a pathological phenomenon. The Berlin design grew out of the wish to merge a twofold function into a single organism."

Its flexibility is reflected inwards: it permeates the dwelling spaces, whose standard type follows the Corciano model, an essential cavity set on two heights plus a series of lightweight elements that can be arranged in a variety of different ways. There is one significant difference, however, the curvilinear designs articulate the volumes into more fluid forms, compared with the rigid delimitation of the cube structure. This is a sign that the expressive system, while losing nothing in efficiency, is becoming more complex and that the geometrical order includes asymmetrical factors.

384

'It is only through this kind of combination that you can bring the city to life. The urban structure cannot be built up out of specialized units, otherwise you end up with something that is, by its very constitution, the opposite of what a city ought to be: a mixture."

384. Location of the project next to the Nationalgalerie.

385-387. Sketches for the residential section.

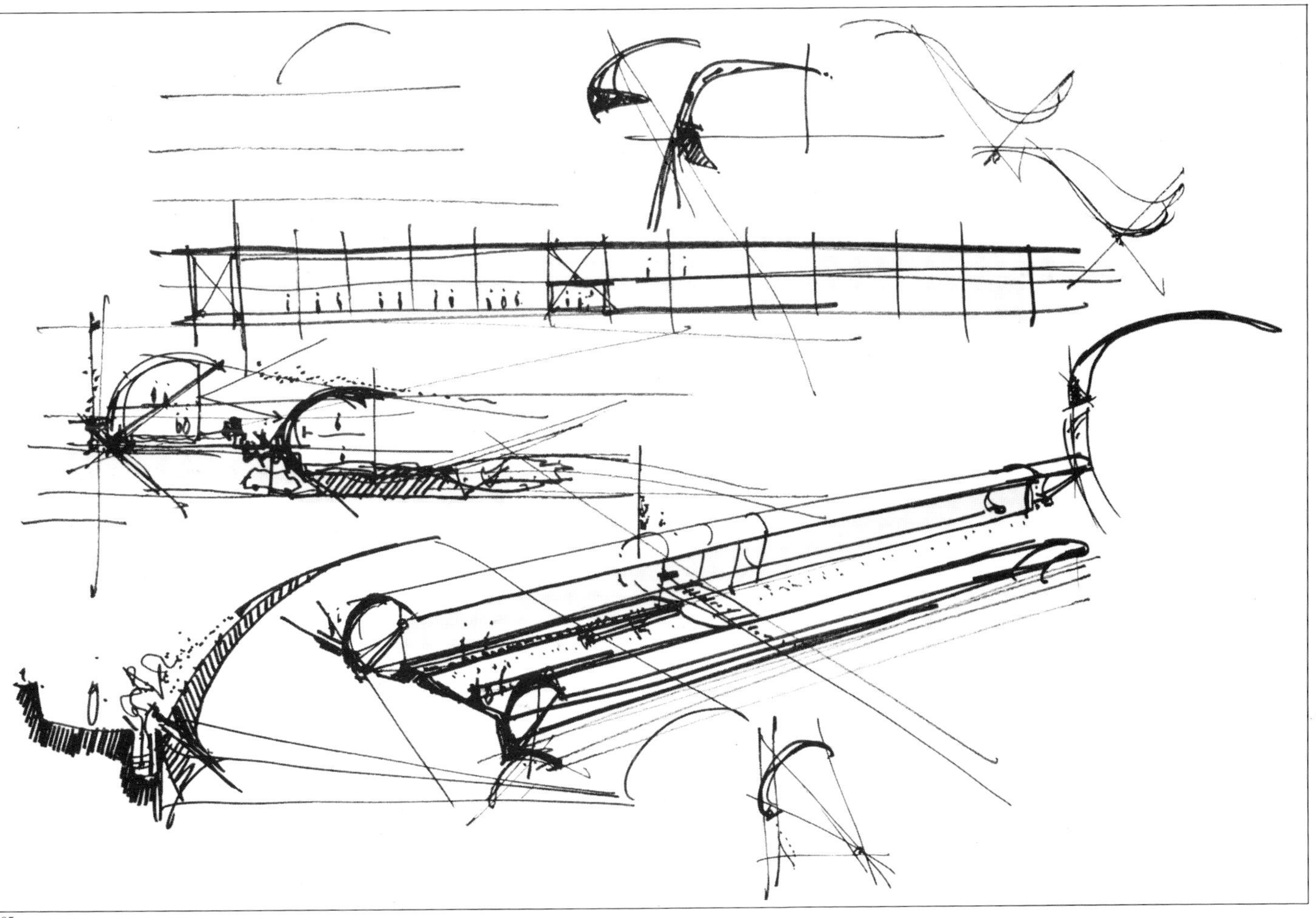

385

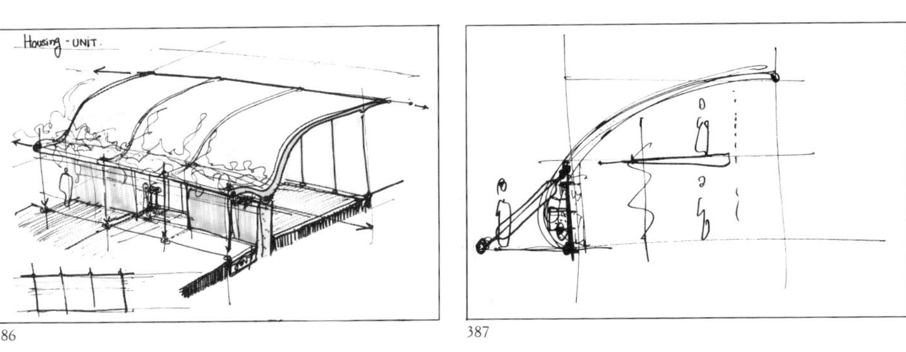

386

387

388. *Model.*

389. *Volumetric plan of the shell-structures constituting the residential section to the south and extension of the Nationalgalerie to the north.*

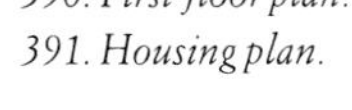

390. *First-floor plan.*

391. *Housing plan.*

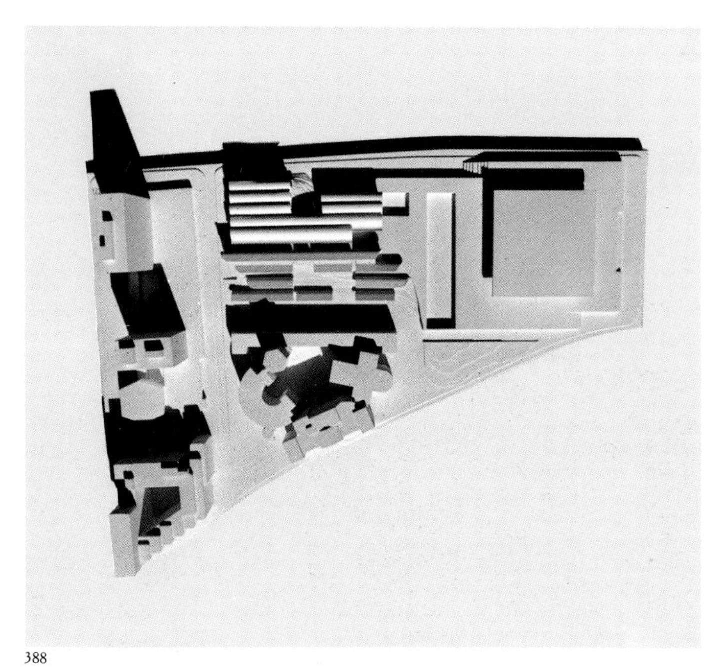

388

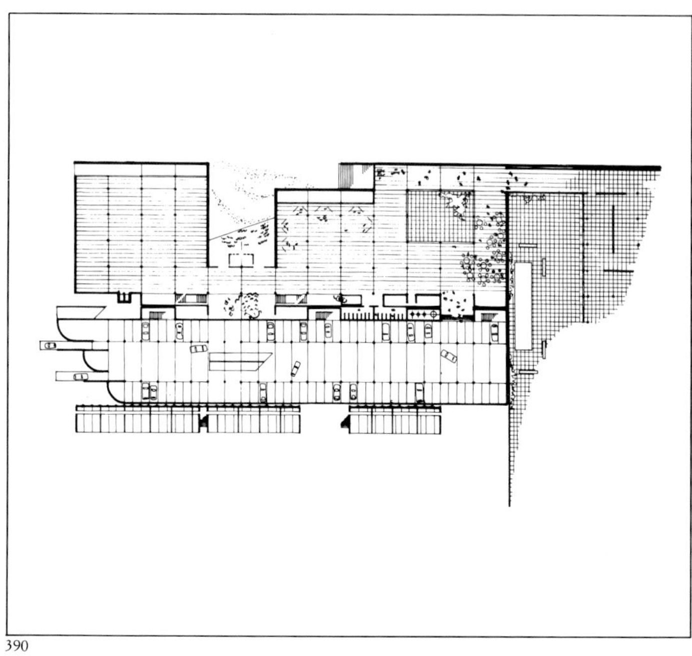

390

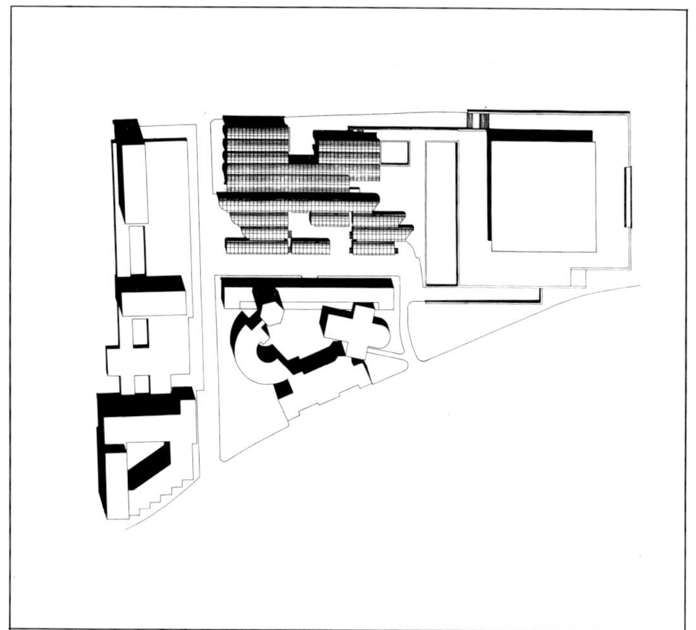

389

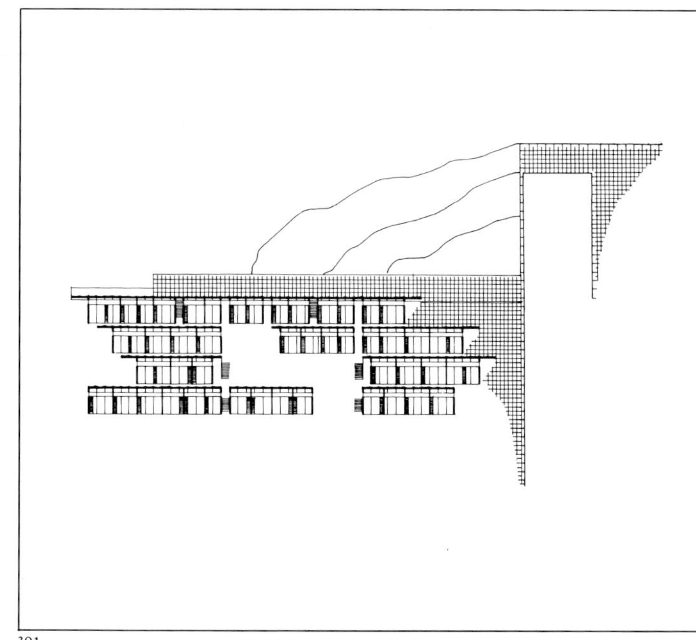

391

392. General plan of the residential and cultural project; to the right, Mies van der Rohe's Nationalgalerie.

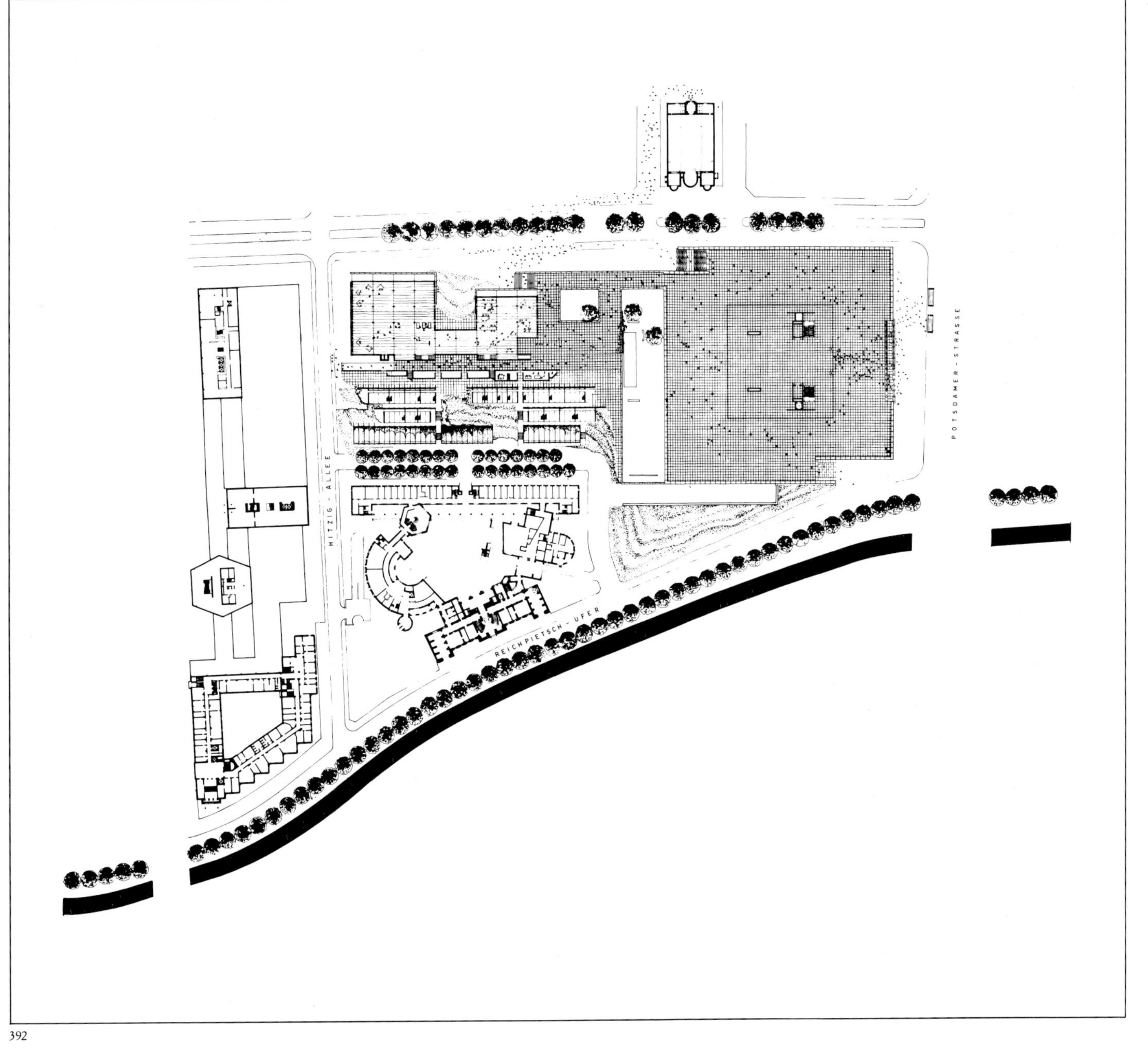

392

393. Section of the side of the Nationalgalerie extension (left) and the area for housing (right). Both structures are simply curved and made of reinforced concrete; the roofing of the exhibition rooms is designed to achieve a double reflection of light and prevent sunlight from entering the rooms directly; the housing has a double reinforced concrete membrane with internal insulation.

394. Section of the proposal; the church of St. Matthew (left).

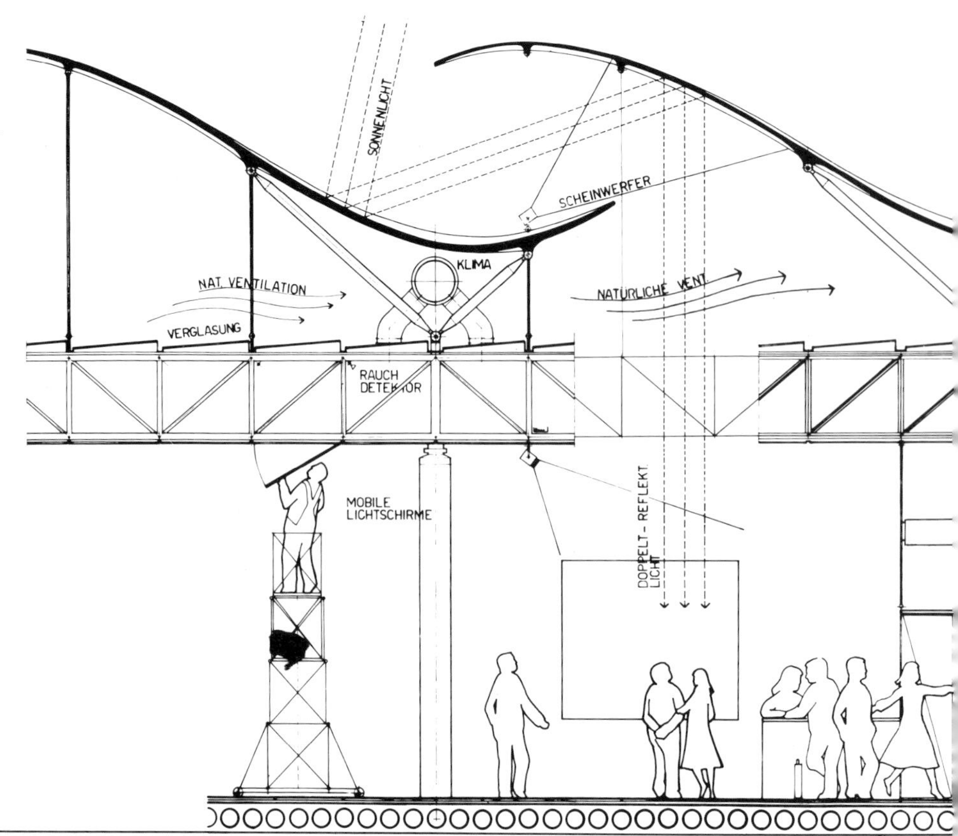

393

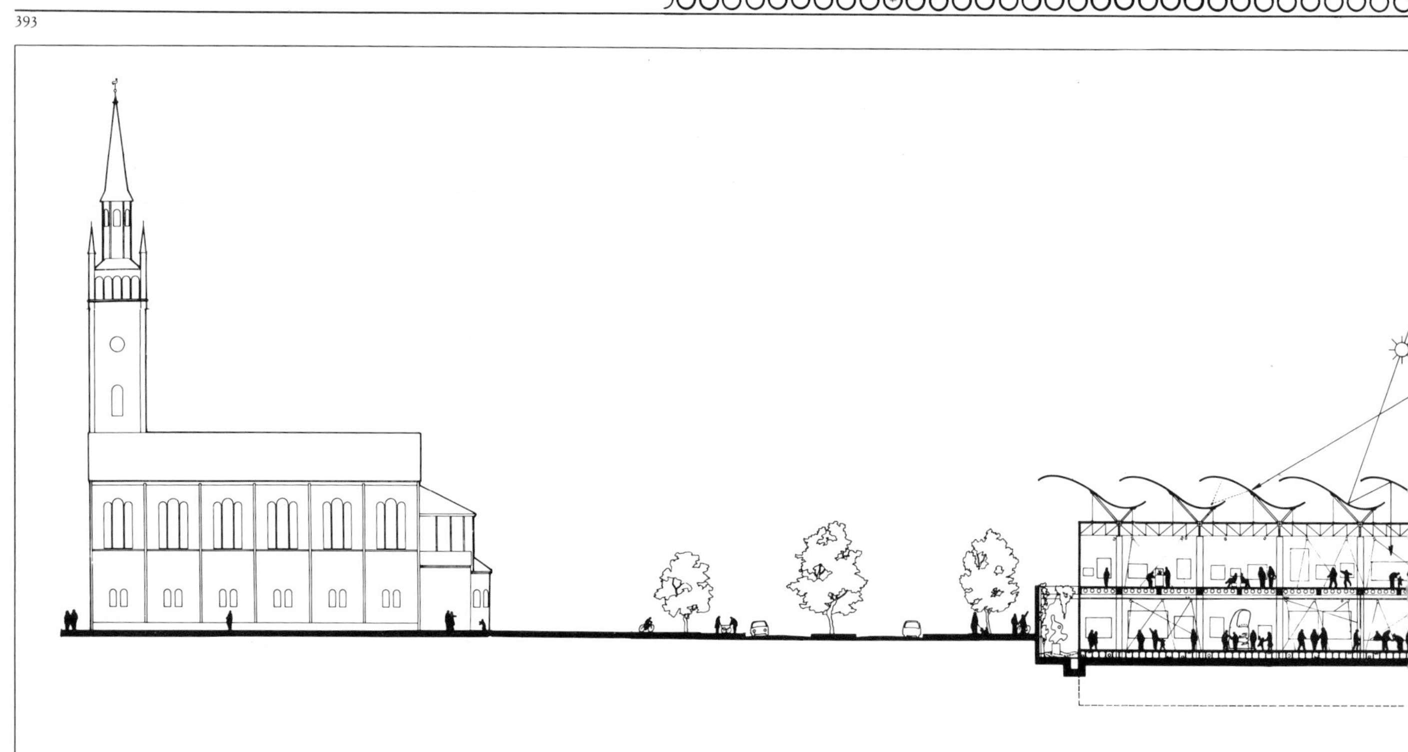

394

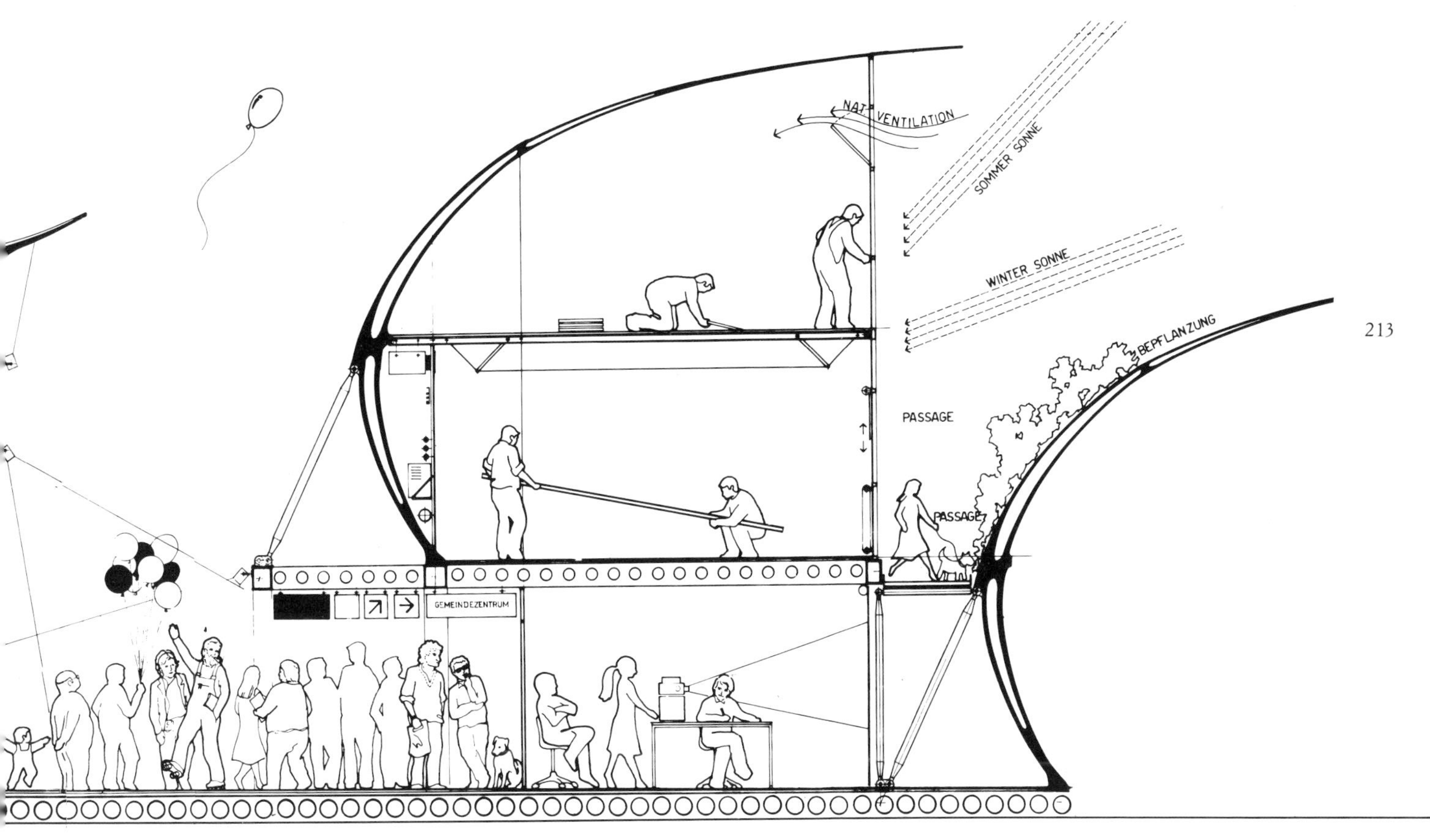
NAT. VENTILATION
SOMMER SONNE
WINTER SONNE
BEPFLANZUNG
PASSAGE
PASSAGE
GEMEINDEZENTRUM

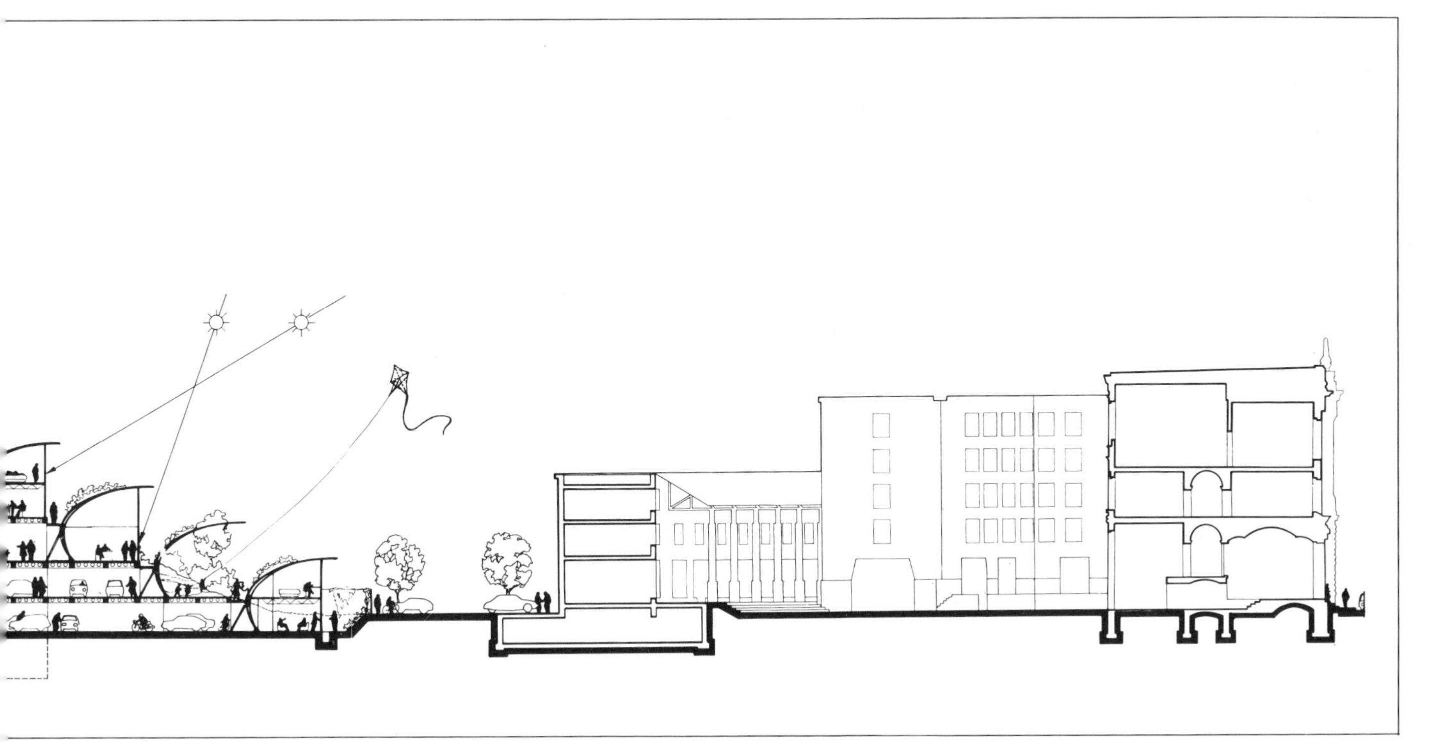

1981 Genoa, Italy
An axis of services

Rediscovery of the sea

Client: Commune of Genoa
Architects: Studio Piano
S. Ishida, A. Traldi
with F. Marano, A. Bianchi, E. Frigerio

Once again an urban plan has to be healed, a barrier to be demolished. The revitalization of the Molo Vecchio inevitably triggers off a chain reaction, by linking the district to the old city center and the city center to the rest of the town. Genoa is a divided city where the continuity in urban planning has long been lost, especially ever since the highway was built, abruptly interrupting the rapport with the sea and creating a physical barrier between the city and the port. Any attempt to recompose the urban fabric will have to start from the peninsula of the Molo which is the sole portion of the city on this side of the highway, where the old dock area of Mandraccio used to lie.

The guiding principle of this project in urban terms is to reestablish the relation between the city and the sea. It is essential to create an area adjacent to the ancient town center. "The Piazza Cavour zone, the area of the old free port, constitutes the main access to the ancient town center: which is by no means marginal, indeed it still is the city's nerve center. It is here at the end of the highway that we have to imagine an interchange between the old city and the outer city." The idea of an axis of services, now a leitmotif in the treatment of ancient city centers, is an interchange center for pedestrians made possible by creating a large underground car park. Since other underground development is inevitable, such as an underground railway station and restructuring of the sewers, it is a natural step to consider the possibility of a subterranean highway allowing the city to heal completely. The terminal is planned as a goods depôt, its function does not conflict with that of the old city center and provides connections by electric driven transport, moving at human speed and non-polluting; in this way the ancient center's essential role as the magnetic pole of commercial activity is reinforced. The concept of the ship-city thus takes shape: three new buildings designed for amenities slope down to the sea, not competing with the existing facilities but stretching into the water like three ships.

In a town like Genoa, with its labyrinthine spaces, Piazza Cavour could constitute a safety valve, a great social condenser, retrieving some of the vitality lost in the 1930s, without interferring with the commercial and maritime vocation of the neighboring areas and, if anything, providing them with less traffic. The old port in turn, having lost its former momentum, concentrates on the tourist industry and pleasure sailing, as well as medium and short-range coastal trade. A few projects such as parking, relocation of the highway underground, construction of the three buildings, endeavor to remove the destabilizing factors and to reconnect the city with its roots in the sea. Furthermore, a monorail could join the terminal's conference center to the Boat Show Center, creating another link in the chain of connections.

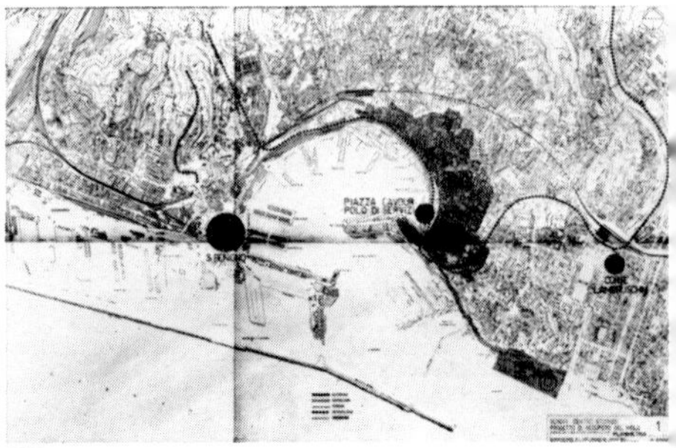

395

The highway abruptly interrupted the rapport with the sea, creating a physical barrier. To reestablish the relation between the city and the sea, it is essential to create an area adjacent to the ancient town center.

395. Piazza Cavour in Genoa constitutes the main access to the city's historical center.

396. Proposal for new structures on the waterfront like three great ships anchored in the port and capable of recreating a relationship between sea and city; these three volumes replace those of the free port and dock installations no longer in use.

397. View of the highway that has a deadening effect on the urban space around Piazza Cavour and cuts off the Molo Vecchio from the rest of the city.

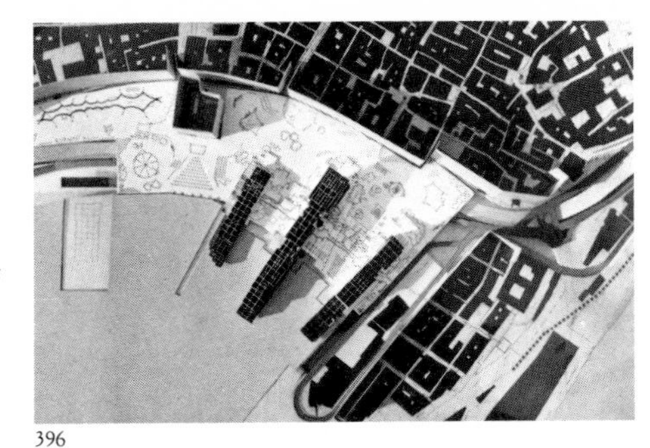

396

397

398. The Palazzo San Giorgio, one of the most significant historic monuments in Genoa, is completely overwhelmed by superstructures, the dock buildings and the highway.

399. Section of the Piazza Cavour pole of services through the ancient town center (right) to the sea, setting the city on the waterfront again.

400. General plan of the area. The proposal is to put the highway underground and provide underground parking for 2,000 vehicles.

398

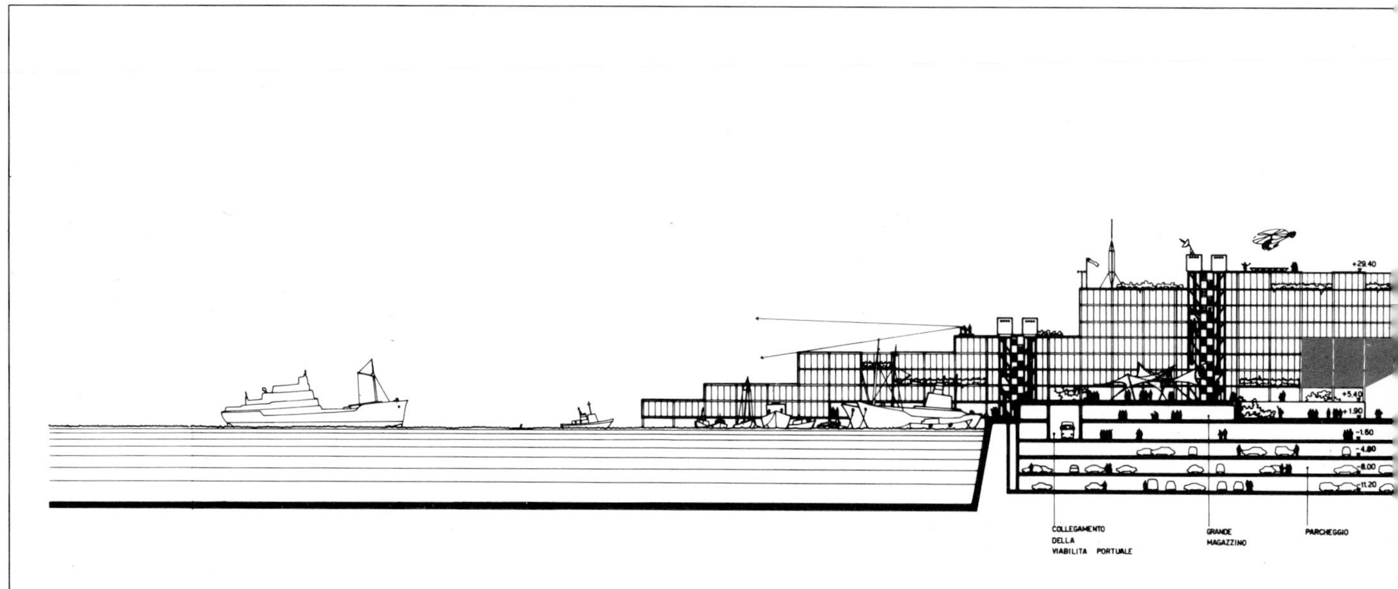

399

AREA IN CORSO DI STUDIO

400

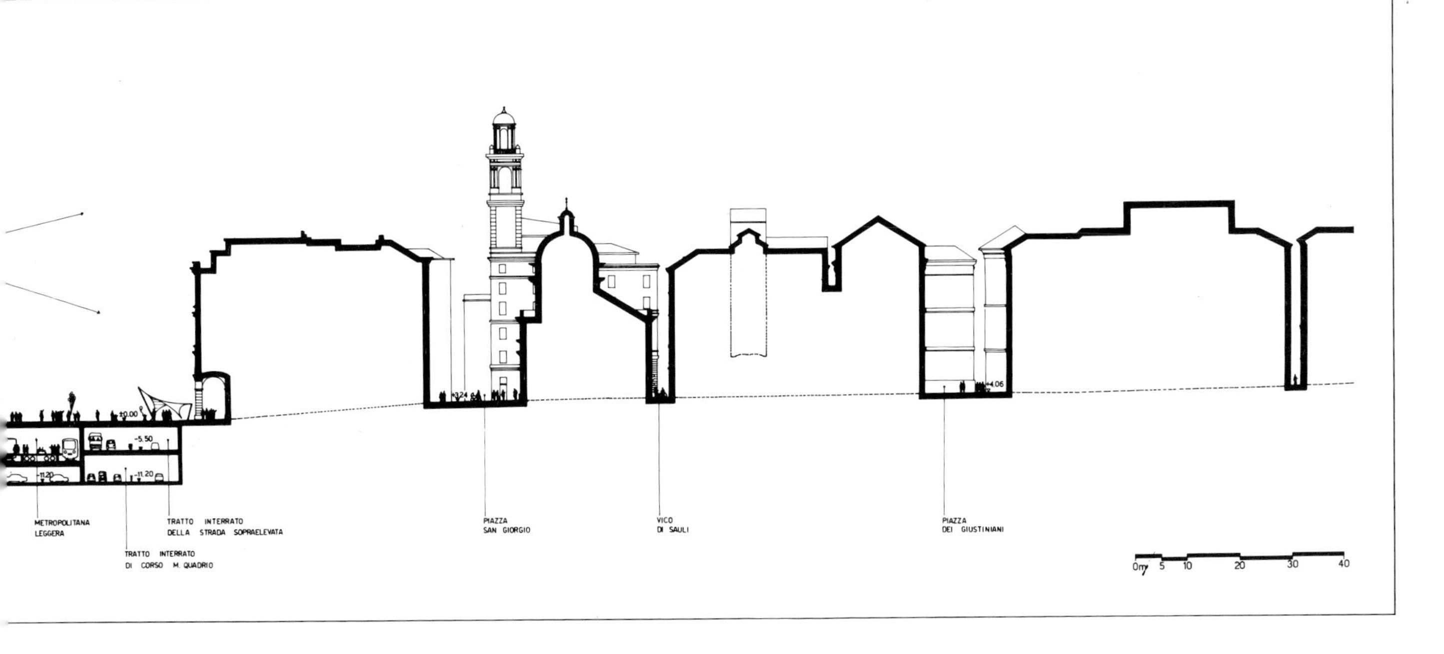
METROPOLITANA
LEGGERA
TRATTO INTERRATO
DI CORSO M. QUADRIO
TRATTO INTERRATO
DELLA STRADA SOPRAELEVATA
PIAZZA
SAN GIORGIO
VICO
DI SAULI
PIAZZA
DEI GIUSTINIANI
0 m 5 10 20 30 40

1979

An experiment in educational television: the program "Open Site"

Misunderstanding giganticism

Client: Radiotelevisione Italiana, Channel 2
Program directed by G. Macchi
Produced by V. Lusvardi

Architects: Piano & Rice & Associates
with S. Ishida, N. Okabe, G. Picardi, S. Yamada, M. Bonino, R. Biondo, G. Fascioli, R. Gaggero

Texts and screenplays by Magda Arduino

401

"In the past architects concerned themselves not just with the end product but designed, organized and worked on the site. Think of the great architects, the cathedral builders, who understood their material, stone, perfectly. The cathedral was a challenge." The reference to the origins of his craft constantly reinforces Piano's experience as an architect. Yet this does not involve style: it is a structural and not a linguistic issue. This means that the journey backwards is directed to the rediscovery of construction techniques rather than a nostalgic recovery of primitive typological categories. In these terms the process acquires controversial implications. Skills have to be recomposed, reviving a concept of architecture that has been lost in the course of time: architecture as design, construction and invention of productive processes and even of the instruments of work, not merely confined to the packaging of aesthetic products.

It is in this sense that the television program *Habitat*, produced by Renzo Piano and Magda Arduino, directed by Giulio Macchi, is charged with significance going far beyond the pure information. The program could be described as a cross section of soft technology building, an illustration of the working methods of Piano's staff and their manifesto. The cathedral, from this standpoint, appears as a theater of creativity, a great research center, a university of engineering where there was as yet no discrimination between manual work and intellectual activity of the sort that eventually developed during the Renaissance. Moreover, apart from technical innovations, the cathedral construction site offered the first historical example of free wage labor, that was strongly motivated: a series of workshops, stone masons, sculptors, ironsmiths and glaziers, was organized on clearly interdisciplinary relationships.

Similarly the study of the yurt, the Mongol tent, also takes on controversial implications. As described by Marco Polo in the *Milione*, the yurt is a dwelling-tool, made up of standardized sections and easily adaptable to the needs of the environment, a small "prefabricated" home workshop. Its structural potential and method of construction was used as an attack on the distortions produced by industrialized building. "The aim of this experiment is to demystify building technology, to show that research into building does not necessarily mean big machines and sophisticated systems. In the field of construction we could describe ours as a period of retarded technology. Big construction sites and huge machines do exist but they do not necessarily mean advanced technology. It is the technology of a large industry systematically removed from the public's comprehension and control."

Another significant stage in the backward journey is the balloon frame system used by the American pioneers during the 19th century. It is a self-build structure based on the use of only two materials: wooden planks and nails. When the pioneers set out on their journey they would load the boards onto the wagons already measured out and numbered; hammer and nails completed the equipment. This was all they needed to build a house. In those days anyone could build and there was no specialization. "Research is at present specialized and often marginal. It also suffers from a misunderstanding about the gigantic proportions necessary to implement it. In reality the equipment truly useful for research can be greatly simplified. Technological progress is all too often confused with excessive technology at both production and site level."

The artisanal dimension in this reevocation of history is also noteworthy. In *Habitat* the information given is continually backed up by experimental tests of the behavior of materials and of manufacturing processes. This is in line with the guiding principles of the Piano workshop, where scientific discipline goes hand in hand with practical execution.

"When the pioneers set out on their journey they would load the boards onto the wagons already measured out and numbered; hammer and nails completed the equipment. This was all they needed to build a house. In those days anyone could build and there was no specialization."

401. Sugako Ishida showing construction of a Mongol yurt tent.

402. Plan of the ten programs of the cycle "Open Site" for Habitat, *shown on Channel 2 of Italian television, with superimposed Giulio Macchi, Magda Arduino and Shunji Ishida.*

CATTEDRALE 1 (storico) 15' durata

LA CAVA della pietra

CATTEDRALE 2 (storico) 15' durata

LA CATTEDRALE

IL COLORE

CATTEDRALE 3 (storico) 15' durata

LA MUSICA

IL LINGUAGGIO

10' durata IL TETTO (storico/propositivo)

15' durata IL SUOLO

IL KOLOSSAL

IL KOLOSSAL

IL LEGNO 1 10' durata

IL LEGNO 2 10' durata

giulio macc

L'ACCIAIO 1 10' durata

IL KOLOSSAL

L'ACCIAIO 2 10' durata

LO SPAZIO EVOLUTIVO 15' durata

77 31/10 77 HAB

402

403, 404. Teaching models made for the program.

405. Model of a cathedral construction site particularly showing the construction processes and development of the equipment.

406. Television sequence on the construction of the cathedral.

403

404

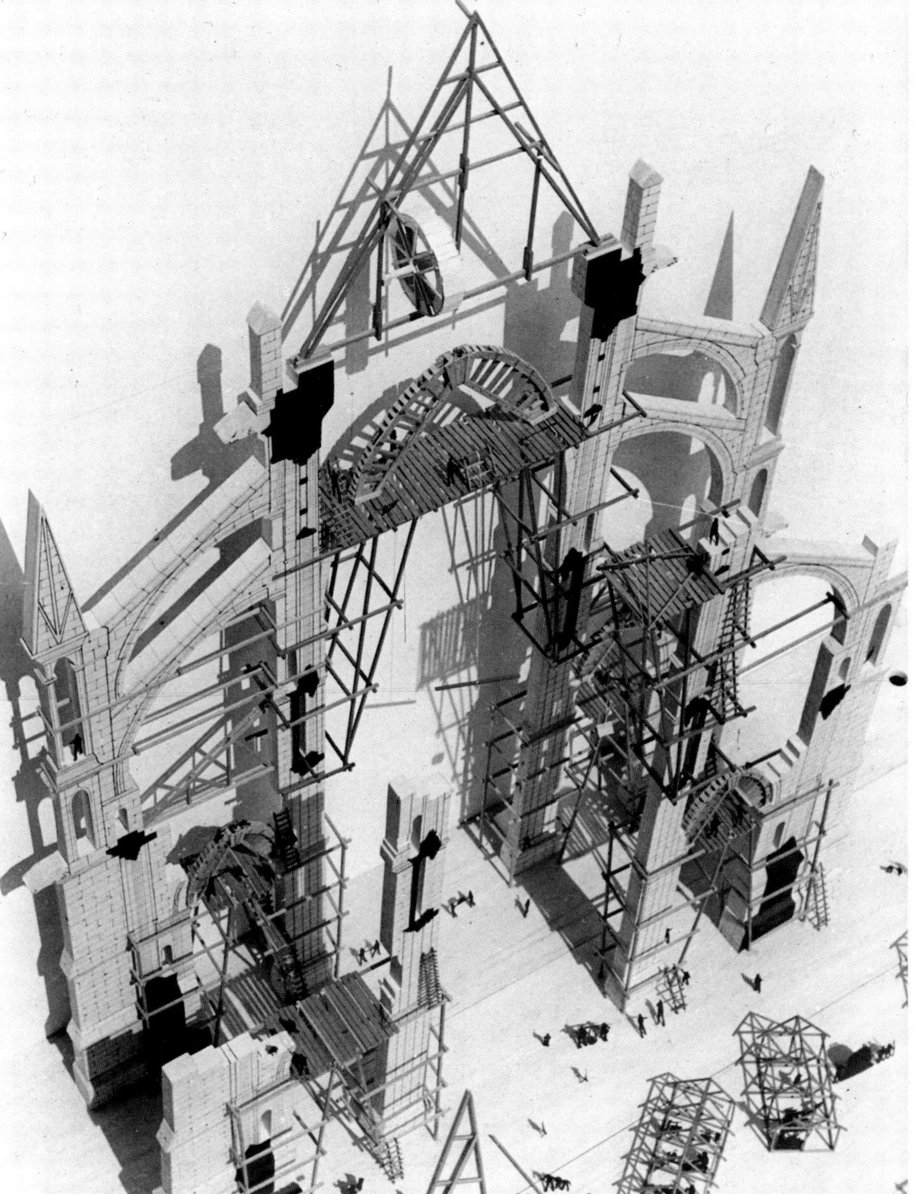

405

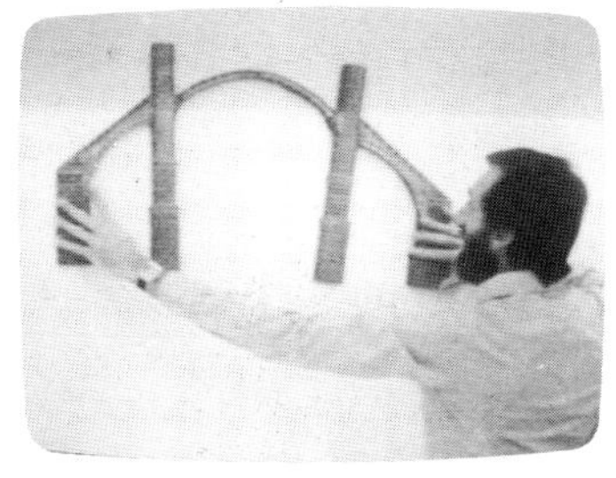

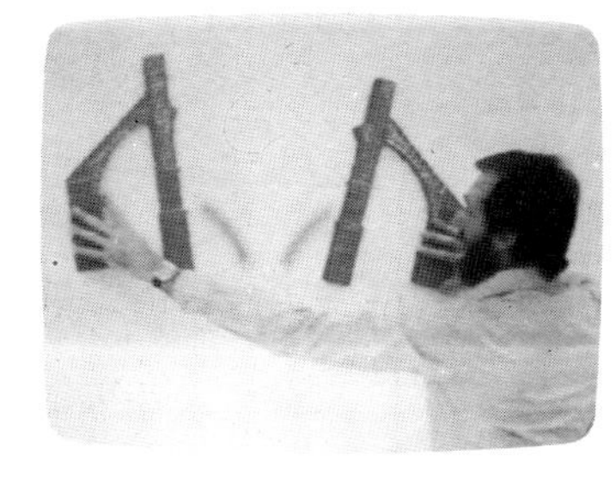

406

407

407. *Preparation for filming construction of a Mongol yurt.*

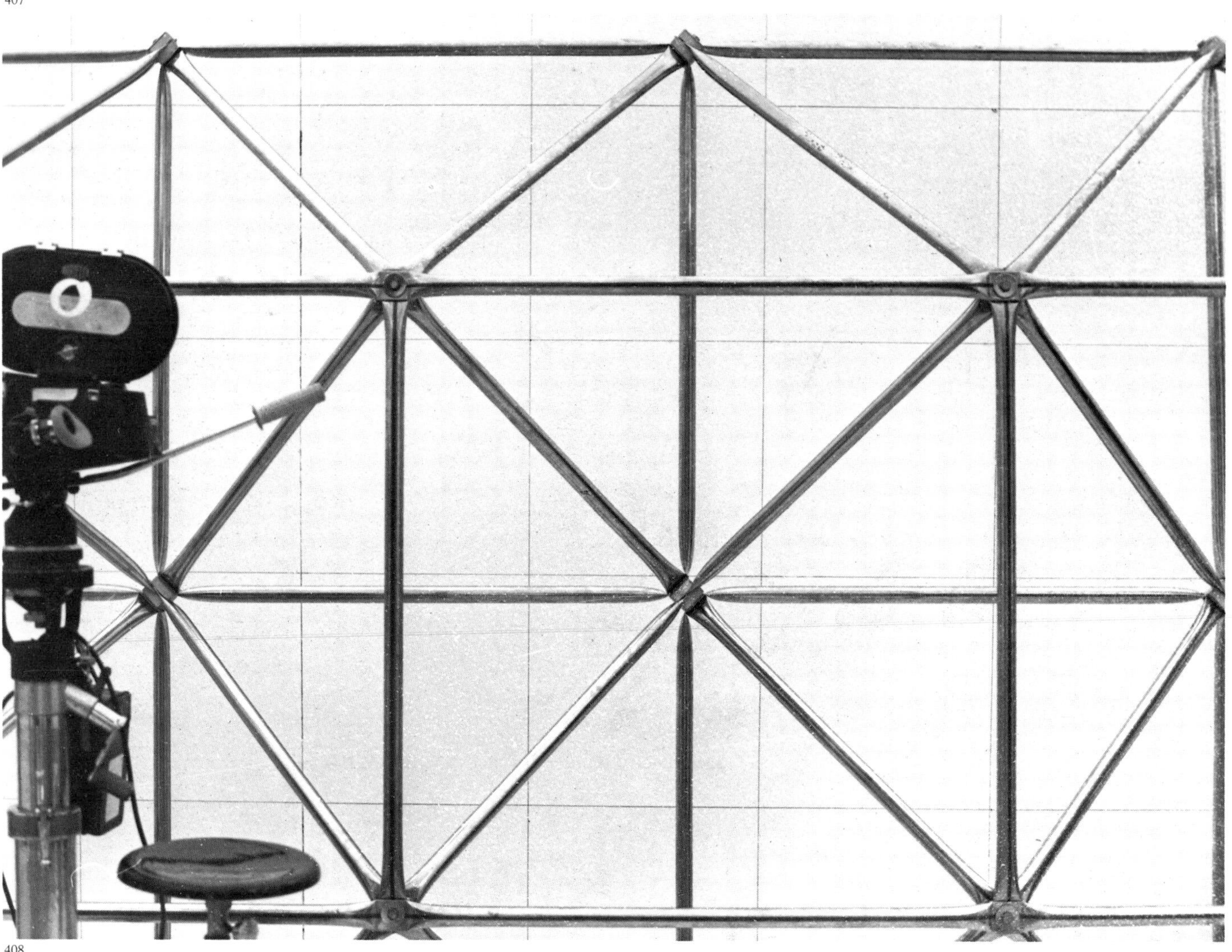

408

408. *Construction of a steel tube grid structure.*

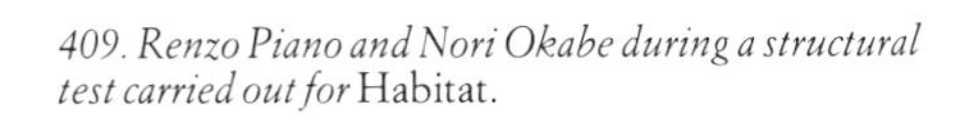

409. Renzo Piano and Nori Okabe during a structural test carried out for Habitat.

410. Curving plywood panels under tension to produce an emergency shelter.

409

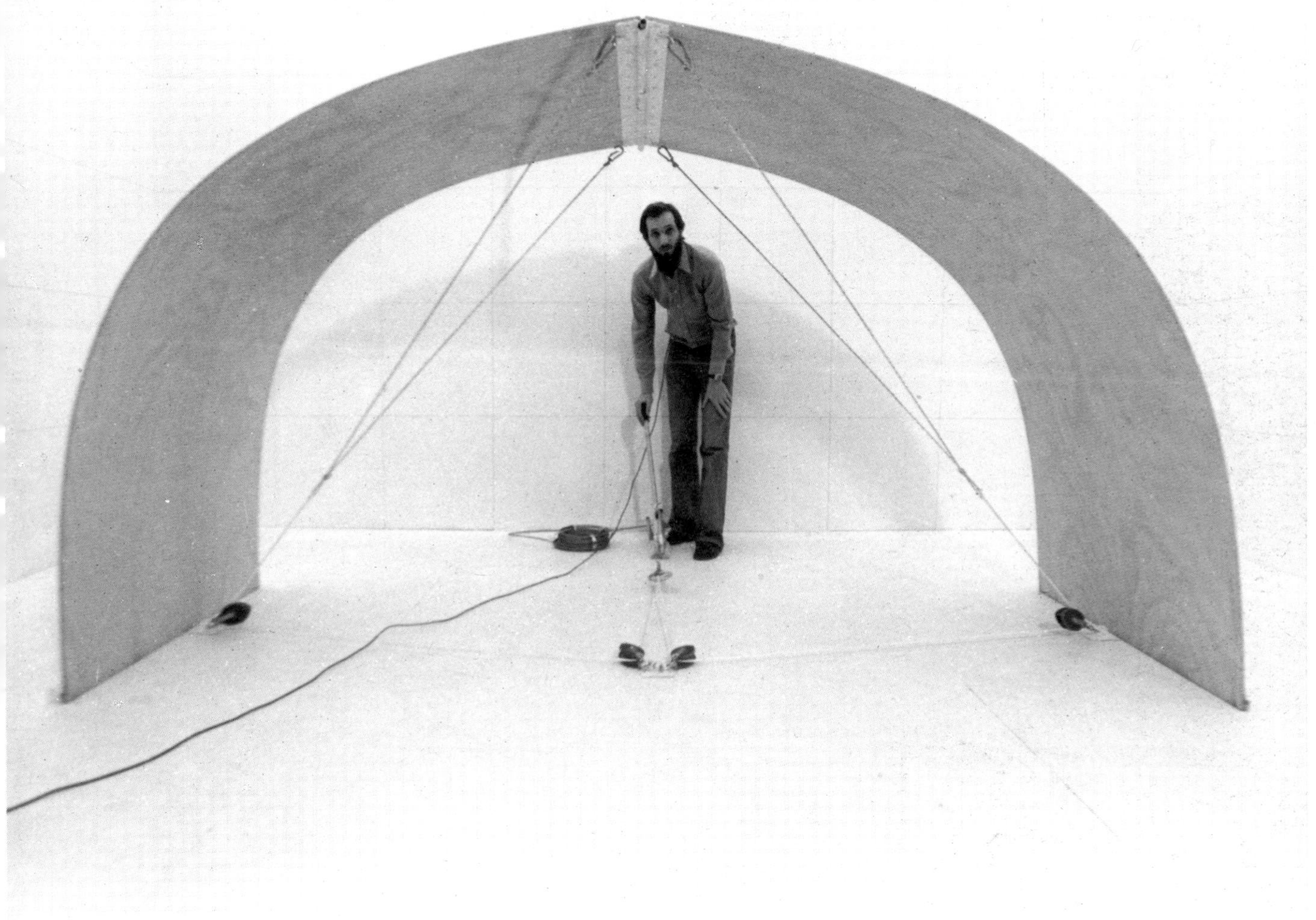

410

Chronology
Biography
Bibliography

1964-1965 Genoa, Italy
1. Reinforced polyester space frames

Experimenting for optimization of reinforced polyester space frames.
Architects: Studio Piano

1965 Genoa, Italy
2. Woodworking shop

Self-supporting structure composed of identical elements of bent sheet metal.
Architects: Studio Piano
with the collaboration of R. Foni, M. Filocca, L. Tirelli
Contractors: E. Piano Contractors

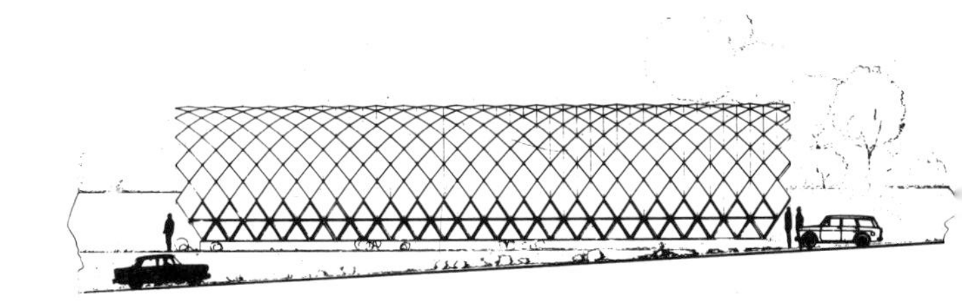

1966 Pomezia, Rome, Italy
3. Mobile structure for sulfur extraction

Self-supporting sectional structure with reinforced polyester elements, used from start to finish following the production line.
Architects: Studio Piano
Contractors: E. Piano Contractors

1966 Genoa, Italy
4. Space frame in small inflatable units

Roofing of inflatable elements which can be rolled up and transported conveniently.
Architects: Studio Piano

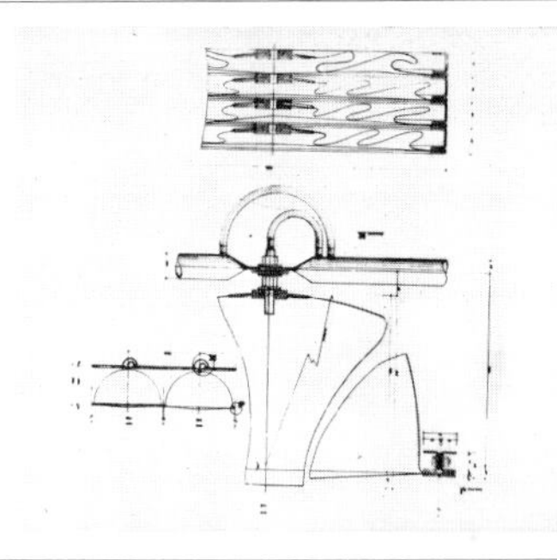

1966 Genoa, Italy
5. Prestressed steel and reinforced polyester structure

Roofing of double-membrane reinforced polyester elements, pretensed with steel cables.
Client: IPE - Genoa
Architects: Studio Piano
with F. Marano
Contractors: E. Piano Contractors

1967 Milan, Italy
6. Shell structural systems: a pavilion for the XIV Triennale

Shell structures in reinforced polyester using production system developed by Studio Piano.
Client: Milan Triennale
Architects: Studio Piano
with F. Marano, O. Celadon,
G. Fascioli

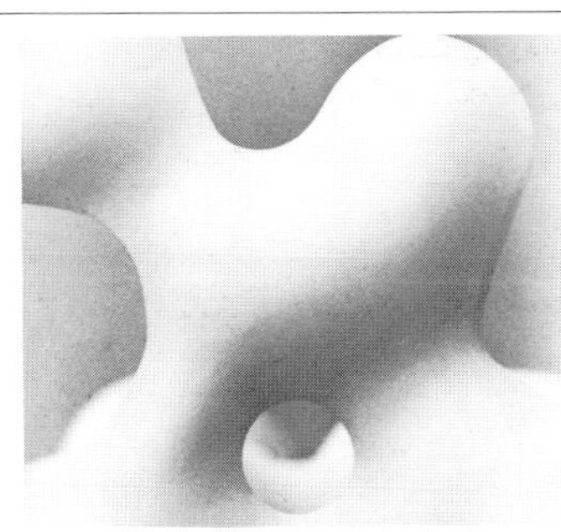

1967 Bologna, Italy
7. Reinforced concrete construction system

Structural system integrating installations and equipment.
Client: Vibrocemento - Bologna
Architects: Studio Piano
with F. Marano, G. Fascioli
and the collaboration of R. Jascone

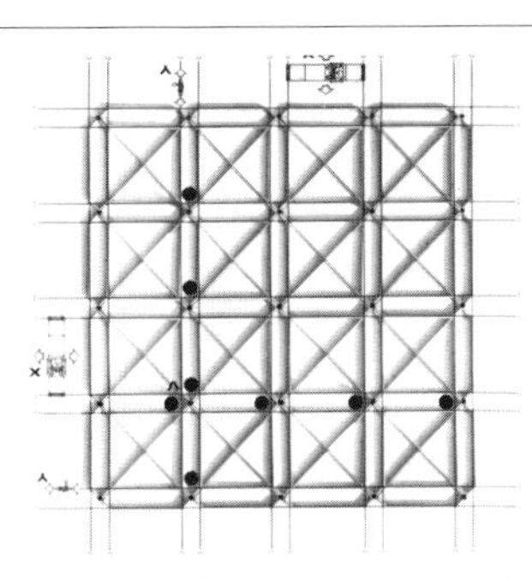

1968 Genoa, Italy
8. Industrialized construction system for a housing estate

Housing of reinforced concrete cells on projecting load-bearing structure of precompressed reinforced concrete.
Client: IPE - Genoa
Architects: Studio Piano
with F. Marano, O. Celadon,
G. Fascioli
Engineers: SERTEC Engineering
Contractors: E. Piano Contractors

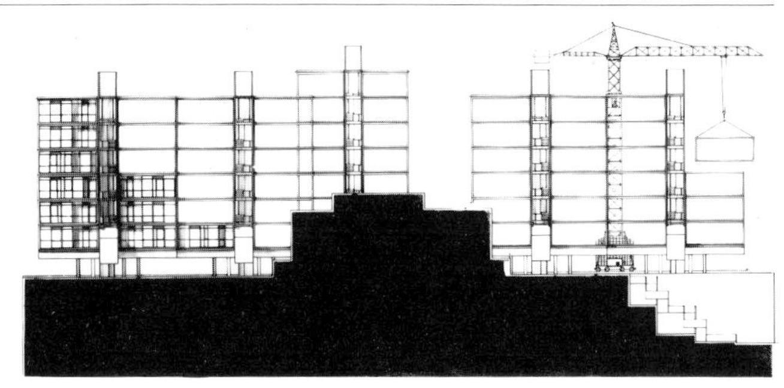

1968 Scarmagno, Ivrea, Italy
9. Roofing for Olivetti works

Study of optimized overhead light-source correlated with ventilation and thermic qualities of the building, executed in reinforced polyester.
Client: Olivetti S.p.A.
Architects: Studio Piano
for the roofing system
with F. Marano, O. Celadon,
G. Fascioli
Marco Zanuso and Edoardo Vittorio
for the design of the works

1968-1969 Genoa, Italy
10. Office workshop for the Renzo Piano studio

Workshop made with structural steel pyramid, microshed polyester roofing, sandwich panel curtain - walls of lightweight concrete.
Client: R. Piano
Architects: Studio Piano
with F. Marano, G. Fascioli,
T. Ferrari
Contractors: E. Piano Contractors

1968-1970 Harrisburg, USA
11. Roofing components for Olivetti Underwood works

Lighting elements with space frame in polyester and aluminum, integrating the cement work.
Client: Olivetti Ltd - Harrisburg
Architects: Studio Piano
for the roofing
with G. Fascioli
Louis I. Kahn for the design of the works
Engineers: SERTEC Engineering

1968-1971 London, England
12. Top-story extension

Added top story for a turn-of-the-century building and conversion to office space.
Client: DRU (Design Research Unit), London, and Piano & Rogers
Architects: Piano & Rogers
with M. Goldschmied, J. Young,
P. Botschi, Y. Kaplicky

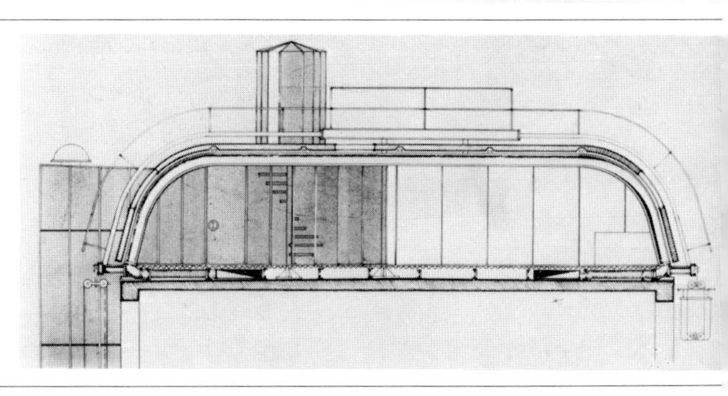

1969-1971 Cambridge, England
13. Fitzroy Street shopping center

Plan for renovation and conversion of Cambridge inner-city area as a shopping center.
Client: Cambridge City Council
Architects: Studio Piano & Rogers with J. Young, M. Goldschmied, J. Morris

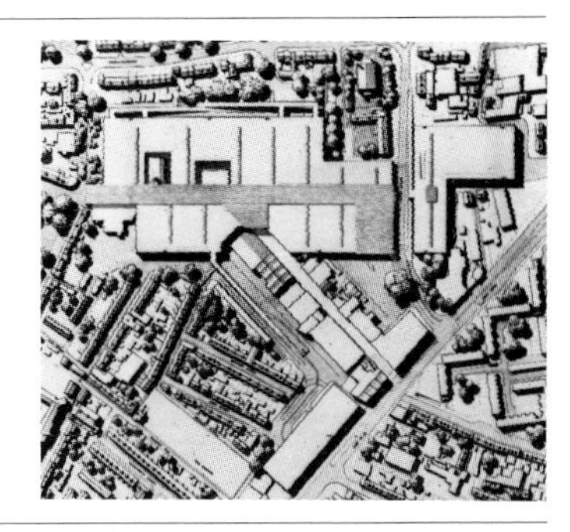

1969 Crema, Cremona, Italy
14. Roofing for Olivetti works

Roofing of lighting elements in reinforced polyester.
Client: Olivetti S.p.A.
Architects: Studio Piano for the roofing system with F. Marano, G. Fascioli
Marco Zanuso and Edoardo Vittoria for the building
Contractors: E. Piano Contractors

1969 Garonne, Alessandria, Italy
15. Open plan home

Plan of roofing, a space frame in wooden pyramidal elements permitting complete flexibility in the layout of the space below.
Architects: Studio Piano with F. Marano, G. Fascioli, T. Ferrari
Contractors: E. Piano Contractors

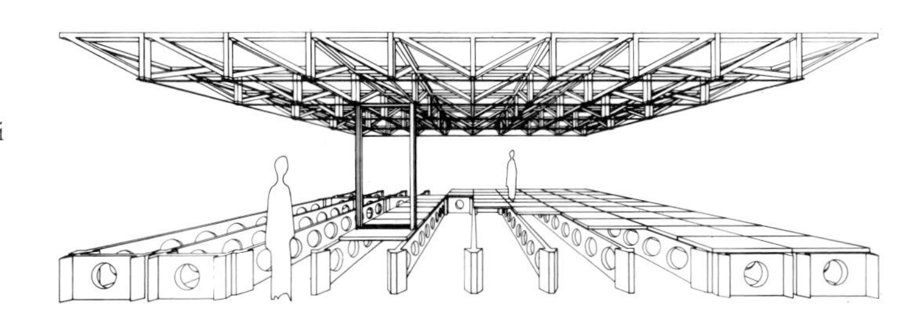

1969-1970 Osaka, Japan
16. Italian Industry Pavilion at the Osaka Expo

Steel tensile structure with reinforced polyester membrane.
Client: Italpublic, Rome
Architects: Studio Piano with F. Marano, G. Fascioli, G. Queirolo, T. Ferrari
Engineers: SERTEC Engineering
Contractors: E. Piano Contractors

1970-1971 Rome, Italy
17. Competition for a new system of prefabricated service stations

Spatial service grid of steel prefabricated elements.
Client: Esso Standard Italy, Rome
Architects: R. Piano, F. Marano, B. Bassetti

1970 Washington, D.C., USA
18. Standardized hospital module

Health service capsule containing all of the hospital's sophisticated equipment.
Client: ARAM (Association for Rural Aids in Medicine), Washington, D.C.
Architects: Studio Piano & Rogers with M. Goldschmied, J. Young, P. Flack

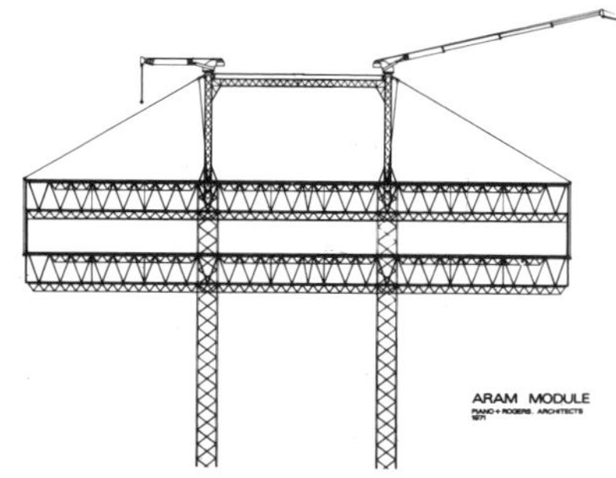

1971-1973 Novedrate, Como, Italy
19. B & B Italy office building

Open-space plan, covered by a steel structure which allows for light penetration and flexibility in the layout of the offices.
Client: B & B Italy S.p.A., Como
Architects: Studio Piano & Rogers with C. Brüllmann, S. Cereda, G. Fascioli
Engineer: F. Marano

1971-1977 Paris, France
20. Georges Pompidou cultural center

Client: Ministry of Cultural Affairs and Ministry of National Education, Paris
Architects: Studio Piano & Rogers
Design team: Renzo Piano and Richard Rogers; G.F. Franchini (competition, program, interiors); W. Zbinden with H. Bysaeth, J. Lohse, P. Merz, P. Dupont (substructure and mechanical services); L. Abbott with S. Ishida, H. Naruse, H. Takahashi (superstructure and mechanical services); E. Holt (façades and galleries); A. Stanton with M. Dowd, R. Verbizh (internal/external audiovisual systems); C. Brüllmann (environment and scenographic space); B. Plattner (coordination and site supervision); M. Davies with N. Okabe, K. Rupard, J. Sircus (IRCAM); J. Young with F. Barat, H. Diebold, J. Fendard, J. Huc, H. Schlegel (interiors); B. Merello, F. Marano (participation in the first phase of design); F. Gouinguenet, C. Spielmann, C. Valensi (secretarial)
Engineers: Ove Arup & Partners
Design team: P. Rice, L. Grut, R. Peirce (structure); T. Barker (plant engineering); M. Espinosa (cost control)
Building contractors: GTM: J. Thaury (job engineer) with: Krupp, Mont-à-Mousson, Pohlig (structures); CFEM (façades); Otis (elevators and escalators); Voyer (secondary structures); Industrielle de Chauffage, Saunier Duval (heating installations)

1972 Genoa, Italy
21. Ferrocement pleasure craft

Client: ATIB S.r.l.
Construction: Renzo Piano with R. Gaggero, F. Marano, C. Brüllmann, G. Fascioli, T. Ferrari

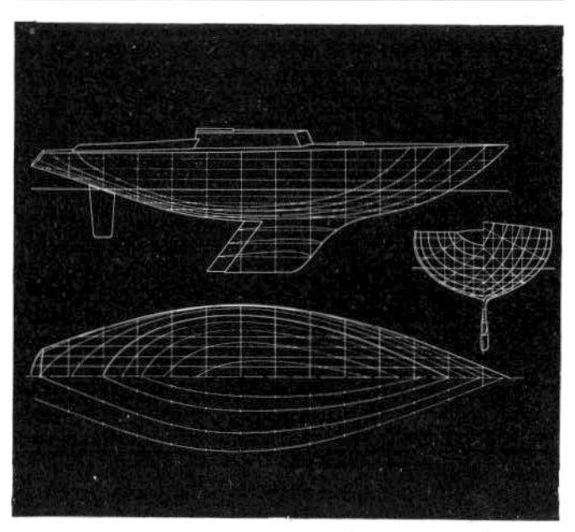

1972 Paris, France
22. Conversion of a river boat

Conversion of a river boat and its adaptation to a studio/workshop.
Client: Piano & Rogers, Paris
Architects: Studio Piano & Rogers with C. Brüllmann, F. Marano

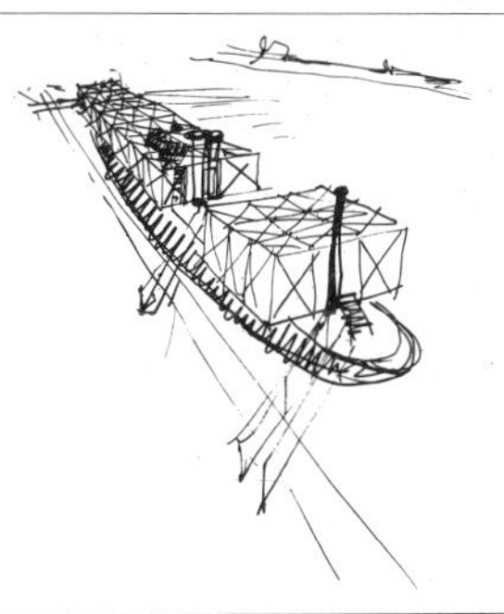

1972-1974 Cusago, Milan, Italy
23. One-family homes

Four single-family homes; steel roofing structure permits free layout of interior.
Clients: Lucci, Giannotti, Simi, Pepe
Architects: Studio Piano & Rogers with C. Brüllmann, R. Luccardini, G. Fascioli, and the collaboration of R. and S. Lucci
Engineer: F. Marano

1973-1974 Ashford, England
24. Chemical laboratory for production of perfumes

Research into the field of integration of organic installations with structure.
Client: UOP Fragrances Ltd, London
Architects: Studio Piano & Rogers with M. Goldschmied, J. Young, R. Bormioli, P. Flack, N. Winder, P. Ullathorne
Engineers: Antony Hunt Associates (structural consultants)

1973-1976 Ovada, Alessandria, Italy
25. Industrial building

Industrial building built with factory-precast reinforced concrete elements.
Client: ATIB S.r.l.
Architects: Studio Piano & Rogers with G. Fascioli
Engineer: F. Marano

1973-1974 Paris, France
26. Atelier Paris

Client: Atelier Piano
Architects: Atelier Piano

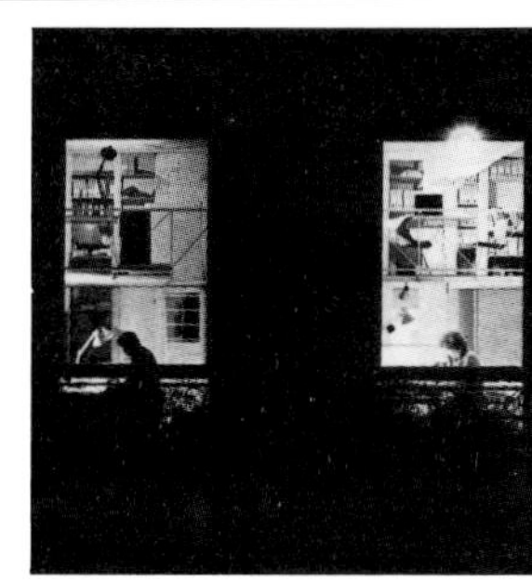

1973-1977 Paris, France
27. IRCAM: Institute for Research and Coordination in Acoustics and Music

A musical implement on the scale of a building, created by collaboration between the architects and musicians, mathematicians, physicists. Constructed underground to reduce and control external acoustic interference.
Client: IRCAM, Paris
Architects: Studio Piano & Rogers with M. Davies, N. Okabe, K. Rupard, J. Sircus, W. Zbinden
Engineers: Ove Arup & Partners
Acoustic consultant: V. Peutz

Scenographic consultant: G.C. François

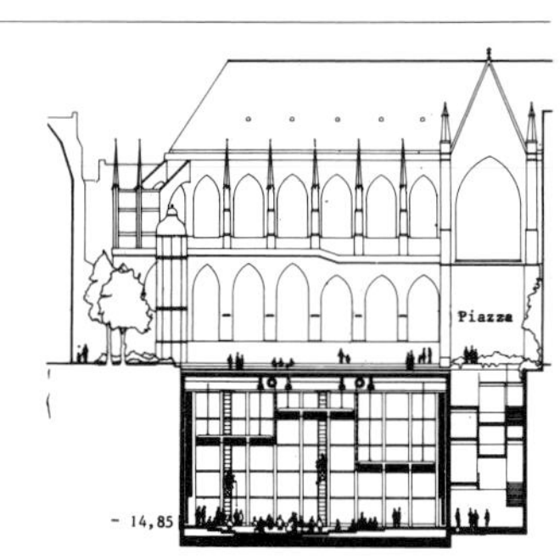

1976 Cambridge, England
28. Electrical engineering workshop

Open plan building with high degree of integration of equipment, intended for research.
Client: PAT Division, Cambridge
Architects: Studio Piano & Rogers with J. Young and M. Goldschmied, M. Burckhardt, D. Gray, D. Thom, P. Ullathorne
Engineer: Felix J. Samuely (structural consultant)

1976
29. Telephone exchanges

Telephone exchanges with modular in-line development predisposed for electronic switchboard systems.
Client: F.lli Dioguardi Contractors
Architects: Piano & Rice & Associates with S. Ishida and N. Okabe

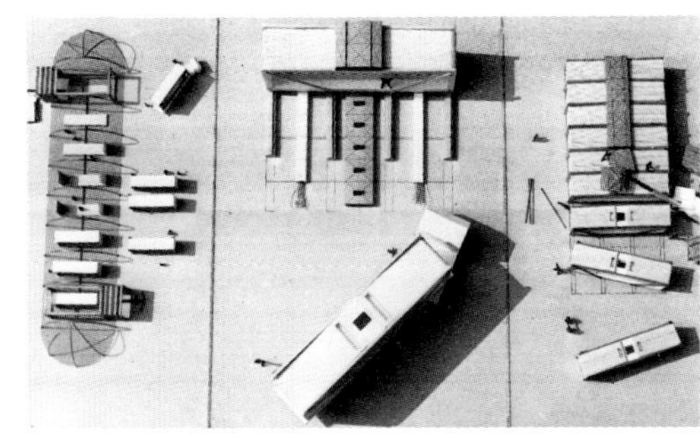

1977 Milan, Italy
30. Office system

Modular system of office furnishing integrating functions of lighting, climate-control, communications.
Architects: Studio Piano & Rice with S. Ishida and N. Okabe

1977-1980 Genoa, Italy
31. Studio/workshop

Pavilion/studio/workshop in the garden of a 17th century building.
Client: Studio Piano
Architects: Studio Piano

1977-1980 Marne-la-Vallée, France
32. Housing and workshops

Housing and buildings for the purifying plant of Lagny.
Client: Etablissement Public de la Ville Nouvelle de Marne-la-Vallée
Architects: Piano & Rice & Associates - Paris
with B. Plattner, W. Zbinden, J. Lohse

1978 Selestat, Strasbourg, France
33. Kronenbourg factory building

Permanent construction site functioning over a ten-year period without interrupting production.
Client: Kronenbourg & Ingetec eng., coordinator
Architects: Piano & Rice & Associates - Paris
with M. Dowd, B. Plattner, R. Verbizh, W. Zbinden
assisted by N. Okabe, J. Lohse, C. Ostrej
Engineers: GETTEC, Inex, NNN

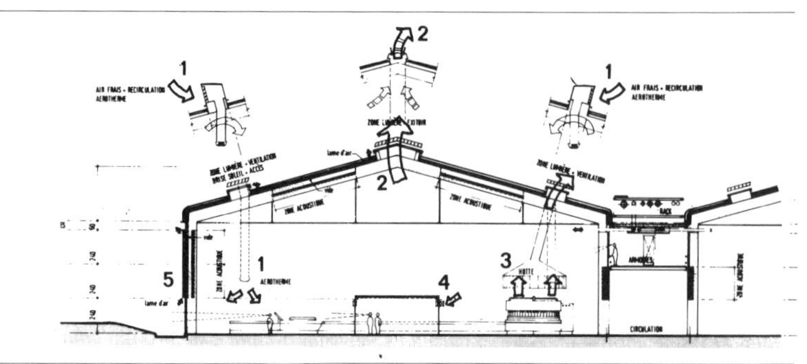

1978
34. Wall system

Emergency housing with modular linear construction system.
Client: F.lli Dioguardi Contractors
Architects: Piano & Rice & Associates
with S. Ishida, N. Okabe

1978 Cergy-Pontoise, France
35. Competition design for a housing estate

Design based on a concept of evolving units currently studied in this period.
Architects: Piano & Rice & Associates - Paris
with M. Dowd, B. Plattner, R. Verbizh, W. Zbinden

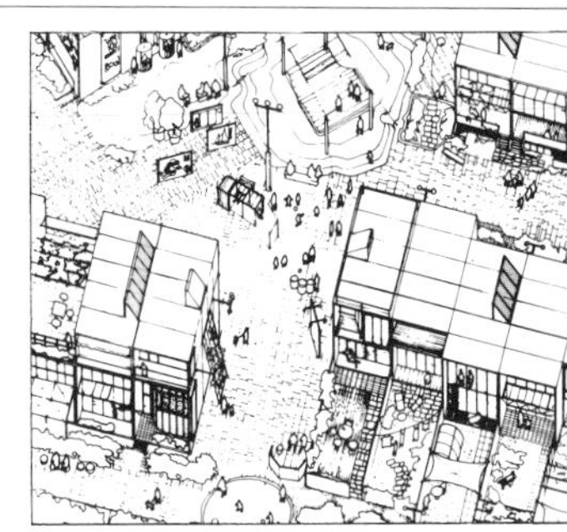

1978 Dakar, Senegal
36. Mobile construction unit for Senegal

Decentralization of construction using small travelling workshops available to occupants.
Client: UNESCO, Dakar regional office; M. Senghor; Breda of Dakar
Architects: Piano & Rice & Associates
with R. Verbizh, O. Dellicour, S. Ishida

1978
37. Competition design

Single-story construction system, climatized by solar energy plant.
Architects: Studio Piano & Rice & Associates
with S. Ishida, N. Okabe, G. Picardi
F.lli Dioguardi Contractors.
with S. Pietrogrande, D.M. Fontana

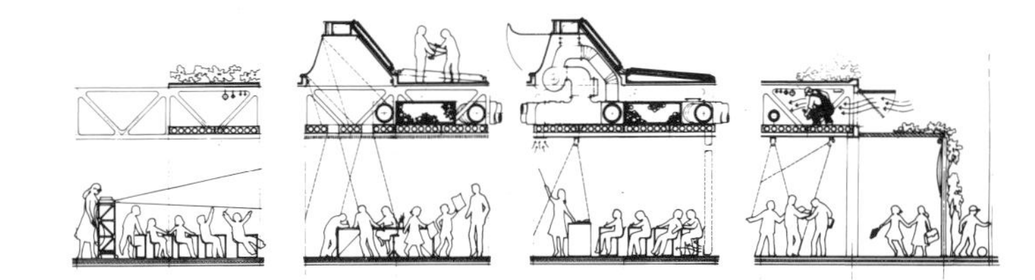

1978 Perugia, Italy
38. Industrialized construction system for evolving-type homes

The concept of evolving space applied to specialized construction of the outer shell and organization of the interior directly controlled by the occupant.
Client: Vibrocemento Perugia S.p.A.
Coordinator: Engineer R. Jascone
Architects: Piano & Rice & Associates
S. Ishida, N. Okabe
with E. Donato, G. Picardi
Engineers: P. Rice assisted by
F. Marano, H. Bardsley

with the collaboration of Vibrocemento Perugia

1978 Turin, Italy
39. Transport vehicle

Basic means of transport for developing countries produced using intermediate technologies and imported mechanical components.
Client: IDEA, S.p.A.
Architects: Piano & Rice & Associates
with S. Ishida, N. Okabe,
IDEA Institute
with F. Mantegazza, W. De Silva

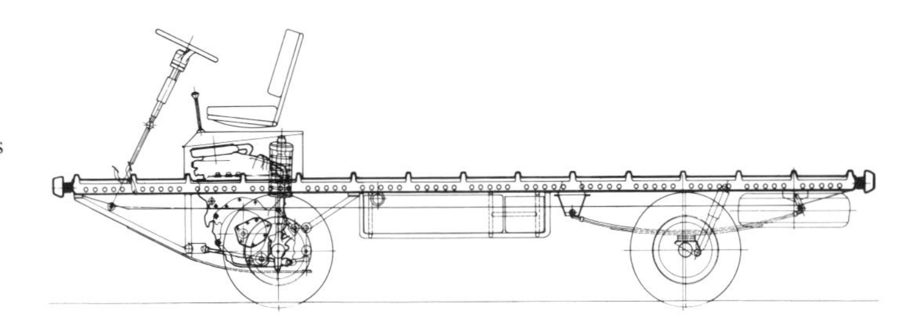

1978-1980 Turin, Italy
40. Fiat VSS experimental vehicle

Experimental car based on separation of structure and the outer shell; research into lightness and safety.
Client: Fiat Auto S.p.A., Turin;
IDEA Institute
Coordination: G. Trebbi/IDEA Institute
Architects: Piano & Rice & Associates
with L. Abbot, S. Ishida, N. Okabe,
B. Plattner, A. Stanton, R. Verbizh
IDEA Institute
with S. Boggio, F. Conti, O. Di Blasi,
W. De Silva, M. Sibona

Engineers: Ove Arup & Partners
(T. Barker and M. Manning)
Acoustics: S. Brown Associates

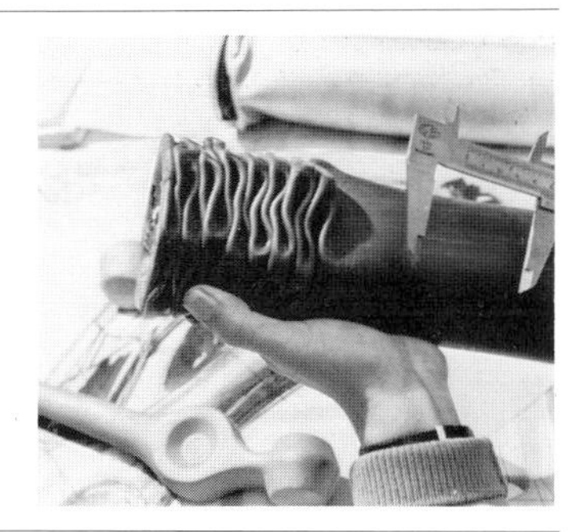

1978-1982 Corciano, Perugia, Italy
41. Quartiere Il Rigo

A residential estate experimenting with occupant participation.
Client: Commune of Corciano
Architects: Piano & Rice & Associates
S. Ishida, N. Okabe, L. Custer, architects in charge
with E. Donato, G. Picardi, O. Di Blasi
Engineers: P. Rice with H. Bardsley, F. Marano
with Edilcooper, RPA Associates, Vibrocemento Perugia
Direction of works: L. Custer with F. Marano.

1978-1982 S. Luca di Molare, Alessandria, Italy
42. Holiday homes

Housing estate experimenting with advanced forms of natural ventilation and solar energy.
Client: Immobiliare S. Luca
Architects: Studio Piano
with S. Ishida, G. Picardi, E. Donato, O. Di Blasi, F. Marano, G. Fascioli
Direction of works: O. Di Blasi

1979
43. An experiment in educational television: the program "Open Site"

Client: Radiotelevisione Italiana, Channel 2
Program directed by G. Macchi
Produced by V. Lusvardi
Architects: Piano & Rice & Associates
with S. Ishida, N. Okabe, G. Picardi, S. Yamada, M. Bonino, R. Biondo, G. Fascioli, R. Gaggero
Texts and screenplays by Magda Arduino

1979
44. Design for office-factory

Study of a new type of work organization in industrial series production and of new equipment adapted for its application.
Client: ANACT
Architects: Piano & Rice & Associates - Paris
with M. Dowd, architect in charge

1979-1981 Macolim, Switzerland
45. Prototype emergency home

Emergency cell easily dismantled and transported for the homeless.
Client: Département des Affaires Etrangères de la Confédération Helvétique
Architects: Studio Piano & Rice & Associates (competition)
B. Plattner, P. Rice (execution)

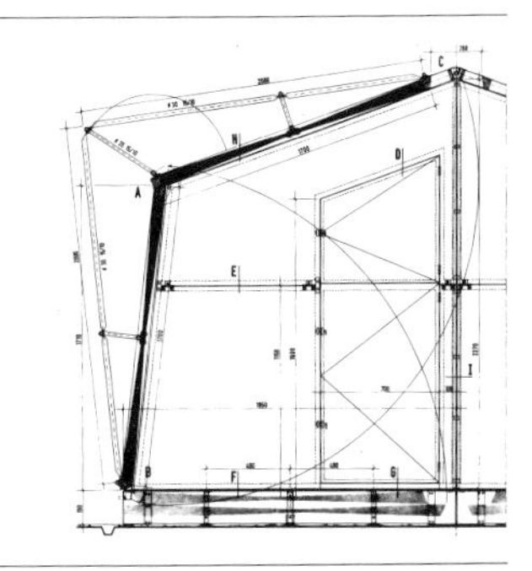

1979 Otranto, Italy
46. Neighborhood Workshop: an experiment in urban reconstruction

Experiment in renovation of the ancient town. Routine and extraordinary maintenance projects with the Neighborhood Workshop.
Client: UNESCO (Establishment division of human and socio-cultural environments)
S. Busuttil, W. Tochtermann
Architects: Piano & Rice & Associates/ F.lli Dioguardi Contractors
with S. Ishida, N. Okabe, R. Verbizh, E. Donato, G. Fascioli, R. Melai, G. Picardi, R. Gaggero
Engineers: Ove Arup & Partners (P. Beckmann), IDEA Institute with the collaboration of G.P. Cuppini, G. Gasparri, F. Marano, F. Marconi, EDITECH with M. Fazio for the Neighborhood Workshop and G. Macchi for the films of the Radiotelevisione Italiana
R. Biondo, M. Bonino
Operational coordination and administration: G. Dioguardi
Program by Magda Arduino

1980 Burano, Venice, Italy
47. Design for restructuring the island of Burano

Neighborhood Workshop involving craftsmen and inhabitants.
Client: Commune of Venice
Architects: Piano & Rice & Associates with P. H. Chombard de Lauwe, S. Ishida, University of Venice and coordination of the Fondazione Tre Oci, G. Macchi and A. Macchi assisted by H. Bardsley, M. Calvi, L. Custer, C. Teoldi
Program by Magda Arduino

1980-1982 Bari, Italy
48. Neighborhood Workshop for local maintenance

Technological consulting workshop, with inhabitants' participation, for the analysis, maintenance and energy improvement of existing buildings at the eastern fringe of Bari.
Client: F.lli Dioguardi Contractors, Bari
Architects and Engineers: Studio Piano/Building Workshop S.r.l. and Dioguardi Contractors
with N. Costantino, S. Pietrogrande, G. Ferracuti, S. Ishida, F. Marano, E. Frigerio, E. Donato, G. Fascioli,
C. Teoldi, SES Engineering
L. Malgieri
assisted by A. Alto, G. Amendola
Program by Magda Arduino

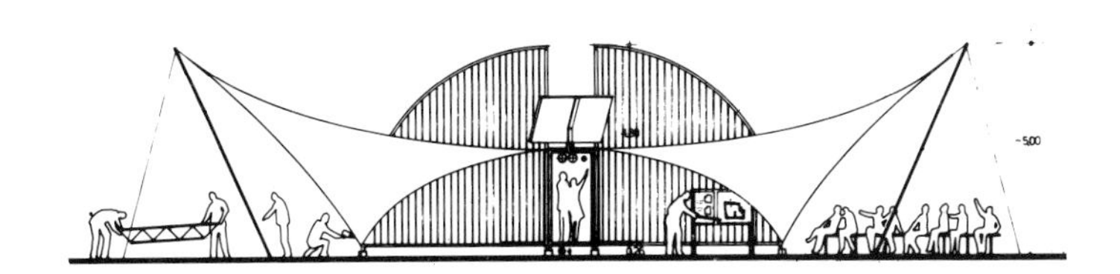

1980 Genoa, Italy
49. Multifunctional food center

Complex of buildings for the city's food markets, using experimental techniques for energy retrieval.
Client: Commune of Genoa
Architects: Studio Piano/Building Workshop S.r.l.
with S. Ishida, F. Marano, E. Donato, F. Doria, G. Fascioli with specialist contributions from F. Torrieri, Ansaldo S.p.A., Elsag S.p.A., Molinari Appalti S.r.l., Aerimpianti S.p.A., Termomeccanica S.p.A.

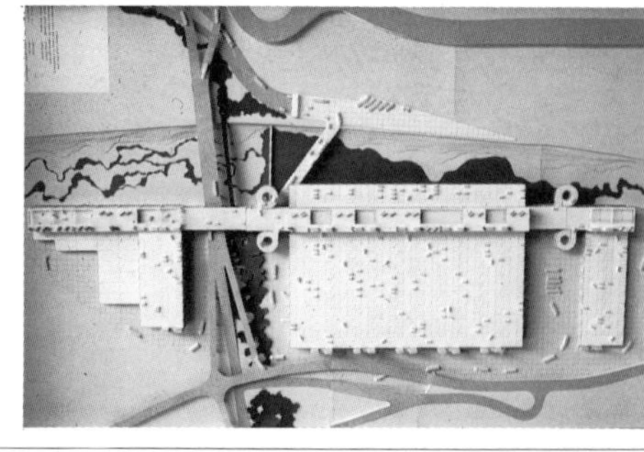

1980-1981 Milan, Italy
50. Load-bearing structure for Milanofiori Conference Center

Structural system with steel beams supporting the building, Italian premises of the World Trade Center.
Client: WTC, Milan
Architects: Studio Piano/Building Workshop S.r.l.
with S. Ishida, F. Marano

1980 Passaggio di Bettona, Perugia, Italy
51. Cultural and exhibition center

Restoration of a 15th century Benedictine abbey and its conversion to use as a cultural and exhibition center.
Client: Sig.ri Lispi
Architects: Piano & Rice & Associates/Building Workshop S.r.l.
with S. Ishida, L. Custer, F. Marano
with the collaboration of F. Icardi, R. Ruocco

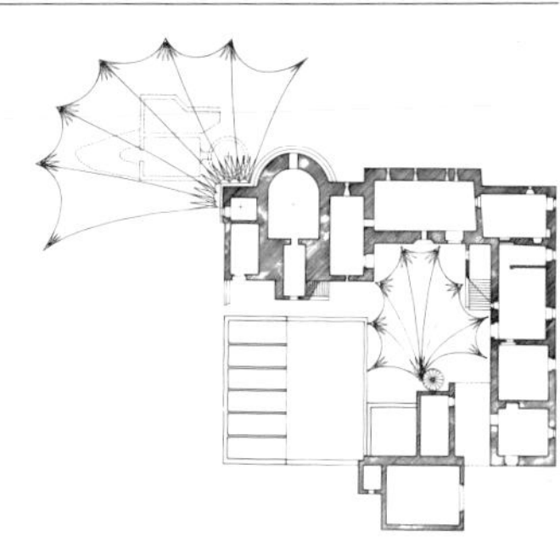

1980 Milan, Italy
52. Exhibition complex

Exhibition area conceived as a great platform equipped with facilities and composed of a spatial grid of reinforced concrete pyramidal elements.
Client: Nidosa - Gruppo Cabassi
Architects: Studio Piano/Building Workshop S.r.l.
with S. Ishida, F. Doria, E. Frigerio, A. Traldi, F. Marano, G. Trebbi (coordinators)
assisted by M. Carroll, O. Di Blasi, E. Miola, G. Fascioli, R. Gaggero
Film documentation: M. Arduino, M. Bonino, S. Battini
Engineers: Ove Arup & Partners, P. Rice, T. Barker, assisted by N. Noble and A. Guthrie, C. Giambelli. D. Zucchi
Consultants: Italian Promoservice (exhibition services)
B. Richards (transport)
G. Lund (technical)
APT (fire prevention and security)

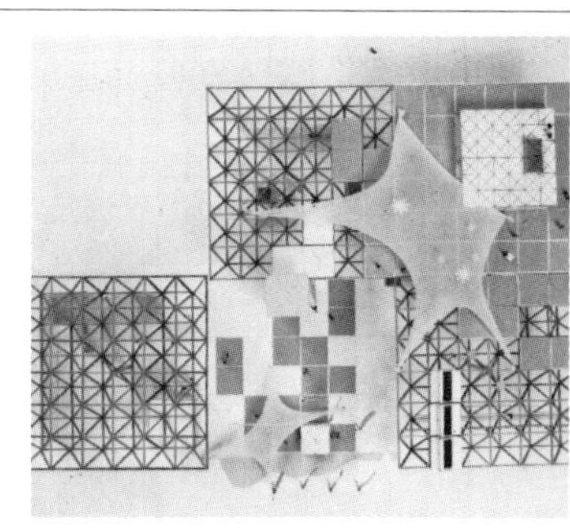

1980 Loano, Savona, Italy
53. Detailed plan for shore and port

Study of detailed development plan for shore and port.
Client: Commune of Loano
Architects: Studio Piano/Building Workshop S.r.l.
with S. Ishida, A. Traldi, F. Doria, M. Carroll, G. Picardi, R. Truffelli
with the specialized collaboration of engineer Brizzolara

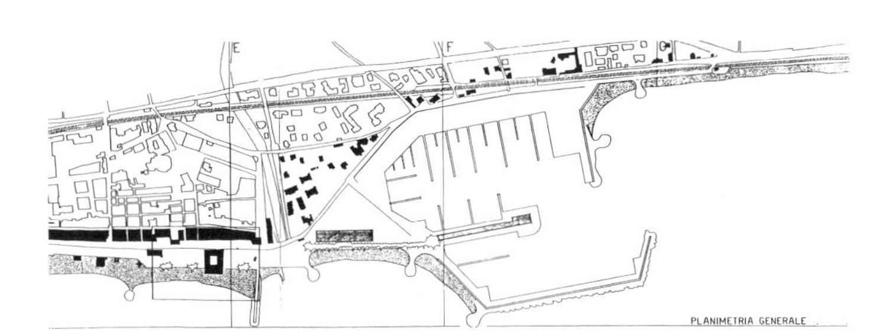

1980 Loano, Savona, Italy
54. Loano civic center

Design of the library and meeting rooms to identify a service dimensioned with reference to existing spaces on the town level.
Architects: Studio Piano/Building Workshop S.r.l.
with S. Ishida, A. Traldi, F. Doria, M. Carroll, G. Picardi

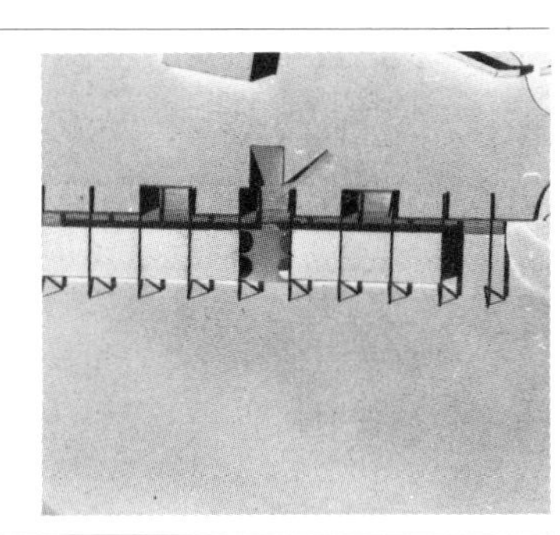

1980-1981, Cremona, Italy
55. Arvedi tubular structural system

An example of integrated design between architects and industry. The design is intended to realize a tubular steel structural system exploiting the manufacturing processes of large-scale industrial works.
Client: Arvedi S.p.A.
Architects: Piano & Rice & Associates/Building Workshop S.r.l.
with S. Ishida, O. Di Blasi
engineers: P. Rice assisted by H. Bardsley
with Arvedi technical department
with engineers Gosio and Galli

1981 Genoa, Italy
56. Renewing the old Quartiere del Molo and an axis of services

Reclamation plan envisaging rehabilitation projects with minor transfers of inhabitants within the ambit of the neighborhood, to be carried out through the Neighborhood Workshop.
Application of special techniques of natural lighting of the lanes and ventilation of lower stories of buildings.
Client: Commune of Genoa
Architects: Studio Piano/Building Workshop S.r.l.
S. Ishida, A. Traldi
with F. Marano, A. Bianchi, E. Frigerio
For the rehabilitation project of the old Quartiere del Molo the collaboration of R. Ruocco, F. Icardi, R. Melai, E. Miola
and for planning aspects
V. Podestà, G. Amadeo of Tekne Planning
with legal consultancy of F. Pagano
Program by Magda Arduino

1981 Turin, Italy
57. Restructuring renewal of a street block in the ancient city center

Rehabilitation project, renewal of structures and facilities, and completion executed directly by the occupants with assistance of the Neighborhood Workshop.
Client: Commune of Turin (Housing Department)
Architects: Studio Piano/Building Workshop S.r.l.
with S. Ishida, F. Marano, R. Ruocco, F. Icardi, E. Frigerio
Program by Magda Arduino

1981-1983 Houston, Texas, USA
58. The Menil Collection

Building consisting of an articulated platform filtering light from above and transmitting it to the interior of the exhibition area. A comprehensive scientific study of light enables the design to provide natural lighting for the works of art. Some functions are distributed in the neighboring buildings.
Client: Menil Foundation
Mme D. De Menil, president;
W. Hopps, director;
P. Winkler, associate director

Architects: Piano & Fitzgerald Architects, Genoa-Houston
with S. Ishida, assisted by M. Carroll, F. Doria, C. Süsstrunk, B. Plattner;
P. Kelly, project director
assisted by L. Turner,
E. Huckaby and M. Downs
Engineers: Ove Arup & Partners
P. Rice, T. Barker, assisted by N. Noble and A. Guthrie
with Gentry Haynes & Whaley and Galewsky & Johnston, structures and fluids;
R. Jensen, fire-protection; E. Brown, security; E.G. Lowry, contractors

1981-1983 Reggio Emilia, Italy
59. Building for the Banca Agricola Commerciale, Italian Automobile Club and collective services

Cluster of services comprising parking, bank premises, shopping center, conference hall and other collective activities linked with the surroundings of the ancient city center of Reggio Emilia.
Client: Banca Agricola Commerciale
Coordinator: S. Ferretti
Architects: Studio Piano/Building Workshop S.r.l.
with S. Ishida, A. Traldi, F. Doria, E. Donato, F. Marano, C. Süsstrunk
Engineer: A. Rossi

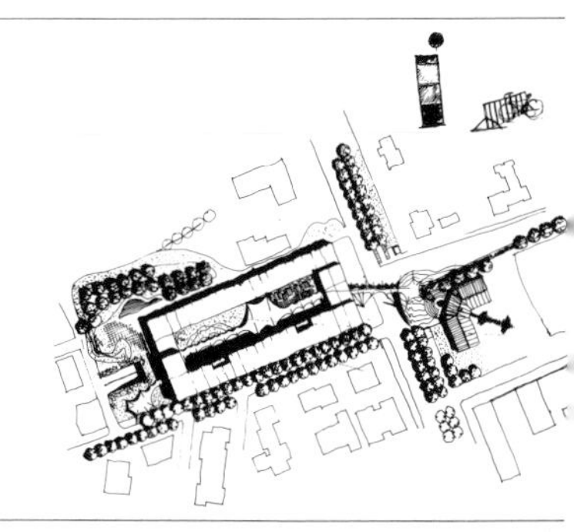

1981-1984 Montrouge, Paris, France
60. Urban conversion of Schlumberger works

Rehabilitation and conversion of an early 20th century industrial complex to parking space, urban park, offices and workshop. The plan envisages grafting present-day architectural vocabulary onto existing structures but without obliterating their memory.
Client: Compteurs Montrouge (Groupe Schlumberger Ltd)
Coordinators: A. Vincent
assisted by R. Lafon and G. Messand
Architects: Atelier Piano

with N. Okabe, B. Plattner, M. Dowd, architects in charge
assisted by S. Ishida, T. Hartman, J.F. Schmit, J. Lohse, G. Saint-Jean
Technical engineers: GEC
Landscaping: A. Chemetoff

1981 Berlin, West Germany
61. IBA design for extension of the Nationalgalerie and housing

Restricted entry competition organized by the IBA for 50 apartments and an extension to the museum.
Client: IBA, Berlin
Architects: Studio Piano/Building Workshop S.r.l.
S. Ishida, C. Süsstrunk, architects in charge
with F. Doria, N. Okabe, A. Traldi, M. Carroll

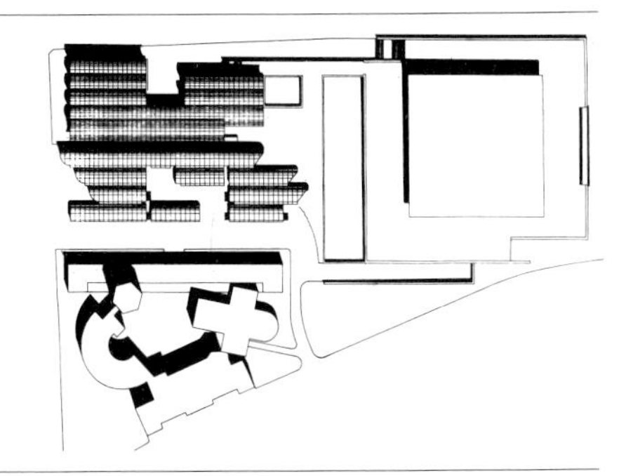

1982
62. Competition for premises of the Organization of Arab Petroleum Exporting Countries in Kuwait

Office building with scope for extension and system of exploitation of the local climate.
Client: Organization of Arab Petroleum Exporting Countries
Architects: Studio Piano/Building Workshop S.r.l.
with S. Ishida, A. Traldi, F. Doria
B. Mehren, M. Carroll, E. Frigerio
Tekne VRC
with C. Bottigelli, Parodi, Seratto

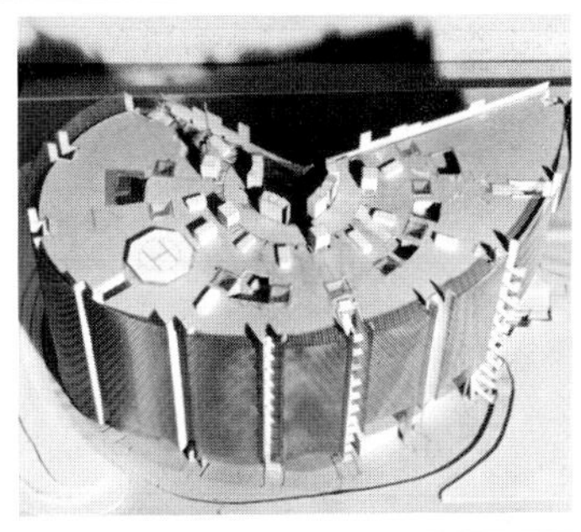

1982
63. IBM travelling exhibition

Temporary exhibition building of polycarbonate pyramidal elements, laminated wood and aluminum, to be placed in urban parks.
Client: IBM
Coordinators: G.L. Trischitta
R. Lanterio, F. Moisset
Architects: Studio Piano/Building Workshop S.r.l.
with S. Ishida, A. Traldi, O. Di Blasi
F. Doria, F. Marano, M. Carroll
G. Fascioli, R. Gaggero
with P. Nestler (Munich), N. Okabe (Paris) and A. Stanton (London)
Engineers: Ove Arup & Partners,
P. Rice, T. Barker, assisted by
A. Guthrie and R. Kinch.
General contractor:
Carablese Engineering S.p.A.
A. Gnoato, M. Valeriani

1982 Turin, Italy
64. Reuse of the Palazzo a Vela for the Alexander Calder retrospective

Client: Commune of Turin, Toro Insurance
Curator: G. Carandente
Architects: Studio Piano/Building Workshop S.r.l.
with S. Ishida, O. Di Blasi, E. Frigerio,
P. Terbüchte, F. Marano, A. Traldi
Engineers: Ove Arup & Partners
Lighting: P. Castiglioni
Graphics: P. Cerri

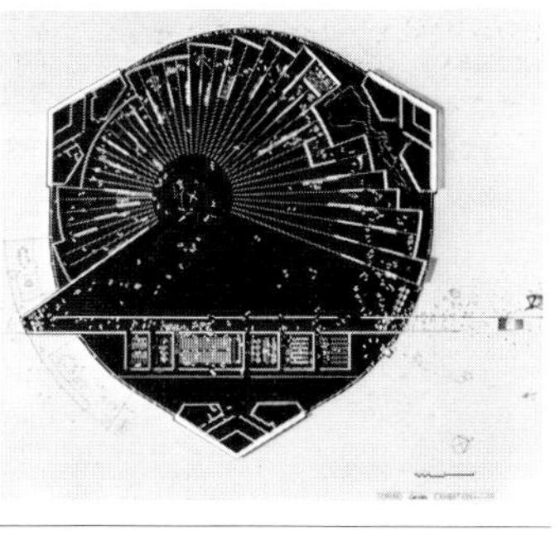

1982 Rome, Italy
65. Centocelle business center

Design for the new Centocelle/ Torrespaccata business center.
Client: Brioschi Finanziaria - Gruppo Cabassi
Architects: Studio Piano/Building Workshop S.r.l., engineer Clerici with S. Ishida, F. Marano, A. Traldi, B. Merhen, M. Carroll, E. Frigerio, A. Bianchi, F. Doria, R. Truffelli

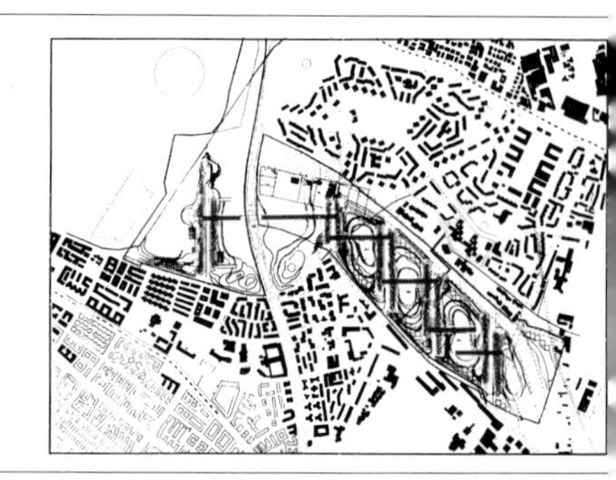

1982 Paris, France
66. Universal exposition 1989

Main entry floating on the Seine.
Client: Ministry of Culture
Architects: Atelier Piano with N. Okabe, J.F. Schmit, G. Petit, C. Clarisse
Engineers: P. Rice with J. Thornton
Historical research: C. Hodeir

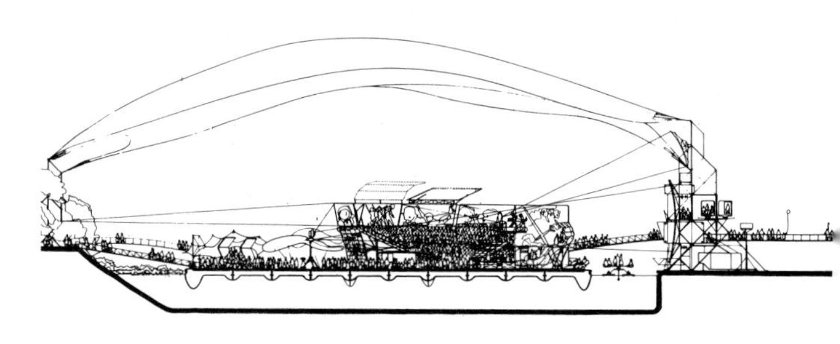

1982 Omegna, Novara, Italy
67. Detailed plan for the "Pietra" area

Study of a detailed plan for the industrial site of the former Cobianchi building.
Client: Commune of Omegna
Architects: Studio Piano/Building Workshop S.r.l. with S. Ishida, F. Marano, A. Bianchi E. Frigerio and with the collaboration of R. Ripamonti

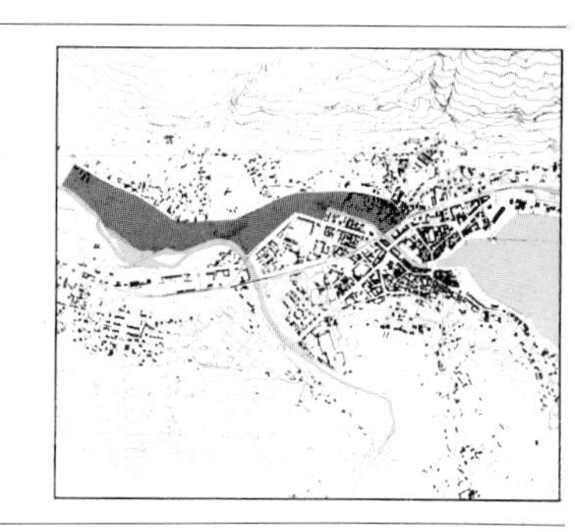

1982 Modena, Italy
68. Branch bank for the Banca Agricola Commerciale

Typological conversion of a printing work into a bank.
Client: Banca Agricola Commerciale
Coordinator: S. Ferretti
Architects: Studio Piano/Building Workshop S.r.l. with S. Ishida, E. Frigerio
Engineers: Ceccoli, Jascone Associated Engineers

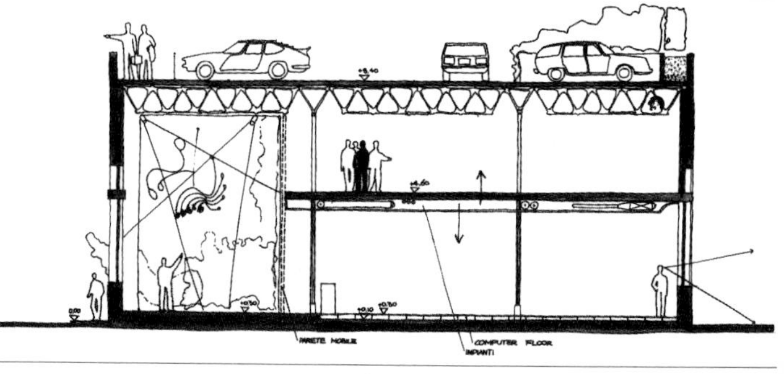

Biography

Born in Genoa on September 14, 1937, Renzo Piano presently lives in Paris. He graduated from the School of Architecture, Milan Polytechnic in 1964, and subsequently worked with his father in Genoa. He worked under the design guidance of Franco Albini from 1962 to 1964. Between the years 1965 and 1970 Piano worked with Z.S. Makowsky in London. His collaboration with Richard Rogers dates from 1971 (Piano & Rogers), from 1977 with Peter Rice (Atelier Piano & Rice) and from 1980 with Richard Fitzgerald in Houston. His work is currently divided between London, Genoa, Paris and Houston.
He has been a visiting professor at Columbia University, New York; University of Pennsylvania, Philadelphia; the Oslo School of Architecture; the Central London Polytechnic; the Architectural Association School of London and has lectured in London, Delft, Bucharest, Paris, Milan, Rome, Tokyo, Venice and Houston.
Piano has won recognition in various national and international architectural competitions. In 1978 he was awarded the Union Internationale des Architects prize in Mexico City, and in 1981 he was awarded the Compasso d'Oro.
He has been awarded the AIA Honorary Fellowship. Exhibitions devoted to his work have been mounted by the Architectural Association, London; the Musée des Arts Décoratifs, Paris; the Milan Triennale; the RIBA, London; the Paris Biennale; IN-ARCH, Rome; the Tre Oci, Venice; the Palazzo Bianco, Genoa; the Sottochiesa di San Francesco, Arezzo; SAIE DUE, Bologna; Castello Svevo, Bari; Museo di Capidomonti, Naples; and the Architectural Museum, Helsinki.

Piano's present collaborators
Genoa office, (Building Workshop S.r.l.):
Shunji Ishida, (associate architect), with Alessandro Bianchi, Mark Carroll, Lorenzo Custer, Ottavio Di Blasi, François Doria, Giorgio Fascioli, Enrico Frigerio, Filippo Icardi, Barbara Mehren, Peter Terbüchte, Raffaele Ruocco, Alessandro Traldi, Renzo Truffelli, architects; Flavio Marano, engineer; Magda Arduino Piano, with Sandro Battini and Manuel Bonino for the media and film production; Anna Serra, graphics; Rinaldo Gaggero, Edoardo Miola, workshop; Rosella Biondo, secretarial department; Gianfranco Biggi, Angela Sacco, administration.
Paris office (Atelier Piano):
Noriaki Okabe, Bernard Plattner, Mike Dowd, Tom Hartman, Johanna Lohse, Gil Petit, Gérard Saint-Jean, Jean François Schmit, Christian Süsstrunk, Bernard Vaudeville, architects; Evelyne Mercier and Mariette Müller, secretarial department.
Houston office (Piano & Fitzgerald):
Paul Kelly, Leland Turner, Ed Huckaby, Mike Downs. Permanent collaboration with Ove Arup & Partners, London: Peter Rice structural engineer, Tom Barker service engineer, with Neil Noble, Alistair Guthrie, J. Thornton and R. Kinch.

Bibliography

R. Piano, R. Foni, G. Garbuglia, L. Tirelli, M. Filocca, "Una struttura ad elementi standard, per la copertura di medie e grandi luci," in *La Prefabbricazione*, January 1966.

Z.S. Makowsky, "Structural plastics in Europe," in *Arts & Architecture*, August 1966, pp. 20-30.

M. Scheichenbauer, "Progettare con le materie plastiche," in *Casabella*, 316, 1967.

"Ricerca sulle strutture in lamiera e in poliestere rinforzato," in *Domus*, 448, March 1967, pp. 8-22.

"Il grande numero," in *Domus*, 466, September 1968.

"Nuove tecniche e nuove strutture per l'edilizia," in *Domus*, 468, November 1968, p. 6.

"Uno studio-Laboratorio," in *Domus*, 479, October 1969, pp. 10-14.

R. Piano, "Progettazione sperimentale per strutture a guscio," in *Casabella*, 335, 1969.

R. Piano, "Experiments and projects with industrialised structures in plastic material," in *P.D.O.B.*, 16/17, October 1969.

Z.S. Makowsky, "Plastic structures of R. Piano," in *Systems, Building and Design,* February 1969, pp. 37-54.

R. Piano, "Nasce con le materie plastiche un nuovo modo di progettare architettura," in *Materie plastiche ed Elastomeri*, 1, 1969.

Z.S. Makowsky, "Les structures et plastiques de R. Piano," in *Plastique Bâtiment,* 126, February 1969, pp. 10-17.

R. Piano, "Italie recherche de structures," in *Techniques & Architecture,* XXX, 5, 1969, pp. 96-100.

Z.S. Makowsky, "Strukturen aus Kunststoff von Renzo Piano," in *Bauen + Wohnen,* 4, April 1970, pp. 112-121.

"Un Cantiere Sperimentale," in *Casabella*, 349, 1970.

R. Piano, "Il padiglione dell'Industria italiana all'Expo 70 di Osaka," in *Acciaio,* 11, November 1970, p. 1.

A. Cereda, "Alcune recenti esperienze nel campo della industrializzazione edilizia - tre architetture di Renzo Piano," in *Lipe,* 3, March 1970, pp. 1-12.

R. Piano, translated by T.M. Stevens, "Architecture and Technology," in *A.A. Quarterly,* 3, vol. 2, July 1970, pp. 32-43.

"Renzo Piano," in *Architectural Design,* 3, March 1970, pp. 140-145.

"Italian Industry Pavilion, Expo 70, Osaka," in *Architectural Design,* 8, August 1970, p. 416.

"Il poliestere rinforzato protagonista del padiglione dell'industria italiana," in *Materie plastiche ed Elastomeri,* 5, May 1970, pp. 470-477.

"Rigging a roof," in *The Architectural Forum,* 2, vol. 132, March 1970, pp. 64-69.

"Renzo Piano verso una pertinenza tecnologica dei componenti," in *Casabella,* 352, 1970, p. 37.

"L'Italia a Osaka," in *Domus*, 484, March 1970.

"Industrialisierung," in *Deutsche Bauzeitung*, 4, April 1971, pp. 405-407.

"Industrial building," in *Architectural Forum*, April 1971.

"Piano & Rogers: Beaubourg," in *Domus*, 503, October 1971, pp. 1-7.

R. Piano, "Per un'edilizia industrializzata," in *Domus*, 495, February 1971, pp. 12-15.

R. Piano, "L'acciaio nell'edilizia industrializzata," in *Acciaio*, 11, November 1971, pp. 1-4.

"Le materie plastiche nella produzione edilizia per componenti," in *Materie plastiche ed Elastomeri*, 5, May 1971.

"Grand Piano," in *Industrial Design*, 8, vol. 18, October 1971, pp. 40-45.

M. Cornu, "Concours Beaubourg 'est-ce un signe de notre temps?'" in *Architecture Mouvement Continuité*, 23, November 1971, pp. 8-9.

"Projet des Lauréats," in *Techniques & Architecture*, 3 special, 34, February 1972, pp. 48-55.

"Le projet lauréat," in *Paris project*, 7, 1972, pp. 48-57.

"Paris Centre Beaubourg," in *Deutsche Bauzeitung*, 9, September 1972, pp. 974-976.

"A Parigi per i Parigini l'evoluzione del progetto Piano + Rogers per il Centre Beaubourg," in *Domus*, 511, June 1972, pp. 9-12.

"Aktualitat: Esso Tankstellen Wettbewerd in Italien," in *Bauen + Wohnen*, 6, 1972, p. 280.

"Padiglione dell'industria italiana all'Expo 70 di Osaka," in *Casabella*, suppl. 363, March 1972.

Rédaction de l'A.A., "Centre Culturel du Plateau Beaubourg," in *L'Architecture d'Aujourd'hui*, 168, July-August 1973, pp. 34-43.

"Piano + Rogers," in *L'Architecture d'Aujourd'hui*, 170, November-December 1973, pp. 46-58.

"Centre Plateau Beaubourg," in *Domus*, 525, August 1973.

"Edificio per gli uffici B & B a Novedrate," in *Domus*, 530, January 1974, pp. 31-36.

"Beaubourg en transparence," in *Architecture Intérieure*, 141, June-July 1974, pp. 72-77.

"Piano," in *Zodiac 22*, pp. 126-147.

"Centre Beaubourg à Paris," in *Techniques & Architecture*, 300, September/October 1974, p. 58.

"Factory, Tadworth, Surrey," in *The Architectural Review*, 934, December 1974, pp. 338-345.

Piano & Rogers, "B & B Italia Factory," in *Architectural Design*, 4, 1974, pp. 245-246.

"Le Centre Beaubourg," in *Chantiers de France*, 68, 1974, pp. 1-6.

"Expressive Einheit von Tragkonstruktion und Installationsanlagen," in *Bauen + Wohnen*, 2, February 1974, pp. 71-74.

"A Parigi musica underground," in *Domus*, 545, April 1975, pp. 9-12.

R. Bordaz, "Le Centre Georges Pompidou," in *Construction*, 9, September 1975, pp. 5-30.

"Etablissement public du Centre Beaubourg, Paris," in *Werk œuvre*, 2, February 1975, pp. 140-148.

P. Rice, "Main Structural Framework of the Beaubourg Centre, Paris," in *Acier. Stahl. Steel*, XL, 9, September 1975, pp. 297-309.

Piano & Rogers, "Piano + Rogers," in *Architectural Design*, 45, May 1975, pp. 75-311.

F. Marano, "Una struttura tubolare per un nuovo edificio per uffici a Novedrate," in *Acciaio*, 2, February 1975, pp. 1-7.

P. Rice, L. Grut, "Renzo Piano. La struttura del C. Beaubourg a Parigi," in *Acciaio*, 9, September 1975, pp. 3-15.

K. Menomi, "Nel prato una struttura policroma. Edificio per uffici B & B," in *Ufficio stile*, IX, 6, 1976, pp. 76-79.

"Piano + Rogers: Architectural method," in *A + U*, 66, 1976, pp. 63-122.

"L'Ircam institut de recherche et coordination acoustique/musique," in *Chantiers de France*, 93, September 1976, pp. 2-13.

"IRCAM design process," in *RIBA Journal*, 2, 1976, pp. 61-69.

"Strukturen und Hüllen," in *Werk œuvre*, 11, 1976, pp. 742-748.

Piano & Rogers, "Beaubourg furniture internal system catalogue," in *Architectural Design*, 46, July 1976, pp. 442-443.

"Novedrate Italia Edificio per uffici," in *A.C.*, XXII, 82, April 1976, pp. 35-37.

"Centre National d'Art et Culture Georges Pompidou, Paris," in *Domus*, special issue (566-575), January 1977, pp. 5-37.

P. Restany, C. Casati, "Parigi: l'oggetto funziona!," in *Domus*, 575, October 1977, pp. 1-11.

"Le défi de Beaubourg," in *A.A.*, 189, February 1977, pp. 40-81.
"Frankreichs Centre National d'Art et de Culture G. Pompidou in Paris," in *Bauwelt*, 11, March 1977, pp. 316-334.
"Piano + Rogers," in *RIBA Journal*, 1, January 1977, pp. 11-16.
"Centre National d'Art et Culture Georges Pompidou," in *Domus*, 566, January 1977, pp. 3-37.
"Centre Georges Pompidou," in *AD Profiles*, 2, 1977.
"Piano & Rogers 4 progetti," in *Domus*, 570, May 1977, pp. 17-24.
"The Pompidolium," in *The Architectural Review*, 963, vol. CLXI, May 1977, pp. 270-294.
M. Fadda, "Dal Beaubourg al progetto collettivo," in *Laboratorio 1*, 1, April-June 1977, pp. 69-73.
G. Neret, "Le Centre Pompidou," in *Connaissance des Arts*, 1977, pp. 3-15.
Y. Futagawa, "Centre Beaubourg: Piano + Rogers," in *G.A. Globe Architecture*, 44, 1977, pp. 1-40.
"Le Centre Beaubourg," in *Ministère des Affaires Culturelles Ministère de l'Education Nationale*, 1977.
"Staatliches Kunst- und Kulturzentrum Georges Pompidou/Paris," in *DLW - Nachrichten*, 61, 1977, pp. 34-39.
"Intorno al Beaubourg," in *Abitare*, 158, October 1977, pp. 69-75.
R. Piano, "Mobilités des hypothèses alternatives de production," in *Werk-Archithese*, 11-12, November/December 1977, p. 32.
C. Mitsia, M. Zakazian, C. Jacopin, "Eiffel vs Beaubourg," in *Werk-Archithese*, 9, 1977, pp. 22-29.
J. Bub, W. Messing, "Centre National d'Art et de Culture G. Pompidou ein Arbeitsbericht von zwei Architekturstudenten," in *Bauen + Wohnen*, 4, 1977, pp. 132-139.
R. Piano, "Per un'edilizia evolutiva," in *Laboratorio*, 2, September/November 1977, pp. 7-10.
"Piano & Rogers," in *Architectural Design*, 7-8, vol. 47, 1977, p. 530.
G. Lentati, "Centro Beaubourg, un'architettura utensile," in *Ufficio stile*, X, 5, 1977, pp. 74-87.
P. Chemetov, "L'opéra Pompidou," in *Techniques & Architecture*, 317, December 1977, pp. 62-63.
M. Cornu, "Ce diable de Beaubourg," in *Techniques & Architecture*, 317, December 1977, pp. 64-66.
A. Darlot, "Le centre national d'art et de culture G. Pompidou," in *Revue Française de l'Electricité*, L, 259, December 1977, pp. 48-55.
R. Continenza, "Il centro nazionale d'arte e cultura G. Pompidou a Parigi," in *L'Ingegnere*, LIII, 6, June 1978, pp. 187-198.
A. Paste, "Il Centro d'Arte e di Cultura G. Pompidou," in *L'industria delle costruzioni*, 76, February 1978, pp. 3-30.
"Centro Beaubourg Paris," in *Informes de la Construcciòn*, XXX, 299, April 1978, pp. 13-23.
G. Biondo, E. Rognoni, "Materie plastiche ed edilizia industrializzata," in *Domus*, 585, August 1978, pp. 25-28.
"Tipologie evolutive," in *Domus*, 583, June 1978, pp. 12-13.
"Esperienze di cantiere. Tre domande a R. Piano," in *Casabella*, 439, September 1978, pp. 42-51.
"Tipologie evolutive, lo spazio costruito deve adattarsi all'uomo," in *Domus*, suppl. 587, October 1978, pp. 30-31.
"IRCAM," in *A.A.*, 199, October 1978, pp. 52-63.
"Da uno spazio uguale due case diversissime," in *Abitare*, 171, January/February 1979, pp. 2-21.
"Wohnboxen in Mailand," in *M.D.*, 6, June 1979.
L. Wright, "Heimatlandschaft," in *The Architectural Review*, 990, vol. 166, August 1979, pp. 120-123.
R. Continenza, "L'opera di Piano & Rogers," in *L'Ingegnere*, LIV, 10, October 1979, pp. 469-485.
"Mobiles-Quartier Laboratorium," in *Bauen + Wohnen*, 9, September 1979, pp. 330-332.
"Per il recupero dei Centri storici. Una proposta: il Laboratorio di quartiere," in *Abitare*, 178, October 1979, pp. 86-93.
"Una recentissima proposta di R. Piano: Laboratorio mobile per lavori di recupero edilizio," in *Modulo*, 7/8, 1979, p. 855.
"Il Laboratorio di quartiere a Otranto," in *Domus*, 599, October 1979, p. 2.
L. Rossi, "Piano + Rice + Ass. Il Laboratorio di quartiere," in *Spazio+Società*, 8, December 1979, pp. 27-42.
"Renzo Piano. The Mobile Workshop in Otranto," in *ILA & UD Annual Report Urbino 1979*, 1979, pp. 60-63.
"Operazione di recupero," in *Casabella*, 453, December 1979, p. 7.
R. Continenza, "Architettura e tecnologia aspetti dell'opera di R. Piano e R. Rogers," in *Costruttori Abruzzesi*, II, 1979, pp. 15-18.
"Free-Plan Four House Group," in *Toshi Jutaku*, February 1980, pp. 14-23.
"Enveloppes identiques diversité interne Milano-Cusago I," in *AC 97*, January 1980, pp. 6-11.
"Fiat's magic carpet ride," in *Design*, 379, July 1980, p. 58.
"Centre Georges Pompidou," in *Nikkei Architecture*, 8, August 1980, pp. 83-85.
"Contemporary design in two cities," in *Building & Remodelling Guide*, July 1980, pp. 108-113.
"La technologie n'est pas toujours industrielle," in *A.A.*, 212, December 1980, pp. 51-54.
"Art news," in *The Geiutsu Sheischo*, September 1980.
"C.G. Pompidou," in *A.A.*, 213, February 1981, pp. 92-95.
M.T. Mirabile, "Centro Musicale a Parigi," in *L'industria delle costruzioni*, 114, April 1981, pp. 68-69.
"Sul mestiere dell'Architetto," in *Domus*, 617, May 1981, pp. 27-29.
"Wohnhausgruppe bei Mailand," in *Die Kunst*, 6 June 1981.
P. Santini, "Colloquio con R. Piano," in *Ottagono*, XVI, 61, June 1981, pp. 20-27.
"Pianoforte," in *Building Design*, 556, July 1981, pp. 11-14.
R. Pedio, "Renzo Piano Itinerario e un primo bilancio," in *L'Architettura*, 11, November 1981, pp. 614-662.
G. Lentati, "Quale Ufficio?," in *Ufficio stile*, 6, 1981, pp. 60-69.
R. Piano, "Renzo Piano, Genova," in *Casabella*, 474/475, November/December 1981, pp. 95-96.
Rainieri e Valli, "Progetto e partecipazione," in *Edilizia Popolare*, 163, November-December 1981, pp. 66-68.
"Piano in Houston," in *Skyline*, January 1982, p. 4.
"Renzo Piano monografia," in *A.A.*, 219, monographic issue, February 1982.
"Fiat vettura sperimentale a sottosistemi," in *Abitare*, 202, March 1982, pp. 8-9.
"Italia," in *Nikkei Architecture*, 2, February 1982, pp. 52-56.
M. Dini, "La città storica," in *Area*, 5, June/July 1982, p. 47.
S. Fox "A Clapboard Treasure House," in *Cite*, August 1982, pp. 5-7.
"Renzo Piano still in tune," in *Building Design*, 606, August 1982, pp. 10-11.
"Piano demonstration in Texas," in *Progressive Architecture*, 9, 1982.
M.T. Carbone, "Sei progetti e un fuoco di paglia," in *Costruire per Abitare*, 5, December/January 1982/83, pp. 76-78.

"Tecnoarchitettura vettura sperimentale a sottosistemi," in *Ottagono*, March 1982.

"People's office e ufficio fabbrica," in *Ufficio stile*, 4, April 1982, pp. 49-52.

"Abitacolo e abitazione," in *Casabella*, 484, October 1982, pp. 14-23.

"Renzo Piano," in *The Architectural Review*, 1028, October 1982, pp. 57-61.

L. Scacchetti, "Si chiude la scena, comincia il congresso," in *Costruire per Abitare*, 3, October 1982, pp. 117-120.

"Il Centro Congressi del World Trade Center Italiano," in *Ufficio stile*, XV, 67, 1982, pp. 24-30.

"Contemporary French Architecture. IRCAM: Piano and Rogers," in *Architecture and Urbanism*, 144, September 1982.

"Il recupero del Centro Storico: Sei progetti e un fuoco di paglia," in *Costruire*, January 1983.

"A Roma cresce l'ottavo colle di Massimo di Forti," in *L'Espresso*, February 6, 1983.

"La macchina espositiva," in *Abitare*, 212, March 1983.

O. Pivetta, "La fiera dei mercanti," in *Casabella*, 489, March 1983.

P.-A. Croset, "Parigi 1989," in *Casabella*, 490, April 1983.

A. L. Rossi, "The well tempered environment," in *Domus*, 638, April 1983.

"Designs on the Future. Jean Nouvel and Renzo Piano Set their Sites for '89," in *Wave*, April 1983.

"Réhabilitation/des technologies nouvelles pour l'habitat ancien," in *Techniques & Architecture*, 348, June-July 1983.

"L'espace – flexible entretien avec Renzo Piano," in *Art Press*, special issue, 2 June-July-August 1983.

"Renzo Piano un architetto controvento," in *Linea Capital*, 6, Spring 1983.

B. Levi, "C'è una firma nel cielo," in *L'Espresso*, August 28, 1983.

"Piano Machine," in *The Architectural Review*, 1038, August 1983.

"Schlumberger à Montrouge," in *Architecture Intérieure/CREE*, 196, August-September 1983.

"Architettura bioclimatica; en/arch 83," in *L'Architettura*, 334-335, August-September 1983.

"Riuso a Parigi. Renzo Piano e la Schlumberger," in *Costruire*, September 1983.

M. Pawley, "Piano's progress," in *Building Design*, September 23, 1983.

"Un chantier experimental a Montrouge," in *Le Moniteur*, 40, September 1983.

"In vista di una riqualificazione di ITALIA '61. L'allestimento di Renzo Piano per la mostra di Calder," in *Casabella*, 494. September 1983.

"Paris 89/une expo de papier," in *Urbanisme*, 197, September 1983.

"Quartiere 'Il Rigo' Corciano. Laboratorio di quartiere Bari," in *Architecture Contemporaine*, 5, '83-'84.

"Calder a Torino," in *Domus*, 544, November 1983.

"L'invention technologique; un espace pour demain," in *Techniques & Architecture*, 350, November 1983.

"The New Workplace; Transformation in Paris," in *The Architectural Review*, 104, November 1983.

International Conference on Space Structures, exhibition catalogue, Dep. of Civil Engineering University of Surrey, 1966, London.

IRCAM, Centre Georges Pompidou, 1977, Paris.

Costruire e Ricostruire, AIP, 1978, Udine.

R. Piano, M. Arduino, M. Fazio, *Antico è bello*, Laterza, 1980, Rome-Bari.

A. Fils, *Das Centre Pompidou in Paris*, Heinz Moos Verlag, 1980, Munich.

Renzo Piano/Pezzo per Pezzo, exhibition catalogue edited by G. Donin, Casa del Libro Editrice, 1982, Rome.

La Modernité un Projet Inachevé, exhibition catalogue, Le Moniteur, 1982, Paris.

C. Jencks, W. Chatikin, *Architecture Today*, Harry N. Abrams, 1982, New York.

H. Bofinger, M. Bofinger, *Junge Architekten in Europa*, Kohlhammer, 1983, Stuttgart.

Photographic credits

G. Berengo Gardin, Milan: pages 8, 9, 10, 11, 12; nos. 78, 85, 101, 102, 103, 104, 105, 106, 107, 108, 109, 112, 116, 118, 119, 122, 123, 124, 125, 126, 127, 128, 129, 137, 138, 140, 160, 161, 162, 164, 166, 199, 225, 226, 227, 228, 230, 231, 232, 233, 234, 235, 236, 237, 252, 253 (and cover), 261, 262, 263, 264, 265, 270, 308, 311, 312, 334, 336; chronology: nos. 9, 19, 26, 31, 32, 46, 47, 60, 63.

Studio Piano, Genoa: page 10 (below); nos. 1, 2, 3, 4, 5, 6, 7, 9, 10, 11, 12, 13, 16, 17, 20, 22, 23, 24, 25, 26, 27, 28, 30, 31, 32, 34, 36, 37, 38, 39, 43, 44, 46, 48, 79, 80, 82, 83, 87, 88, 90, 97, 113, 143, 145, 146, 147, 148, 149, 150, 151, 152, 153, 155, 156, 157, 159, 172, 196, 197, 224, 362, 366, 370, 371, 377, 378, 398; chronology: nos. 1, 3, 5, 10, 16, 17, 34, 36, 54, 55.

S. Ishida, Genoa: nos. 49, 50, 51, 54, 65, 66, 180, 182, 183, 184, 186, 187, 193, 276, 277, 282, 284, 286, 293, 303, 325, 328, 388, 396, 401, 403, 404, 405, 406, 407, 408, 409, 410; chronology: nos. 29, 30, 38, 41, 42, 62.

FIAT Auto, Turin: nos. 55, 61, 70, 75, 76.

F. Doria, Genoa: nos. 62, 213, 275, 292, 294; chronology: nos. 40, 49.

EDITECH., Florence: no. 115.

B & B Italia, Como: no. 168.

R. Einzing, London: nos. 174, 176, 177, 178; chronology: no. 23.

S. Caffini, Milan: nos. 200, 201; chronology: nos. 50, 52.

B. Vincent, Paris: nos. 223, 239, 242, 244, 245, 248, 249, 250, 257.

Bel Air Photo, Houston: no. 274.

D. Crossly, Houston: nos. 278, 283, 285.

Ove Arup & Partners, London: nos. 298, 299, 300.

Publiaerfoto Italia: no. 309.

Foto Bergami, Genoa: no. 315.

R. Melai, Genoa: nos. 319, 327.

N. Okabe, Paris: nos. 329, 337, 349, 351, 402; chronology: no. 43.

Archives Schlumberger, Paris: nos. 331, 353.

P. Astier, Paris: nos. 350, 352.

Compagnia Generale Riprese Aeree, Rome: no. 397.

Montecatini Edison S.p.A.: chronology: no. 14.

A. Holmes, London: chronology: nos. 24, 28.